Comprehensive
Multicultural Education

Comprehensive Multicultural Education

Theory and Practice

Christine I. Bennett
Indiana University at Bloomington

Allyn and Bacon, Inc.
BOSTON   LONDON   SYDNEY   TORONTO

Library of Congress Cataloging-in-Publication Data

Bennett, Christine I.
  Comprehensive multicultural education.

  Bibliography: p.
  Includes index.
  1. Intercultural education—United States.
I. Title.
LC1099.3.B46 1986   370.19′6′0973   85–26796
  ISBN 0–205–08587–3

Series editor: Susanne F. Canavan
Developmental coordinator: Lauren Whittaker
Production coordinator: Helyn Pultz
Editorial-production services: P. M. Gordon Associates
Cover coordinator: Linda K. Dickinson

Printed in the United States of America

10 9 8 7 6 5 4 3 2   90 89 88 87

This book is dedicated to my grandmothers,
Christine Iverson Bennett and Anna Marie Kahn,
one my lifelong inspiration, one my strongest source of ethnicity

Brief Contents

Contents

Preface

Multicultural competence may soon become one of the basic skills that schools are required to teach. Just as some states have recently added decision-making or thinking skills to the traditional basics of reading, writing, and computation, so might they require competence in multiple ways of perceiving, evaluating, and doing.

Given that we live in a multicultural world, multicultural education is for everyone. Most of today's schools, however, remain monocultural in scope. They are hampered by societal policies and practices, often beyond their control, that impede reform of formal and hidden curricula. Shortage of funds and lack of understanding, for example, make it difficult for schools to replace or supplement biased books and films, to hire new personnel who can provide positive role models from a variety of ethnic groups, or to study alternatives to discriminatory school practices in areas such as co-curricular activities or student discipline. How teachers might meet the challenge of fostering multicultural competence through multicultural education is this book's raison d'être.

The book's approach to multicultural education is unique for three reasons. First, its content is comprehensive and interdisciplinary in scope and practical in focus. Key concepts from education and the social sciences are fully explained, often with primary source material, and the implications for teaching and learning are fully developed. Because teachers may not have the opportunity to develop knowledge about cultural diversity through their course work and experiences beyond those provided by schools of education, an introduction to the social sciences is included. The book is designed to help teachers use this knowledge by applying important concepts to classroom settings. Practicing and prospective teachers need assistance in bridging the gap between theory and practice, especially in the area of multicultural education.

Other books on multicultural education lack this combined thrust of theory and practice. Either they focus on important data about ethnic groups, or they focus on strategies for students while presenting only superficial knowledge about cultural diversity. This book aids development of skills and understanding in both areas: knowledge about key concepts from a variety of disciplines, including the history and culture of various ethnic groups, and knowledge about related strategies and personal decision making in schools and classrooms—for example, classroom management, instructional strategies, and multicultural curriculum development in all areas of the curriculum.

Second, this book is unique in that it develops an interaction between cultural and individual differences. Teachers often fear that by noting cultural differences among their students, they will be labeled as racist or prejudiced. This fear is related to an ill-founded tendency to equate color consciousness with racism. It also stems from feelings that differences are bad or inferior, and from the mistaken notion that the recognition of differences implies a necessity to imitate or adopt these differences. Many cultural awareness and human relations workshops have failed because these basic concerns of the participants were not dealt with. On the other hand, most teachers do believe in individualizing or personalizing their instruction. Most would agree that their ultimate goal as teachers is to foster the intellectual, social, and personal development of all students to each one's greatest potential. This book shows that the ability to reach this goal can be strengthened by an understanding of both cultural alternatives and individual differences.

Third, this book adds needed conceptual clarity to the field of multicultural education. Literature as well as practice in multicultural education has not been grounded in well-developed theory and lacks clearly defined terminology. This book addresses the problem by defining frequently used (and misused) concepts such as culture, assimilation, ethnic group, cultural pluralism, and racism. It also includes important concepts and theories that hold promise for multicultural education but are not widely known among preservice and practicing teachers—for example, social contact theory and the complex problem of stereotyping.

The vignettes presented here are based on fact, but the names have been changed. The inclusion of characters from my previous writings, notably Kevin and Rachael, seemed appropriate in this larger work. They are as relevant today as they were when I met them eight years ago.

Numerous individuals have contributed to the development of this book in important ways. My former professors, the late Alan P. Merriam and the late Henry Bullock, as well as Roger D. Abrahams are lasting sources of inspiration. My thoughts have also been profoundly influenced by the work of Gordon Allport and Asa Hilliard, and by my colleagues and friends James A. Banks and Geneva Gay.

Several colleagues and friends at Indiana University read and reacted to portions of the manuscript as it emerged. I am especially grateful to Karen Schuster Webb, who has also written the section on bilingual education in Chapter 8, and to Robert Arnove, George Nakhnikian, David F. Hummons, Cheryl Cohen, Irving Katz, and Tim Niggle. l am also deeply grateful for the strength provided by fellow members of Indiana University's Committee on Interracial Understanding, particularly Michael Gordon, Bill Shipton, and Derek Kotze. My appreciation also extends to the numerous students I have known at Indiana University who have taught me much about the teaching of multicultural education, and I am especially grateful to Gayle Reiten, David Page, Elizabeth Ellis, Allison Hoadley Hanscom, Rhea Townley, Brad Purlee, Arlessa Barnes, Lori Bauer, Susan Goodman, Jean Seger, Sally Goss, Teresa Hogue, Janice Bristow, Debra York-Heck, and E. Van Campbell, whose lessons appear in this book.

Outside reviewers contributed extensively to the development of the manuscript. My thanks go to Dr. Donald S. Seckinger of the University of Wyoming, Dr. Phillip T. K. Daniel of Northern Illinois University, Dr. Francis Femminella of the State University of New York at Albany, Dr. Edith W. King of the University of Denver, and Dr. Richard Pacheco of San Diego State University.

I especially want to thank Hiram Howard, Managing Editor at Allyn and Bacon, who was a source of inspiration and encouragement during the early stages of the book. Thanks also go to Lauren Whittaker, Developmental Coordinator, for her cheerful correspondence and many efforts to help me pull together the final draft. Douglas Gordon, of P. M. Gordon Associates, has been fantastic in handling the minutiae of obtaining the many permissions required for this text. I also wish to thank Sue Logsdon for her patience and expertise in typing the preliminary and final drafts of the manuscript.

My parents, Matthew and Claire Bennett, have been a lifelong source of encouragement. Their understanding and assistance have been especially significant during the past several years while I was writing this book. My sons, Matthew and Adam, and their friends Doug, Todd, Omar, and David, have taken great delight in the development of this book. Their enthusiasm and interest, particularly regarding the book's vignettes, added much enjoyment to its creation.

Finally, I wish to express my appreciation and affection for Tom Rowland, who has provided both intellectual strength and emotional support.

C.I.B.

Part One

The Concept of Culture: Implications for Teaching and Learning

A student who was preparing to become a public school teacher recently wrote the following comments in his journal for an education class.

> Why be concerned about culture? After all, we all live in the same country. Most of us speak the same language, and those who don't have the chance to learn English in school. Most of us dress the same, bathe every day, and enjoy the same foods and entertainment and comforts. If you don't think so, just spend some time in a really foreign country. Then you'll see just how American you are. . . . Sure, I plan to be a teacher . . . and I see it as my responsibility to help everyone learn to the best of their ability and to fit in to the American society. When we start to look at differences between the races and other groups we tend to develop stronger stereotypes. . . . Besides, I think it's prejudiced to look at a person's race or cultural differences especially in the classroom where we're supposed to treat everyone equally. [Education Major, 1983]

This book is based on the assumption that our major goal as teachers is to foster the intellectual, social, and personal development of our students to their highest potential. The goal is to provide each student with an equal opportunity to learn. The education major previously quoted seems to agree; however, the question still remains, "Why be concerned about culture?"

Consider the school experiences of three different American students: Fred Young, Sarah Stein, and Jimmy Miller.

Fred Young[1]

Fred Young grew up in the traditional world of the Navajo. Today, after having earned a doctorate in nuclear physics, Fred works at the Los Alamos scientific labs, where America's best scientists seek to understand the universe.

As a child, Fred lived in desperate poverty. He helped support his family at a very young age by hunting game, and sometimes he dug for food in the garbage cans outside Gallup, New Mexico, homes. During these early years, Fred also developed a deep curiosity about the world of nature, wondering what it was made of.

Fred's parents sent him to a boarding school at Ignacio, Colorado, so that he could eat regularly. His curiosity and love of nature continued, and he wondered if perhaps clocks could tell the time of day because they were controlled by the sun. His years at the boarding school were filled with hurt and resentment. "In the White world the basic assumptions are so different that something that would be taken for granted by all my classmates wasn't obvious to me at all," Fred says. "So they thought I was scared or dumb or both. It was embarrassing at times, and it made me angry." The daily insults and arrogance Fred experienced in school built up feelings of resentment and hostility, and he sometimes ran off from school and returned to his family in Monument Valley. His intense curiosity and desire to know always brought him back to school where he put up with the hurt in order to satisfy his quest for knowledge. When Fred attended the University of New Mexico on a tribal scholarship, a textbook explanation of how the rainbow works so excited him that he decided to become a physicist.

Today, despite his accomplishments in the world of White America, Fred is still bewildered about how Anglo society works. And there is still hurt. "Even now strangers will sometimes treat me like a dumb Indian," Fred says.

Sarah Stein[2]

Sarah Stein grew up in New York City, where she was close to her maternal grandmother, an Orthodox Jew. Although some members of Sarah's extended family consider themselves to be Reform Jews, her parents are Conservative. They observe the Jewish Sabbath and holidays, and Sarah has attended Hebrew schools twice a week throughout her school years. The family also follows many of the traditional dietary rules.

Sarah has moved to the Midwest, where her parents took new jobs at a large university in a city that has retained its small-town flavor. Sarah attends one of the two high schools in the community where she excels in all of her classes. Nevertheless, like Fred Young, Sarah is experiencing pressures in school and at home.

A bright and eager student who is accustomed to a learning environment where students are continually encouraged to ask questions and discuss while new learning is going on, Sarah has begun to turn off many of her new teachers and classmates. She frequently interrupts lecturers with questions of clarification, violating school expectations that students should be quietly attentive until the teacher's presentation is over. She is often perceived as rude, obnoxious, and pushy.

For the first time, Sarah feels embarrassment over missing school during special holidays. She worries about missing important schoolwork during her absences, and this year she missed two days of the Iowa Tests because they were scheduled during Rosh Hashanah.

In her desire to make new friends, Sarah wants to participate in Friday evening activities, such as school parties and football games. However, this conflicts with her parents' demands that she share the Sabbath meal before going to the synagogue. Other conflicts have caused her to drop out of the school band, although she still continues private clarinet lessons.

Sarah is becoming aware of being an exception, if not in conflict with the way of life in her new school and community. She feels set apart when she wants to feel accepted.

Jimmy Miller

Jimmy Miller spent his earliest years in the verdant mountains of Kentucky. He moved to a large industrial city in the Midwest when his father was forced to give up the family farm and found work in an automobile factory.

When Jimmy lived in Kentucky there was no kindergarten and he started school in the first grade. When his family moved north he was placed in kindergarten rather than moving up to the second grade. Jimmy was a shy child who was large for his age, and the notable size difference between him and his classmates became a source of taunting.

Jimmy remembers the first day in his new school. He and his mother were called hillbillies by some of the children; his mother, confused and fearful, was unable to complete all the required forms. The teacher told him the first day that he had better learn to "talk right" and punished him thereafter when he spoke in his dialect, the only language he had known until that time. The school tested his IQ and placed him in the low ability classes. Jimmy was unfamiliar with many of the items on the test. His family didn't "fly planes," "go on vacations," "have company," "take lessons," or "pack luggage." The common, everyday middle-class world was strange and frightening to him.

Today Jimmy is in the ninth grade, waiting to drop out of school. He rarely, if ever, speaks out in class and does poorly in all his academic subjects except math, where, much to the school's amazement, he excels. His general science teacher might be surprised to know that when Jimmy was in the first grade he saw his mother save his sister's life by performing a tracheotomy when medical assistance was unavailable. Jimmy learned much about breeding and raising animals and managing crops from his grandfather, and at age five he grafted his first apple tree. The chorus teacher at school has no idea that Jimmy comes from a family of skilled dulcimer crafters. Jimmy is a gifted performer on the dulcimer, but he thinks no one at school cares about this talent.

As in the cases of Fred Young and Sarah Stein, Jimmy Miller feels alienated in school. He feels a *dichotomy* between school and home.

Students like Fred Young, Sarah Stein, and Jimmy Miller often find themselves to be an exception to, if not in conflict with, "the American way of life." They feel the pressures of a dual identity as a result of living within two cultures. Consider that Fred, Sarah, and Jimmy are just three examples of what millions of students experience to some degree in our schools every day. How do we proceed?

The purpose of this book is to show how multicultural education can help teachers better achieve their major goal: the intellectual, social, and personal development of all students to each one's highest potential. If we are going to equalize the opportunities we provide, we *must* consider culture. We must be aware of our own cultural expectations and the expectations of our students, which may be different from our own.

It is important to develop deeper insights into society's core culture and the ways it shapes our schools, and into the cultural differences that exist in most classrooms. Many students have felt alienated in public schools because they experienced conflict between the cultural expectations of the home and school. The greater the difference between home and school expectations, the more likely a student will experience so-called transitional trauma in the classroom.

Chapters 1 and 2 are designed to clarify the meanings of some important basic concepts from anthropology, sociology, and psychology that are frequently misused and misunderstood. Chapter 1 begins by defining culture and by examining this society's macroculture. The importance of world view is discussed and illustrated, primarily with examples of the Navajo perspective. The chapter then focuses on social values, a central aspect of world view, and considers social scientists' observations about the macroculture in the United States. The chapter concludes with examples of cultural conflict in classrooms modeled after the macroculture, providing illustrations primarily from a perspective of Black youth from low-income inner-city areas.

Notes

1. Based on "The Long Walk of Fred Young," television documentary, *Nova*, 1978. Reproduced by permission of the British Broadcasting Corporation.

2. All names are fictitious unless noted otherwise.

Chapter 1

Why Study Culture?

What Is Culture?

Anthropologists and sociologists have defined culture in a variety of ways. Edward Tylor, for example, defined culture as "that complex whole which includes knowledge, belief, art, morals, law, custom, and any other capabilities and habits acquired by man as a member of society."[1] Others, such as James Spradley and David McCurdy, define culture as "the acquired knowledge that people use to interpret experience and to generate social behavior,"[2] and develop the position that cultural knowledge "is like a recipe for producing behavior and artifacts." Ward Goodenough writes that

> A society's culture consists of whatever it is one has to know or believe in order to operate in a manner acceptable to its members, and do so in any role that they accept for any one of themselves. Culture, being what people have to learn as distinct from their biological heritage, must consist of the end product of learning: knowledge, in a most general, if relative, sense of the term. By this definition, we should note that culture is not a material phenomenon; it does not consist of things, people, behavior, or emotions. It is rather an organization of these things. It is the forms of things that people have in mind, their models for perceiving, relating and otherwise interpreting them. As such, the things people say and do, their social arrangements and events, are products or by-products of their culture as they apply it to the task of perceiving and dealing with their circumstances.[3]

Culture may also be defined as the learned, shared, and transmitted social activities of a group, the human-made part of the environment that satisfies all basic needs for survival and adaptation to the environment.[4] Subjective culture refers to "world view or the way a cultural group perceives its environment, including stereotypes, role perceptions, norms, attitudes, values, ideals, and perceived relationships between events and behaviors, and may be distinguished from material or concrete culture which includes the objects and artifacts of a culture."[5] All of these definitions are useful in understanding culture, but a common framework will be established here with Spradley and McCurdy's definition of culture: "the acquired knowledge that people use to interpret experience and to generate social behavior."[6]

Where we happen to be born, and when, largely determines the culture we acquire. The family, the neighborhood, the region, and the nation can all make a difference. Initially, we have little control over the language we learn to speak, the concepts and stereotypes we acquire, the religion we accept, the gestures and expressions that amuse or reassure us, or the behavior that offends or pleases us. Furthermore, we tend to assume that our way is the best way. Reactions of international visitors and students in the United States are instructive. Some regard dating and romantic love as a source of severe psychological strain and are thankful that their families select their mates. Some are offended by the chemical odor of antiperspirants and soaps, or body odor associated with eating beef. Many become sick after eating food with which they are unaccustomed. Many perceive the nursing home phenomenon as evidence that older family members are not loved or valued.

To study any culture or to make cross-cultural comparisons, anthropologists have identified basic universal characteristics of culture. Despite their cultural differences, people share basic similarities, and human behavior in any culture can be studied according to patterns within a culture's universal characteristics. Wherever we are born, the culture we learn provides the following:

1. Language and communication, including signs, symbols, and verbal and nonverbal messages
2. A social structure that includes family or kinship systems, age sets and the accompanying rites of passage, territorial grouping, and systems of rank and stratification
3. An economic system that provides for the distribution of goods and services to meet biological and social needs
4. A political system or some form of government for implementing public policies, assigning power and responsibility, keeping order, and settling disputes
5. A religious system that includes explanations of the supernatural, values, and world view
6. Aesthetic expression, including music, art, architecture, and costuming
7. Scientific knowledge and technology
8. Protection against invasion
9. Enculturation, or systematic ways of teaching people the accepted standards for perceiving, evaluating, behaving, and doing

Sociologists typically study culture in terms of basic institutions or social organizations related to education, economics, government, religion, and family life. Together, sociology and anthropology provide a useful conception of culture.[7]

Culture can be seen, simply, as a cluster of factors (social institutions and aspects changing over time) that influence socialization, or the process by which members of a society learn to conform to standards for perceiving, evaluating, behaving, and doing (see Figure 1.1). The cube may be sliced vertically and horizontally, producing forty or more rectangular sections, the possible factors. The configuration of factors may differ for groups and for individuals, and there are a range of differences within any one factor. United States families, for example, tend to be monogamous, patrilineal, and nuclear. There are, however, cases of serial monogamy, children retaining the mother's name, and extended families. Somewhat different roles, customs, and values (as well as other aspects of culture) may emerge with differing family practices. Yet there are limits, such as no polygamy.

This conception shows how cultural influences help unify a society by providing a common base of communication and understanding, and by regulating its social life through rules, customs, mores, and taboos. It also reveals ways of examining cultural differences between different societies and within a single culturally pluralistic society, such as the United States. To the degree that different individuals and groups share similar socialization experiences, they will be similar in their cultural ways. The greater the difference within any one cultural factor, and the more factors included, the stronger the cultural differences will be among individuals, groups, or societies.

Acquired cultural knowledge is like a recipe for producing behavior, artifacts, and interpretations of one's reality. Understanding our own and other cultures clarifies why we behave in certain ways, how we perceive reality, what we believe to be true, what we build and create, what we accept as good and desirable, and so on. In a complex and relatively young society that combines peoples of diverse national origins, such as the United States, a variety of cultures co-exist, along with the Anglo–Western European macroculture. The macroculture is the predominate culture that has developed primarily out of Anglo and Western European traditions, and has largely determined the formal institutions, official language, social values, and other aspects of life in this society. It is important to understand the macroculture as well as the microcultures that have survived among different ethnic groups within United States society. (Of course, as is evident in Chapters 4 and 5, it is also important to be aware of individual differences that affect learning; by recognizing these differences, we can escape ethnic stereotyping.)

Avoiding ethnocentric explanations of students' behavior—that is, not interpreting their behavior from our own culturally biased view-

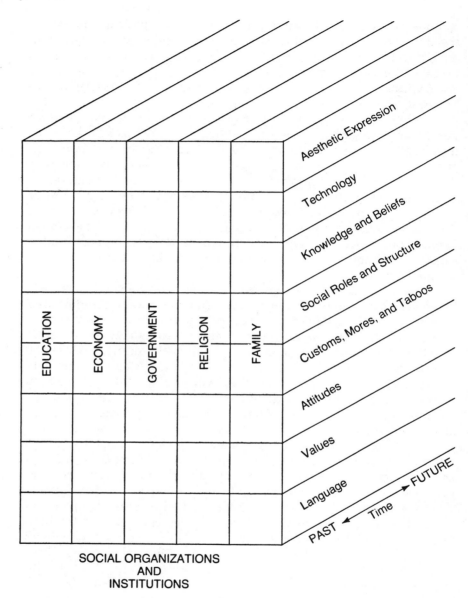

Figure 1.1 *Factors of Culture and the Structure of Socialization: A Proposed Conceptualization*

point—requires awareness of our own cultural expectations. Reyes
Martha Ramos illustrate this need in their criticism of sociologic<
search, which they believe has led to erroneous concepts used t
scribe La Raza. They list the following descriptions as examples c
nocentric conclusions about Mexican Americans that abou
literature.

1. Present-time oriented and desires immediate gratificatio
2. Nonintellectual, that is, formal education is not valued
3. Nongoal, nonsuccess oriented
4. Fatalistic and superstitious
5. Prefers living within the extended family group
6. Believes in machismo and a male dominated society[8]

The writers challenge the validity of each of these long-held generalizations and suggest that each may be based on ethnocentric interpretations of evidence.

> Consider the Ortiz family, who followed the crops from Texas to
> Michigan. Every fall they arrived in Colorado to pick sugar beets.
> Although they lived there only for the picking season, the children
> enrolled in school and were signed up for the government-
> subsidized hot lunch program. The Ortiz family felt that there was
> some reluctance on the part of the school personnel to give the
> children free lunches. After all, the school personnel observed, the
> parents drove the children to school in a new car and had probably
> bought it with no thought for the children's future.
>   Why does the Ortiz family own, or at least have a down pay-
> ment on, a new car when they cannot buy lunches? It is simply
> because it is impossible to be a migrant worker without dependable
> transportation, and when one car breaks down another must re-
> place it. Actually, the car represents the future rather than the pres-
> ent. If the Ortiz family can forego some essentials today, the
> chances are that with the aid of a new car, they can travel faster and
> pick more crops to get ahead in the future. As Mr. Ortiz once told
> me, his hope is that the car will get his family to the jobs before the
> other pickers arrive and thus enable him to get the better jobs. On
> the surface the Ortiz family's actions appear to confirm the present-
> time orientation, but upon considering the circumstances we find
> the opposite to be true.[9]

The Problem of Defining the Macroculture

It would seem that, for the sake of clarity, there should be a name for the
macroculture, but which of the frequently used labels does one select?
Anglo-Saxon? Anglo-European? White Anglo-Saxon Protestant? Euro-
American? Western European? None of these is totally accurate or universally acceptable.

The official language in the United States is standard American English, English having been selected over German after vigorous debate. Most of our political, social, and economic institutions are derived from English and Western European tradition. Because most immigrants prior to 1880 were from either the British Isles or Western Europe, Anglo–Western European world views and customs were transplanted here relatively unchallenged during the formative years of the macroculture. (American Indian, Black, and Hispanic influences were kept separate or suppressed.) Therefore, the most accurate (if nonflowing) name for the macroculture is Anglo–Western European. Although this label does not connote mediating experiences in the Americas, as does Euro-American, it does signify the intense Americanization and/or exclusionary experiences faced by Eastern and Southern Europeans as well as by immigrants and would-be immigrants from the Eastern and Southern Hemispheres.

In this book, the Anglo–Western European macroculture is frequently, but not always, referred to. The microcultural perspective makes a difference: Afro-American and Euro-American; Mexican American and Anglo-American; Indian and non-Indian; Japanese and Caucasian (including Black Americans); Italian American, Greek American, or Slavic American, and Anglo-Saxon or White Anglo-Saxon Protestant (WASP).

In the case of defining the macroculture, consistency does not illuminate. Ironically, inconsistency does because it sheds light on each group's perception of the macroculture. In the following pages, every attempt has been made to select the best label for each context to better reflect the differing intercultural interactions.

The Importance of World View

World view refers to the way a cultural group perceives people and events. While individual idiosyncrasies do exist, it is also true that the people who share common dialects and primary experiences learn to see reality in the same ways. They develop similar styles of cognition; similar processes of perceiving, recognizing, conceiving, judging, and reasoning; and similar values, assumptions, ideas, beliefs, and modes of thought.[10] What we see as good or bad depends on whether or not it supports our view of reality.

> It is thus apparent that there is no absolute reality, nor is there a universally valid way of perceiving, cognizing, and/or thinking. Each world view has different underlying assumptions. Our normal state of consciousness is not something natural or given, nor is it universal across cultures. It is simply a specialized tool, a complex structure for coping with our environment.[11]

Because schools are patterned after the macroculture, it is essential to understand the macrocultural world view that has originated primarily in Britain and Western Europe. This is not an easy task for those who happen to share this view of the world and take it for granted. Lessening the transitional trauma many students face in our classrooms, however, requires awareness of what many teachers unconsciously expect students to fit into.

Anthropologist Clyde Kluckholm has written that "studying [other cultures] enables us to see ourselves better. Ordinarily we are unaware of the specialized lens through which we look at life."[12] Consider the Navajo way (see Box 1.1), as compared with the non-Indian way, as a means of understanding the macrocultural world view.

It should be easier now to identify ways in which our schools are consistent with the non-Indian way. School days are organized into strict time schedules punctuated by the bell. The competitive learning environment rewards individual excellence. Students learn ways to control disease, and they dissect frogs in the science lab. They debate the rightness or wrongness of public policies such as nuclear arms control, school prayers, and school desegregation. Many questions are asked; quick answers are associated with intelligence, slow ones with dullness. The list could go on.

Different world views often lead to mutual misperceptions, hostility, or conflict. For example, an American professor and his wife visiting Thailand for the first time were greeted with inquiries about their weights and salaries. A Japanese businessman terminated dealings with an insensitive American because the latter, not wishing to waste time or pry, initiated business discussions without the customary inquiries about family and other personal matters.

Evidence indicates that the same process of misperception that operates between members of different nations who are unaware of each other's world view also operates in many schools and classrooms. The Panther Prowl, an annual homecoming celebration at a high school in central Florida, where Black and White students experience little interracial contact, illustrates this misperception and cultural conflict. Two different musical groups, one Black and one White, had been hired to perform at the assembly. When the Black musicians began to perform, Blacks in the audience responded by clapping, stomping, singing, and dancing. The Black performers kept cool, interacted with the Black audience, and were clearly enjoying it. A group of White students became very upset, demanded quiet, and finally walked out. Black students, in turn, felt the Whites were being purposefully rude and unresponsive to the Black performers. Later that evening, several interracial fights broke out on campus.

According to anthropologist Roger Abrahams, what happened at the Panther Prowl is an example of the different performance traditions

Box 1.1

The Navajo Way

To a Navajo, time is ever flowing; can't be broken. Exactness of time is of little importance.

To a non-Indian, time is of the utmost importance and must be used to its fullest extent.

To a Navajo, the future is uncertain. Nature, which is more important than man, may change anything. This life is what counts—there is no sense that life on earth is a preparation for another life.

Non-Indians prepare for the future. Such items as insurance, savings, and plans for trips and vacations show to what extent non-Indians hold this value.

Patience: Navajo. To have patience and to wait is considered a good quality.

Non-Indian. The man who is admired is the one who is quick to act.

Age: Navajo. Respect is for the elders. Experience is felt to bring knowledge. Age has priority though increasing power is going to those who speak English well. Knowledge is power.

Non-Indian. The great desire is to look younger and live longer. Much money is spent to pursue these efforts.

Family: Navajo. The Indian cultures consider many more individuals to be relatives than do non-Indians. Clan relationships are strong. The Navajo is wary of nonrelatives and foreigners.

Non-Indian. Biological family is of utmost importance, and relationships are limited within this group.

Wealth: Navajo. Wealth is to be consumed and used as security—always to be shared. Many Indians are suspicious of individuals who collect material possessions. Some tribes give love gifts and enjoy this practice.

Non-Indian. Non-Indian cultures have measured wealth in terms of material things. Many such possessions often constitute status symbols and are considered highly desirable.

Nature: Navajo. Humanity lives in perfect balance with nature. The earth is here to enjoy. Heed signals from nature—learn from animals. People are an integral part of this universe and must do their part to maintain harmony and balance among the parts of the cosmos.

Non-Indian. Culture here is a constant search for new ways for control and mastery of the elements around. Artificial lakes are made; natural waters are controlled; electricity is generated and controlled. Such accomplishments are looked upon with pride.

Cultural premises among the Navajos may be summarized as follows:

1. The universe is orderly.
2. There is a basic quest for harmony.
3. The universe, though personalized, is full of dangers.

4. Evil and good are complementary and both are ever present in all things, thus human nature is neither basically good nor evil.
5. Everything exists in two parts, male and female, which belong together and complete each other.
6. The future is uncertain—nature (which is more powerful than people) might change anything.
7. This life is what counts—there is no sense that life on earth is a preparation for another existence.
8. Time and place are symbols of recapitulation.
9. Events, not actors or quality, are primary.
10. Time is ever flowing, can't be broken.
11. Concept of life as one whole—Navajos have a hard time thinking in terms of social, economic, and political distinctions.
12. Like produces like . . . the part stands for the whole.

Source: "Teacher-Aide Guide for Navajo Area," product of a conference at the Dzilth-na-o-dith-hle Community School, Bloomfield, N.M., June 8–12, 1970. Reprinted by permission of the Bureau of Indian Affairs, Eastern Navajo Agency—OIEP.

in Black and White cultures. The Anglo-European tradition places a virtuoso performer on a pedestal. The audience is passive recipient, and appreciation is expressed with applause at acceptable times. For many Black Americans, however, the essence of the performance is an active interchange between performer and audience. Great performers, including public speakers and ministers, are those who keep their "cool" while getting their audience "hot."[13] Many Blacks and Whites have, of course, learned to appreciate and enjoy each other's music and performance traditions. Where this mutual understanding has not occurred, however, conflicts such as the Panther Prowl can be expected.

Social Values of the Macroculture

Social values are an important aspect of world view. Values are beliefs about how one ought or ought not to behave, or about some end-state of existence worth or not worth attaining. Values are abstract ideals, positive or negative, which represent a person's beliefs about ideal modes of conduct and ideal terminal goals.[14] Core values refer to the most general beliefs about desirable and undesirable goals and behaviors, and are especially important for the selection of cultural behavior from among alternatives.[15]

Consider some of the macrocultural values that are predominant in United States society: cleanliness, hard work, material comforts and material wealth, private property, health and youth, promptness, problem solving and progress, formal education, and the right to dissent.

These values are reflected in many of our folk expressions. For example:

"Cleanliness is next to godliness."
"It's better to have tried and failed than never to have tried at all."
"Time is money."
"Never put off until tomorrow what you can do today."
"Early to bed and early to rise makes a man healthy, wealthy, and wise."
"If at first you don't succeed, try, try again."

One of the most effective ways to gain insight into our own cultural values is to learn how we are perceived by people from other cultures.

Anthropologist Francis Hsu describes a series of postulates about U.S. society, based on his experience in both the United States and China. His observations may provide insight into macrocultural values in the United States. Hsu's Blueprint (see Box 1.2) can also guide reflections about our own personal social values that may or may not be consistent with the macroculture. This reflection is well worth the effort, for in the words of Socrates, "the unexamined life is not worth living."

Many Americans do not accept all or even most of these core values as their own. Often they find their values in conflict. Anthropologists find that the rules and values of every culture sometimes conflict. The excerpt from Robert Lynd's *Knowledge for What? The Place of Social Science in American Culture* is instructive about value conflicts within the macrocultural core (see Box 1.3).

Teachers often are unaware of, or fearful of recognizing, their students' cultural alternatives. Yet even the most sensitive and dedicated teachers can be frustrated in their attempts to reach individual learners if they are unaware of how their own cultural orientations cause learning difficulties for some children.

The greater the differences between the world view of teachers and students, the more likely it is that students' and teachers' preferred ways of communicating and participating are different. Those teachers who are unaware of their pupils' needs and preferences force the learner to do most of the adjusting. Those pupils who cannot make the adjustment cannot learn much in the classroom.

Cultural Conflicts in the Classroom

It is impossible to fully understand the cultural orientations of all students. Nevertheless, there are at least two common components of any cultural orientation that teachers can cue into: preferred mode of communication (verbal and nonverbal) and preferred mode of participation. Consider the example of Black students who have grown up primarily outside the macroculture and who attend predominantly White schools. It must be emphasized that numerous Black Americans are bicultural

Postulate I. An individual's most important concern is his self-interest: self-expression, self-development, self-gratification, and independence. This takes precedence over all group interests.

Corollary 1. After self-interest the individual's responsibility toward his wife and minor children (in that order) takes precedence over all else.

Corollary 1'. Parents must cultivate the friendship of their children and keep communication lines with them open.

Corollary 1". Parents should assist but not interfere with their children, especially when the youngsters have married or reached majority.

Corollary 2. The individual has little responsibility toward his parents and no responsibility toward other kinsmen.

Corollary 3. Upon reaching majority an individual is free to do anything, form or join any group, and go anywhere that is not illegal.

Corollary 4. An individual should seek the good life and pursue happiness.

Corollary 4'. The good life and happiness consist primarily of the maximization of bodily comforts, food, and sexual enjoyment. Pursuit of knowledge for its own sake and worship of God through eternal abstention and asceticism are not favored. Health and sexual attractiveness must be defended at all costs.

Corollary 4". Altruism is examined for ulterior motives.

Corollary 5. Selection of a mate is the concern of the individual partner only, for marriage is for individual happiness.

Corollary 5'. Sex must be based on love.

Corollary 5". Marital affairs are matters for the marital partners alone. Parents should stay out.

Corollary 6. An individual must decide on his own career or occupation and advance on his own.

Corollary 6'. An individual is responsible for his own actions unless he is a minor or insane.

Corollary 7. Individual initiative, excellence, and creativity are highly desirable.

Corollary 7'. Individual ambition and competition are highly desirable virtues.

Corollary 7". To be content is to stagnate, to be uncreative, and to be unworthy.

Postulate II. The privacy of the individual is the individual's inalienable right. Intrusion into it by others is permitted only by his invitation.

Corollary 1. An individual's body is inviolate.

Corollary 2. An individual's property is inviolate.

Corollary 2'. Violation of property is to be punished severely.

Corollary 3. An individual's conscience is to be respected.

Corollary 3'. Conscientious objection to serving the country is possible.

Continued

Box 1.2

Continued

Corollary 4. Sharing one's private life is a costly matter. Since all close relations contain limitations, it is often better to share one's personal life with strangers or paid servants (for example, analysts, psychiatrists, or counselors).

Postulate III. Because the government exists for the benefit of the individual and not vice versa, all forms of authority, including government, are suspect. But the government and its symbols should be respected. Patriotism is good.

Corollary 1. Sacrifice for the government is only justified during a national emergency.
Corollary 1'. An individual may be partially excused from this sacrifice if his conscience forbids it.
Corollary 2. The government should protect the individual, thereby justifying its existence.
Corollary 3. The government should not encroach upon the freedom and privacy of the individual.
Corollary 4. The government should be run by representatives chosen by and from among the people.
Corollary 4'. The people in government are the same as ordinary people.
Corollary 5. People with great power are likely to have better ways of furthering their own self-interests. They are likely to act contrary to the general good.
Corollary 6. The people must watch the government and check it when it misbehaves or fails to deliver the goods.
Corollary 7. Broad charisma (popular appeal) is important for leaders in government. This means they must be responsive to the people's needs. Even actors, television personalities, and even professional athletes may become political "leaders."

Postulate IV. An individual's success in life depends upon his acceptance among his peers.

Corollary 1. An individual must combine with peers to further his self-interest.
Corollary 2. An individual must maintain his flexibility for vertical or horizontal mobility by not being involved too much with specific peers at any time.
Corollary 3. Being a member of exclusive clubs is the most important sign of the individual's success.
Corollary 3'. Nothing succeeds like success among one's peers.

Postulate V. An individual should believe or acknowledge God and should belong to an organized church or other religious institution. Religion is good. Any religion is better than no religion.

Corollary 1. Individuals who do not belong to churches are socially abnormal.
Corollary 1'. Individuals who deny the existence of God or who think churches are bad are suspect.
Corollary 2. There is only one God.

Postulate VI. Men and women are equal.

Corollary 1. There are developmental differences between the sexes.

Corollary 2. There are differing needs between the sexes.

Corollary 3. Men and women should receive the same formal education, occupational considerations, etc.

Postulate VII. All human beings are equal.

Corollary 1. Differences of race, class, national origin, religion, education, and natural attributes make people unequal, but with each generation these inequalities are reduced. Social inequality is temporary.

Corollary 2. Education will serve to make people more equal.

Corollary 3. Inequalities in occupational prestige and salaries are consistent with the value placed on individual initiative, and legitimate as long as individual opportunities for achievement are equal.

Postulate VIII. Progress is good and inevitable. An individual must improve himself (minimize his efforts and maximize his returns); the government must be more efficient to tackle new problems; institutions such as churches must modernize to make themselves more attractive.

Corollary 1. Education and its elaboration are absolutely good. Education is one of the two chief means for all kinds of progress.

Corollary 2. Wealth and its increase are absolutely good. Wealth is the other chief means for all kinds of progress.

Corollary 2'. Most or all problems can be solved by judicious monetary appropriations.

Corollary 2". A great deal of any appropriation should go to research (physical, medical, industrial, psychological, and even sociological) which will bring about progress.

Corollary 3. Good and evil each are absolute. They cannot coexist. However, the world is temporarily divided between good and evil. Progress means the systematic extermination of evil by the good.

Corollary 4. Youth is good. The future is before the young. Old age is bad. Old people have no role in the scheme of things.

Corollary 4'. Opinions and wishes of children are to be taken more seriously than those of the elderly.

Corollary 4". Crimes against children are more heinous than those against adults.

Corollary 5. The fight against evil requires the active participation of everyone.

Postulate IX. Being American is synonymous with being progressive, and America is the utmost symbol of progress.

Corollary 1. The United States has a mission to spread Americanism to all peoples of the world.

Corollary 2. Obstructions to the spread of Americanism are intolerable and must be destroyed (by war, if necessary) until the good prevails.

Continued

Box 1.2

Continued

> Corollary 3. Americans are willing to go a long way to help those who acknowledge the superiority of Americans and Americanism, so that they will become Americanized.
> Corollary 3'. Americans have the power and know-how to build the world anew, where the weak will be protected.
>
> *Source:* Francis L. K. Hsu, *The Study of Literate Civilizations* (New York: Holt, Rinehart and Winston, 1969), pp. 78–82. Reprinted by permission of author and copyright holder.

and have learned to move in and out of the macroculture as necessary in order to thrive in this society. This is particularly true among upper- and middle-income Black families, and in low-income families where parents have stressed academic achievement and other macrocultural values.

Linda Myers describes some basic differences between the Western world view and the African world view. She places these diverse world views at the heart of the present cultural differences between the Euro-American core and Afro-American culture.

> The Western world view is segmented; the African world view is holistic. . . . Western culture tends to compartmentalize reality and focus on the parts. The African cultural focus is on the whole, and the tendency is to integrate all perceived existence into the total reality. . . . Western culture assumes a reality that is materialist and limited to comprehension via the five senses. . . . African culture assumes a reality that is both material *and* spiritual viewed as one and the same. This view allows for a reality that goes beyond the comprehension of the five senses and is known in an extrasensory fashion.[16]

The possible classroom implications of these cultural differences are striking. Evidence increasingly reveals that many Afro-American students have learning style preferences, related to their African cultural origins, that put them at a disadvantage in our schools. Consider the following Afro-American preferences related to modes of participation and communication.

1. *Cooperation and Competition.* Most academic activities are based on competition and individual achievement. Many macrocultural children, therefore, learn best working on their own, sometimes with the help of an adult. Most learn to expect and accept, and some need and thrive on this competitive structure. Tests in school are nearly always individual rather than group exercises. Whole systems of instruction are individualized (programmed texts, learning labs, computer-assisted instruction, and independent study projects). Educators motivate students with classroom games modeled after competitive sports and quiz shows

Box 1.3*

Core Values
and Conflict-
ing Values
in American
Culture

1. The United States is the best and greatest nation on earth and will always remain so.

2. Individualism, "the survival of the fittest," is the law of nature and the secret of America's greatness; and restrictions on individual freedom are un-American and kill initiative.

But: No man should live for himself alone; for people ought to be loyal and stand together and work for common purposes.

3. The thing that distinguishes man from the beasts is the fact that he is rational; and therefore man can be trusted, if let alone, to guide his conduct wisely.

But: Some people are brighter than others; and, as every practical politician and businessman knows, you can't afford simply to sit back and wait for people to make up their minds.

4. Democracy, as discovered and perfected by the American people, is the ultimate form of living together. All men are created free and equal, and the United States has made this fact a living reality.

But: You would never get anywhere, of course, if you constantly left things to popular vote. No business could be run that way, and of course no businessman would tolerate it.

5. Everyone should try to be successful.

But: The kind of person you are is more important than how successful you are.

6. The family is our basic institution and the sacred core of our national life.

But: Business is our most important institution, and, since national welfare depends upon it, other institutions must conform to its needs.

7. Religion and "the finer things of life" are our ultimate values and the things all of us are really working for.

But: A man owes it to himself and to his family to make as much money as he can.

8. Life would not be tolerable if we did not believe in progress and know that things are getting better. We should, therefore, welcome new things.

But: The old, tried fundamentals are best; and it is a mistake for busybodies to try to change things too fast or to upset the fundamentals.

9 Hard work and thrift are signs of character and the way to get ahead.

Continued

Box 1.3

Continued

But: No shrewd person tries to get ahead nowadays by just working hard, and nobody gets rich nowadays by pinching nickels. It is important to know the right people. If you want to make money, you have to look and act like money. Anyway, you only live once.

10. Honesty is the best policy.
But: Business is business, and a businessman would be a fool if he didn't cover his hand.

11. America is a land of unlimited opportunity, and people get pretty much what's coming to them here in this country.
But: Of course, not everybody can be boss, and factories can't give jobs if there aren't jobs to give.

12. Capital and labor are partners.
But: It is bad policy to pay higher wages than you have to. If people don't like to work for you for what you offer them, they can go elsewhere.

13. Education is a fine thing.
But: It is the practical men who get things done.

14. Science is a fine thing in its place and our future depends on it.
But: Science has no right to interfere with such things as business and our other fundamental institutions. The thing to do is to *use* science, but not let it upset things.

15. Children are a blessing.
But: You should not have more children than you can afford.

16. Women are the finest of God's creatures.
But: Women aren't very practical and are usually inferior to men in reasoning power and general ability.

17. Patriotism and public service are fine things.
But: Of course, a man has to look out for himself.

18. The American judicial system insures justice to every man, rich or poor.
But: A man is a fool not to hire the best lawyer he can afford.

19. Poverty is deplorable and should be abolished.
But: There never has been enough to go around, and the Bible tells us that "The poor you have always with you."

20. No man deserves to have what he hasn't worked for. It demoralizes him to do so.
But: You can't let people starve.

(for example, baseball and "Jeopardy"). They reward individual achievement with gold stars, "happy face" stamps, and privileges.

Within the Black world view, these preferences are often reversed: competition and individual excellence in play and cooperation in work situations. Geneva Gay and Roger Abrahams focus on inner-city Black youth and suggest that the preference for cooperation in work may develop "because so much of the transmission of knowledge and the customs of street culture takes place within peer groups [and thus] the Black student is prone to seek the aid and assistance of his classmates at least as frequently as he does the teacher's."[17] What is nearly always interpreted by teachers as cheating, copying, or frivolous socializing may in fact be the child's natural inclination to seek help from a peer (borrowing a pencil or talking after a test has begun).

2. *The Speaker-Listener Relationship.* The typical macrocultural mode is for the teacher to talk and students to listen. Students are passive recipients. Indeed, research indicates that teachers do over 75 percent of the talking in classrooms. The cardinal rule is that students must raise their hands and may not speak until given permission. One must never interrupt another who is speaking, especially the teacher.

This may sound like good classroom management, and often it is, especially for "middle-class" children. In many macrocultural homes, adult questioning of children is common practice. Parents enjoy that kind of interaction and often use it to develop the child's ability to speak; thus the child is not confused when adults in school continue the process. For many inner-city Black children, however, question and answer elicitation may be wrongly interpreted as hostile because it occurs most frequently in their homes when the adult is angry at the child.

What about students who learn best in a more informal setting that encourages an active interchange between the speaker and the audience? Think back to the Panther Prowl and the different participation styles of the Blacks and Whites in that audience. Communication expert Jack Daniels shows how for many Blacks communication and participation involve the whole self in a simultaneous interaction of intellect, intuition, and sensuality.[18] Because communication and participation are central to learning, students with the Black world view apparently learn best in settings that encourage a simultaneous response of thought, feeling, and movement. Silence and sitting still are often signs that the Black child is bored.

In the macroculture, on the other hand, intellectual, emotional, and physical responses are easily separated. Messages become distinct from people in the form of memos, and ideas are analyzed in their written form only. Society assumes that individuals, such as lawyers, sometimes argue viewpoints they do not believe, and in school teachers often ask students to sharpen their thinking by arguing a position they cannot accept. In some cultures, these are impossibilities.[19] Children of the macrocultural world view can be comfortable in the classroom role of passive recipient. They can learn to be rational and to remove emotions and feelings from decisions. Many are unable to concentrate in a more active, noisy environment.

3. *Written Versus Oral/Aural Tradition.* The macroculture emphasizes visual learning through the written word. In Euro-American tradition, seeing is believing, and it is commonly accepted that the highest levels of thinking are possible only for humans who can reflect upon thoughts recorded on the written page. No equivalent to the African *griots*, those living/singing encyclopedias, exists in the Euro-American core culture.

Many Black Americans have grown up in an oral tradition. Melville Herskovitz claims this orientation is a carry-over from Africa. Traditional Africa, for example, had elaborate communication systems using drums, singing, and dance rituals. From the time Blacks first arrived in the United States, music and the spoken word have been at the heart of the Black experience.[20] Their oral/aural tradition thrives in the New World. Classroom examples of the oral/aural tradition are easily illustrated. One geography teacher in California (this author) discovered that her students, mostly Black or Latino males labeled remedial, scored considerably higher on tests when she read the questions provided in written form. Another teacher, working with Black and Latino eighth graders in Texas, found that their comprehension of a United States history text was better if they listened to a tape of the text while reading it. Many of her White pupils preferred to read without hearing the tape. Similar examples are abundant, and helpful, provided that they do not lead to racial stereotypes and assumptions that all Blacks learn aurally and all Whites learn visually.

4. *The Uses of Words: Communication Versus Manipulation.* Both Blacks and Whites use words to communicate and to manipulate or gain power over others. The macrocultural mode is usually to find meaning in the words themselves. How accurately a message is interpreted depends upon the similarity of the meaning senders and receivers attach to the words. Among Blacks, however, words often become power devices, and the style of delivery is as important as the words expressed.

Within both cultures, whether one becomes a leader or a follower depends upon the ability to influence and control others. Control and influence in the White community usually accompany wealth. Among Blacks, for whom wealth is more difficult to obtain, adeptness with words and skill at performance lead to power and influence. Abrahams and Gay have clearly identified some critical classroom implications:

> Language in the largest sense plays a fundamental role in the process of survival in ghetto neighborhoods, in addition to being the basis of acquiring leadership, status, and success. The popularly

held belief that it takes brute physical strength to survive in the ghetto is a myth. It may help one endure temporarily, but fists alone are not the answer to survival. Survival is based on one's versatility and adeptness in the use of words. The man-of-words is the one who becomes the hero to ghetto youth. Consider the current conditions and compile a profile of spokesmen of ghetto action groups. These persons in the spotlight are dynamic speakers whose jobs are frequently dependent on the effective use of words, such as lawyers and ministers. Verbal ability can make the difference between having or not having food to eat, a place to live, clothes to wear, being accepted or rejected by one's peers, and being personally and emotionally secure or risking a complete loss of ego. . . . Teachers make their mistakes by looking at individual words or phrases as proof that the children are limited in their verbal abilities. For example, they fail to understand that what they choose to call profanity and coarse four letter words may be used as tools to indicate importance and emphasis. Street people are not inclined to use words for the mere sake of using them. They are used for their performance qualities.

To understand the relationship that exists between herself and her students, and the students' classroom behavior, the middle-class teacher needs to realize that her older Black students use a variety of verbal techniques, and that they use these techniques to discover her strengths and weaknesses, to find out where she stands on issues ranging from how "hip" she is to racial attitudes, and to locate her breaking point. Once these are discovered they help the student to exert some control over the situation.

Because street culture is an oral culture, and is dependent largely upon the spoken word for its perpetuation and transmission, its language is very colorful, creative, and adaptive. It is in a constant state of flux and new words are always being invented. Further, new slang words are constantly created as a way of maintaining an in-group relationship and of excluding outsiders. Thus, there emerges something of a secret code that only in-group members completely understand. It is used by students and others in street culture to convey messages to each other about the "enemy," even in his presence. Of course, some of these terms have been picked up by White "hipsters," but often the meaning is changed because of the different cultural perspective.[21]

5. *Standard American English.* The almost exclusive use of standard American English in United States schools is a striking example of the macrocultural orientation. Whether or not all school children should develop enough skill in standard English to make its use a functional option is not being debated. The cultural conflict many children experience in schools that ignore or repress the language they have known since birth, however, should be examined. According to Mario Benitez:

All the pre-primers available on the market assume a level of development in oral languages that the Mexican American child has not reached at the beginning of first grade. Phonologically speaking he neither hears nor discriminates certain sounds. Accustomed as he is to hearing Spanish mostly at home, he hears Spanish in the classroom instead of English and tries to decode accordingly. The result is frustration and awareness that he is failing at something [while] the other children are succeeding.[22]

The truth of Benitez's remarks is usually accepted when referring to Latino, American Indian, and East Asian American children—those whose first language often is not English. Rarely, however, it is recognized that standard American English may create similar learning problems for Black children.

A group of elementary teachers in a rural school in central Florida noted that, as early as first grade, White students surpassed Blacks in reading. Until they listened to tapes of Black students speaking, they were oblivious to the distinct Black dialect. They then realized that asking these children to learn to read available materials was like asking Whites to begin reading Old English.

Conclusions

Differences in modes of communication, participation, and world view enter the classroom when students and teachers represent different ethnic groups and/or different nationalities. Equalizing the learning opportunities for students becomes more difficult to achieve when teachers and students have alternative world views. It is a challenge to find out how learners can be taught when we do not understand their language, when we misinterpret their behavior, when our tried and true methods of diagnosing and motivating fail. Most of us expect cultural differences when meeting someone from another country, such as Vietnam, Saudi Arabia, or France. Fewer of us are aware that cultural differences can also occur between members of the ethnic groups that comprise our own society. Even in the 1980s, despite the fact that we live in a polycultural society, most of our schools remain monocultural. To teach effectively in pluralistic classrooms, which characterize most schools in the United States, teachers must recognize the validity of the cultures present. Students from different ethnic groups bring with them cultures that are to some degree distinct from the school's macroculture.

Many of us are unclear about our own ethnicity, or sense of ethnic identity, and about what ethnic groups are. Many of us do not understand the term *race* and how it is distinguished from culture. These topics will be clarified in Chapter 2.

1. Culture and macroculture 2. Ethnocentrism and cultural universals 3. World view and socialization 4. The Navajo way and the non-Indian way	**Compare and Contrast**

1. Experience *Bafá Bafá*, a cross-cultural simulation. (In general, sixteen to forty participants are required.) The simulation creates a situation that allows participants to explore the idea of culture, creates feelings similar to those one would encounter when exposed to a different culture, gives participants experience in observing and interacting with a different culture, and provides numerous insights that can be applied to culturally pluralistic classrooms.[23]

Activities and Questions

2. Conduct international interviews on perceptions of the macroculture. Work with another class member, or partner, to interview an international student on campus or a visitor in the community. Each partner should each interview a different individual, preferably from different families, to discover their perceptions of the macroculture. Overall, an attempt should be made to interview people from different world regions as well as several from the same nation. The interviews can be discussed in small groups organized by geographic areas of the world, and results compiled prior to reporting these data to the large group as a whole. Comparisons of perceptions about the macroculture can be displayed and discussed.

3. Complete the following chart:

Perspectives of Major Social Values in the Macroculture

HSU'S PERCEPTIONS	NAVAJO PERCEPTIONS	YOUR PERCEPTIONS
1. _____	1. _____	1. _____
2. _____	2. _____	2. _____
3. _____	3. _____	3. _____
4. _____	4. _____	4. _____
5. _____	5. _____	5. _____

What similarities and differences do you see in these three different sources? Can you find evidence of how the perceptions of each was shaped by the person or group's original culture (Chinese, Navajo, and your own)?

4. Robert Lynd published his views on core values and conflicting values in American culture during the 1930s. Which of these conflicts still exist today? What new value conflicts have emerged?

5. Using the examples of Fred Young, Sarah Stein, Jimmy Miller, and any other students you know about, including yourself, give one or more examples of transitional trauma due to cultural conflict between home and school for each category.

| Student | Type of Transitional Trauma | | | |
	Language	Nonverbal Communication	Social Values	Other?
Fred Young				
Sarah Stein				
Jimmy Miller				
Yourself				
Other?				

6. Reconsider the student's journal entry that opens this chapter, "Why Study Culture?" What are some of the points you agree with (if any)? List as many as you can. What major assumptions does the student make? What points do you disagree with (if any)? List as many as you can and briefly explain why.

7. Read the book *Black Elk Speaks*, by John G. Neihardt. What inferences can you make about Lakota culture, based on Black Elk's story? (For example, significance of the circle; how historical events are noted; the naming of people, places, events, and celebrations; and the concept of private property.) What contrast do you see between the Lakota world view (especially social values) and that of the macroculture? What similarities? How might North American history be written differently from the Lakota perspective?

8. Consider the conceptualization of culture proposed in this chapter on page 10. What other factors would you add? Create an alternative conceptualization of your own.

9. What *is* an American? In your opinion, what is the best descriptive name for the macroculture? Explain.

Notes

1. Sir Edward B. Tylor, *Primitive Culture*, 2 vols. (1871; reprint, New York: Harper Torchbooks, 1958).

2. James P. Spradley and David W. McCurdy, *Anthropology: The Cultural Perspective* (New York: John Wiley and Sons, 1975), p. 5.

3. Ward H. Goodenough, *Cultural Anthropology and Linguistics*, Georgetown University Monograph Series on Language and Linguistics, no. 9, 1957, p. 167.

4. Ashley Montagu, "What Anthropology Is," *Instructor* 75 (November 1965):48–49.

5. Harry C. Triandis, "Culture Training, Cognitive Complexity and Interpersonal Attitudes," in *Cross-Cultural Perspectives on Learning,* ed. Richard W. Brislin, Stephen Bachner, and Walter J. Lonner (New York: John Wiley and Sons, 1975).

6. Spradley and McCurdy, *Anthropology.*

7. See, for example, Peter I. Rose, ed., *The Study of Society: An Integrated Anthology* (New York: Random House, 1967).

8. Reyes Ramos and Martha Ramos, "The Mexican American: Am I Who They Say I Am?" in *Chicanos: As We See Ourselves,* ed. D. Trejo Arnulfo (Tucson: University of Arizona Press, 1979), p. 1. This list and the following extract from the same source are reprinted by permission. Copyright 1979.

9. Ibid., pp. 55–56.

10. Alfred J. Kraemer, "A Cultural Self-Awareness Approach to Improving Intercultural Communication Skills," ERIC ED 079 213 (April 1973).

11. Tulsi B. Saral, "Consciousness Theory and Intercultural Communication" (paper presented at the International Communication Association, Portland, Oreg., April 14–17, 1976).

12. Clyde Kluckholm, *Mirror for Man* (Greenwich, Conn.: Fawcett, 1965), p. 19.

13. Roger D. Abrahams, "Cultural Conflict in the Classroom" (videotape from symposium sponsored by the Alachna County Teacher Center, Gainesville, Fla., January 30, 1975).

14. Milton Rokeach, *Attitudes, Values and Beliefs* (San Francisco: Jossey-Bass, 1969).

15. Spradley and McCurdy, *Anthropology,* p. 495.

16. Linda James Myers, "The Nature of Pluralism and the African American Case," *Theory into Practice* 20, no. 1 (Winter 1981):3–4.

17. Geneva Gay and Roger D. Abrahams, "Black Culture in the Classroom," in *Language and Culture Diversity in American Education,* ed. Roger D. Abrahams and Rudolph C. Troike (Englewood Cliffs, N.J.: Prentice-Hall, 1976).

18. Jack Daniels et al., "Teaching Afro-American Communication," ERIC ED 082 247 (November 1972).

19. Milton Bennett, "Culture and Changing Realities" (Society of Intercultural Education Training and Research (SIETAR), pre-conference workshop, Third Annual SIETAR Conference, Chicago, February 25, 1977).

20. Melville I. Herskovitz, *The Myth of the Negro Past* (Boston: Beacon Press, 1969). See also Charles Keil, *Urban Blues* (Chicago: University of Chicago Press, 1966); and Leroi Jones, *Blues People: The Negro Experience in White America and the Music That Developed from It* (New York: William Morrow, 1963).

21. Roger D. Abrahams and Geneva Gay, "Talking Black in the Classroom," in *Language and Culture Diversity in American Education,* ed. Roger D. Abrahams and Rudolph C. Troike, © 1972. Pp. 201–2. Reprinted by permission of Prentice-Hall, Inc., Englewood Cliffs, N.J.

22. Mario Benitez, "A Blueprint for the Education of the Mexican American," ERIC ED 076 294 (March 1973), p. 7.

23. R. Garry Shirts, *Bafá Bafá: A Cross Culture Simulation,* 1977. Published by Simile 11, 218 Twelfth Street, P.O. Box 910, Del Mar, Calif. 92014.

Chapter 2

Cultural Diversity in the United States: The Conflicting Themes of Assimilation and Pluralism

This book focuses on teaching in a pluralistic society. It emphasizes understanding human diversity as it relates to both race and culture, as well as to a student's personal attributes. If we limit our focus to race or culture, we run the risk of stereotyping. If, on the other hand, we ignore students' cultural attributes and rely totally on our own culturally biased lenses, we are likely to limit the chances for successful learning to those who are most "like us."

This chapter defines four important, frequently misunderstood concepts: race, racism, ethnic group, and minority group. It then explains the degree to which some of the major ethnic groups have been assimilated or absorbed into the Anglo-Western European core culture. Five ethnic capsules illustrate ethnic pluralism in society and the need for multicultural education.

What Is Meant by "Race"?

Race is an anthropological concept used to divide humankind into categories based on physical *characteristics of size and shape of the head, eyes, ears, lips, and nose, and the color of skin and eyes.* Following the eighteenth-century trend among European scientists to classify all living things, J. F. Blumenback first identified five racial types that have lasted: Negroid, Caucasoid, Mongoloid, Malayan, and American Indian.[1]

Darwin attacked the scientific use of race, and many anthropologists prefer to abandon the concept because it has not provided useful knowledge in understanding human nature.[2] Anthropologists also point out that there are greater physical differences among individuals within a given race than there are between people of different races. According to Ashley Montagu, who calls race man's most dangerous myth, "[I]t is not possible to make the sort of racial classifications which some anthropologists and others have attempted. The fact is that all human beings are so mixed with regard to origin that between different groups of individuals . . . 'overlapping' of physical traits is the rule."[3] Nevertheless, the concept of race persists and remains a primary basis for categorizing self and others within United States society.[4]

Race and culture are certainly not synonymous. There are Whites who act Black and vice versa, and tremendous racial diversity exists within the Puerto Rican and other Hispanic communities. It is true, however, that racial isolation has been a fact of history for large segments of the population; as a result, cultural differences that can be associated with race have survived. The fact that cultural differences are associated with racial differences confirms myths and stereotypes associated with race. Blacks, for example, are often perceived as having more "rhythm" and as being natural athletes. Jews are often perceived as being miserly and more intelligent. These perceptions are usually based on the belief that genetic racial factors, rather than cultural factors, explain what is perceived. The concept of race has lead to the development of racist ideologies such as the Nazi ideology, which argued for the distinction between Aryans and Jews and led to the extermination of over six million European Jews during the 1930s and 1940s.

The terms *race* and *racism* are closely related and are often misunderstood. Some people mistakenly believe that simply recognizing a person's race is racist. Sometimes teachers say, "I love *all* of my children. I don't even know what color they are." Given social reality, to be unaware of a student's race is being dishonest. Don't we notice whether a student is male or female—has blue eyes or brown? Granted, we cannot always know if a student is Black or White or Indian, but where race is obvious why not recognize the fact? It is only when we lower our expectations, accept stereotypes, or discriminate that racial identity can conjure up negative attitudes and behaviors. The recognition of physical racial differences does not mean racism.

What Is Racism?

Racism is the belief that one's own race is superior to another. This belief is based on the erroneous assumption that physical attributes of a racial group determine their social behavior as well as their psychological and intellectual characteristics. A racist, therefore, is an individual who believes that members of another race are inferior because of their physical traits. The racist further believes that a person's behavior, morality, and intellectual qualities are shaped by these physical traits. Ultimately, the racist believes this inferiority is a legitimate basis for inferior social treatment.[5]

Racism also involves institutions. Institutional racism consists of "those established laws, customs, and practices which systematically reflect and produce racial inequalities in American society . . . whether or not the individuals maintaining those practices have racist intentions."[6] That the United States Constitution considered a slave three-fifths of a man, that anyone whose grandfather was a slave was denied voting rights, and that the Supreme Court upheld racial segregation are all examples of institutional racism from the past. White abolitionists who may not have been individually racist—that is, they may not have believed in the racial inferiority of Black Americans in slavery—were nonetheless part of a society whose institutions were racist. Current examples of institutional racism include formal and informal real estate practices that prohibit some races from buying or renting in particular sections of town, and practices that deny certain races access to clubs and organizations such as fraternities and sororities. Textbooks and educational materials that present erroneous information about certain racial groups or omit their contributions are other examples of institutional racism.

Cultural racism (within the United States) is the belief in the inferiority of the implements, handicrafts, agriculture, economics, music, art, religious beliefs, traditions, language, and story of non-Anglo-European peoples, and the belief that these people *have no* distinctive culture apart from that of mainstream White America.[7]

James Jones describes Carolus Linnaeus, "the eminent Swedish biologist who developed the system for classifying animals and plants that is still in use today," as an example of the cultural racism that pervades Western society. Box 2.1 includes Linnaeus's system for classifying humans, Peter Farb's criticisms, and Jones's discussion.

In summary, racism is a complex concept that includes attitudes of racial superiority, institutional power that suppresses members of the "inferior" race, and a broadly based ideology of ethnocentrism or cultural superiority.

What Is an Ethnic Group?

Ethnic group is defined as *a group of people within a larger society that is socially distinguished or set apart, by others and/or by itself, primarily on the basis of racial and/or cultural characteristics,* such as religion, language, and tradition. This definition is based on Milton Gordon's broad definition of an ethnic group as a social group distinguished "by race, religion, or national origin."[8] The central factor is the notion of set-apartness; the distinctiveness may be based on either physical or cultural attributes, or both. Ethnicity applies to everyone; people differ in their sense of ethnic identity. Everyone, however, has an ethnic group. James Banks wrote:

> All Americans are members of an ethnic group, since each of us belongs to a group which shares a sense of peoplehood, values, behaviors, patterns, and cultural traits which differ from those of

Box 2.1

Mammalian
Homo Sapiens
Classified by
Carolus Lin-
naeus

1. HOMO. Sapiens. Diurnal; varying by education and situation.
2. Four-footed, mute, hairy.   WILD MAN
3. Copper-coloured, choleric, erect.   AMERICAN
   Hair black, straight, thick; nostrils wide, face harsh; beard scanty; obstinate, content, free. Paints himself with fine red lines. Regulated by customs.
4. Fair, sanguine, brawny.   EUROPEAN
   Hair yellow, brown, flowing; eyes blue, gentle, acute; inventive. Covered with close vestments. Governed by law.
5. Sooty, melancholy, rigid.   ASIATIC
   Hair black, eyes dark; severe, haughty, covetous. Covered with loose garments. Governed by opinions.
6. Black, phlegmatic, relaxed.   AFRICAN
   Hair black, frizzled; skin silky; nose flat, lips tumid; crafty; indolent, negligent. Anoints himself with grease. Governed by caprice.
   [*Systema Naturae*]

Commenting on Linnaeus's descriptions of the main categories of human races, Farb notes two fundamental problems:

> First of all, skin color, hair texture, and facial features have no genetic relation to personality, mental abilities, or behavior—notwithstanding that such a belief has long been an intellectual assumption by people in Western societies. . . . The second thing wrong with Linnaeus' classification is that whole segments of humankind cannot be categorized according to a few visible traits.

Western society has had a tendency to categorize human groups according to simple visible traits and to infer mental, behavioral, and sociocultural capacities and tendencies from them. It is also profoundly the case that the evaluation of these traits and their presumed correlates places those attributed to Western people and societies squarely at the top, and all others in varying degrees of subordinate status.

As long as the only standard of cultural responsibility continues to be those models of European heritage and upper-class white America, ethnic and racial minority groups will always be at a disadvantage. Black Americans as a group cannot claim parity, even relative parity, as long as their legacy is an African past and their adaptational reality is viewed as lower-class, urban ghetto. The popular notion of "cultural deprivation" as a description of black children attests to a wholesale disregard of black life and culture.

Source: James M. Jones, "The Concept of Racism and Its Changing Reality," in *Impacts of Racism on White Americans*, ed. B. D. Bowser and R. G. Hunt (Beverly Hills, Calif.: Sage, 1981), p. 118. Copyright © 1981 by Sage Publications, Inc. Reprinted by permission of Sage Publications, Inc.

other groups. However, one's attachment and identity with his or her ethnic group varies greatly with the individual, the times of his or her life, and the situations and/or settings in which an individual finds himself or herself. Ethnicity is extremely important for some individuals within our society and is of little or no importance to others.[9]

Table 2.1 displays the populations of ethnic groups in the United States according to the 1980 census. The data were not broken down by ethnic origins for White Americans, but figures for Jewish Americans have been estimated from other sources.[10]

Some people in the United States identify primarily with the Anglo–Western European core culture, frequently labeled White Anglo-Saxon Protestant (WASP). This group comprised the host society, or macroculture, which received the nationality groups that have immigrated to this country since about 1820. Examples of ethnic groups based on these nationality groups are the Germans, Irish, Italians, Jews, Greeks, Chinese, Japanese, and Poles. Other ethnic groups are people whose ancestors were indigenous or who controlled the land before the westward expansion of the Anglo–Western European core culture. These groups include the American Indians and the Mexican Americans, whose Spanish and Indian or Mestizo ancestors had settled large portions of the West and controlled what now consists of eight states in the Southwest. Still another ethnic group is the Afro-American or Black American group whose ancestors were brought here as slaves. Also recognized as an ethnic group are the geographically isolated mountain people of Appalachia, who have maintained many traditions related to their Scotch-Irish roots.

When Is an Ethnic Group a Minority Group?

The label *minority group* is confusing; today, many individuals prefer not to be labeled a "minority." The term connotes inferior or lesser status vis-à-vis the majority. Furthermore, minority is often confused with numerical minority, when in fact a numerical minority may control a numerical majority. White slave owners, for example, were a numerical minority on the large southern plantations, and today in many small towns throughout the South and Southwest, White minorities hold political and economic control despite the larger numbers of Black or Mexican American citizens.

From a sociological perspective, whether or not an ethnic group is also a minority group depends on whether or not it holds a subordinate status in the society. Louis Wirth defined minority group in terms of subordinate position, as "a group of people who, because of their physical or cultural characteristics, are singled out from others in the society

Table 2.1 *Estimated Population of Ethnic Groups in the United States, 1980*

ETHNIC GROUP	1980 TOTAL	1980 PERCENTAGE
Total	235,381,820[a]	100%
White Americans	189,035,012	80.3
(Jewish Americans)	(5,800,000)[b]	(3)
Afro-Americans	26,482,349	11.30
American Indians	1,478,523	0.60
Eskimos	42,098	—
Aleuts	13,715	—
Chinese Americans	812,178	0.40
Filipino Americans	781,894	0.30
Japanese Americans	716,331	0.30
Korean Americans	357,393	0.15
Native Hawaiians	172,346	0.10
Hispanic Americans	14,603,683[c]	6.20
Asian Indians	387,223	.16
Vietnamese	245,025	.10
Guamanians	30,695	—
Samoans	39,520	—
Others	183,835	.10

Sources: Based on data in the *1980 Census of Population*, Volume 1, *Characteristics of the Population*, Table 75 (Washington, D.C.: Bureau of the Census, 1981); and in *Statistical Abstract of the United States*, 105th edition (Washington, D.C.: Government Printing Office, 1985).

[a]Totals differ slightly among various census reports due to different sampling and measurement techniques.

[b]Reported in James A. Banks, *Teaching Strategies for Ethnic Studies*, 3rd ed. (Boston: Allyn and Bacon, 1984), p. 187.

[c]Persons of Spanish origin may be of any race; the group includes those of Mexican, Puerto Rican, Cuban, and other national origins.

in which they live for differential and unequal treatment and who therefore regard themselves as objects of collective discrimination."[11] Joe Feagin asserts that Charles Wagley and Marvin Harris have provided the most comprehensive definition of minority groups as

1. Suffering discrimination and subordination within a society
2. Set apart in terms of physical or cultural traits disapproved of by the dominant group

3. Sharing a sense of collective identity and common burdens
4. Having membership determined by the socially invented rule of descent
5. Characterized by marriage within the group[12]

A review of United States history reveals that most, if not all, ethnic groups have experienced minority group status, usually during the early stages of immigration. From the Wagley and Harris definition, it is clear that some ethnic groups have remained minority groups for many generations and others have not.

The degree to which an ethnic group retains minority group status depends on how it is received by and/or receives the host society. Does it experience long-term segregation? Is it quickly absorbed into the mainstream? Does it wish to retain its own cultural traditions?

The next section of this chapter focuses on the major ethnic groups that co-exist in our society. Teachers must consider the extent to which their students may have retained aspects of an original culture that differs from the macroculture, which shapes schools.

When Cultures Meet: The Conflicting Themes of Assimilation and Pluralism

Cultural assimilation is *a process in which persons of diverse ethnic and racial backgrounds come to interact, free of constraints, in the life of the larger community. It is a one-way process through which members of an ethnic group give up their original culture and are absorbed into the core culture, which predominates in the host society.*[13] Cultural assimilation, or the melting pot theory, has been a strong theme throughout American history.

The United States is a nation of immigrants. Between 1820 and 1970, more than forty-five million immigrants, most from European nations, entered the United States. The prevalent view was that the newly arrived ethnic groups would give up their unique cultural attributes and accept the Anglo-American way of life. The school was expected to play the major role in this enforced assimilation. As was so vividly expressed by the educational historian Ellwood Cubberly:

> Everywhere these people [immigrants] tend to settle in groups or settlements and to set up their own national manners, customs and observances. Our task is to *break up* their groups and settlements, to assimilate or amalgamate these people as a part of the American race, and to implant in their children, so far as can be *done*, the Anglo-Saxon conception of righteousness, law, order, and popular government, and to awaken in them reverence for our democratic institutions and for those things which we as people hold to be of abiding worth.[14]

The melting-pot theory is still widely accepted, especially by classroom teachers. In an attempt to educate in "the American way," many teachers are blind to their students' personal and cultural strengths and view cultural differences as deficits and disadvantages. Many Spanish-speaking students who could not read English were placed in classes for the mentally retarded after scoring low on IQ tests that were written in English. Students like Fred Young were perceived as "dumb."

In recent years the theory of cultural pluralism has emerged as an alternative to the melting pot. *Cultural pluralism, in its purist form, is a process of compromise characterized by mutual appreciation and respect between two or more ethnic groups.*[15] *In a culturally pluralistic society, members of different groups are permitted to retain many of their cultural ways, as long as they conform to those practices deemed necessary for the survival of the society as a whole.* The stained-glass window, tapestry, and mosaic are images frequently associated with cultural pluralism. Each part retains some of its uniqueness while contributing to the beauty and strength of the whole composition.

The concept of cultural pluralism was developed early in the twentieth century by democratic philosopher Horace Kallen, who wrote that each ethnic group had the democratic right to retain its own heritage.[16] Kallen immigrated to this country from Poland and argued vehemently against enforced Americanization of immigrants. His views, however, were not given much credence until after the civil rights movement in the United States during the 1960s and 1970s.

Geneva Gay described the psychological and political impact of the civil rights movement in our society:

> Newly formed student activist organizations, as well as the older established civil rights groups, began to demand restitution for generations of oppression, racism, and cultural imperialism. The shifting ideological focus of the movement was captured in such slogans as "Black is beautiful," "Yellow is mellow," "Black power," and "Power to the people." Moreover, as the slogans suggest, the civil rights movement for Afro-Americans gradually became a movement for recognition of *all* minority groups, including Mexican-Americans, Native Americans, Asian-Americans, and Puerto Ricans.[17]

What began as a Black Power movement spread to include all minority groups and women. It also helped inspire and rekindle ethnic consciousness among numerous White ethnic groups, particularly among the third and fourth generation of Southern and Eastern European immigrants. As a result, today's society is much more aware and even appreciative of its cultural diversity.

A common misconception is that cultural pluralism is dangerous to society because it heightens ethnic group identity and leads to separatism, polarization, and intergroup antagonism. This view overlooks a critical ingredient of cultural pluralism: All groups must conform to certain rules, which are necessary for the survival of the society as a whole. The question of what is good and necessary for the survival of a society is a difficult one, and the processes of social boundary maintenance between different ethnic groups are complex. Negative prejudice and stereotypes about members of the out groups may serve a useful purpose for keeping ethnic traditions alive. The Amish provide a good example of the struggle for cultural pluralism in this society. In some regions they are allowed to maintain their own communities, schools, and traditions, but are expected to abide by the rules of the larger society.

Sources of Cultural Diversity in the United States

Those who accept the myth of the melting pot overlook the fact that assimilation was never intended for everyone. Various nonassimilationist strategies were used to deal with indigenous Americans, the Indians. These included policies of genocide, reservations, and subordination through forced labor or slavery. The most blatant evidence against the melting-pot myth is the oppression of Black Americans under slavery, and later during Jim Crowism. With the 1896 U.S. Supreme Court decision in Plessy v. Ferguson, separate but equal facilities for Blacks became the law of the land. For the next sixty years an extreme dual system pervaded all aspects of life in the American South. Jim Crow laws were passed to keep "Coloreds" separate from Whites in schools, public transportation, restaurants, theaters, baseball fields, public bathrooms, swimming pools, doctors' offices, and so on. Many courtrooms had separate Bibles for giving oaths. Intermarriage was illegal in thirty-eight states until the mid-twentieth century, and Blacks were denied their right to vote through grandfather clauses, poll taxes, and outrageous literacy tests until the voting rights legislation between 1964 and 1970. Gerrymandering is still used to divide Black neighborhoods in order to dilute their power through the ballot box. Many Mexican Americans have experienced segregation and oppression similar to Black Americans, particularly darker-skinned persons.

During the late 1800s and early 1900s, nativist prejudice and stereotyping were directed at European immigrants, particularly those from Southern Europe. There was fear that the American race would become mongrelized. One prominent journalist wrote:

> Races cannot be cross-bred without mongrelization, any more than breeds of dogs can be cross-bred without mongrelization. The American nation was founded and developed by the Nordic race, but if a few more million members of the Alpine, Mediterranean and Semitic races are poured among us, the result must inevitably

be a hybrid race of people as worthless and futile as the good-for-nothing mongrels of Central America and Southeastern Europe.[18]

Such sentiments may be found in our nation's congressional record and in the major scholarly textbooks of that time.

The second and third generations of White ethnic groups who did not appear racially different from the Caucasian core could, if they so chose, give up their language and traditions, change their names, and assimilate. However this was not possible for Black Americans, East Asian Americans, Native Americans, or darker-skinned Mexican Americans. Members of these racially different ethnic groups who wanted to melt in were prevented from doing so. Thus a society that perceived itself as being based on the American way, actually fostered the development of diverse cultures within its national boundaries. Policies of segregation meant that isolated groups would retain aspects of their original culture and create a new culture that is distinct from the Anglo–Western European core.

Afro-American culture exemplifies this process of creating culture in the Americas.

> The millions of enslaved Africans could only bring with them certain parts or aspects of their ancestral cultures—whatever they could carry in their minds. One includes here speech characteristics (pitch, entonation, timbre), folklore heroes and motifs, religious beliefs or values, artistic skills and preferences, and the like. But the slaves had only harshly limited opportunities to maintain anything like the full content of their original cultures.[19]

Social organizations could not be transmitted, for example the priesthood associated with a religion, a guild of smiths associated with ironworking, and a royal lineage associated with a regal tradition. Therefore, the new American setting required that they "innovate, fabricate, synthesize, and adapt whole new patterns of and for existence."[20] While the material aspects of African cultures—technology of ironworking, wood carving, and weaving—died out or were greatly transformed, nonmaterial aspects survived. Leroi Jones wrote that music, dance, and religion are the most significant legacies of the African past, even to the contemporary Black American.[21] In the past it was believed that slaves were stripped of their original culture, but most scholars today would agree that African cultural origins have helped shape the Afro-American cultures that were created throughout the Western Hemisphere.[22]

Who Has Assimilated?

To what extent have ethnic groups assimilated into the predominant core? Envision cultural assimilation at one end of a continuum in opposition to cultural suppression at the other end. There are degrees of as-

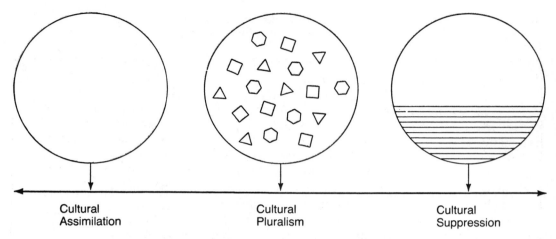

Cultural Assimilation	Cultural Pluralism	Cultural Suppression

Figure 2.1   *What Happens When Cultures Meet?*

similation and suppression, with cultural pluralism falling somewhere between the extremes.

Figure 2.1 illustrates the continuum between theoretical extremes of total assimilation and total segregation. Box 2.2 lists characteristic responses among ethnic minority groups under conditions of assimilation, pluralism, and suppression in contrast with macrocultural responses. The true test of assimilation is when members of an ethnic group experience the following conditions:

> Change of cultural patterns to those of the host society; large-scale entrance into cliques, clubs, and institutions of the host society on the primary group level; large-scale intermarriage; development of a sense of peoplehood based exclusively on the host society; absence of prejudice; absence of discrimination; and absence of value and power conflict.[23]

This chapter's examination of the extent to which various ethnic groups have been assimilated is based on the work of Joe R. Feagin, who has completed one of the most comprehensive analyses on the subject. According to Feagin, none of the ethnic groups he studied, with the possible exception of Irish American, could be considered totally assimilated into the Anglo-Saxon core culture. His study included Irish Americans, Italian Americans, Jewish Americans, Native Americans, Black Americans, Mexican Americans, and Japanese Americans.

Advocates of the melting-pot theory often use examples of white ethnic groups, such as the Irish, to support their position: Indeed, the Irish have moved up the socioeconomic ladder and are strong influences in our nation's political and economic spheres. Some would argue that

Box 2.2

Ethnic Minority Group Versus Macroculture Responses

ASSIMILATION	PLURALISM	SUPPRESSION
The ethnic minority group:	*The ethnic minority group:*	*The ethnic minority group:*
• Gives up its original culture • Identifies with and is absorbed into the predominant Anglo–Western European culture • Is no longer identifiable as distinct from the predominant Anglo–Western European culture	• Retains many of its traditions, such as language, religion, artistic expression, and social customs • Adopts many aspects of the predominant Anglo–Western European culture such as language; monogamy; military service; local, state, and federal laws; and full civil rights of citizenship • Develops an ethnic perspective and also identifies with the nation as a whole • Respects and appreciates different ethnic traditions that it may or may not choose to experience	• Is segregated from the rest of society, including schools, churches, jobs, housing, restaurants, and clubs • Develops a unique culture, retains its original culture, or a combination of both • May develop a "dual consciousness" in order to survive
The macroculture:	*The macroculture:*	*The macroculture:*
• Accepts members of other ethnic groups once they give up their original ethnic identity • Views other cultures as unacceptable, inferior, or a threat to social harmony and national unity • Suppresses the culture and contributions of other groups	• Respects and appreciates ethnic diversity • Encourages ethnic minorities to keep many of their traditions alive • May or may not adopt some of society's different ethnic traditions and current way of life	• Regards the ethnic minority as inferior • Controls society's economy, government, schools, churches, news and other media • Accepts the doctrine of White supremacy and sets up policies to preserve it • Suppresses the culture and contributions of other groups

the sense of Irish ethnic identity among Irish Americans is fading. Feagin offers valuable insights into assimilation of the Irish, but also provides evidence that there is still an Irish ethnic group to be recognized.*

Ethnic Capsule 1

Irish Americans

While Irish Protestants seemed to have begun blending in relatively early, for Irish Catholics, because of nativistic attacks and discrimination, ethnic identity was less voluntary in the first few decades than it was to become later. In the beginning the Irish Catholic group, concentrated in the cities, had a cultural heritage which was distinctly different from that of the British-dominated host culture; yet there were some modest similarities in language and customs. Over several generations of sometimes conflictual interaction the Irish adapted substantially to the host society. Yet in this interaction process was created a distinctive Irish ethnic group which reflected elements both of its nationality background and of the host culture revised to fit the subordinate situation of the Irish.

This Irish Catholic group changed over several generations of contact with the public school system and mass media, but it also retained enough distinctiveness from its nationality heritage and its experience as a subordinate group in the nineteenth century to persist as a distinctive ethnic group for many decades, even into the last third of the twentieth century. With future assimilation it may be that this distinctiveness will come to be more in the area of behavior and less in the areas of ethnic identity and sense of one's ethnic heritage. Thus the Irish seem to be moving at cultural, structural, and marital levels in the direction of the core society. But the Irish remain. It is useful to distinguish here between ethnic *identity* and ethnic *impact*. Ethnic identity for the Irish, the sense of the past, may be weakening, while the impact of the Irish background on Irish behavior is still obviously strong. . . .

Indeed, an example of the persistence of Irish ethnicity, even of distinctive ethnic communities, and its positive and negative functions, can be seen in the desegregation struggle which took place in Boston in the mid-1970s. There a working-class and lower-middle-class Irish community, South Boston, was involved in a judge's school desegregation plan; the plan was vigorously, even violently, opposed by the Irish. As one reporter noted: "Antibusing demonstrators, wearing tam-o-shanter hats in the neighborhood high school colors, have broken up rallies of

---

*The following ethnic capsules and other quotations from Joe R. Feagin, *Racial and Ethnic Relations*, © 1978, are reprinted by permission of Prentice-Hall, Inc., Englewood Cliffs, N.J.

women's groups and dogged Senator Edward M. Kennedy's appearances. The usually jovial St. Patrick's Day parade was a procession of antibusing floats." This is more than a legal desegregation struggle. Different views of schooling and of urban communities are reflected in the controversy; the South Boston Irish see the schools as a socializing force, reinforcing traditional family and community values, whereas frequently blacks and suburban, Protestant whites now view them as avenues of upward mobility for nonwhite minorities. Irish resistance to the racial desegregation of central city neighborhoods is based in part on protecting one's own ethnic community against all intruders, whoever they may be.[24]

Italian Americans are another example of an ethnic group that overcame initial prejudice, discrimination, and violence and moved upward into the economic and political spheres of the host society. Even though the social mobility of Italian Americans over the past three or four generations makes them an American "success story," these people have not been completely assimilated into the macroculture. Most "have remained enmeshed in kinship-friendship networks predominantly composed of other Italian Americans";[25] most prefer Italian American neighborhoods and marry within the Italian American community. Non-Italian marriage partners tend to be from other Catholic groups—Irish, German, or Eastern European.[26]

Ethnic Capsule 2

Italian Americans

Italians came to the United States with significant differences from the dominant British group, but they at least shared some European historical background and a Christian tradition with that group. By virtue of interaction in the public schools and the influence of the mass media, the linguistic and custom gap narrowed substantially, but by no means completely. Nationality characteristics, the immigrant heritage, have had a persistent impact. Italian Americans became in some ways similar to members of the host culture, but in other ways they retained their distinctiveness. Over time, because of their heritage, together with segregation and strong community and kinship networks, a distinctive American ethnic group was spawned. In the complex adaptation process an Italian American group was formed, distinctive in terms of both certain persisting nationality characteristics and unique experiences in the United States. No longer an Italy-centered group dominated by its heritage, neither has it simply become British Protestant American or simply American. Substantial adaptation without complete assimilation at a number of levels characterizes Italian Americans. The third and fourth generations appear to retain a great deal of Italian Americanness, in their commitment to the family and Italian community. Particularly for working-class Italian Americans there is still a rich family community life in the 1970s.[27]

Japanese Americans are often regarded as yet another example of the American success story. Stereotyped earlier as the "yellow peril," now they are often stereotyped as the model minority. Japanese Americans have the highest literacy rate of any ethnic group in our society, tend to be financially well off, and have been assimilated into the predominant language and religion. The similarity between traditional Japanese values and attitudes and the macroculture may be a superficial mask hiding some deep cultural differences.

Ethnic Capsule 3

Japanese Americans

Acculturation for the Japanese has in some ways been less difficult, because of a rough similarity in certain Japanese and core culture values. Certain traditional Japanese values such as *enryo*, the deferential or self-denying behavior in a variety of situations, and the ancient Buddhist-Confucian ethic of hard work aimed at individual honor and the success of the group have been useful for the Japanese operating in the United States context. *Enryo* was useful in coping with oppression and bears some similarity to the Protestant Ethic. As a result, Japanese Americans have sometimes been viewed in recent years as "just like whites." Yet the basic values are, in a number of ways, still fundamentally Japanese. In this sense, then, complete acculturation has not been fully attained. What appears to be Anglo-conformity acculturation may not always be so.[28]

The success of Japanese Americans in United States society is often used as an example of what other nonwhites, particularly Blacks and Mexican Americans, could also accomplish. However, Feagin points out a number of factors that contributed to the success of Japanese Americans and Jewish Americans, which were not available to larger oppressed groups, such as Blacks.

The success of Japanese Americans, seen as rooted in their values and family styles, has been cited by numerous writers as a paramount "bootstraps" example of what other nonwhites, particularly blacks and Mexicans, could be if they would only conform to these patterns. Stereotyping that sees the Japanese as an Asian Horatio Alger story and as paragons of hard-working, docile, not-rocking-the-boat virtues has been noted as carrying a clearly negative undercurrent. Critics of this cultural background interpretation have noted a number of other factors at least as important in shaping Japanese economic success: the role of the Japanese government in supporting immigrants, the availability of a ghettoized, small business niche on the West Coast, and the effect of intense racial discrimination in the surrounding environment in forging group solidarity. . . . Japanese Americans created small businesses to serve one another and the basic economic needs of a frontier economy. This hostile situation fostered a situation where both Japanese employers and employees saw themselves as a single racial "class" versus the outside world. Out of dire economic necessity, employers and employees, often with kinship or regional ties, worked together against white competitors. Success came at the price of being ghettoized in the small business economy and, later, in certain professions. As with Jewish Americans, Japanese Americans have "made it" as a group in American society in a distinctive way, a process (and result) of adaptation not in line with certain idealistic assimilation or inclusion models. Thus the long-term effects of past discrimination are still reflected in the concentration of Japanese Americans in the small business economy or in certain professional/technical occupations. Smaller oppressed groups, it seems, have a better chance of establishing an economic niche, where they go because of widespread prejudice and discrimination, but where they can also attain some measure of success, particularly in an expanding economy. It appears that such niches are not as readily available to larger oppressed groups such as black Americans.[29]

Although Jewish Americans represent an economically prosperous group and although Judaism has become partially Americanized, Jewish Americans have not assimilated into the Anglo-Saxon core. Anti-Semitism, or discrimination against Jews, is still a factor today in both social and economic forms.

From the late nineteenth century onward Jewish Americans have been excluded from hotels, restaurants, social clubs, voluntary associations, and housing. Such discrimination has persisted into the 1960s and 1970s. Thus the social ties of Jewish Americans have been firmly cemented together, at least partially, for defensive reasons. The Jewish community and the extended Jewish family—one can underscore this point—have provided the critical defensive context for survival in the face of anti-Semitism. The "Jewish mother" stereotypes have a nucleus of truth in the vigorous protective actions taken by Jewish mothers—and fathers—in defending their children from the onslaughts of non-Jews. Even in recent decades Jewish families have remained cohesive bastions of defense for their members.

Ethnic Capsule 4

Jewish Americans

Consequently, in recent decades the intermarriage rate has not been as high as some analysts have predicted, given the high level of acculturation of Jewish Americans.[30]

Hispanics represent the second largest minority group population in the United States today. Hispanics are also the most rapidly growing minority population and are expected to become the largest ethnic minority group within a decade. In "Pluralism and the Hispanic Student: Challenge to Educators," David and Donna Melendez and Angela Molina wrote:

> In 1978, there were twelve million people of Hispanic origin living in the United States. Of those, 7.2 million were of Mexican origin, 1.8 million were of Puerto Rican origin, 0.7 million were of Cuban origin, and 2.4 million were of other Hispanic origin (*Statistical Reporter*, 1979). The educational needs of Hispanic Americans are clear; as a group, Hispanics are the most undereducated of Americans. Only 40 percent have completed high school, vs. 46 percent of U.S. blacks and 67 percent of whites. In some urban areas, dropout rates frequently reach over 80 percent, and clearly, language is a major handicap to school success.
>
> Major cultural differences influence attitudes and behavioral patterns of the three largest Hispanic groups. In addition, the experience of each group has varied as a result of its geographical location. The Mexican American experience is largely out of the Southwestern United States and Mexico; the Cuban experience reflects the Spanish culture, colonial dominance and Southeastern United States presence; the Puerto Rican is a migrant whose mainland experience is basically a Northeastern and urban experience. The common thread is the Spanish culture, including the Spanish language.[31]

Historical issues of territory are essential in understanding Mexican American perspectives. As Carey McWilliams pointed out, Mexican Americans differ from European immigrant groups in that initially "Mexicans were *annexed by conquest*, along with the territory they occupied, and, in effect, their cultural autonomy was guaranteed by a treaty."[32] This was the Treaty of Guadalupe Hidalgo—a treaty that was not honored. Mexican migrants have moved within one broad geographical area, all of which was at one time controlled by their own people.[33]

Feagin writes that there has been substantial cultural persistence among Mexican Americans, whether they have experienced the traditional life of rural villages or the faster-paced life of the urban barrios. The Spanish language is the most notable example and has persisted as a primary language or as part of a bilingual pattern.

The relative isolation of many Mexican Americans in the Southwest, their closeness to Mexico, and the constant movement across the border have been given as important reasons for the persistence of loyalty to the Spanish language. Recent surveys in Los Angeles and San Antonio found that most wished their children to retain ties to their Mexican culture, particularly language, customs, and religion. Commitment to Catholicism remains strong even in later generations. There are still strong pressures within the group for a bicultural pattern of adaptation which resists full acculturation.

Widespread prejudice and severe discrimination faced the Mexicans who were conquered in the aggressive expansion of the United States, as well as the waves of first-generation migrants entering the United States since 1900. However, as time passed, some lighter-skinned Mexican Americans in larger cities were treated with much less prejudice and discrimination. Darker-skinned persons have often been treated just as black Americans. There still remains considerable prejudice and discrimination directed against Mexican Americans, the great bulk of whom are in the working-class and lower-class groups.

Structural absorption at the primary-group level and marital assimilation have not yet reached the point where one can speak of moderate-to-high assimilation for Mexican Americans as a group.[34]

Ethnic Capsule 5

Mexican Americans

Feagin reported that most marriages are within the Mexican American group, ranging from about 75 to 95 percent depending on the geographical area. He also wrote that most Mexican Americans maintain their identity as persons of Mexican descent.

Pressures brought by outside oppression forced many, particularly in earlier decades, to try to hide their Mexican origin under the euphemism of "Spanish," "Latin," or "Hispanic" Americans, but this cannot necessarily be taken as a sign of identificational assimilation. It was the middle- and upper-class Mexican American who in the 1920s began to use such terms as these in an attempt to overcome prejudice. In recent years there has been a shift back to "Mexican" and "Mexican American." In a mid-1960s survey the overwhelming preference was for "Mexican" or "Mexican American" in Los Angeles, while in San Antonio the preference of a majority was still for "Latin American." Given the great stigma still attached to "Mexican" in Texas, this latter result is not too surprising. However, few in either city wanted to be called just "American." In the last decade "Chicano" has come to be used by activists and has spread widely throughout the Mexican American population, particularly among the young persons, as a sign of accented group pride.[35]

Mexican Americans are not like European immigrant groups whose level of segregation has declined over the generations. Intentional discrimination exists at *many* levels.[36] In reporting the colonial perspective, Feagin wrote:

> The rise of a Mexican American middle class, and the mobility obvious therein, can be seen as a way of maintaining the subordination of most Mexican Americans rather than as a vanguard phenomenon leading to assimilation of the majority. From this viewpoint equal-opportunity advocates have distorted the meaning of this economic upgrading. A small segment of the Chicano population is dramatically moving upward, but as a token elite used to control the rest of the population. Just as classic colonialism points to a colonial elite controlling the masses, internal colonialism needs a small middle class.[37]

Conclusions

The preceding evidence shows that United States society is culturally pluralistic. Many ethnic groups have not melted into the Anglo–Western European core culture, and schools are filled with children from diverse cultural backgrounds.

At the same time, in the face of this ethnic diversity, everyone shares to some degree in the more general Euro-American or Anglo-Saxon core culture. Furthermore, as will be seen later in this book, the Anglo–Western European core is not pure. Rather, it has borrowed extensively from other cultures, including the Afro-American, Hispanic, and Native American Indian. Ironically, the power of our cultural similarities may blind us to the legitimacy of our differences and cause us to view others as deficient, or inhumane when they do not meet our expectations of what all humans should be like.

Students like Fred Young, Sarah Stein, and Jimmy Miller sometimes find themselves to be an exception to, if not in conflict with, the American way of life. Virtually every school in the society has students who, like Fred and Sarah and Jimmy, feel the pressures of a dual identity as a result of living within two cultures. Multicultural education has developed in recognition of the ethnic pluralism within our schools. The case for multicultural education is explained in Chapter 3.

Compare and Contrast

1. Culture and race
2. Individual and institutional racism
3. Ethnic group and minority group
4. Cultural assimilation and cultural pluralism
5. Plessy v. Ferguson and Brown v. the Board of Education of Topeka

---

1. *Ethnic Roots Essay.* Your analysis may take weeks or months and could be shared with other members of your class or workshop. Photo essays could be an alternative. Describe your ethnic background in terms of:

   a. Where your ancestors came from, when they arrived in this country, and where they settled.

   b. The immigrating ancestor or family member who has had the strongest influence on your own development. Tell why this person immigrated and when he or she settled. Describe the most difficult problem(s) this person faced upon arrival, and how he or she (or later family members) dealt with the problem(s).

   c. Description of your family in terms of cultural assimilation, accommodation, segregation or separatism, and amalgamation.

Using Longstreet's definition of ethnicity, describe your own ethnicity in terms of your

   a. Verbal communication
   b. Nonverbal communication
   c. Orientation modes
   d. Values
   e. Intellectual modes
   f. Other

Be specific and explain how your early experiences shaped each of these aspects of your ethnicity. Briefly explain the degree to which your own ethnicity helped you meet school expectations (grades K–12). If you experienced any areas of mismatch, be specific.

2. Experience illustration one (page 216) in Chapter 7.

3. Is it always necessary that members of an ethnic group "trade off" some aspects of their traditional culture?

4. Experience illustration twelve (page 244) in Chapter 7. Create an original lesson modeled after the one provided. Share it with other members of your class or workshop.

5. Divide into small groups of approximately six. Have each member share his or her earliest memory of race and most recent memory of race. Share the results with the large group and if possible develop comparisons and contrasts by race and gender.

Notes

1. Jack Kelso, "The Concept of Race," *Improving College and University Teaching* 15, no. 95 (Spring 1967):7.

2. Ibid.

3. Ashley Montagu, *Man's Most Dangerous Myth: The Fallacy of Race*, 5th ed. (New York: Oxford University Press, 1974), p. 7.

4. H. J. Ehrlich, *The Social Psychology of Prejudice* (New York: John Wiley and Sons, 1973).

5. James M. Jones, "The Concept of Racism and Its Changing Reality," in *Impacts of Racism on White Americans,* ed. Benjamin D. Bowser and Raymond G. Hunt (Beverly Hills, Calif.: Sage, 1981), p. 118.

6. Ibid., p. 131.

7. Ibid., p. 148.

8. Milton M. Gordon, *Assimilation in American Life* (New York: Oxford University Press, 1966).

9. James A. Banks, *Teaching Strategies for Ethnic Studies*, 2d ed. (Boston: Allyn and Bacon, 1979), p. 10.

10. Banks, *Teaching Strategies* (3d ed., 1983), p. 187.

11. Louis Wirth, "The Problem of Minority Groups," in *The Science of Man in the World Crisis*, ed. Ralph Linton (New York: Columbia University Press, 1945).

12. Joe R. Feagin, *Racial and Ethnic Relations* (Englewood Cliffs, N.J.: Prentice-Hall, 1978), p. 11.

13. David L. Sills, ed., "Assimilation," in *International Encyclopedia of the Social Sciences*, vol. 1 (New York: Macmillan/Free Press, 1968), p. 438.

14. Ellwood P. Cubberly, *Changing Conceptions of Education* (Boston: Houghton Mifflin, 1909), p. 16.

15. David L. Sills, ed., "Pluralism," in *International Encylcopedia of the Social Sciences*, vol. 12 (New York: Macmillan/Free Press, 1968).

16. Horace M. Kallen, *Culture and Democracy in the United States* (New York: Boni and Liveright, 1924); Milton R. Konvitz, "Horace Meyer Kallen (1882–1974): Philosopher of the Hebraic American Idea," in *American Jewish Yearbook, 1974–1975*, ed. Morris Fine and Milton Himmelfarb (Philadelphia: Jewish Publication Society of America, 1974), pp. 65–67.

17. Geneva Gay, "Multiethnic Education; Historical Developments and Future Prospects," *Phi Delta Kappan* 64, no. 8 (April 1983):560–61.

18. Kenneth L. Roberts, *Why Europe Leaves Home,* reprinted in "Kenneth L. Roberts and the Threat of Mongrelization in America, 1922," in *In Their Place*, ed. Lewis H. Carlson and George A. Colburn (New York: John Wiley and Sons, 1972), p. 120.

19. Sidney W. Mintz, "Creating Culture in the Americas," *Readings in Anthropology 75/76* (Guilford, Conn.: Dushkin, 1974), p. 202.

20. Ibid.

21. Leroi Jones, *Blues People: The Negro Experience in White America and the Music That Developed from It* (New York: William Morrow, 1963), p. 21.

22. Stanley Elkins, *Slavery: A Problem in American and Institutional Intellectual Life* (Chicago: University of Chicago Press, Universal Library ed., 1963). Laura Foner and Eugene Genovese, ed., *Slavery in the New World* (Englewood Cliffs, N.J.: Prentice-Hall, 1969). Melville I. Herskovitz, *The Myth of the Negro Past* (Boston: Beacon Press, 1969).

23. Sills, "Assimilation," p. 438.

24. Feagin, *Racial and Ethnic Relations*, pp. 108–9.

25. Ibid., p. 140.

26. Ibid.

27. Ibid., pp. 141–42.

28. Ibid., p. 356.

29. Ibid., pp. 359–60.

30. Ibid., pp. 179–80.

31. David Melendez, Donna Cole Melendez, and Angela Molina, "Plural-

ism and the Hispanic Student: Challenge to Educators," *Theory into Practice* 20, no. 1 (Winter 1981):8–9.

32. Carey McWilliams, *North from Mexico: The Spanish-Speaking People of the United States* (New York: Greenwood Press, 1968), p. 207.

33. Ibid., p. 321.

34. Feagin, *Racial and Ethnic Relations*, pp. 318–19.

35. Ibid., p. 320.

36. Ibid., p. 322.

37. Ibid.

Chapter 3

The Case for Multicultural Education: Goals, Rationale, Meaning, Assumptions, and Necessary School Conditions

Is multicultural education necessary? Is it possible? How do multicultural schools differ from monocultural schools? This chapter begins with the goals and rationale of multicultural education and an explanation of what it means. A discussion of basic assumptions of multicultural education and the complex problem of stereotypes follows. The chapter concludes with necessary conditions for multicultural schools and uses school desegregation in urban setting as an illustration.

Why Multicultural Education?

Demand for the reform of schooling in America has been a continuing theme throughout the twentieth century. The educational reform movement gained new momentum in the mid-1980s, beginning with the Reagan administration's report "A Nation at Risk." Nearly a dozen additional major reports on American schooling appeared in 1983 alone. The common thread throughout these reports is demand for a national commitment to true excellence in education.

What many of these reports did not acknowledge, however, is that educational excellence in our schools cannot be achieved without educational equity. Equity in education means equal opportunities for all students to develop their fullest potential. Potentials may differ, and at times equity requires different treatment according to relevant differences. Equity in education must not be confused with equality or sameness of result, or even identical experiences. Achieving educational excellence requires an impartial, just educational system.

The major goal of multicultural education is to change the total educational environment so that it will develop competencies in multiple cultures and provide members of all cultural groups with equal

educational opportunity. Equity is at the heart of multicultural education. Although one's ethnic group is just one of a number of identity
sources available, ethnicity is at the heart of the equity problem in this
society. Therefore, discussions about achieving educational excellence
require concern about those ethnic groups that have been consistently
cut off from equal access to a good education.

There is a lot of rhetoric in education about the human potential and
the need for equality of opportunity. Multicultural education moves
beyond the rhetoric and recognizes that the potential for brilliance is
sprinkled evenly across all ethnic groups. When social conditions and
school practices hinder the development of this brilliance among students outside the macroculture, as is the case within this society, the
waste of human potential affects us all. The cumulative loss of talented
scientists, artists, writers, doctors, teachers, spiritual leaders, and
financial and business experts is staggering. The concern for developing
human potential goes beyond individuals with special talents and gifts,
however. High levels of development and achievement are believed
possible for nearly everyone. Only those who are known to be of limited
mental capacity, or to be psychologically deeply disturbed, are considered to be beyond the school's resources.

Multicultural education contributes to excellence in a second important way. The traditional curriculum is filled with inaccuracies and omissions concerning the contributions and life conditions of major ethnic
groups within our society. These inaccuracies and omissions also exist
for nations across the globe.[1] Obviously, the attainable levels of excellence are limited by curriculum content that is untrue.

There are other important reasons that help build the case for multicultural education. Before continuing, however, it is important to
clarify what multicultural education means. Multicultural education has,
over the past few decades, become a popularized slogan, and the power
and potential of the approach has been lost to many. Progress has been
impeded to a large degree by lack of conceptual clarity concerning its
goals and content. Different proponents of multicultural education attach different, if overlapping, meanings to the phrase. Some of the
major approaches to multicultural education, for example, include bilin-
gual/bicultural education, education for the culturally different, education about cultural differences, and education for cultural pluralism.[2]

In her analyses of approaches to multicultural education in the
United States, anthropologist Margaret Gibson has pointed out that although each approach contains some necessary aspects of multicultural
education, each has serious limitations. Education for the culturally different is basically a condescending approach that assumes that cultural
differences cause school failure. Although education about cultural differences is designed to teach students to value cultural differences, to
understand the meaning of the culture concept, and to accept others'

right to be different, the approach suffers major shortcomings due to unintended outcomes. It leads to stereotyping by ignoring the similarities among all groups and by neglecting differences within any one group. Another limitation of this approach is that it overlooks the impact of racism. As Gibson has indicated, there is no reason to assume that developing ethnic literacy and cultural appreciation will put an end to prejudice and discrimination or solve basic problems of inequity.[3]

Gibson is justifiably critical of multicultural education based on education for cultural pluralism if it is conceptualized as a strategy for the extension of ethnic groups' sociopolitical interests. (As previously noted, this is a common misconception about what cultural pluralism means.) She has identified major shortcomings of the bilingual/bicultural approach, including the tendency to equate culture with language or ethnic group, and an overemphasis on ethnic identity to the exclusion of other sources of identity.

What is an appropriate conception of multicultural education? The most promising definition has been proposed by Gibson as "the process whereby a person develops competencies in multiple systems of standards for perceiving, evaluating, behaving, and doing."[4] This approach offers some important advantages and is harmonious with the goals of cultural pluralism as defined in Chapter 2. First, culture and ethnic group are no longer equated. Stereotypes can be avoided because diversity within an ethnic group is recognized. Second, the schools are relieved of the entire burden of education because there is a consideration of relationships with informal school and out-of-school learning. Third, ethnically separate schools are antithetical since "the development of competence in a new culture usually requires intensive interaction with people who already are competent."[5] Fourth, it clarifies the fact that individuals can be multicultural. They need not reject their cultural identities to function in a different cultural milieu—for example, the school. Fifth, this approach avoids divisive dichotomies between native and mainstream culture, and brings about an increased awareness of multiculturalism as "the normal human experience."[6]

Given the reality of cultural diversity in our society we must recognize that many citizens have perceptions, values, and customs different from our own. These differences can lead to greater ethnocentrism, polarization, and conflict. Gibson's view of multicultural education acknowledges that cultural conditioning is so strong that people who have not been exposed to other cultures simply cannot understand a communication based on a different set of norms and cannot even comprehend the misunderstanding.[7] Multicultural education provides curriculum and instruction that clarify cultural orientations and foster intercultural understanding. It also provides a curriculum that corrects inaccuracies and omissions.

Chapter 2 established the fact that society in the United States is composed of numerous ethnic groups. Current patterns of immigration, particularly with the influx of people from Southeast Asia, Latin America, and the Caribbean, ensure that ethnic pluralism will continue to be the American way in the foreseeable future. Multicultural education provides knowledge about ways to achieve greater social harmony in a society and world currently faced with intercultural conflict. Because it is based on the ideology of cultural pluralism, multicultural education represents a compromise between cultural assimilation on the one hand and cultural separatism or segregation on the other.

Cultural pluralism is considered dangerous to society by those who believe it heightens ethnic group identity and leads to separatism, intergroup antagonism, and fragmentation. This misconception overlooks a crucial ingredient of pluralism that was noted earlier: All ethnic groups are expected to conform to those elements of the macroculture that are necessary for societal well-being. Cultural pluralism seems possible in a nation such as the United States, which, from a non-Indian perspective, is a nation of immigrants.[8] With the exception of American Indians and certain segments of the Latino population, land is not an issue in ethnic identity for most groups. In contrast to those areas of the world where cultural pluralism has resulted in fragmentation—for example, portions of Europe—many ethnic groups in the United States contributed to the development of the macroculture or were immersed in an already existing macroculture when they arrived.[9]

Our schools are faced with educating a culturally pluralistic population. Pluralistic schools must identify base-line expectations for learning and behavior that are expected of all students. Every attempt must be made to lessen the cultural conflict that may result from cultural bias in this base line. Some groups may perceive certain rules as culturally biased, for example, the prohibition of hats in a school serving Orthodox Jews, or unexcused absenses during religious holidays. The scheduling of extracurricular activities after school discourages students who travel to school by bus; certain school traditions may also symbolize the preeminence of a particular group.

Consider a final note on equity, which is not only a matter of uplifting the nation's educational system. Equity in education is required if we value the American creed. The essential goals of human rights, social justice, respect for alternative life choices, and equal opportunity for all are part of this nation's basic democratic ideals. In theory it is un-American to be racist or sexist, but because many teachers are fearful about teaching attitudes and values, they ignore the issues of prejudice and discrimination. Multicultural education confronts the fact that this is a racist society with a history of White supremacy. An effective curriculum would point out that White racism has greatly influenced how people perceive, evaluate, believe, and act—and that legacy persists. Because its aim is to reduce the ignorance that breeds racism and to develop the understanding and actions people need to become antiracists, multicultural education can help overcome the greatest barrier to achieving pervasive excellence in education.

Basic Assumptions of Multicultural Education and the Complex Problem of Stereotypes

A basic assumption of multicultural education is that different ethnic groups can retain much of their original culture if they so choose, and can be multicultural at the same time. In other words, it is believed that people can learn about multiple ways of perceiving, behaving, and evaluating so that they can conform to those aspects of the macroculture that are necessary for societal well-being, without eroding acceptance of their original ethnicity. It is assumed that ethnic traditions and beliefs can be preserved under conditions of intercultural contact that will reduce myths and stereotypes associated with previously unknown groups. These are big assumptions. Some will argue that because stereotyping and prejudices help develop strong in-group feelings they are necessary if cherished traditions and beliefs are to be preserved. Can we destroy ethnic stereotypes and still maintain cultural pluralism?

First, consider what is meant by stereotypes. A stereotype is a mental category that is based on exaggerated and inaccurate generalizations about a group of people that are either favorable or unfavorable. It is prejudiced thought used to describe all members of the group.

As explained by Harry Triandis and others, stereotyping is natural.[10] All humans develop categories to help make sense of their environment. In some disciplines, such as anthropology, this is an acceptable procedure. In the area of group behavior,

we behave in response to many similar events as though they were identical. We do this because it is impossible for the human brain to employ all the information present in man's environment. Furthermore, there is a natural tendency to simplify our problems and to solve them as easily as possible. A "pet formula" such as "Mexicans are lazy" makes it possible for an Anglo employer to eliminate much of his mental effort by simply not considering Mexicans for jobs in his firm. If he were to check on each applicant and to understand the causes of his behavior he would have to work much harder. Furthermore, categorization helps perception. When somebody tells us, "Careful, a drunken driver!" our driving instantly becomes more defensive. The category "drunken" implies many behaviors on the part of the other driver, and we adjust to them quickly and usefully.

But categorization also has a penalty. The broader the categories, the more inaccurate they are likely to be. The more they help us, in that they allow us to simplify our problems, the more likley they are to cause us to perceive the world incorrectly.[11]

Often there is just enough fact to make a stereotype seem true. Triandis distinguishes between sociotypes, which are accurate characterizations of social groups, and stereotypes, which are what people believe about another group of people. Sometimes there is a kernel of truth to a stereotype, but sociotypes and stereotypes overlap only imperfectly.[12]

Theoretically, it could be argued that stereotypes can foster intergroup understanding when they happen to fit the person being stereotyped. For example, a teacher might better understand such a student's needs if he or she knew what to look for. Most often, however, stereotypes are dangerous because when based on a negative prejudice they can lead to discrimination or scapegoating. There are very few positive stereotypes. Those that do exist are about those who dominate the society and give justification for their preeminent position.

Those who believe in the feasibility of cultural pluralism will find support in the words of Gordon Allport, considered by many to be the greatest authority on prejudice and the personality. Allport agrees that humans prefer the familiar, but he explains that this is because of "the principles of ease, least effort, congeniality, and pride in one's own culture," not prejudice. He visualizes social relationships among groups along a continuum from friendly to hostile. He proposes that we "define the degrees of hostile relationships that are readily distinguishable, starting with predilection, the mildest and most normal form of group-exclusion, through active prejudice and discrimination, to scapegoating itself."[13] (See Figure 3.1 and Box 3.1.)

Allport has written that group loyalty does not necessarily mean one feels hostile toward out-groups. "Hostility toward out-groups helps strengthen our sense of belonging, but it is not required."[14] To illustrate his point, Allport has diagramed some of the in-groups to which one might belong, with the central core being most potent and the outermost circle being the weakest (see Figure 3.2). There is no intrinsic reason, however, why loyalty to humanity ("mankind"—the outermost circle) must be weakest. Allport writes:*

> Race itself has become the dominant loyalty among many people, especially among fanatic advocates of "Aryanism" and among certain members of oppressed races. It seems today that the clash between the idea of race and of One World (the two outermost circles) is shaping into an issue that may well be the most decisive in human history. The important question is, Can a loyalty to mankind be fashioned before interracial warfare breaks out?
>
> Theoretically it can, for there is a saving psychological principle that may be invoked if we can learn how to do so in time. The

---

*The following quotation from Gordon Allport, *The Nature of Prejudice*, ©1979, Addison-Wesley, Reading, Massachusetts, is reprinted with permission of the publisher.

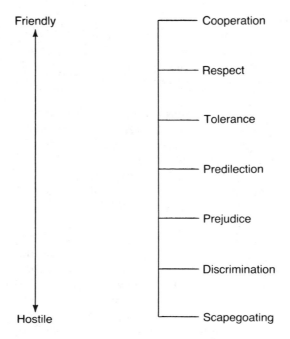

Figure 3.1 *A Continuum of Social Relationships Among Human Groups. From Gordon Allport,* ABC's of Scapegoating *(New York: Anti-Defamation League of B'nai B'rith, 1979). Reprinted by permission of the Anti-Defamation League of B'nai B'rith.*

principle states that concentric loyalties need not clash. To be devoted to a large circle does not imply the destruction of one's attachment to a smaller circle. The loyalties that clash are almost invariably those of identical scope. A bigamist who has founded two families of procreation is in fatal trouble with himself and with society. A traitor who serves two nations (one nominally and one actually) is mentally a mess and socially a felon. Few people can acknowledge more than one alma mater, one religion, or one fraternity. On the other hand, a world-federalist can be a devoted family man, an ardent alumnus, and a sincere patriot. The fact that some fanatic nationalists would challenge the compatibility of world-loyalty with patriotism does not change the psychological law. Wendell Willkie and Franklin Roosevelt were no less patriots because they envisioned a United Nations in One World.[15]

If we accept Allport's reasoning, it is clear that loyalty to an ethnic group need not preclude loyalty to the nation and vice versa. Respect and cooperation among different groups can replace prejudice, discrimination, and scapegoating.

The assumption that everyone is prejudiced is neither helpful nor accurate. There are individual differences in the extent to which we

Box 3.1

Degrees of
Hostile
Relation-
ships

Predilection is the simple preference of an individual for one culture, one skin color, one language as opposed to another. If you like Mexican culture and I do not, there is no use disputing about our respective tastes. We are privileged to disagree on such matters, and, as a rule, we respect one another's choice. Predilections are inevitable and natural. But they are the first step toward scapegoating if and when they turn into more active biases, that is to say, into:

Prejudice. Here we have a rigid, inflexible, exaggerated predilection. A prejudice is an attitude in a closed mind. Impervious to evidence and to contrary argument it makes for prejudgment. Some Europeans think all Americans are loud-mouthed spendthrifts. This stereotyped judgment is fixed. It is hard to change. It is a prejudice. An Oxford student is said to have remarked, "I despise all Americans, but I've never met one I didn't like." This anecdote suggests that prejudgments may stand even when every particle of available evidence is against them. Some people with prejudices think all Negroes are stupid, all Scotsmen are tight-fisted, all women inferior to men.

Prejudice, if not *acted out*, if kept to oneself, does no great social harm. It merely stultifies the mind that possesses it. But prejudice expressed leads to:

Discrimination, which differs from scapegoating chiefly in the amount of aggression shown. Discrimination is an act of exclusion prompted by prejudice. Generally it is based not on an individual's intrinsic qualities but on a "label" branding the individual as a member of a discredited group. It means separating forcibly and unjustly from our vocation, our neighborhood, our schools, even our churches, a person against whom we are prejudiced because he bears an unsavory label. Note well, it is not *we* who move out, prompted by our predilection, but *they* whom we forcibly exclude from intruding into "our domain."

Scapegoating is full-fledged aggression in word or deed. The victim is abused verbally or physically. He usually cannot fight back, for we see to it that we pick only on minority groups weaker than ourselves. The essential cowardliness of scapegoating is illustrated by our persecution of the Salem "witches," a small, frail handful of neurotic women and elderly people who could not offer effective resistance.

As long as human beings have choices to make, they will make them on the basis of some inclination. Predilections are the basis for such choices, normal enough and inevitable. But unjust generalizations on the basis of these predilections lead to the formulation of prejudices which, if uncontrolled, breed discrimination. Finally, if conditions are ripe—if frustration, ignorance, and propaganda combine in proper proportions—discrimination breaks over into scapegoating.

Source: Gordon Allport, *ABC's of Scapegoating* (New York: Anti-Defamation League of B'nai B'rith, 1979), pp. 8–10. Reprinted by permission of the Anti-Defamation League of B'nai B'rith.

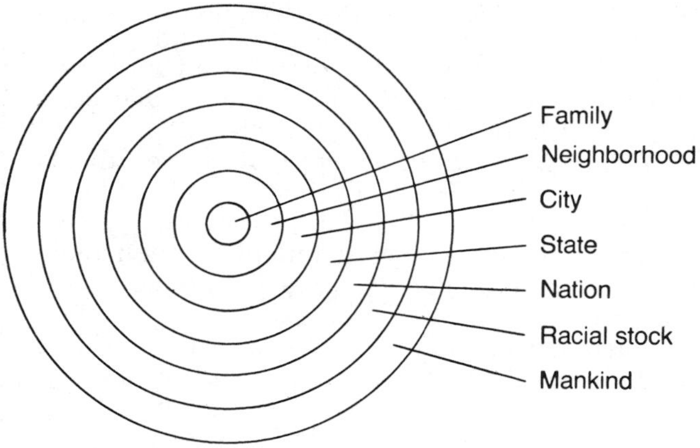

Figure 3.2 *Hypothetical Lessening of In-Group Potency as Membership Becomes More Inclusive. From Gordon Allport,* The Nature of Prejudice, © *1979, Addison-Wesley, Reading, Massachusetts. Reprinted with permission of the publisher.*

reject outsiders. Furthermore, it has been established that the person who rejects one out-group is likely to reject any out-group.[16] Although no single theory adequately explains the development of prejudice, it appears that less prejudiced people have fewer aggressive needs, hold a generally favorable view of their parents, and perceive their environment as friendly and nonthreatening. No child is born prejudiced. Prejudices are learned within a context influenced by personal needs and social influence.

Research by Glen Pate suggests that some people reject prejudiced thinking because of intellectual and psychological strengths.[17] He identifies four areas of defense against prejudice: positive view of self, positive view of society (for example, belief in democratic values of equality and justice), positive view of other people, and logical thinking. An individual with low self-esteem is more likely to be prejudiced than one with high self-esteem. A positive view of society means:

> A person should have basically democratic views with a belief in equality and a sense of justice. A positive view of other people includes a degree of empathy, a feeling that people are basically worthwhile, and an aversion to manipulating people for selfish reasons. Logical thinking is just that—a quality of reasoning ability which does not jump to conclusions, see only the superficial, reach faulty conclusions, confuse cause and effect, or overgeneralize.[18]

Obviously teachers are limited in what they can do to modify the deeply prejudiced personality. We should remember, however, that not everyone who accepts stereotypes is deeply prejudiced. Furthermore, there is no known reason why we cannot or should not attempt to reduce ethnic group stereotypes and at the same time foster within our students a healthy sense of ethnic pride and respect. Those who feel genuine pride (not superiority) in their own ethnic group are most apt to accept other ethnic groups. Stereotypes impede that acceptance.

Some Necessary Conditions for Multicultural Schools: The Example of Effective School Desegregation in Urban Settings

Under what conditions do students benefit from desegregated schooling? Most desegregated schools were forced to do so before this question was answered. The assumption over the past quarter century seems to have been that segregated schools are inherently bad, and desegregated schools inherently good.

To the degree that segregated schools foster unwarranted fears, misconceptions, and negative stereotypes between isolated groups, in addition to unequal educational opportunities, this assumption is correct. It is false, however, to assume that simply desegregating a school will eliminate these inherent problems. Both research and casual observation in the vast majority of desegregated schools document the existence of resegregation through formal practices such as tracking, grouping, and scheduling of extracurricular activities, and through informal practices such as student seating preferences in classrooms and cafeterias. Many desegregated schools face the problems of racial tension, apathy, and absenteeism as a reaction to forced busing and desegregation. All these conditions mediate against personal growth and achievement among students.

Unfortunately, there has rarely been time for advance consideration of the question, "Under what conditions do students benefit from desegregated schooling?" In most United States schools, teachers, students, and administrators have been forced to desegregate without the help of guidelines to establish good race relations and academic achievement among minority and majority students alike. However, answers to the question do exist. The purpose of the remainder of this chapter is to provide a synthesis of important, but not widely used, concepts and theories that hold promise for school desegregation, and to suggest guidelines for effective desegregation in a variety of settings.

The focus will be on the urban setting, which typically has involved racial desegregation. Urban desegregation highlights the process that occurs unrecognized in many other school settings where race may not be a factor. Numerous possibilities come to mind: rural versus urban, labor versus management, wealthy versus poor, military versus civilian, Christian versus non-Christian, Polish American versus Italian American, and Indian versus non-Indian.

How the Host School Responds

There are at least four possible ways schools can respond to school desegregation: business-as-usual, assimilation, pluralistic coexistence, and integrated pluralism. These possible responses have been identified and described by H. A. Sagar and J. W. Schofield, as a result of their research in desegregated schools.[19] This author believes that the first three are unacceptable and that integrated pluralism—or, simply, integration—is a goal to strive for. Thomas Pettigrew makes a distinction between desegregated schools, which refers to the physical mixing of formerly isolated ethnic groups in the same school, and integrated schools.[20] Integration is a form of desegregation whereby all desegregated groups are recognized and accommodated—in other words, the conditions of cultural pluralism.

Business-as-usual may be characterized as follows:

> Insofar as possible, these interracial schools tried to maintain the same basic curriculum, the same academic standards, and the same teaching methods that prevailed under segregation. . . . Furthermore, they strove to enforce the same behavioral standards, to espouse the same values, and to apply the same sanctions to student offenses. In short, the schools did not perceive themselves as having to adjust their traditional practices in order to handle the new student body. Rather, the students were expected to adjust to the school.[21]

This type of response does not consider whether old rules or procedures are desirable when the nature of the student population has changed.

Compatible with the business-as-usual approach to desegregation is the assimilationist response.

> The assimilationist ideology holds that integration will have been achieved when the minority group can no longer be differentiated from the white majority in terms of economic status, education, or access to social institutions and their benefits. This will be accomplished by fostering a "color-blind" attitude where prejudice once reigned . . . and by imparting to minority persons the skills and value orientations which will enable them to take their place in the currently white-dominated social structure. . . . No significant change is anticipated since the newly assimilated minority individuals will be attitudinally and behaviorally indistinguishable from the majority. Stated in its baldest form, the assimilationist charge to the schools is to make minority children more like white children.[22]

Those who do not assimilate are resegregated, drop out, or are suspended or expelled. The fact that students' race and culture may make a difference, say in students' and teachers' perceptions of each other and expectations about appropriate classroom behavior, is not considered. This response is often based on an erroneous assumption that to recognize race is to be racist.

Schools that desegregate with the business-as-usual or assimilation response appear similar. The subtle difference is that under the assimilation response a conscious decision has been made by the host school about expectations for new students. Business-as-usual schools proceed as they have in the past and, perhaps unconsciously, expect all new students to fit in.

Like the business-as-usual and assimilation response, the pluralistic coexistence response also involves resegregation. But in contrast to the assimilation response, where only those students who do not fit in are resegregated, pluralistic coexistence is based on separation of different racial or ethnic groups. Students are allowed to maintain different styles and values, but within a school environment comprised of separate turfs for different racial groups. Typically, there are different schools within a school, and little or no attempt is made to encourage students to mix. Describing one such school, Sagar and Schofield wrote:

> The principal tolerated almost complete informal resegregation of the students, to the point where there were considered to be "two schools within a school." The school's annex, for example, became known as a black area, or the "recreational study hall," while the library served as a white area, or "non-recreational study hall."[23]

In this formerly all-White school, the Black principal tried to appease White parents by maintaining advanced academic programs to prevent them from withdrawing their children, who had become the minority. In this school situation, separate was clearly unequal.

In contrast with these three responses to school desegregation, integrated pluralism actively seeks to avoid resegregation of students.

> [It] is pluralistic in the sense that it recognizes the diverse racial and ethnic groups in our society and does not denigrate them just because they deviate from the white middle class patterns of behavior. Integrated pluralism affirms the equal value of the school's various ethnic groups, encouraging their participation, not on majority-defined terms, but in an evolving system which reflects the contributions of all groups. However, integrated pluralism goes beyond mere support for the side-by-side coexistence of different group values and styles. It is integrationist in the sense that it affirms the educational value inherent in exposing *all* students to a diversity of perspectives and behavioral repertoires and the social value of structuring the school so that students from previously isolated and even hostile groups can come to know each other under conditions conducive to the development of positive intergroup relations. . . .

> Integrated pluralism takes an activist stance in trying to foster in-
> teraction between different groups of students rather than accept-
> ing resegregation as either desirable or inevitable.[24]

Research on the characteristics of effectively integrated schools shows
that a policy consistent with integrated pluralism has the best potential
for encouraging good race relations, academic achievement, and personal development among students. This assertion will be explained
more fully later in this chapter.

Three necessary conditions underlie cultural pluralism in the
school, or the integrated pluralism response: positive teacher expectations, a learning environment that encourages positive intergroup contact, and a pluralistic curriculum. This chapter concludes with a discussion of the first two of these conditions. Chapters 4 and 5 deal more fully
with learner characteristics that often interact with teacher expectations,
and Chapter 8 expands on effective classroom strategies. Chapters 6 and
7 will develop condition three: a pluralistic curriculum.

Condition One: Positive Teacher Expectations

Teachers often make snap judgments about students and treat them
differently, based on their perceptions of them. Many teachers interact
with students differently according to the student's race and socioeconomic status. Barbara Lightfoot has aptly referred to teachers as "judges
of deviance."

Much has been written about the power of teacher expectations.
Research also supports the basic assumption that teacher attitudes influence student achievement. Probably best known is the controversial
study by Robert Rosenthal and Lenore Jacobson, who reported their
success in influencing student achievement by giving teachers phony
data about their students.[25] Approximately 20 percent of the student
population, selected at random, were identified as "bloomers" on an
intelligence test. Teachers were given the names of these supposedly
high-potential students, to be held in confidence, and these students did
indeed achieve at significantly higher levels than their classmates. Although the methodology used in this study has been questioned by
some, even its critics accept the notion that teacher expectations often
affect student achievement.[26]

In another study, social studies student teachers were asked by
their university supervisors to rank their students from high to low in
terms of academic ability after two days in the classroom.[27] The student
teachers did so without expressing uncertainty or difficulty. During the
semester, their interactions with the high and low students were coded
by their university supervisors. Results showed that lows were less
frequently encouraged to participate in class discussion or to interact

with the teacher, either directly by being called on or indirectly by receiving extended teacher feedback when they volunteered. Teachers tended to neglect the students they rated low.

In another study involving student teachers, all White females, the women were asked to teach a comparable current events lesson to a biracial group of students.[28] Each was given a class roster that contained phony IQ data for each student. High and low IQs were distributed at random, but evenly for Black and White students. Classroom observers recorded no significant difference in student behavior during the lesson, but the student teachers perceived the bright Black students as more hostile and disruptive. A likely explanation is that these student teachers felt threatened by students who did not fit their expectations (that is, they were not expecting a group of Black students who were also bright).

A growing body of evidence indicates that many White teachers have lower expectations for their non-White students. In one midwestern study of high school student discipline in two large urban school corporations, for example, teachers who responded to an anonymous questionnaire felt Black students had less innate potential than White students on every variable, except basketball, where Blacks were perceived as having equal potential. Other variables included band, orchestra, drama, and scholastics.[29]

Another study of classroom interaction in forty-one middle school classrooms showed that when teachers have equal achievement expectations for Black and White students there is more interracial friendship and interaction among the students. A classroom climate of acceptance among students was more likely to exist when teachers did not distinguish between the learning potential of Black and White students.[30] Other studies have shown that a classroom climate of acceptance is related to increased student achievement, especially among minorities in the classroom.

Studies by Geneva Gay, Ray Rist, and the U.S. Civil Rights Commission have shown that many teachers have lower expectations for Black and Mexican American students.[31] In the Rist study, which involved Black teachers and students, the teacher had lower expectations for the darker-skinned children. All three studies showed that teachers interacted with low-expectation students in intellectually limiting ways and were more supportive and stimulating with their White or light-skinned students.

Given the fact that teacher expectations strongly influence student achievement, and given the fact that many teachers hold lower expectations for Black and Hispanic students, is integrated education possible? This author believes it is. Not all administrators, teachers, and students are racially prejudiced and not all have lower expectations. These facts attest that racial prejudice is not necessary to the human condition.

Furthermore, many teachers, administrators, and students who are racially prejudiced can develop the kinds of understanding required to become less so. This is a major goal of multicultural education among adults.

Lower teacher expectations for particular racial or ethnic groups are based on negative racial or ethnic prejudice. Prejudice is an erroneous judgment, usually negative, which is based on incomplete or faulty information. Prejudice becomes a stereotype when it is used to label all or most members of a group. Racial prejudice, therefore, is an erroneous and typically negative judgment made about members of a racial group. Teachers, like all people, often are not aware of their prejudices; thus they may not be aware of their lower expectations for some students.

A major theme in this book is the belief that if teachers are to have equally positive expectations for students of all races they must understand the cultural differences that often exist in the desegregated classroom. The fact that cultural differences frequently are associated with racial differences often confirms myths and stereotypes associated with race. Teachers need guidelines to help them observe and interpret culturally different behavior. Such guidelines can help prevent blanket assumptions that certain behaviors and values go with certain racial features.

There is an argument against the study of cultural differences that, while not found in scholarly literature, is frequently expressed in courses and workshops designed to help educators work with culturally diverse students. Even though its major premise is false, as will be shown, the argument warrants discussion because it can seriously undermine efforts to achieve integrated pluralism in schools.

The argument holds that to dwell on cultural differences is to foster negative prejudices and stereotypes, and that it is human nature to view those who are different as inferior. Some students, during early phases of studying different ethnic groups, have reported that they were developing new negative prejudices; the excerpt from the student journal on page 1 is an example of this. The truth is, however, that there are numerous cultural differences as well as basic similarities of being human, and to gloss over these differences doesn't change this reality. If it is also true that different people are viewed as being inferior, then it would seem that the ability to interpret cultural differences and understand their origins to avoid intercultural conflict would be an imperative goal of education. Myths and stereotypes about different cultures and races are based on incomplete and erroneous information.

A major fallacy of the argument that perception of difference fosters negative prejudices and stereotypes is that it ignores the fact that humans differ in their capacity to accept and appreciate diversity, and that humans may become more (or less) open-minded as life progresses. This assertion is supported by the work of scholars such as E. S. Bogardus, Robert Levine, and Milton Rokeach, who have developed different measures of open-mindedness, particularly openness to racial and ethnic diversity.[32] Chapter 5 will present recent conceptualizations of stages of ethnic identity, which are generating research efforts that will clarify how humans differ in their ability to accept differences. These studies suggest that teachers must understand the diversity among members of an ethnic group—in terms of their sense of ethnic identity—if they are to make appropriate decisions in desegregated settings. Furthermore, if teachers are to provide equal opportunities for learning, their expectations for student success must be positive and equitable. In ethnically diverse classrooms, teachers need a healthy sense of their own ethnic identity in order for this to occur.

Condition Two: A Learning Environment That Supports Positive Interracial Contact

Too often, with different groups of students who share a history of isolation from each other, we simply bring them together and hope for the best. The best rarely happens. Casual contact between different ethnic groups may reinforce existing negative stereotypes or generate new ones. This fact was exemplified recently in a kindergarten classroom in a Florida school district during its initial attempts at desegregation. As the school year began, White students, most of whom had already had several years of nursery school, could be found busily working in one of the higher-ability achievement groups. Their Black classmates, who had been bused from across town and had not had preparatory nursery school experience, ran wildly around the room until they could be settled into one of the remedial or lower-achievement groups. White parents who advocated school desegregation were dismayed by their children's negative reports. For many of these White kindergartners, initial contact with Black children appeared to be creating negative racial prejudices. For most of the Black kindergartners, the vicious cycle of low expectations and low academic achievement was beginning.

Scenes like this can be avoided when school policies and practices are guided by social contact theory. In 1954, the year of the landmark school desegregation decision, Gordon Allport first published his theory of positive intergroup contact. He summarized his theory as follows:

> Given a population of ordinary people, with a normal degree of prejudice, we are safe in making the following general prediction: Prejudice (unless deeply rooted in the character structure of the individual) may be reduced by equal status contact between majority and minority groups in the pursuit of common goals. The effect is greatly enhanced if this contact is sanctioned by institutional supports (i.e. by law, custom or local atmosphere), and if it is of a sort

that leads to the perception of common interests and common humanity between members of the two groups.[33]

It is unlikely that the young children described in this scene harbored deep-seated racial prejudice. If this is also true for the teacher, classroom practices can be implemented to encourage academic achievement and good race relations. Social contact theory provides a framework that can help educators identify policy guidelines for effective school desegregation, as well as promising practices that have been uncovered by recent research in desegregated schools.

According to contact theorists, at least four basic conditions are necessary if social contact between groups is to lessen negative prejudice and lead to friendly attitudes and behaviors:

1. Contact should be sufficiently intimate to produce reciprocal knowledge and understanding between groups.
2. Members of various groups must share equal status.
3. The contact situation should lead people to do things together. It should require intergroup cooperation to achieve a common goal.
4. There must be institutional support—an authority and/or social climate that encourages intergroup contact.[34]

These four conditions of positive social contact can be used as guidelines for observing desegregated schools and for detecting problem areas. One of the most difficult conditions for most schools to establish is an equal status environment for the different racial groups within the student body. Often there are sharp socioeconomic differences, as well as differences in the initial achievement levels of Black and White classmates. Tracking and grouping practices may be viewed as necessary, but they may also lead to resegregation. A history of racial discrimination in education and hiring practices means schools often face a limited pool of available Black and Hispanic administrators and teachers who can serve as high-status role models.

Other potential violations of the conditions of positive intergroup contact stem from school rules, discipline practices, extracurricular activities, and symbols and traditions. Some rules are perceived as inequitable (for example, prohibition of bad language and hats). Scheduling extracurricular activities after school excludes students who travel by bus and limits opportunities for intergroup contact in co-curricular activities. School traditions often become a problem during initial stages of desegregation and act as symbolic indicators of where the school's authority stands on integrated pluralism.

If "new" students come to an "old" school, there is a frequent tendency for both racial groups to perceive the school as "belonging" to the "old" group. The school name, team nicknames, school songs, and titles of school publications are a few of the many symbols that may symbolize preeminence of a particular racial group. There are other, more subtle, customs that may symbolize segregation in ways not anticipated. If editors have always been college preparatory students, and there are few college preparatory students in the "new" group, continuation of the tradition will symbolize unequal status. . . .

"Preserving traditions" can be an euphemism for "putting minorities in their place." Opposition to integration may focus on defense of symbols. When this happens, school personnel need to realize what is happening and deal with the reality.[35]

Underlying these relatively visible concerns is a hidden problem: a mutual lack of knowledge about communication modes, values, and perceptions among culturally different students and teachers, which often leads to misunderstanding and conflict. For example, many White teachers and students are unknowingly ignorant about the structures and meanings of Black vernacular. The double negative "ain't got no" may signify a "low-class," uneducated person, while use of the term "nigger" among Blacks may be viewed by Whites as insulting or threatening. Black students, on the other hand, might regard all Whites as racist and interpret the behaviors of White teachers and classmates from that perspective. As long as students and teachers are left to their own devices, there is little opportunity for the kind of intimate contact between culturally different students that could foster mutual understanding. Informal segregation is typically the rule throughout the school.

Social contact theory can be used as a guide to alleviate obstacles to school integration. Although visions of integrated schools may differ, there are at least two necessary observable characteristics. First, there is a relaxed interracial mixing among the majority of students and teachers in casual and informal settings at school. Second, there is real academic achievement and personal growth among all students, as seen in formal course work and extracurricular activities. These two characteristics appear to be interactive. Where good race relations exist student achievement is higher, and the reverse is also true.

There is no standard recipe for integrating the desegregated school. Neither are there specific requisite practices. There are, however, necessary conditions for positive intergroup contact (equal status, knowledge, cooperation, and institutional support) that schools can use as a guide in making decisions about specific desegregation practices. For example, some form of ability grouping might be appropriate in creating an equal-status environment in one school but not in another. What is important is that ability groups do not produce racially visible differences.

Research by scholars such as Elizabeth Cohen suggests ways of creating equal status among racially different students who bring differ-ing entry-level skills to the classroom.[36] In one study Cohen provided special instruction to lower achievers prior to their participation in small-group cooperative learning. The lower achievers could then make unique contributions to their group, which helped equalize their class-room status. Furthermore, achievement and interracial friendship were enhanced.

A recent study conducted by Garlie Forehand and Marjorie Ragosta focused on school characteristics of effectively desegregated schools.[37] The researchers defined effectiveness in terms of student achievement and race relations. Data were collected from tests, questionnaires, and interviews in nearly 200 schools. All the schools were racially mixed and represented a wide range of socioeconomic, demographic, and geo-graphic conditions.

The results identified school conditions under which benefits in integrated education were maximized in a wide variety of settings, sometimes even where large socioeconomic differences existed within the student population. In their *Handbook for Integrated Schooling*, which developed from their findings, the researchers have presented a number of practices that characterize effectively desegregated schools. Table 3.1 presents an overview of these and other research findings, and shows their relationship with the conditions of positive intergroup contact.

Other research shows that biracial work and play teams among students are one of the most powerful ways to improve race relations. As seen in Table 3.1, this practice meets the four conditions of positive intergroup contact. One promising strategy that builds on this fact is *team learning*, an approach developed by Robert Slavin and his associates at the Center for Social Organization of Schools at The Johns Hopkins University. Team learning can help establish an equal-status environ-ment among students who bring different entry skills to the classroom because the tasks can be designed to fit student strengths. (Team learn-ing is examined in Chapter 8.)

Conclusions

Teachers must be relatively free of racial prejudice and ethnocentrism if they are to be effective with students of diverse cultural, racial, and socioeconomic backgrounds. Although prejudice and ethnocentrism are natural to the human condition, it is assumed that teachers should be less prejudiced and ethnocentric than the average person. Furthermore, it is possible for teachers to become so.

A multicultural society requires educational programs that are mul-ticultural, not monocultural, in design. Most students in every racial group can achieve the basic requirements in school under the proper conditions. Most students (regardless of race or socioeconomic status)

Table 3.1 *Strategies for School Integration: Summary of Research Findings*

	CONDITIONS OF POSITIVE INTERGROUP CONTACT			
SCHOOL PRACTICE	EQUAL STATUS	KNOWLEDGE/ ACQUAIN- TANCE	COMMON GOAL	INSTITU- TIONAL SUPPORT
Multiethnic curriculum	✓	✓		✓
Extracurricular activities scheduled during school day	✓	✓	✓	✓
Open discussion of race and racial issues in classroom		✓		✓
Biracial work and play teams among students	✓	✓	✓	✓
Biracial seating patterns		✓		✓
Rules and discipline: equal punishment for equal offense	✓			✓
Equitable rules. (If punishment for the infraction of a rule appears to be associated with race, determine whether the rule is equitable.)	✓			✓
Academic achievement and good race relations established as explicit goals				✓
Biracial staffing that reflects school's racial composition	✓			✓
Biracial staffing in high-status positions				✓
Student-focused human relations activities	✓	✓	✓	✓
Class and program assignments that do not result in racially identifiable groups	✓	✓		✓
Individualized instruction that rewards improvement as well as academic absolutes	✓			✓

can master basic knowledge at the accepted grade-level standards. Similar proportions of gifted and talented students are found across all racial groups, and most individuals are capable of achieving a degree of personal excellence.

Schooling in the United States should be racially integrated. Furthermore, there are positive actions that can be taken to maximize the benefits of integrated schooling. In most United States urban schools, however, teachers, students, and administrators have been forced to desegregate without helpful guidelines to establish good race relations and foster academic achievement among both minority and nonminority students. Many educational programs designed to assist teachers and students in desegregated schools have ignored the fact that great differences in psychological readiness are likely to exist among the participants (for example, differences in their degree of open-mindedness and sense of ethnic identity). Psychological orientations such as these can be directly related to an individual's previous interracial and intercultural contact experiences, particularly the intensity and positive or negative nature of these experiences.

This chapter opened with a case for multicultural education and concluded with necessary conditions for establishing effective integrated schools in urban settings. These conditions also apply to schools where teachers and students have developed stereotypes and misunderstandings because of the absence of intergroup contact, either through personal experience or through books and other media.

Part I has emphasized culture and ethnicity as factors in teaching and learning. Part II will describe individual differences that affect the classroom, for as important as culture is, "people are not merely microcosmic examples, rubber stamps, of the culture to which they are heirs. They are individual personalities who handle cultural norms in different ways with varying degrees of adeptness, with their own personal styles. Some even choose to ignore the norms—which is in itself an important cultural decision.[38]

Compare and Contrast

1. Monocultural and multicultural education
2. Equity and equality
3. Stereotype and sociotype
4. Prejudice, predilection, and discrimination
5. School desegregation and school integration
6. Social contact theory and defenses to prejudice theory

Activities and Questions

1. You have been asked to present a major address at the Annual Meeting of the Society for Intercultural Education, Training, and Research (SIETAR). This year's meeting is in Paris during the month of

July. All your expenses are paid, including a three-week European study tour with educators from around the world. Choose your topic: "The Case Against Multicultural Education" or "The Case for Multicultural Education." Plan a rigorous and inspiring speech.

2. Can a stereotype ever be good? Explain fully.

3. Interracial contact: a personal history. Complete the interracial contact sheets on pages 74–76, or ask your students to complete them. Results can be shared in small and large groups.

4. Under what conditions can school desegregation lead to positive race relations among students and staff? According to contact theorists, at least four basic conditions are necessary if social contact between different isolated groups is to lessen negative prejudice and lead to friendly attitudes and behaviors. These conditions are listed below. As you read each one, note current practices in your school or classroom that would impede the development of that condition (negative practice) as well as practices that would help establish it (positive practices). Finally, note practices not in use that could be implemented to help build this condition in your school or classroom (possibilities).

   a. Contact should be sufficiently intimate to engender knowledge and mutual understanding between different ethnic or racial groups that have been isolated from each other.

NEGATIVE PRACTICES	POSITIVE PRACTICES	POSSIBILITIES
(1) —————	(1) —————	(1) —————
(2) —————	(2) —————	(2) —————
(3) —————	(3) —————	(3) —————

   b. Members of the various ethnic groups should share equal status.

NEGATIVE PRACTICES	POSITIVE PRACTICES	POSSIBILITIES
(1) —————	(1) —————	(1) —————
(2) —————	(2) —————	(2) —————
(3) —————	(3) —————	(3) —————

   c. The contact situation leads people to do things together; it requires intergroup cooperation to achieve a common goal.

NEGATIVE PRACTICES	POSITIVE PRACTICES	POSSIBILITIES
(1) —————	(1) —————	(1) —————
(2) —————	(2) —————	(2) —————
(3) —————	(3) —————	(3) —————

Interracial Contact: A Personal History

FREQUENCY OF INTERRACIAL CONTACT

QUALITY AND NATURE OF CONTACT

P = Positive feelings N = Negative feelings
V = Neutral feelings 0 = No contact

	Daily, or often as same race	Often, weekly	Rarely, several times a year	Never	Home Adults	Home Peers	Neighborhood / Community Adults	Neighborhood / Community Peers	School Adults	School Peers	Friends Team sports	Friends Clubs	Friends Your house	Friends His/Her house	Friends Best friends	Work Adults	Work Peers	Other important life events/ experiences
Birth																		
School Entry																		
Junior High																		
High School																		

The Interracial Contact Scale: Current Campus Profile A

QUALITY AND NATURE OF CONTACT

P = Positive feelings   N = Negative feelings
V = Neutral feelings   O = No contact

Type of Contact	FREQUENCY OF CONTACT				QUALITY AND NATURE OF CONTACT					
	Daily	Often	Rarely	Never						
With racially different students					In classes	On teams	Special interest groups, clubs	Roommates	Parties	Work
With professors					In classes	Prof's office	Teams, clubs	Committees	Social	Work
With staff					Formal, in offices		Informal			
Extra-campus										

75

The Interracial Contact Scale: Current Campus Profile B

Twelve types of campus activities are listed. Circle any that you are now participating in or have participated in during the past year. For each activity you circle, check *yes* if the condition is true and *no* if the condition is not.

Campus Activity	INTERRACIAL CONDITIONS							
	Minorities and nonminorities have a chance to get to know each other personally		Minorities and nonminorities have equal status		Minorities and nonminorities cooperate to achieve a common goal		People in authority, or the social climate, encourage contact between minorities and nonminorities	
	No	Yes	No	Yes	No	Yes	No	Yes
1. Church group								
2. Club								
3. Team								
4. Musical or theatrical performance								
5. Class								
6. Party								
7. Dorm								
8. Work								
9. Fraternity/ Sorority								
10. Political								
11. Student committee								
12. Organization								
13. Other								

d. There is institutional support—an authority and/or social climate
    that encourages intergroup contact.

NEGATIVE PRACTICES   POSITIVE PRACTICES   POSSIBILITIES

(1) —————————   (1) —————————   (1) —————————

(2) —————————   (2) —————————   (2) —————————

(3) —————————   (3) —————————   (3) —————————

5. When might racially segregated schools be better than integrated
schools?

6. Consider the characteristics Glen Pate has identified as defenses
to prejudice: highly positive view of self, strong belief in equality and
justice, highly positive view of other people, and ability to think logi-
cally and critically. How do you rate yourself on each category? Teachers
you know? Students? Assuming Pate's theory is valid, how can schools
help strengthen defenses to prejudice among teachers, administrators,
and students? What could be done in your specific teaching area?

Notes

1. See, for example, *Asia in American Textbooks: An Evaluation* (New York:
The Asia Society, 1976); Jonathan Friedlander, *The Middle East: The Image and the
Reality* (Los Angeles: University of California Press, 1980); Susan J. Hall, *Africa in
U.S. Schools, K–12: A Survey* (New York: The African Institute, 1978); and *In
Search of Mutual Understanding,* Japan/United States Textbook Study Project, Joint
Report (Washington, D.C.: National Council of the Social Studies, January
1981).

2. Margaret Gibson, "Approaches to Multicultural Education in the United
States: Some Concepts and Assumptions," *Anthropology and Education Quarterly*
7, no. 4 (November 1976):7–18. Reprinted in *Anthropology and Education Quarterly*
15, no. 1 (Spring 1984). The summary and quotations from Gibson's work are
used by permission of the author and *Anthropology and Education Quarterly.*

3. Ibid.

4. Ibid.

5. Ibid.

6. Ibid.

7. Alfred J. Kraemer, "A Cultural Self-Awareness Approach to Improving
Intercultural Communication Skills," ERIC ED 079 213 (April 1973).

8. Michael Walzer, Edward T. Kantowicz, John Higham, and Mona Harrington, *The Politics of Ethnicity* (Cambridge, Mass.: Belknap Press of Harvard
University Press, 1982).

9. Ibid.

10. Harry C. Triandis, *Attitude and Attitude Change* (New York: John Wiley
and Sons, 1971).

11. Ibid., pp. 102–3. Quotation reprinted by permission of the publisher.
Copyright © 1971 by John Wiley & Sons, Inc.

12. Ibid.

13. Gordon Allport, *ABC's of Scapegoating* (New York: Anti-Defamation League of B'nai B'rith, 1979).

14. Gordon Allport, *The Nature of Prejudice* (Reading, Mass.: Addison-Wesley, 1979), p. 42.

15. Ibid., p. 44.

16. Ibid.

17. Glen S. Pate, "The Ingredients of Prejudice" (paper presented at the College and University Faculty Assembly of the National Council for the Social Studies, Boston, November 24, 1982).

18. Ibid.

19. H. A. Sagar and J. W. Schofield, "Integrating the Desegregated School: Problems and Possibilities," in *Advances in Motivation and Achievement: The Effects of School Desegregation on Motivation and Achievement*, ed. D. E. Bartz and M. L. Maehr (Greenwich, Conn.: JAI Press, 1984), vol. 1, pp. 203–42. Quotations from this article are reprinted by permission of Janet Schofield and JAI Press.

20. T. Pettigrew, "The Case for the Racial Integration of the Schools," in *Report on the Future of School Desegregation in the United States*, ed. O. Duff (Pittsburgh: University of Pittsburgh, Consultative Resource Center on School Desegregation and Conflict, 1973).

21. Sagar and Schofield, "Integrating the Desegregated School," p. 208.

22. Ibid., p. 212.

23. Ibid., pp. 220–21.

24. Ibid., pp. 231–232.

25. R. Rosenthal and L. Jacobson, *Pygmalion in the Classroom: Teacher Expectation and Pupils' Intellectual Development* (New York: Holt, Rinehart and Winston, 1968).

26. R. Snow, "Unfinished Pygmalion," *Contemporary Psychology* 14 (April 1969):197–99.

27. C. Cornbleth, O. L. Davis, Jr., and C. Bennett Button, "Expectations for Pupil Achievement and Teacher-Pupil Interaction," *Social Education* 38 (January 1974):54–58.

28. Described in Geneva Gay, "Differential Dyadic Interactions of Black and White Teachers with Black and White Pupils in Recently Desegregated Social Studies Classrooms: A Function of Teacher and Pupil Ethnicity," OE Project no. 2F113 (January 1974).

29. Christine Bennett and J. John Harris III, "Suspensions and Expulsions of Male and Black Students: A Study of the Causes of Disproportionality," *Urban Education* 16, no. 4 (January 1982):399–423.

30. C. Bennett, "A Study of Classroom Climate in Desegregated Schools," *The Urban Review* 13, no. 3 (1981):161–79.

31. Gay, "Differential Dyadic Interactions"; Ray Rist, "Student Social Class and Teacher Expectations: The Self-Fulfilling Prophecy in Ghetto Education," *Harvard Education Review* 40 (August 1970); U.S. Civil Rights Commission, *Teachers and Students. Report V: Mexican-American Education Study. Differences in Teacher Interaction with Mexican-American and Anglo Students* (Washington, D.C.: Government Printing Office, March 1973).

32. Robert A. Levine and Donald Campbell, *Ethnocentrism: Theories of Conflict, Ethnic Attitudes and Group Behavior* (New York: John Wiley and Sons, 1972).

33. Allport, *The Nature of Prejudice*, p. 281.

34. Ibid.

35. G. A. Forehand and M. Ragosta, *A Handbook for Integrated Schooling* (Princeton, N.J.: Educational Testing Service, 1976), p. 79.

36. Elizabeth Cohen, "Status Equalization in the Desegregated School" (pa-

per presented at the Annual Meeting of the American Educational Research Association, San Francisco, April 1979); and idem, "Student Influence in the Classroom" (paper presented at the Annual Meeting of the American Educational Research Association, Toronto, 1978).

37. Forehand and Ragosta, *Handbook for Integrated Schooling.*

38. Andrew Weiss, ed., Introduction to "Society and Personal Experience," in *Readings in Anthropology 75/76* (Guilford, Conn.: Dushkin, 1974), p. 36.

Part Two

Individual Differences
That Affect Teaching and Learning

The schools you are about to visit are real. Although their names have been changed, the teachers and students you will meet are actual people, and the incidents described have recently taken place.

There is nothing unique or unusual about these schools, teachers, or students. Some of the people and events will seem familiar, which is partly why they are included. Other people and events may seem exaggerated or unrealistic. These examples serve to illustrate that efforts to develop individual and cultural perspectives in teaching and learning must be broad in scope. Concern should not be limited to inner-city schools or settings where most students are ethnic minorities, but should include any classroom where students are not achieving because of personal and cultural characteristics that conflict with what predominates in a classroom. Is there a classroom in existence that does not merit this concern?

The Case of Warren Benson's Classroom

It is 2:00 P.M., beginning of the sixth period class, and Warren Benson, a young teacher, looks around the room. Only eight students out of a possible thirty are present.

"Where is everybody?" he demands. "They don't like your class," a girl volunteers. Three girls saunter in. Cora, who is playing a cassette recorder, bumps over to her desk in tune with the music. She lowers the volume. "Don't mark us down late," she shouts. "We was right here."

Benson, a first-year teacher who spent four years in the navy between high school and college, had requested this school. Here you find students from poverty homes, students who can't read, students who hate school and teachers, students with drug problems, students waiting to drop out. Almost one-third of the students come from homes where one or both parents speak only Spanish.

For years Benson's dream was to teach on an Indian reservation. He believed this school would be good preparation. Now, after two months in the classroom he has real doubts. Doubts about these kids. Doubts about himself.

Benson tells everyone to take out today's vocabulary words. "Aw, come on man, give us a break," a student called Spark moans. Cora turns up the volume and croons, "Hey-ey-ey, bay-bee . . . ah wants ya to know-o-o-o . . ." Then, lowering the volume, she asks, "Mr. Benson, you got a pencil?" Another straggler walks in. "You late, boy," one student says. "So what, boy," the straggler answers. Benson asks for a definition of the first word, *tariff*. No response. "Ricardo?" "What?" Ricardo asks, tuning in briefly. A few students busily leaf through the text, trying to locate the glossary.

Spark tells some nearby students his ancestors are Aztec Indians. "You an Indian?" Ricardo asks. "You got a tomahawk and all?" Benson defines tariff for Ricardo, who listens for a second, then throws a paper airplane over Benson's head and hits a girl in the neck. Benson continues. "Number two is Treaty of Guadalupe. Who can tell us what the Treaty of Guadalupe is?"

"Mr. Benson," Cora interrupts, "I got to go to the bathroom." Benson tells her no. "Goddammit, mother f——, I got to go to the bathroom," she yells. "I'll give you a pass today," says Benson, "but this is the last time."

Benson tries to get back into the lesson. "Who can tell us what the Treaty of Guadalupe is?" "Ain't no word Treaty of Ha-wa-da-loop in here," shouts Spark. A blonde student sits silently in a corner chair; everyone else is talking.

Cora returns to the classroom. She grabs Benson's hand and pats it. "You ain't mad, is you?" Benson ignores her. Then he shouts to make himself heard above the din of conversation. "Get quiet!" Benson slams his fist on the lectern. Then he glares at the students until he has their attention. "Okay. It's obvious that you haven't learned these words. Everybody take out a paper. I'm going to give you a vocabulary test."

It is evident that Warren Benson's class typifies one of the most difficult and challenging teaching situations imaginable. The problems Benson faces—problems of poorly skilled students, high absenteeism, and unruly classes—are faced by teachers throughout the nation.

One theme of the next two chapters is that we must learn to teach others as they would be taught (that is, learn), rather than necessarily as we would teach or have others teach us. We must be able to cue into the critical characteristics of learners in our classroom (critical meaning those characteristics that strongly affect the way a person learns). Some of these characteristics are accurately labeled individual differences. Others stem from cultural differences and alternatives.

Read the following incident, which took place recently in the Midwest. The case of Kevin Armstrong illustrates that it is often difficult to distinguish between individual and cultural characteristics, unless a teacher knows what to look for.

The Case of Kevin Armstrong

It is the second day of a new school year, 2:15 P.M. The phone rings and Mrs. Armstrong answers it.

"Hello, Mrs. Armstrong?" a voice inquires. "This is Mrs. Dixon over at Wildwood Elementary School. Kevin's teacher. I—"

Mrs. Armstrong, a striking Black woman in her early thirties, interrupts, "What's wrong?"

"Nothing is wrong," answers Mrs. Dixon. "I'm just calling to let you know that we've decided to put Kevin back in second grade. He just isn't ready for third grade work."

Mrs. Armstrong is stunned. Prior to their move from Denver to a midwestern university town, Kevin had done superior work in a desegregated school that was considered good. Over half the students were White. "What do you mean he isn't ready for third grade?" she asks coldly. "Teacher last year didn't say nothin' about him having problems."

"Mrs. Armstrong, what I'm suggesting is for Kevin's own good. He's way behind the other children in my class. He'll feel like a failure if he stays."

"How you think he'll feel if you put him back?" she snaps. "He been lookin' to third grade all summer long."

"I hoped you would understand that we want to do what's best for Kevin," responds Mrs. Dixon. "Would you like to come to the school and talk this over with the principal?"

"We comin'." Mrs. Armstrong hangs up and turns to face her husband.

Wildwood is considered by many to be the best elementary school in town. Standardized achievement test scores are among the highest in the state and the school boasts many innovative academic programs. Except for a few who, like Kevin, live in a string of apartment buildings bordering the school district, most of the children come from wealthy homes. The community is largely professional. A handful of Black and Latino children attend the school, and most have been adopted by Anglo parents.

Mr. Peters, the principal, explains to Mr. and Mrs. Armstrong why he and Mrs. Dixon believe Kevin would be better off in second grade. Mrs. Dixon, also present, remains silent.

"Kevin is too immature for third grade. Mrs. Dixon picked this up immediately. Physically he is small for his age, and his attention span is very short. During music class he is unable to sit still. In class he can't wait for his turn to speak and in general it's clear that he hasn't learned to control himself the way our other third graders do. Mrs. Dixon has already given the children some pretests to see how much they remember. And, of course, Kevin's reading, writing, and math skills are way below grade level."

"Can't you give him a chance? This is just the second day. Can't we get him some tutoring or something? I read somewhere about some special programs for kids in the district who have problems," Mr. Armstrong asks.

"Some schools in the city do, but not us. We don't have enough students who need them to justify the expense. If we keep Kevin in third grade, he'll be isolated from his classmates, working by himself. That doesn't seem fair to Kevin."

"But still that's better than puttin' him back," counters Mrs. Armstrong. "We'll be goin' back to Denver in a year and a half."

Stating that it is against their best judgment, Mrs. Dixon and Mr. Peters agree to keep Kevin in the third grade on a trial basis.

Mrs. Dixon's conclusion that Kevin was not capable of third-grade work after less than two days of observation warrants questioning. She was aware of his geographical move The adjustment to a new home, new school, and new friends can be difficult for any child. The additional adjustments a Black child must make to a setting such as Wildwood can be traumatic. Many children like Kevin are raised in a cultural environment that is significantly different from what predominates at school. For these children, the school's expectation of appropriate behavior requires so much energy that little remains for the business of learning.

White children from middle- and upper-income backgrounds can also find it difficult to adjust to new schools. Thrust into a desegregated setting, they often misinterpret and are misunderstood, and they are sometimes fearful and vulnerable.

The Case of Marcia Patton

Marcia Patton is the twelve-year-old daughter of Mavis and Lew Patton, two politically active lawyers who practice law in a large midwestern city. Marcia is one of the first group of White children to attend Jefferson Junior High School, traditionally a school for inner-city Blacks. Although most of the children in her neighborhood attend a high-powered prep school, Marcia's parents are sending her to Jefferson as a matter of principle.

Today is her second day at Jefferson. She clutches her books tightly to her chest as she enters Mrs. Samson's language arts class. Mrs. Samson, a Black woman in her mid-forties, neatly dressed in a rose-colored suit, smiles as she greets Marcia. Then she steps into the hall to speak with several noisy students who are scrambling around the drinking fountain.

At that moment a group of five classmates burst into the room. They slam their books down on the desk and crowd in around Marcia.

"You got pretty hair," offers Rheba as she handles one of Marcia's blonde braids. Marcia is tight-faced, her blue eyes unusually wide.

"You like it here?" quizzes Jackson, a big, muscular twelve-year-old who sits on Marcia's desk top.

"Yes, I—I guess so," whispers Marcia, her voice barely audible.

"C'mon Rheba, let her hair alone," Jackson shouts as he swats the braid out of Rheba's hand and shoves her away from Marcia.

"Keep yo hands offa me, you mother ——," yells Rheba, her eyes flashing.

Marcia is pale and sitting erect. Her fingers press into the seat of her desk. Mrs. Samson enters and the students find their places.

"Me and Marie, we take you to the cafeteria today at lunch," offers Rheba as she sits down next to Marcia.

That evening Marcia writes a letter to Miss Bryant, her teacher last year, in the secrecy of her bedroom.

"When I first walked in, I saw all these dark faces and for the first time I felt so White. There was nothing but laughing, noisy, dark-skinned faces. My heart was beating so fast I thought I would drop dead for sure. I guess a lot of them won't like me. Still, most of the kids are real nice to me. But even so, I'm scared. Everyone is so loud and sometimes they get so close I can hardly breathe.

"The teachers are real nice to me but I wish Mrs. Samson wouldn't call on me so much. We use the book we used in your class last year, and lots of the kids in the class can't read it.

"I've been there over a week now and was feeling better until today. A horrible thing happened and I can't tell anybody but you.

"I went to the bathroom after lunch and two girls I don't

know told me to give them all my money or they would hurt me. I gave them twelve dollars, all I had. They said they'd slash my face if I told anybody. I'm afraid to go back."

Marcia's situation, that of being one of a few White students in a predominantly Black school, is a reversal of what many Black, Latino, Asian, and Native American children often face. Marcia's situation is complicated by the fact that her parents are using her to act in accordance with their belief in school desegregation. Liberal White parents are frequently criticized for not sending their children to inner-city schools.

Students like Marcia need a good deal of emotional support. Marcia is afraid of disappointing her parents; she confuses her fears and anxieties about her classmates with being racist and thus is unable to confide in her parents.

While most of the Black students are willing to accept Marcia and try to make her feel welcome, there are some students who will take out their anger and frustration on Marcia. Because she is a symbol of White oppression, her safety is endangered.

Reconsider the case of Kevin Armstrong, and meet one of his schoolmates, Rachael Jones. Their teachers perceive them strictly as failing individuals. These teachers like *all* their children and believe in treating each one the same. Ironically, by treating Kevin and Rachael the same as their classmates, teachers are probably stacking the deck against them. In order to provide equal opportunity for all students, it is sometimes necessary to offer unequal treatment, according to relevant (though not frivolous) differences.

Mrs. Dixon is fearful of probing into Kevin's Blackness and dismisses that fact as irrelevant. She is unable to entertain the thought that Kevin might have special needs because deep inside she fears this may be a racist notion. Mrs. Dixon has had a Black student before, the adopted daughter of a prominent physician in town. The girl conformed beautifully in class, was a top student, and confirmed Mrs. Dixon's view that there are smart Blacks and dumb Blacks, and Kevin falls into the second category.

Rachael is White. The conditions of her life are largely unknown to her teacher who, thus, has no reason to believe that there is any possible explanation for her failure other than her lack of ability to learn. Her Whiteness masks the possibility that she might need unequal treatment in order to attain success in school.

Kevin Reconsidered

Anyone who knows Kevin around the apartment complex is struck by his clever wit, his mischievous nature, and the way he gets other kids of all ages to do just what he wants. Whether it is an after-school snack, a bicycle, or a toy sale (other kids' toys, of course), Kevin somehow manages to outsmart the other children and many of their parents as well. The apartment children often get into a lot of trouble, though usually it's not too serious. Kevin is always there, but somehow he always escapes blame. Physically, he is tough. Although he is very small for his age, he can get the better of kids almost twice his size.

One day, close to Mother's Day, a newspaper reporter came around asking all the youngest kids what was special about their mothers. Most of the children mentioned their mothers' good cooking and things their mothers buy them. Kevin, however, said his mother is special because she collects frogs—all kinds, all sizes. Fully enjoying the reporter's surprise, Kevin later added that most of the frogs weren't real ones.

On rainy days Kevin usually plays in a friend's apartment. He often builds complicated structures with a borrowed Erector set. He seems to know all the television programs, channels, and times by heart, but can read the *TV Guide* if necessary (as well as *Jaws* and Captain Marvel comics). Kevin was the organizer of a week-long toy sale and earned a commission as manager. He kept all the financial records and supervised the cash flow for an entire week. To the casual observer, Kevin is a bright and lively eight-year-old.

It is a different story inside Mrs. Dixon's classroom, where Kevin is far behind everyone else in class. He works by himself in a cubby much of the time. Kevin sits in his desk a lot better than he did at the first of the year. But he still hams it up any chance he gets. The other kids love that and see Kevin as a kind of class clown.

Mrs. Dixon is concerned about Kevin. His progress this year is very slow, slower than any child she has known in her three years of teaching (all at Wildwood). Kevin does not concentrate on one activity long enough to finish anything, and he is easily distracted by his classmates. Often he does not listen to her directions and, thus, cannot do the assignments, or does them incorrectly. Although she is often amazed at his creative and unusual ideas, Mrs. Dixon is distressed by his sloppy and careless writing habits and his lack of effort in math.

The Case of Rachael Jones

Rachael lives in Kevin's apartment complex and is a second grader at Wildwood. This is her first year there too.

Rachael's mother, a hardworking and good-hearted woman

in her thirties, cleans apartments in the complex. Her work has become so steady that she is off ADC for the first time in six years. Although Rachael's stepfather has a college degree, he has been unable to find work in his field and works as a city bus driver. Rachael's natural father (and her eldest brother as well) is a man who is continually in and out of prison and pays no support for any of his five children. While money is a continual problem for the family, the remarriage of Rachael's mother has brought a degree of stability and security.

Like Kevin, Rachael is at the bottom of her class. She is often sick and is frequently absent from school. Rachael complains to her mother that her schoolwork is too hard. Homework assignments are usually put off until 9:30 or 10:00 P.M., and Rachael's mother is unable to help her. On occasion she will ask one of the women she works for to help Rachael. Unlike Kevin, Rachael fears adventure, even the three-quarter-mile walk to school, and has few friends. Her long blonde hair hangs limply and her clothes seldom fit properly, a fact that sometimes elicits cruel remarks from schoolmates.

Miss Bryant, Rachael's second-grade teacher, sees Rachael as a shy, quiet little girl who is doing the best she can. She has placed Rachael in her slowest reading and math group, where Rachael's progress is so slow that it is doubtful she will be able to go on to third grade next year.

The Case of Max Britten

There had always been something different about Max that his teachers couldn't quite understand. As early as kindergarten his teachers sensed something. He tuned out a lot during class, and his work was inconsistent, ranging from very high to very low. The teacher suspected he was capable of doing better, although a learning disability was also a strong possibility. At the school's request Max was completely tested by the head of the Children's Neurology Clinic. The physician reported that Max was a bright, exceptionally independent child who could learn anything he wanted to learn. But that would be the key: his interest. Max also suffered from a severe case of sibling rivalry regarding his younger brother that might require future attention.

After kindergarten Max's parents (both college professors) were divorced and he moved with his mother and brother to the Midwest, where he attended the same school as Rachael and Kevin. Max became quite shy and had a difficult time making friends. At school he was often teased and scapegoated in subtle ways unobservable to his teachers. At home he was continually taunted by his peers with the exception of one friend who suffered similar rejection.

Max's schoolwork deteriorated. His teacher felt he was immature, easily distracted, and did not listen well. He was in the lowest reading and math groups. In contrast, Max's younger brother was a top student at Wildwood. He was well liked by teachers and classmates and was involved in sports and music. As one teacher said to Max's mother, "Your sons are like night and day, salt and pepper." In the third grade, for some unknown reason, the school did not receive the results of Max's Iowa tests. There was no record of his past test scores, and the fourth-grade teacher wondered if Max were mildly retarded or perhaps suffered from some sort of learning disability.

Despite his parent's divorce, Max's home environment was highly supportive and during summer vacations with his maternal grandparents Max was a different person. He was an avid stamp collector and through stamps had come to know more about geography than most adults. He read *Time* and *National Geographic* regularly, and frequently consulted his *World Book* encyclopedias, a gift from his grandparents. Yet it became clear that Max was becoming increasingly miserable at school. One day he cut school and hid at home. When his mother returned from work he told her he just couldn't go back. The school decided to test Max to see if he was eligible for Special Education.

The confidential psychological evaluation of Max in the fourth grade stated that "Max is a handsome, blond-haired, blue-eyed boy. He is somewhat quiet but friendly. Max reportedly gets along well with his classmates although the teacher notes that he tends to keep to himself. . . . Max frequently does not attend to critical instructions regarding assignments which often results in missed work and/or poor performance on assignments. When singled out for individual attention Max's work tends to improve; his work also improves when he is specifically requested to redo an unsatisfactory assignment."

On the day Max was given a variety of IQ tests, his teacher excitedly told him to tell his mother that he had done a fantastic job on the tests. He had done so well in fact, that none of the socioemotional tests were administered.

The written report stated that "The results of the current psychological evaluation show Max to be a child of superior intellectual ability. . . . Interviews with Max's teacher suggest that Max can perform academically when he is given large amounts of individual attention or when required to redo unsatisfactory assignments. However, there is only a limited amount of individual attention that can be afforded to any individual child in a typical classroom.

"There is some suggestion that Max finds the individual attention he receives very soothing and rewarding and therefore sees little incentive in performing well consistently. This is not unusual in view of Max's family situation. . . . It is recommended that Max be reassured about his academic ability but also, it should be explained that he must satisfy certain criteria in order to complete the fourth grade successfully. Max is not eligible for special services at the present time."

Later, during the case conference Ms. Johnson stated that Max became a different person as a result of doing well on the tests, and the schoolwork began to improve. Max's mother reported that he was beginning to make new friends in the neighborhood and that he seemed happier at home.

Suppose Max, for emotional reasons, was unable to perform well on the test. What would have happened in that event? The case of Max illustrates that factors related to school success are very complex and not necessarily linked to cultural conflicts or racial differences. Both Max and his teacher were from White, economically advantaged backgrounds.

It is possible that problems faced by children like Kevin, Marcia, and Rachael and the students in Warren Benson's classroom grow out of conflict between their world view and that which predominates in school, or to negative prejudices on the part of teachers and classmates. It is also possible that, like Max, their failure is due to a mismatch between teaching and learning styles, or to some special personal qualities that need to be understood. Teachers must be sensitive to all the possibilities, which is not an easy task.

When we observe what goes on in most classrooms, the basic assumption seems to be that students are basically the same. The fact that there are important individual differences along with the obvious similarities seems to be overlooked.

The next two chapters analyze individual differences that are known to affect learning. These characteristics are complex and interrelated and must not be regarded as mutually exclusive categories. The list that follows could be conceptualized in a variety of ways, but experience has shown that it is helpful in guiding and clarifying teachers' observations of students.

1. Learning styles
2. Need for structure
3. Learning skills

  4. Aptitudes and achievements
  5. Motivation
  6. Self-concept
  7. Interests
  8. Physical attributes
  9. Peer relationships
 10. Family conditions
 11. Values, attitudes, and beliefs
 12. Sense of ethnic identity

Chapter 4 provides an introduction to students' learning styles and need for structure, two key variables that often affect school success. Chapter 5 provides an overview of the ten remaining characteristics and discusses the importance of how teachers perceive individual and cultural differences.

Chapter 4

Learning Styles: Interactions Between Culture and the Individual

Students differ in the way they approach learning. Some work well in groups; others prefer to work alone. Some need absolute quiet in order to concentrate; others do well with noise and movement. Some need a great deal of structure and support; others are more independent and self-motivated. Some students grasp oral instructions quickly; others need to see the instructions in writing. Some require a warm personal rapport with the teacher, while others do not. Some are intuitive; others prefer inductive or deductive reasoning. Some learn best in a formal environment, while others prefer a more relaxed informality. The list of differences could go on.

Psychologists have been researching the nature of learning styles for a number of decades. Only recently has the utility of this research been made known to educators. Typically, we look for emotional reasons to explain why a child is not learning; we look for an emotional block or conflict, or a learning disability. Many teachers ignore the possibility that children are not learning because they are not given an opportunity to use their own style of learning in the classroom.

Take, for example, a child like Max who has a slow warm-up period of twenty to thirty minutes. He does not easily get into something new, but once involved he may show a good deal of perseverance. He may be a physical learner who needs to become involved in the learning process. This takes time. Once immersed, he may go deeper than his classmates. The quick changes of learning activity typical in most elementary classrooms can make it impossible for the slow-to-warm-up learner to get past the point of warming up. Thus, he is rarely able to complete work expected by the teacher. The frequent change of activity may also be frustrating and discouraging because once into an activity he has difficulty shifting to a new one. If he makes it past the eighth grade, the slow-to-warm-up learner will also find it difficult to learn within the rigid time schedules of most secondary schools. Unless helped, the slow-to-warm-up student gets caught in a vicious cycle of anxiety, inability to concentrate, and failure.

The idea that we must gear our teaching to students' learning style needs if they are to succeed is revolutionary. Furthermore, it triggers the fear that we sometimes create the conditions of failure for some students. Fortunately, the movement has progressed far enough to provide some of the tools we need to discover the important differences that affect learning and to design appropriate instructional strategies and materials.

What Is Learning Style?

The National Task Force on Learning Style and Brain Behavior adopted the following definition of learning style with the understanding that it would be revised if necessary:

> Learning style is that consistent pattern of behavior and performance by which an individual approaches educational experiences. It is the composite of characteristic cognitive, affective, and physiological behaviors that serve as relatively stable indicators of how a learner perceives, interacts with, and responds to the learning environment. It is formed in the deep structure of neural organization and personality which molds and is molded by human development and the cultural experiences of home, school and society.[1]

The fact that this definition is offered as tentative should alert us to the fact that learning style is an emerging concept. Despite decades of research, there are more questions than answers about learning styles. Nevertheless, knowledge about learning styles has become one of the most promising avenues to the improvement of schooling. We must be careful, however, not to view learning styles as the panacea that will eliminate failure in the schools. To address learning styles is often a necessary, but never sufficient, condition for effective teaching.

Why Be Concerned About Learning Styles?

The rationale behind learning styles is similar to the broader rationale for multicultural education. Knowledge about learning styles provides insights that help us move beyond the rhetoric associated with "individual differences," "human potential," and "creating the independent learner."[2] First of all, when a student is having difficulty learning it is now possible to pinpoint which of the many individual differences affect his or her learning. Understanding individual differences has been especially challenging for teachers beyond elementary school. Gerald Kusler wrote:

Most secondary teachers want to know the students they teach. But, two factors tend to block even the most committed. First, teachers don't really know what they need to know about learners. . . . Second, the typical secondary teacher spends about 90 hours in class with between 125 and 150 youngsters. "Getting to know you" can become "putting the name with the face (or the seat)."[3]

Recent developments in learning style research have produced a variety of efficient ways to gather information about students. Thus, if a student has a strong modality preference, a teacher can provide visual, auditory, or kinesthetic experiences that will enhance the student's learning. Teachers can provide more structure for those who need it, or assist reflective thinkers in developing skills needed for standardized tests. The possibilities are endless.

Second, by focusing on how students learn we assume that they can learn. This is basic to the humanists' view that all of us have the capacity to grow and develop to our fullest potential. Third, when students are taught *how* they learn they become involved in a teaching-learning partnership. In schools where learning styles are assessed and shared with learners, students become involved in structuring how they will learn what is taught. This is an important step in creating the independent learner.[4]

The concept of learning style can also provide some of the teeth needed to move us beyond the rhetoric of educational equity for those ethnic groups who have not yet been well served by our nation's schools. This notion warrants some discussion.

One can assume that teachers, unless they learn to do otherwise, expect their students to learn the same way that they themselves do. Teachers who dislike group work rarely use it with their students. Teachers who require the written word remember to write the assignment on the board, but they may not think of taping the text for their auditory learners. Teachers who are incremental learners tend to spell out short-term objectives, while the intuitive teachers may seem less organized. A teacher's learning style doesn't have to become a teaching style straitjacket; teachers can learn to be flexible and teach in a variety of ways. Being flexible is important because research shows that students do better in classes taught by teachers with the same learning style as their own. Students also tend to like these teachers better.[5]

Learning style is believed to be a combination of both heredity and environment. While it is to some degree rooted in the individual's neurological structure, learning styles do change with age and experience. Young children, for example, seem to be more kinesthetic and tend to develop a visual or auditory preference as they mature. Furthermore, in highly technical societies, such as the United States, cognitive styles tend to move in the direction of analytical thought. Researchers such as Manuel Ramirez and Alfredo Castañeda have found, however, that Latino and American Indian children who have been educated in their own highly humanistic microcultures maintain a more global cognitive style.[6]

To the extent that teachers teach as they have been taught to learn, and to the extent that culture shapes learning style, students who share the teacher's ethnic background will be favored in class. It is not strictly a matter of ethnicity, of course, as was seen in the case of Max, who needed close supervision and few distractions in order to do good work. A number of scholars now conclude, however, that different ethnic groups may be characterized by different learning styles and that some of these styles are at odds with the schools.

Asa Hilliard, for example, asserts that Afro-Americans who have grown up outside the macroculture process information differently from what predominates in schools.[7] His observations suggest that Afro-Americans have the following tendencies:

1. They view things in their environment in entirety rather than in isolated parts.
2. They prefer intuitive rather than deductive or inductive reasoning.
3. They approximate concepts of space, number, and time rather than aiming at exactness or complete accuracy.
4. They prefer people stimuli rather than nonsocial or object stimuli.
5. They rely on nonverbal as well as verbal communication.[8]

John Phillips's description of how many Navajo children learn to learn suggests that Navajo students could also have problems participating in many of our nation's schools.

First American students customarily acquire the various skills of their culture (i.e. hunting, tanning, beadwork) in a sequence of three steps. First, the child over a period of time watches and listens to a competent adult who is performing the skill. Secondly, the child takes over small portions of the task and completes them in cooperation with and under the supervision of the adult, in this way gradually learning all of the component skills involved. Finally, the child goes off and privately tests himself or herself to see whether the skill has been fully learned: a failure is not seen by others and causes no embarrassment, but a success is brought back and exhibited to the teacher and others. The use of speech in this three-step process is minimal. . . .

When these same children go to school they find themselves in a situation where the high value placed on verbal performance is only the first of their cross-cultural hurdles. . . . Acquisition and demonstration of knowledge are no longer separate steps, but are expected to occur simultaneously. Furthermore, this single-step process takes place via public recitations, the assumption apparently being that one learns best by making verbal mistakes in front of one's peers and teachers. Finally, the children have little opportunity to observe skilled performers carrying out these tasks, for the other children who perform are as ignorant and unskilled as they. Under these circumstances, it is small wonder that these First American students demonstrate a propensity for silence.[9]

The concept of learning styles offers a value-neutral approach for understanding individual differences among ethnically different students. Many learning styles are bipolar, representing a continuum from one extreme of a trait to another. Usually, no value judgment is made about where one falls on the continuum. "It is acceptable for example, to be a kinesthetic or an audio visual learner, to reason abstractly or concretely."[10] The assumption is that everyone can learn, provided teachers respond appropriately to individual learning needs.

Numerous instruments now exist for discovering student learning style. In her selected bibliography of learning style assessment instruments, for example, Claudia Cornett lists thirty.[11] James Keefe and others have organized the available measures into four categories: cognitive style instruments, affective style instruments, physiological style instruments, and comprehensive or multidimensional instruments.[12] Cognitive style instruments are those that measure "the learner's typical mode of perceiving, thinking, problem solving, and remembering."[13] Affective style instruments are those that measure personality traits related to attention, emotion, and valuing. Physiological style instruments are those that measure biologically based responses, such as sex-related differences, personal nutrition and health, and reaction to the physical environment. Comprehensive or multidimensional instruments are those that assess more than one of the three categories of learning style and several dimensions within these categories.[14] Because comprehensive instruments that can measure all three aspects of learning style (cognitive, affective, and physiological dimensions) do not yet exist, it is wise to select instruments from two or more categories to better understand a student's learning style.

The four learning style approaches to be described in this chapter represent a cross section of these categories. Each strategy has been extensively researched and is used successfully by classroom teachers across the country. Assessment instruments and instructions for each may be obtained by writing to individuals noted at the end of this chapter, where a selected annotated list of other learning style instruments is also included.

Four Strategies for Discovering Learning Styles

Field Independence–Dependence

Imagine yourself in a psychology laboratory, seated on a chair in a tilted room. The experimenter asks you to adjust the chair and your body to the true upright position. Can you do it?

Now imagine that you are seated in a darkened room with a luminous rod in a luminous picture frame, which is set aslant. You are instructed to set the rod to the true vertical position. Are you able to do so?

These two experiments were part of the dramatic research begun by Herman Witkin and his associates in 1954, which illustrates the field independence–dependence dimensions of learning style. Those participants labeled field dependent consistently aligned themselves to the tilt of the room, leaning perhaps as much as thirty degrees but perceiving themselves to be sitting upright. They also tended to be influenced by the slant of the picture frame and were unable to place the rod in its true upright position. Other participants, those labeled field independent, ignored their immediate surroundings. In the tilted room test they used internal cues to adjust their bodies to an upright position. In the luminous rod test, they tended to ignore the frame and set the rod in its true upright position.[15]

Diagnosis of field independence–dependence is now greatly simplified through use of a simple embedded figures test. Figure 4.1 illustrates the task as it appears in the Hidden Figures Test.[16] If we visualize people along a continuum from extreme field dependence to extreme field independence, we find that people at the field-dependent end are unable to locate simple figures embedded in the complex pattern. Field-independent people, on the other hand, can quickly separate the simple figure from the background.

For years, knowledge generated about learning styles by Witkin and others has been unavailable to teachers and counselors. Only recently have classroom implications been discussed. When trying to identify relatively field independent–dependent students, think in terms of clusters of personality and intellectual characteristics. These clusters include the following characteristics:[17]

Field-Independent Learner	Field-Dependent Learner
1. Perception of discrete parts	1. Global perception
2. Good at abstract analytical thought	2. Poor at analytical problem solving
3. Individualistic and insensitive to emotions of others, poorly developed social skills	3. Highly sensitive and attuned to social environment, highly developed social skills

This is a test of your ability to tell which one of five simple figures (A–E) can be found in a more complex pattern. Beneath the row of figures is a row of patterns. Each pattern has a row of letters beneath it. Indicate your answer by putting an X through the letter of the figure which you find in the pattern.

Note: There is only one of these figures in each pattern, and this figure will always be right side up and exactly the same size as one of the five lettered figures.

Part 1 (10 minutes)

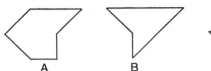

A   B   C   D   E

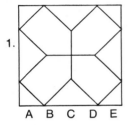

1.

A   B   C   D   E

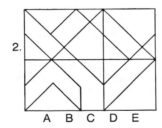

2.

A   B   C   D   E

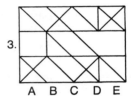

3.

A   B   C   D   E

Figure 4.1 *Hidden Figures Test. Adapted from Hidden Figures Test (Cf-1),* Kit of Factor-Referenced Cognitive Tests, *copyright 1962 by Educational Testing Service. Reprinted by permission.*

4. Favors "inquiry" and independent study, provides own structure to facilitate learning

5. Intrinsically motivated, unresponsive to social reinforcement

4. Favors a "spectator approach" to learning, adopts organization of information to be learned as given

5. Extrinsically motivated, responsive to social reinforcement

Field independence–dependence does not appear to be correlated with intelligence, with the exception of analytical intelligence, which requires the separation of component parts from the whole. It is not related to other aspects of intelligence, such as verbal comprehension. However, most schools and tests tend to be geared to the highly analytical learner who can think abstractly (field-independent learners). Some psychologists suggest that people can be helped to develop cognitive strategies, that people can be taught to make conscious choices about which cognitive process to use in certain situations. Thus, field independents might learn to be more sensitive to other people, and field dependents might increase their analytical skill.

Research by Castañeda and Ramirez suggests that learning style is related to world view, that certain learning styles tend to be predominant in certain cultures.[18] As noted earlier, they indicate that Mexican Americans tend to be relatively field dependent or global in orientation. Furthermore, their research suggests that bilingual individuals tend to be bicognitive; that is, fluent speakers of Spanish and English tend to have greater cognitive flexibility than monolinguists, being able to move back and forth between global and analytical orientations as needed.

The field independence–dependence approach to learning styles is the most widely researched, with over two thousand studies completed to date.[19] However, one problem with the embedded figures test is that it makes field dependents, now more frequently known as field-sensitive learners, feel like failures. The more field sensitive the individual, the less likely he or she will be successful in locating a simple figure within a complex whole. Given the school's emphasis on testing, it becomes difficult to convince the student who scores between zero and eight out of thirty-two possible points that the test reveals little about learning potential. Therefore, the EFT or GEFT should be administered with care and with a full discussion of the insights it offers into how the individual approaches learning.

Castañeda and Gray report observation guidelines based on field independence–dependence research, which can help teachers discover where a student falls on the continuum without testing. They also describe the teacher characteristics and curriculum approach that are most compatible with each learning style. These are summarized in Boxes 4.1, 4.2, and 4.3.[20]

Students' Need for Structure

Students in any classroom may differ greatly in their ability to rely on themselves, to take on new assignments, to make choices, and to organize themselves and their materials. Some need frequent reassurance from the teacher and continually ask if what they are doing is right and what they should do next.

Students also differ in their need for an explanation of the instructions before beginning a test or assignment. Teachers often give instructions to a group of thirty to forty students, expecting all of them to understand the first or second time. A teacher may become irritated at

Box 4.1

Field
Sensitivity

FIELD-SENSITIVE BEHAVIORS

Relationship to peers:
1. Likes to work with others to achieve a common goal
2. Likes to assist others
3. Is sensitive to feelings and opinions of others

Personal relationship to teacher:
1. Openly expresses positive feelings for teacher
2. Asks questions about teacher's tastes and personal experiences; seeks to become like teacher

Instructional relationship to teacher:
1. Seeks guidance and demonstration from teacher
2. Seeks rewards which strengthen relationship with teacher
3. Is highly motivated when working individually with teacher

Characteristics of curriculum that facilitate learning:
1. Performance objectives and global aspects of curriculum are carefully explained
2. Concepts are presented in humanized or story format
3. Concepts are related to personal interests and experiences of children

FIELD-SENSITIVE TEACHING STYLE

Personal behaviors:
1. Displays physical and verbal expressions of approval and warmth
2. Uses personalized rewards which strengthen the relationship with students

Instructional behaviors:
1. Expresses confidence in child's ability to succeed, is sensitive to children who are having difficulty and need help
2. Gives guidance to students; makes purpose and main principles of lesson obvious; presentation of lesson is clear with steps toward "solution" clearly delineated
3. Encourages learning through modeling; asks children to imitate
4. Encourages cooperation and development of group feelings, encourages class to think and work as a unit
5. Holds informal class discussions; provides opportunities for students to see how concepts being learned are related to students' personal experiences

Curriculum-related behaviors:
1. Emphasizes global aspects of concepts; before beginning lesson ensures that students understand the performance objectives; identifies generalizations and helps children apply them to particular instances
2. Personalizes curriculum; teacher relates curriculum materials to

Continued

Box 4.1

Continued

the interests and experiences of students as well as to her or his own interests
3. Humanizes curriculum; attributes human characteristics to concepts and principles
4. Uses teaching materials to elicit expression of feelings from students; helps students apply concepts for labeling their personal experiences

Source: Alfredo Castañeda and Tracy Gray, "Bicognitive Processes in Multicultural Education," *Educational Leadership* 32 (December 1974). Reprinted with permission of the Association for Supervision and Curriculum Development. Copyright © 1974 by the Association for Supervision and Curriculum Development. All rights reserved.

students who never seem to listen or pay attention. In many cases, perhaps the student is not paying attention; however, students can differ in their need for directions from the teacher. Students at all age levels differ from one another in their ability to carry out independent projects and activities. Some can handle long-term assignments while others can work independently only for short periods of time.

Need for structure is sometimes regarded as a manifestation of learning style. David Hunt, of the Ontario Institute for Studies in Education, conceptualizes learning style on the basis of the amount of external structure needed by the student. He identifies the characteristics of students who require much, some, and little structure and teaching approaches that are most desirable for students who require a certain degree of structure.

The paragraph completion method has been used since the 1960s by Hunt and his associates to assess a student's need for structure, or conceptual level.[21] This method, which requires special training to administer, asks the learner to complete six to eight open-ended statements by writing two or three sentences about his or her feelings for each one (What I think about rules . . . , When I am criticized . . . , What I think about parents . . . , When someone does not agree with me . . . , When I am not sure . . . , When I am told what to do . . . , and so on).[22] Learner responses are then coded and scored according to the structure of the response, not the content. The result is a general indication of the amount of structure the student needs at the time. Hunt stresses that students' need for structure usually varies over time. He also emphasizes that there are many high-ability students who require structure and warns that many teachers confuse learning style with ability. This confusion is particularly likely with younger (i.e., grade six) students because "teachers tend to equate high level verbal ability with a learning style that requires little structure."[23] While many high achievers do require structure, it is less likely that students who are at lower achieve-

Box 4.2

Field Independence

FIELD-INDEPENDENT BEHAVIORS

Relationship to peers:
1. Prefers to work independently
2. Likes to compete and gain individual recognition
3. Task oriented; is inattentive to social environment when working

Personal relationship to teacher:
1. Rarely seeks physical contact with teacher
2. Formal; interactions with teacher are restricted to tasks at hand

Instructional relationship to teacher:
1. Likes to try new tasks without teacher's help
2. Impatient to begin tasks; likes to finish first
3. Seeks nonsocial rewards

Characteristics of curriculum that facilitate learning:
1. Details of concepts are emphasized; parts have meaning of their own
2. Deals with math and science concepts
3. Based on discovery approach

FIELD-INDEPENDENT TEACHING STYLE

Personal behaviors:
1. Is formal in relationship with students; acts the part of an authority figure
2. Centers attention on instructional objectives; gives social atmosphere secondary importance

Instructional behaviors:
1. Encourages independent achievement; emphasizes the importance of individual effort
2. Encourages competition between individual students
3. Adopts a consultant role; teacher encourages students to seek help only when they experience difficulty
4. Encourages learning through trial and error
5. Encourages task orientation; focuses student attention on assigned tasks

Curriculum-related behaviors:
1. Focuses on details of curriculum materials
2. Focuses on facts and principles; teaches students how to solve problems using shortcuts and novel approaches
3. Emphasizes math and science abstractions; teacher tends to use graphs, charts, and formulas in teaching, even when presenting social studies curriculum
4. Emphasizes inductive learning and the discovery approach; starts with isolated parts and slowly puts them together to construct rules or generalizations

Source: Castañeda and Gray, as cited in Box 4.1.

Box 4.3

Curricula for
Field Sen-
sitivity and
Field Inde-
pendence

FIELD-SENSITIVE CURRICULUM

Content:
1. Social abstractions: Field-sensitive curriculum is humanized through use of narration, humor, drama, and fantasy. Characterized by social words and human characteristics. Focuses on lives of persons who occupy central roles in the topic of study, such as history or scientific discovery.
2. Personalized: The ethnic background of students, as well as their homes and neighborhoods, is reflected. The teacher is given the opportunity to express personal experiences and interests.

Structure:
1. Global: Emphasis is on description of wholes and generalities; the overall view or general topic is presented first. The purpose or use of the concept or skill is clearly stated using practical examples.
2. Rules explicit: Rules and principles are salient. (Children who prefer to learn in the field-sensitive mode are more comfortable given the rules than when asked to discover the underlying principles for themselves.)
3. Requires cooperation with others: The curriculum is structured in such a way that children work cooperatively with peers or with the teacher in a variety of activities.

FIELD-INDEPENDENT CURRICULUM

Content:
1. Math and science abstractions: Field-independent curriculum uses many graphs and formulae.
2. Impersonal: Field-independent curriculum focuses on events, places, and facts in social studies rather than personal histories.

Structure:
1. Focus on details: The details of a concept are explored, followed by the global concept.
2. Discovery: Rules and principles are discovered from the study of details; the general is discovered from the understanding of the particulars.
3. Requires independent activity: The curriculum requires children to work individually, minimizing interaction with others.

Source: Castañeda and Gray, as cited in Box 4.1.

ment levels will need less structure. Hunt writes, therefore, that "learning style and ability show a low, but significant relation, yet they are distinct from one another . . . [furthermore] the relation decreases as students grow older."[24]

Hunt's approach to learning style is practical for teachers, most of whom know that certain students are more independent than others, and that others need more guidance and support. Hunt makes it possible for teachers to sharpen these observations by providing specific behaviors to look for. Boxes 4.4, 4.5, and 4.6 summarize some of these behaviors and can be used as guidelines for identifying a student's need for structure. Suggestions about teaching strategies that best meet a student's need for structure are summarized in Boxes 4.7, 4.8, and 4.9.

Box 4.4

Characteristics of Students Who Require Much Structure

1. They have a short attention span, cannot sit still for the period—in constant movement.
2. They have no inner control as individuals, do not know how to function in group situations (many physical and verbal fights).
3. They (usually boys) are physical with each other and try the rules often.
4. They ask for direction often. (They do not rely on themselves or want to think.)
5. They are literal and unable to make inferences or interpretations.
6. They lack self-confidence, generally have a poor self-image.
7. They have difficulty organizing themselves and their materials.
8. They do not reveal anything of themselves or express personal opinions—everything is very objective. They are afraid to get emotionally involved with a story or film.
9. They have a wide range of abilities.
10. They see things in black and white with no gray in between.
11. They want to know the basic information or process and are not interested in the sidelights.
12. They are incapable of handling general questions or thinking through a problem; they guess and let it go at that.
13. They do not assume responsibility for their own actions.
14. They work only because the teacher tells them to work and look to peers for approval.
15. They are laconic; they give brief answers with little elaboration.

Source: Adapted from David E. Hunt, "Learning Style and Student Needs: An Introduction to Conceptual Level," in *Student Learning Styles: Diagnosing and Prescribing Programs* (Reston, Va.: National Association of Secondary School Principals, 1979). By permission of the author.

Box 4.5

Characteristics of Students Who Require Some Structure

1. They are oriented to the role of the good student (one who gets the right answers, has neat work, and good work habits).
2. They seek teacher approval and strive to please the teacher; they go along with what the teacher says.
3. They want to work alone at their own desks.
4. They are reluctant to try anything new; they do not like to appear wrong or dumb.
5. They do not express personal opinions.
6. They do not ask questions.
7. They are confused by choices.
8. They are incapable of adjusting to a different teacher; they are upset by visitors or alterations of the schedule.
9. They look for reassurance and frequently ask, "Is this right?" "What should I do now?" "What should I write?"
10. They are not particularly imaginative.
11. They participate well in the class as a whole but do not work well in small groups.
12. They are grade conscious.

Source: David E. Hunt, as cited in Box 4.4.

Box 4.6

Characteristics of Students Who Require Little Structure

1. They like to discuss and argue; everybody wants to talk at once with few listening; therefore, the noise level is high and progress somewhat slower.
2. They will question and volunteer additional information.
3. They want to solve things themselves; they don't want the teacher's help until they have exhausted all resources.
4. They are averse to detail and dislike going step by step, are able to see the entire picture and tend to ignore the steps required to get there, are creative and like to formulate and act on their own ideas, and often get so involved that they do not hear the teacher.
5. They are capable of abstract thinking; they do not require concrete objects.
6. They are less afraid of making mistakes than other students, are more imaginative, go off on sidetracks, and are able to see alternatives.
7. They can stay at one thing for a longer time and can work by themselves with little or no supervision.
8. They have greater depth of emotions and are more open about themselves than other students.
9. They display greater ability in making interpretations and drawing inferences than other students do.
10. They are somewhat self-centered and not very concerned with others.

Source: David E. Hunt, as cited in Box 4.4.

Box 4.7

Teaching
Approaches
for Students
Who Require
Much Struc-
ture

1. Have definite and consistent rules—let them know what is expected of them.
2. Give specific guidelines and instructions (step by step); even make a chart of the steps.
3. Make goals and deadlines short and definite—give them the topic, how many lines/pages, how it is to be done and the exact date it is due.
4. Provide a variety of activities during the period, incorporating some physical movement whenever possible.
5. Make positive comments about their attempts; give immediate feedback on each step; give much assurance and attention; praise often.
6. Use visuals and objects they can see, feel, and touch.
7. Get them to work immediately and change pace often.
8. Display their work—it is a form of reinforcement to which they respond.
9. Capitalize on their interest to assist them in learning the various skills (for example, stories or projects dealing with cars with grade nine boys).
10. Begin with factual material before discussion.
11. Move gradually from seat work to discussion; provide more group work as they are able to handle it.
12. Leave them at the end of each period with the satisfaction of having learned new material and having success in what they have been studying—almost a complete lesson each period with a minor carry-over to the next period with the mention of something interesting to come.
13. Give short quizzes and objective tests initially.
14. Provide opportunities for choice and decision making as they appear ready for them.

Source: David E. Hunt, as cited in Box 4.4.

Many of these suggestions may seem like common sense. The point is, however, that most teachers do not act on it; instead, they insist on the same amount of structure for all students. Hunt provides guidelines for flexibility as educators match their teaching with the amount of structure a student requires.

Perceptual Modalities

The Edmonds Learning Style Identification Exercise (ELSIE) is an effective technique for discovering perceptual modes. Classroom teachers can administer, score, and roughly evaluate the ELSIE in less than a half-hour of class time. The ELSIE can be used in grades seven to adult, and possibly as early as fourth grade.

Box 4.8

Teaching Approaches for Students Who Require Some Structure

1. Arrange students initially in rows and gradually get them working in pairs, then in small groups.
2. Have definite and consistent rules—let them know what is expected of them.
3. Use creative skits to encourage spontaneity, self-awareness, and cooperation.
4. Tell them what to do each day. Some teachers find that initialing the students' work daily provides the contact they desire and the impetus to continue—they can see how much they have accomplished.
5. Provide nonthreatening situations where they have to risk an opinion.
6. Provide a lot of praise and success-oriented situations.
7. Give them group problems to encourage sharing.
8. Provide opportunities for choice and decision making as students appear ready for them. Push them gently into situations where they have to make decisions and take responsibility.

Source: David E. Hunt, as cited in Box 4.4.

Box 4.9

Teaching Approaches for Students Who Require Little Structure

1. Allow them to select their own seats.
2. Give them many topics from which to choose.
3. Set weekly or longer assignments and allow students to make up their own timetables.
4. Encourage them to use each other as resources.
5. Allow more mobility and give them more opportunities to take part in planning and decision making.
6. Give them freedom to pursue projects on their own.
7. Have them work in groups with the teacher serving as a resource person.
8. Train them to listen to instructions (and to listen in general) as they tend to go off on their own.
9. Remind and encourage them to take an interest in others.

Source: David E. Hunt, as cited in Box 4.4.

The ELSIE provides a profile of modality strengths, based on the individual's response to a selected list of fifty common English words that are read once at ten-second intervals. Students are asked, as they hear each word, to indicate on their answer sheet which of the following responses is their "own immediate and instantaneous reaction to the word itself."[25]

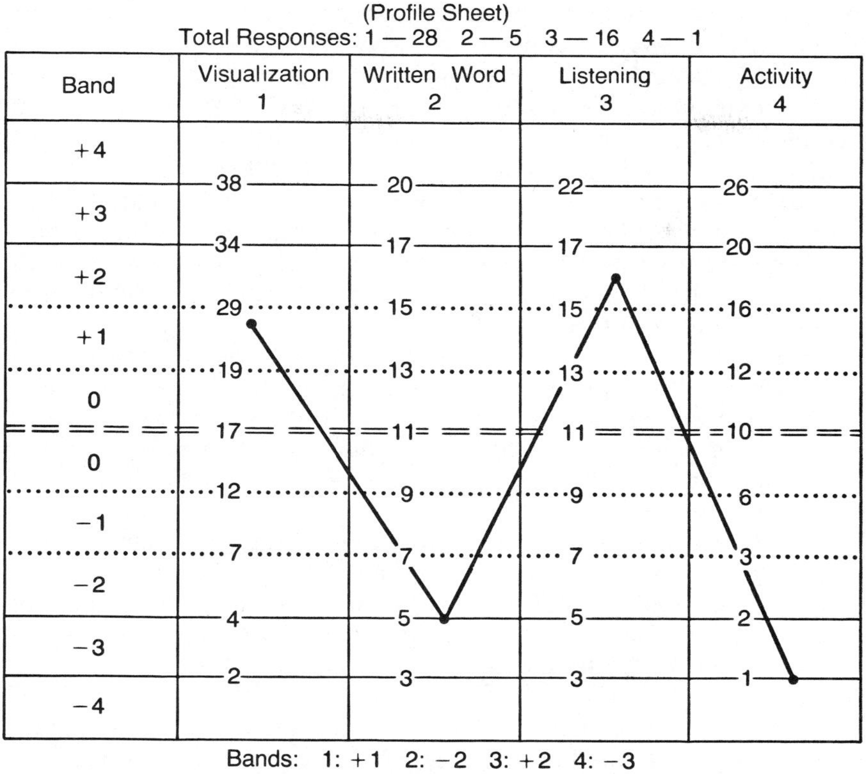

(Profile Sheet)
Total Responses: 1 — 28   2 — 5   3 — 16   4 — 1

Band	Visualization 1	Written Word 2	Listening 3	Activity 4
+4				
+3	38	20	22	26
+2	34	17	17	20
+1	29	15	15	16
0	19	13	13	12
0	17	11	11	10
−1	12	9	9	6
−2	7	7	7	3
−3	4	5	5	2
−4	2	3	3	1

Bands: 1: +1   2: −2   3: +2   4: −3

Figure 4.2 *Edmonds School District, Learning Style Identification Exercise. From Harry Reinert, "One Picture Is Worth a Thousand Words? Not Necessarily!" The Modern Language Journal 60 (April 1976):164. Reprinted by permission of the author.*

1. Visualization: a mental picture of some object or activity
2. Written word: a mental picture of the word spelled out
3. Listening: the sound of the word with no mental picture
4. Activity: a "physical or emotional feeling about the word, such as a tightening of a muscle or a feeling such as warmth, sorrow, etc."[26]

Students can tally the number of responses in each response category and then plot their own profiles to discover their own perceptual strengths and weaknesses. The learner's scores in all four categories are charted on a stanine scale displayed as bands above and below the mean. A sample profile is shown in Figure 4.2. These profiles are interpreted such that "the further the individual varies from the mean in any one of the four categories, the stronger or weaker will be that mode of learning for that individual, i.e. the more (or less) easily the individual is able to learn by using that approach. Scores at the extremes (either in the ±3 or ±4 band) may be considered indicative of a strongly dominant influence—positively or negatively—of that mode."[27]

Students who score high on visualization learn best when they can actually see objects and activities. Visual media such as films, pictures, demonstrations, and models would enhance their learning.

Learners who score high on the written word portion learn best by reading about what is to be learned. "Persons scoring very high in this category have a great dependency on the written word. . . . Persons scoring very low in this category may read quite well, but they tend to translate written words into another category (visual images or sounds) rather than being able to get meaning from the words immediately."[28]

Learners with a modality strength in listening are auditory learners. The higher the score for listening, the better the individual can learn from hearing the spoken language without recourse to some other mode. Listening labs and tapes are usually very effective with auditory learners.

Learners who score high on activity require some manner of physical activity in order to facilitate learning. Many activity or kinesthetic learners are compulsive underliners or notetakers "in class or at lectures (and even films), but they will seldom need to refer to their notes at a later time, for the activity of writing seems to impress the information on their memory."[29]

Harry Reinert reports finding far greater diversity between individual learning profiles than he had originally anticipated and suspects that "many slow learners are 'slow' only because they have never had a chance to learn in the way they could have learned."[30] The ELSIE provides teachers with specific information about students' learning strengths and weaknesses, making it possible for teachers to give individual students the kind of help they need. For some students, drills, outlining, or copying definitions is helpful; for others it is a waste of time. Some students benefit from listening to a tape of the text as they read; some even require it if they are to comprehend. For others, auditory stimuli are a hindrance.

The ELSIE can also be valuable for understanding the overall learning style makeup of a particular class. Reinert suggests that each class has a unique profile. Once teachers know what it is, they can plan instruction that should be most effective for the class as a whole. For example, Reinert gives evidence that casts doubt on the overall effectiveness of films with some groups. One picture is not always worth a thousand words.

Learning Style Inventory

The Learning Style Inventory (LSI) developed by Rita Dunn, Kenneth Dunn, and Gary Price is a multidimensional approach to learning styles.

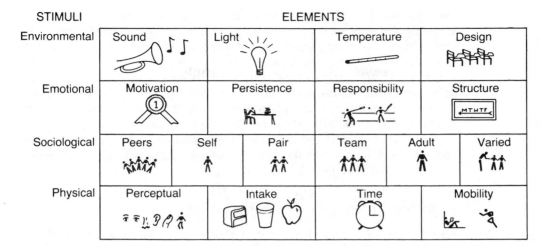

STIMULI   ELEMENTS

Environmental	Sound		Light		Temperature		Design	
Emotional	Motivation		Persistence		Responsibility		Structure	
Sociological	Peers	Self	Pair		Team	Adult	Varied	
Physical	Perceptual		Intake		Time		Mobility	

Figure 4.3   *Diagnosing Learning Style. From Rita Dunn and Kenneth Dunn, "Learning Styles/Teaching Styles: Should They . . . Can They . . . Be Matched?"* Educational Leadership 36 *(January 1979). Reprinted with permission of the Association for Supervision and Curriculum Development. Copyright © 1979 by the Association for Supervision and Curriculum Development. All rights reserved.*

Oriented to the classroom teacher, it is currently the approach most widely used. The Dunns define learning style as "the manner in which at least eighteen different elements from four basic stimuli affect a person's ability to absorb and retain."[31] (See Figure 4.3.) Stimuli are environmental (sound, light, temperature, and design); emotional (motivation, persistence, responsibility, and structure); sociological (peers, self, pair, team, adult, varied); and physical (perceptual, intake, time, mobility).

Two versions exist, one for the primary grades and one for grade four to adult. The LSI consists of a 104-item self-report questionnaire, which may be scored and analyzed by computer. If computerized scoring is used, each student receives a printout that includes a profile and narrative describing the learner's preferences related to classroom environmental conditions and their own emotional, sociological, and physical needs. The LSI identifies needs such as peak learning times, informal or formal classroom arrangement, perceptual modality, structure, and motivation.

The Dunns' definition of learning style has been criticized for overlooking cognitive processes and overemphasizing how four basic stimuli (environmental, emotional, sociological, and physical) affect a person's ability to absorb and retain information. According to some critics, their definition is unclear, seriously flawed, and raises more questions than it answers. "How did these educators decide on these eighteen elements and four types of stimuli? How do these eighteen elements interact? Is there a synergistic effect that any one element has when it interacts with two or three others analogous to the way certain drugs react differently in continuation than when alone? . . . Where is the element of intelligence?"[32] Some leaders of the learning style movement are more favorable. James Keefe, for example, writes that the LSI "is a practitioner-oriented instrument with commendable validation and widespread application, particularly in elementary and middle-level schools."[33] It should also be recognized that the Dunns have recently expanded their approach to include cognitive processes (analytic/global, cerebral preference, and reflective/impulsive).

Learning Styles and Teaching Styles

As teachers we tend to teach the way we learn best, unless we make a conscious effort to do otherwise. We can, therefore, discover a great deal about our teaching style by analyzing our learning style. Indeed, this is important, for just as students may be negatively affected by learning style mismatches, teachers are often negatively affected by teaching style mismatches.

Anthony Gregorc wrote: "Teachers whose teaching styles closely approximate their *major learning preferences* report comfort, ease, and authenticity."[34] Teachers who consistently mismatch their learning and teaching styles "report feelings of awkwardness, lack of efficiency and authenticity, and pain—mental and physical."[35] Many teachers are not aware of their teaching style and learning style preference and view pain and fatigue as natural results of hard work and study—"not as possible indicators of dis-ease." Many teachers attempt to conform to a distinct image of what a teacher should be, even if the image is unnatural for them. Others are influenced by traditional or required practice. "There are teachers, for example, who tell us that 'poetry *must* be taught this way,' and that 'we can't individualize and still meet mandated behavioral objectives,' or that 'students are not permitted to move around my room.' "[36] Stress and teacher burnout can result from extended periods of mismatch. Thus, educators' understanding of their own learning and teaching styles benefits them as much as their students. Fortunately, it is not difficult to attain this self-awareness.

Teachers find the ELSIE and the GEFT useful approaches for assessing their own perceptual modality preferences and their tendency toward field insensitivity–sensitivity or field independence–dependence. Most often these teachers agree that they expect their students to learn the same way they do. They also report that this self-awareness gives them insight into some of the "dis-ease" they experience when trying to be more flexible in their teaching. The insight itself often leads to feeling greater ease as they add new teaching styles to the old.

The idea of teaching style must not be confused with a teacher's method of instruction, such as the lecture, small group work, or oral reports. Teaching style refers to the teacher's pervasive personal behaviors and media used during interaction with learners. It is the teacher's characteristic approach, whatever the method used.[37] One useful description of teaching styles has been developed by Barbara and Louis Fischer. This approach consists of six teaching style categories, which are not intended to be entirely exclusive of each other (see Box 4.10). The categories can serve as guidelines for examining oneself and identifying predominant modes as well as possible combinations of modes.

In one recent review of learning style research, Rita Dunn examined a large number of "well-designed and carefully conducted research"[38] studies. She reported that when students are taught through their individual learning styles, their academic achievement increases significantly, their attitudes toward school improve significantly, and school discipline problems are significantly reduced.[39] Furthermore, "students have significantly more positive attitudes toward a subject when their learning styles are similar to their teachers' teaching styles."[40] Other research has documented that students perform better in classes taught by teachers with learning styles similar to the student.[41] This makes sense if one assumes that most teachers teach in ways that match their own learning styles. Only recently have demands been made that teachers become more flexible and use a variety of teaching styles in order to respond to the diversity of learning styles among their students.

Learning Styles and Effective Teaching

When a majority of students fail to learn, teachers are thought to have taught incompetently; the learning style movement, therefore, represents a tremendous challenge to teachers. It rejects the notion that good intentions are enough. Competence is required and is measured in terms of student growth and development.

Competence among teachers is often compared to competence in other professions. A well-intentioned doctor whose patients do not recover may still be called a doctor, and a well-intentioned architect whose buildings crumble may still be called an architect; neither, however, could be labeled competent in his or her profession. Similarly, a teacher who attends class every day with the intention of teaching is referred to as a teacher, even if no one learns. A competent teacher, however, is one who facilitates high levels of learning. The overall implication is that learning failure is due to teaching failure.

On the other hand, the learning style movement is conducive to higher levels of teacher competence than formerly. Defining effective teaching has been difficult in the past because judgments have been based on one teacher's impact on a large group of learners doing the

Box 4.10

Six Teaching
Style Cate-
gories

1. *The Task Oriented.* These teachers prescribe the materials to be learned and demand specific performance on the part of the students. Learnings to be accomplished may be specified on an individual basis, and an explicit system of accounting keeps track of how well each student meets the stated expectations.

2. *The Cooperative Planner.* These teachers plan the means and ends of instruction with student cooperation. They are still "in charge" of the learning process, but with their adult experience and professional background, they guide the students' learning. Opinions of the learners are not only listened to, but are respected. These teachers encourage and support student participation at all levels.

3. *The Child Centered.* This teacher provides a structure for students to pursue whatever they want to do or whatever interests them. The genuinely emergent curriculum would fit this style, for preplanning by the teacher always takes a back seat to the interest and curiosity of the child. This style is not only extremely rare, it is impossible to imagine in its pure form because the classroom, with its adult-child ratio and adult-responsible environment, automatically encourages some interests and discourages others.

4. *The Subject Centered.* These teachers focus on organized content to the near exclusion of the learner. By "covering the subject," they satisfy their consciences even if little learning takes place.

5. *The Learning Centered.* These teachers have equal concern for the students and for the curricular objectives, the materials to be learned. They reject the overemphasis of both the "child-centered" and "subject-centered" styles, and instead help students, whatever their abilities or disabilities, develop toward substantive goals as well as in their autonomy in learning.

6. *The Emotionally Exciting and Its Counterpart.* These teachers show their own intensive emotional involvement in teaching. They enter the teaching-learning process with zeal and usually produce a classroom atmosphere of excitement and high emotion. Their counterparts conduct classrooms subdued in emotional tone, where rational processes predominate, and the learning is dispassionate though just as significant and meaningful as in the classrooms of the emotionally more involved teachers.

Source: Barbara Bree Fischer and Louis Fischer, "Styles in Teaching and Learning," *Educational Leadership* 36 (January 1979):251. Reprinted with permission of the Association for Supervision and Curriculum Development. Copyright © 1979 by the Association for Supervision and Curriculum Development. All rights reserved.

same activity. This is misleading; few teaching strategies are appropriate for all or even a majority of students; thus the results of studies to determine teaching strategies and successful programs are disappointing. Nothing seems to make a significant difference; however, if researchers could examine the potential impact of specific strategies on individual students, research might be much more valuable.

Consider three first-grade teachers in one midwestern elementary school as an example. Hoping to evaluate the relative effectiveness of the phonetic, visual, and kinesthetic approaches to reading, each teacher chose one. Their comparisons of student growth in reading at the end of the year showed no significant differences; thus they concluded that the three approaches were equally effective and that it made little difference which one was selected. These teachers accepted the belief that every class should have some students progressing below, at, and above grade level. Had they examined program impact on individual students (especially on the failures) rather than on the class as a whole, they may well have found that the approach does make a difference. Many failing or below grade-level readers within each class might have progressed with one or more of the other approaches. In these, as in all first-grade classrooms, different students would have benefited from different kinds of teaching.

To equalize opportunities for success, it is imperative to use unequal teaching methods that respond to relevant differences among students. Paul Torrence wrote:

> Alert teachers have always been intuitively aware of the fact that when they change their method of teaching that certain children who had appeared to be slow learners or even non-learners became outstanding achievers and some of their former star learners became slow learners. They have also learned that when they change the nature of the test used for assessing achievement, such as from a multiple choice test to one requiring creative applications of knowledge and decision making, the star learners may change position in class ranking markedly.[42]

The goal is to maximize the number of stars who can exist simultaneously in the classroom—to formulate a plan that can work even with the most diverse group of students. Research documents the fact that a wide range of learning styles exists among students in every classroom.[43] Add to this the list of individual differences that will be considered in the next chapter. Equity in the classroom will require alternative ways of learning, often simultaneously. Yet many of us are uncomfortable with what feels like creeping chaos in the classroom, which seems easier to manage when students are all doing the same activity. Although individuals or small groups often are allowed to progress at their own rate or read at their own level, we rarely let students learn in the different ways dictated by the learning style movement. Those who continue to teach diverse groups of learners in nonflexible classrooms must not be lulled into complacency by the fact that some students are learning. Perhaps many are. If they can adjust, teachers ask, why can't everyone else?

Without alternative paths to success, we will continue to thwart the learning of some, and often many. If classroom expectations are limited by our own cultural orientations, we impede success for learners guided by another cultural orientation. If we only teach according to the ways we ourselves learn best, we are also likely to thwart success for learners who may share our cultural background but whose learning style deviates from our own.

Everyone knows of gifted teachers whose awareness and human sensitivity enable them to bridge cultural and individual gaps. They manage to provide each student with what he or she needs to be successful. But to what extent this flexibility and openness depend on basic personality traits may never be known. In any case, this author takes the position that every teacher who wants to can take steps that will open the channels of success to all learners, regardless of their cultural or individual ways. To do this, we should adopt the following guidelines:

- Know our own teaching and learning styles.
- Determine how far we can stray from these strengths and preferences and still be comfortable.
- Begin with a few students, those who are having difficulty in our classes.
- Know the learning style patterns that seem to characterize various ethnic groups.
- Build classroom flexibility slowly, adding one new strategy at a time.
- Use all modes (visual, auditory, tactile, and kinesthetic) when teaching concepts and skills.

Compare and Contrast	1. Cognitive, affective, and physiological dimensions of learning style 2. Field-sensitive and field-independent learning 3. Learning style and teaching style 4. Need for structure and modality strengths
Activities and Questions	1. When might it be best for teachers to mismatch their teaching styles with students' learning styles? Are there times when a match is absolutely necessary? Explain. 2. The idea that certain learning styles are related to certain ethnic groups is both dangerous and promising. Explain.

3. Analyze your own learning style. (Instructors and workshop leaders can obtain permission to use many of the learning style measures listed at the end of this chapter.) What insights did you gain about the way you teach or are likely to teach?

4. The following list describes four students according to one or more aspects of learning style. Consider each student; based on the limited information provided, write what you believe would be the most effective instructional and evaluation strategies you could use in a subject area of your choice. Be specific and refer to actual materials and/or resources available to you.

STUDENT	GRADE LEVEL, SKILL, OR CONCEPT TO BE TAUGHT	APPROPRIATE TEACHING STRATEGY/ MATERIALS	APPROPRIATE EVALUATION STRATEGY
1. Peggy Joyce—requires structure and has visual preferences.			
2. George—requires a quiet learning environment, is teacher motivated, prefers learning alone, is a tactual and kinesthetic learner, and requires mobility.			
3. Moses—lacks persistence, is a peer-oriented learner, has auditory preferences, requires food intake, and learns best in the morning.			
4. Doris—requires a formal learning environment, is persistent, responsible, peer oriented, adult and teacher motivated, and can learn in several ways.			

5. Identify a concept or skill you are likely to teach and create a lesson that allows you to develop it both inductively (for field-

independent learners) and deductively (for field-sensitive learners).

6. Select one or more learning style measures and administer it to one or more groups of students, or individuals. Which approach to learning styles did you select, and why? How effective did the approach appear to be? What are its advantages/disadvantages? What problems, if any, did you encounter? Did you discover any new insights or teaching implications for your classroom? If yes, explain fully. If not, was the exercise a waste of time? Explain.

7. Read further about learning styles. What is your current assessment of the learning style movement as an approach for enhancing student achievement? Is it another educational fad, or is there real potential here? Explain.

Selected Bibliography of Learning Style Assessment Instruments[44]

Multidimensional Instruments

Child Rating Form by Manuel Ramirez and Alfredo Castañeda. In *Cultural Democracy, Bicognitive Development, and Education.* New York: Academic Press, 1974. A direct observation checklist yielding frequency of behavior based on field independence/sensitivity and cultural differences. Teacher rates younger students; older students can rate themselves. Administration time varies. A revised version will soon appear in *New Frontiers* to be published by Pergamon Press, Inc.

Cognitive Style Interest Inventory by Joseph Hill. In *Personalized Education Programs Utilizing Cognitive Style Mapping.* Bloomfield Hills, Mich.: Oakland Community College, 1971. A self-report instrument based on a rank ordering that measures abstractions; visual, tactile, and auditory perceptions; motor coordination; and social interaction. Can be used with elementary students and up. Takes approximately fifty minutes.

Learning Style Identification Scale by Paul Malcom, William Lutz, Mary Gerken, and Gary Hoeltke. Publishers Test Service (CTB/McGraw-Hill), 2500 Garden Road, Monterey, Calif. 93940, 1981. A short (twenty-four-item), self-scored rating scale based on the concept of learning style as the "method students use to solve any problem that they encounter in their educational experiences." Five styles are identified based on classification of information reception and use, cognitive development, and self-concept.

Learning Styles Inventory by Joseph Renzulli and Linda Smith. Mansfield Center, Conn.: Creative Learning Press, 1978. Both teacher and student forms are available for this sixty-five-item instrument designed to measure attitude toward nine modes of instruction. Students and teachers indicate their reasons using a Likert scale ranging from very unpleasant to very pleasant. Forms are on optical scanning sheets and are scored by computer. Requires thirty minutes to administer and can be used in grades four through twelve.

Learning Style Inventory (students, 1978) and *Productivity Environmental Preference Survey* (adults, 1977) by Rita Dunn, Kenneth Dunn, and Gary E. Price. Price Systems, Box 3271, Lawrence, Kans. 66044. Self-report questionnaires yielding information about how a given student learns. There are thirty-six sub-scales covering eighteen elements in four areas: Environmental, Emotional, Sociological, and Physical. It is computer scored.

Learning Style Inventory: Primary Version by Janet Perrin. Jamaica, New York: St. John's University, 1981. Based on the *Learning Style Inventory* of Dunn, Dunn, and Price and designed for young children. The questionnaire consists of twelve charts, each containing a series of pictures and questions that assess a different element of learning style. The inventory is individually administered and scored on a student profile form. Takes about twenty minutes.

Learning Styles Inventory by Albert A. Canfield and Judith S. Canfield. Humanics Media, (Liberty Drawer) 7970, Ann Arbor, Mich. 48107, 1976. Self-report instrument based on a rank ordering of choices for each of thirty questions. For use with junior high and up. Takes about fifteen minutes.

Myers-Briggs Type Indicator by Isabel Briggs Myers and Katherine C. Briggs. Consulting Psychologists Press, Inc., 577 College Avenue, Palo Alto, Calif. 94306, 1976. A measure of personality dispositions and interests based on Jung's theory of types. Suitable for early adolescents through adults. Provides four bipolar scales that can be reported as continuous scores or reduced to types. Requires special training to administer.

Short Inventory of Approaches to Studying by Noel Entwistle. In *Styles of Learning and Teaching*. New York: John Wiley and Sons, 1981. A thirty-item test, using a Likert scale, in which students respond to statements concerning their achieving orientation, reproducing orientation, meaning dimension, comprehension style, operation style, and versatile approach. An index of learning pathologies can be obtained by summing three subscales. There is also a prediction of success score. Takes about thirty minutes. Appropriate for junior high and up.

Student Learning Styles Questionnaire by Anthony F. Grasha and Sheryl W. Riechmann, Institute for Research and Training in Higher Education, University of Cincinnati, Cincinnati, Ohio 45221, 1974. A hand-scored, self-report inventory of ninety items designed to elicit student attitudes toward the courses taken in college or high school and to identify related learning style. Six styles are described: Independent, Avoidant, Collaborative, Dependent, Competitive, and Participant.

Cognitive Style Instruments

Cognitive Profiles by Charles A. Letteri. In *Cognitive Profile: Basic Determinant of Academic Achievement*. Burlington, Vt.: Center for Cognitive Studies, 1980. Seven tests of cognitive style that, in combination, predict student achievement as measured by standardized achievement test scores. The seven dimensions are: (1) Field Independence/Dependence, (2) Scanning/Focusing, (3) Breadth of Categorization, (4) Cognitive Complexity/Simplicity, (5) Reflectiveness/Impulsiveness, (6) Leveling/Sharpening, and (7) Tolerant/Intolerant.

Concrete-Operational Reasoning Test and Logical Reasoning Test. In Robert Sund. *Piaget for Educators*. Columbus, Ohio: Charles E. Merrill, 1976. Two paper-and-pencil, group-administered tests to reveal formal or concrete operational reasoning. The problems are multiple choice.

Group Embedded Figures Test (also Embedded Figures Test and *Children's Embedded Figures Test)* by Herman A. Witkin et al. Consulting Psychologists Press, Inc., 577 College Ave., Palo Alto, Calif. 94306, 1971. EFT was originally designed for research with the field independent–field dependent aspect of cognitive style and was used to assess analytic ability, social behavior, body concepts, etc. The GEFT is a group version of the test. Field independence and dependence characterize analytical vs. global styles of information processing. The latter test takes about fifteen minutes.

Inventory of Learning Processes by Ronald R. Schmeck, Fred Ribich, and Nerella Ramanaiah. In "Development of a Self-Report Inventory for Assessing Individual Differences in Learning Processes," *Applied Psychological Measurement* 1 (1977):413–31. A sixty-two-item, true-false, self-report inventory grouped by factor analysis into synthesis/analysis, study methods, fact retention, and elaborative processing, reflecting a continuum of student information processing preferences from deep and elaborative to shallow and repetitive. Approximate administration time is twenty minutes.

Learning Strategies Questionnaire by Norman Kagan and David R. Krathwohl. In *Studies in Human Interaction*, Washington, D.C.: HEW/USOE Bureau of Research, 1967. A short self-report questionnaire developed for use at the college level to describe learner strategies that either focus on the details of a learning situation (focusers) or attempt to piece together the larger picture (scanners), on a continuum of discrete to global orientation. A scanning strategy is related to field independence and to academic success.

Learning Style Inventory by David Kolb. In "Disciplinary Inquiry Norms and Student Learning Styles: Diverse Pathways for Growth." In *The Modern American College*, edited by Arthur Chickering. San Francisco: Jossey-Bass, 1981. A five- to ten-minute self-report based on a rank ordering of four words in each of nine different sets. Each word represents one of four learning modes: feeling (Concrete Experience), watching (Reflective Observation), thinking (Abstract Conceptualization), and doing (Active Experimentation). For use with upper-grade students. Administration time is approximately ten minutes.

Matching Familiar Figures Test by Jerome Kagan. In "Impulsive and Reflective Children." In J. Krumboltz. *Learning and the Educational Process.* Chicago: Rand McNally, 1965. MFFT assesses individual differences in the speed and adequacy of information processing and concept formation on a continuum of reflective to impulsive. The testee is shown twelve pictures and, in each case, six similar alternatives, only one of which is correct. Reflectives tend to take longer and to produce more correct solutions than impulsives.

Schematizing Test by R. W. Gardner et al. In "Cognitive Control: A Study of Individual Consistencies in Cognitive Behavior." *Psychological Issues* 1 (4) (1959). Assesses individual variations in memory processing on a continuum of leveling to sharpening. Each subject is asked to judge in inches the sizes of 150 squares successively projected on a screen. The squares range in size from one to fourteen inches on a side and are shown in a prescribed order. Levelers are likely to over-generalize, while sharpeners may over-discriminate.

Transaction Ability Inventory by Anthony F. Gregorc. Department of Secondary Education, University of Connecticut, Box U-33, Storrs, Conn. 06268. A self-report instrument based on a rank ordering of four words in each of ten sets revealing four combinations of learning preference dualities: (1) Abstract Sequential, (2) Abstract Random, (3) Concrete Sequential, and (4) Concrete Random. Observation and interviews are suggested as adjuncts to the instrument. Administration time is approximately five minutes. Can be used with junior high students and up.

Your Style of Learning and Thinking Forms A & B by E. Paul Torrance, Cecil R. Reynolds, T. R. Riegel, and O. E. Ball. *Gifted Child Quarterly* 2 (1977):563–73.

A thirty-six-item, self-report, multiple-choice questionnaire that classifies subjects according to right hemisphere, left hemisphere, and integrated information processing. Each item presents three choices for the three modes based on an analysis of the research on brain hemispheric functioning. Approximate administration time is twenty minutes. Can be used with upper-grade students and adults.

Affective Style Instruments

Intellectual Achievement Responsibility Questionnaire by V. C. Crandall, W. Katkovsky, and V. J. Crandall. In "Children's Belief in Their Own Control of Reinforcements in Intellectual–Academic Achievement Situations," *Child Development* 36 (1965):91–109. The IAR scale is designed to assess internal-external perceptions of the control one exerts specifically in intellectual and academic situations. There are elementary and secondary school versions of the questionnaire.

Student Motivation Information Form by Raymond J. Wlodkowski. University of Wisconsin, Milwaukee, 1978. (Available from NEA.) A thirty-five-item, incomplete sentences test that elicits information about what motivates the person, e.g., intrinsic or extrinsic rewards. Could be administered orally to younger children.

Paragraph Completion Method by David E. Hunt et al. In *Assessing Conceptual Level by the Paragraph Completion Method.* Ontario Institute for Studies in Education, 252 Bloor Street, West, Toronto, Ont. M5S 1V6, 1978. A semi-projective method to assess the degree of classroom structure needed by students. Conceptual level shown by completing six incomplete statements involving conflict or uncertainty. (1) What I think about rules . . . , (2) When I am criticized . . . , (3) What I think about parents . . . , (4) When someone does not agree with me . . . , (5) When I am not sure . . . , (6) When I am told what to do. . . . Special training required to administer.

People in Society (Internal/External) Scale by Julian B. Rotter. In "Generalized Expectations for Internal Versus External Control of Reinforcements." *Psychological Issues* 1 (4) (1959):11–12. A questionnaire to find out how people react to certain important events that they experience in their society. Measures the degree of control persons feel over their world.

Perceptual Modality Instruments

Swassing-Barbe Modality Index by Walter Barbe and Raymond Swassing. Columbus, Ohio: Zaner-Bloser, 1979. This is a series of three tasks involving visual, auditory, and kinesthetic-tactile processing of the order of geometric shapes. It can be used with learners of any age but must be individually administered. Results tell the percentage of the time each mode is used successfully. Kit includes a textbook on modality instruction and a filmstrip and tape.

Swassing-Barbe Checklist of Observable Modality Strength Characteristics. This is a one-page brochure for use by teachers as they recall student characteristics. Columbus, Ohio: Zaner-Bloser.

"Find Your Modality Strengths" by Walter Barbe. In *Instructor* (January 1980). This is a series of ten incomplete sentences that are supposed to give "a rough idea of the relative strength of each of your modalities." Can be used by teachers and older students.

Learning Methods Test by Robert Mills. Available from The Mills School, 1512 E.

Broward Blvd., Ft. Lauderdale, Fla. 1955. The LMT determines the "students' abilities to learn new words under different teaching procedures." The tasks involve visual, kinesthetic, phonic, and combination presentations of words. Since immediate and delayed recall is assessed, the test takes four days, fifteen minutes each day. It is individually administered.

Edmonds Learning Style Identification Exercise by Harry Reinert. In "One Picture Is Worth a Thousand Words? Not Necessarily!" *The Modern Language Journal* 60 (1976):160–68. ELSIE provides a profile of students' preferred perceptual styles based on patterns of responses to fifty common English words. Four general categories are defined: Visualization, Written Word (reading), Listening, and Activity (kinesthetic).

SRI Student Perceiver Interview Guide. Selection Research, Incorporated, 2546 South 48th Plaza, P.O. Box 6438, Lincoln, Neb. 68506, 1978. A structured interview process designed to elicit student perceptions grouped under sixteen themes that are predominantly affective in nature. Institutes leading to trained certification are held regularly in designated cities. Administration time is approximately forty-five minutes. Can be used with intermediate students and up.

Notes

1. James W. Keefe and Marlin Languis, *Learning Stages Network Newsletter* 4, no. 2 (Summer 1983):1.
2. Gerald E. Kusler, "Getting to Know You," in *Student Learning Styles and Brain Behavior* (Reston, Va.: National Association of Secondary School Principals, 1983), p. 13.
3. Ibid., pp. 11–12.
4. Ibid.
5. Herman A. Witkin, Carol Ann Moore, and Frederick J. McDonald, "Cognitive Style and the Teaching/Learning Processes," American Educational Research Association Cassette Series 3F, 1974.
6. Manuel Ramirez and Alfredo Castañeda, *Cultural Democracy, Bicognitive Development and Education* (New York: Academic Press, 1974).
7. Asa Hilliard, "Alternatives to IQ Testing: An Approach to the Identification of Gifted Minority Children" (final report to the California State Department of Education, 1976). See also Barbara J. Shade, "Afro-American Cognitive Style: A Variable in School Success?" *Review of Educational Research* 52, no. 2 (Summer 1982):220.
8. Shade, "Afro-American Cognitive Style," p. 220.
9. J. C. Phillips, "College of, by and for Navajo Indians," *Chronicle of Higher Education* 15 (January 16, 1978):10–12.
10. James Keefe, "Assessing Student Learning Styles: An Overview," in *Student Learning Styles and Brain Behavior* (Reston, Va.: National Association of Secondary School Principals, 1983), p. 44.
11. Claudia E. Cornett, *What You Should Know About Teaching and Learning Styles*, Fastback 191 (Bloomington, Ind.: Phi Delta Kappa Educational Foundation, 1983).
12. Keefe, "Assessing Student Learning Styles."
13. Samuel Messick, ed., *Individuality in Learning* (San Francisco: Jossey-Bass, 1976).
14. Keefe, "Assessing Student Learning Styles."
15. Witkin, Moore, and McDonald, "Cognitive Style."

16. Hidden Figures Test (Cf-1), from the *Kit of Factor-Referenced Cognitive Tests* (Princeton, N.J.: Educational Testing Service, 1962).

17. Witkin, Moore, and McDonald, "Cognitive Style."

18. Ramirez and Castañeda, *Cultural Democracy.*

19. Patricia Cross, *Accent on Learning* (San Francisco: Jossey-Bass, 1976), p. 116.

20. Alfredo Castañeda and Tracy Gray, "Bicognitive Processes in Multicultural Education," *Educational Leadership* 32 (December 1974):203–7, tables 1–3.

21. David E. Hunt, "Learning Style and Student Needs: An Introduction to Conceptual Level," in *Student Learning Styles: Diagnosing and Prescribing Programs* (Reston, Va.: National Association of Secondary School Principals, 1979).

22. David E. Hunt, quoted in Cornett, *What You Should Know About Teaching and Learning Styles*, p. 36.

23. Ibid., p. 31.

24. Ibid.

25. Harry Reinert, "One Picture Is Worth a Thousand Words? Not Necessarily!" *The Modern Language Journal* 60 (April 1976):163. Reinert's article is summarized and quoted here by permission of the author. *The Modern Language Journal* is published by the National Federation of Modern Language Teachers Associations (Madison: University of Wisconsin Press).

26. Ibid., p. 162.

27. Ibid., p. 165.

28. Ibid., p. 169.

29. Ibid., p. 166.

30. Ibid., p. 161.

31. Rita Dunn and Kenneth Dunn, "Learning Styles/Teaching Styles: Should They . . . Can They . . . Be Matched?" *Educational Leadership* 36 (January 1979):239.

32. Ronald Hyman and Barbara Rosoff, "Matching Learning and Teaching Styles: The Jug and What's in It," *Theory into Practice* 23 (Winter 1984):36.

33. Keefe, "Assessing Student Learning Styles," pp. 52–53.

34. Anthony F. Gregorc, "Learning/Teaching Styles," in *Student Learning Styles: Diagnosing and Prescribing Programs* (Reston, Va.: National Association of Secondary School Principals, 1979), p. 24.

35. Ibid.

36. Ibid.

37. Barbara Bree Fischer and Louis Fischer, "Styles in Teaching and Learning," *Educational Leadership* 36 (January 1979):245–54; see also Gregorc, "Learning/Teaching Styles."

38. Dunn and Dunn, "Learning Styles/Teaching Styles," p. 142.

39. Ibid.

40. Ibid., p. 145.

41. Witkin, Moore, and McDonald, "Cognitive Style."

42. Paul Torrence, "Cultural Discontinuities and the Development of Originality of Thinking," *Exceptional Children* 29 (September 1962):2–3.

43. Dunn and Dunn, "Learning Styles/Teaching Styles," p. 145.

44. The Selected Bibliography is from Cornett, *What You Should Know About Teaching and Learning Styles*, pp. 32–37; © 1983, Phi Delta Kappa Educational Foundation. Reprinted by permission of Phi Delta Kappa.

Chapter 5

Beyond Learning Style: An Overview of Other Key Individual Differences

An appropriate response to students' learning styles is often a necessary condition for success in the classroom, but it is rarely sufficient. Learning style represents one of a cluster of characteristics that may also need to be considered. A student may be so interested in a particular subject, for example, that he or she will learn it regardless of the teacher's style. On the other hand, students who lack confidence, or who experience severe problems outside the classroom, may be unable to learn under even the best classroom conditions. This chapter explains ten individual characteristics that, along with learning styles and need for structure, often make a difference in how students learn. The chapter concludes with a discussion of teacher perceptions of individual differences as being culturally disadvantaged or culturally different.

Learning Skills

Learning skills refer to a student's abilities to change or attain new capabilities. Learning skills would include a child's ability to accurately receive aural and visual stimuli, to control large and small muscles, and to coordinate eye-hand activities. Other examples are decision-making skills and critical thinking, such as the ability to distinguish fact from opinion and the ability to generate alternative solutions to a problem and understand the consequences of each.

Why do students of the same age often differ in their learning skill? How we answer this question is influenced by our conception of intelligence (an individual's ability to learn from experience, or to acquire and retain knowledge). Those who believe that intelligence is predetermined at birth would also believe that it is only natural for the brightest students to have the strongest learning skills. Others believe that intelligence develops primarily through environmental experiences. According to this view, students could not be expected to possess specific learning skills unless they had been taught or had had an opportunity to develop them through experience.

Probably the best response to the old nature-nurture controversy surrounding intelligence is that the individual's highest potential is determined at conception, and that the degree to which this potential is fulfilled depends largely on what the individual experiences during the formative years. The mother's emotional and physical health during pregnancy, as well as the nutrition provided the infant and young child, can influence how this potential is developed. It can be assumed that, barring cases of extreme nutritional and emotional deprivation, the vast majority of students have the capacity to develop the learning skills necessary to succeed in school. What must be remembered, however, is that they are not all ready to do so at the same time. Just as children mature physically at different rates, so do they mature mentally at different rates. Because mental development is more difficult to observe, we often do not know what the child is ready for.

Culturally different students, such as Fred Young and Jimmy Miller, and students from a low-income family, such as Rachael Jones, are often perceived as being culturally disadvantaged, "deficient," and lacking in ability to develop learning skills. Later in this chapter, teacher perceptions will be explained more fully.

Jean Piaget and his associates at the Geneva Institute have generated strong evidence that all humans in all cultures move through a hierarchy of four stages as they develop intellectually.[1] Although everyone moves through the same stages, and in the same order, how quickly one moves through these stages depends on the combination of maturation (growth of brain tissues and development of the endocrine system), physical experiences, social interactions, and ego balance or a general progression of equilibrium through assimilation or accommodation of new learnings.

The first of these stages, *the sensorimotor intelligence stage*, usually operates during the first two years of life. During this period the infant's behavior is primarily motor, and the basic intellectual processes are developed through physical interaction with the environment. Objects exist for the child only if they can be seen, touched, or heard.

The second stage, *preoperational thought*, usually extends from ages two to seven. Verbal and conceptual abilities expand during this stage, and the child is capable of intuitive thought, though it tends to be illogical and ethnocentric.

The third stage, *concrete operations*, is entered at about age seven. Here the child shows striking new abilities to think in a logical way and to solve concrete problems. Thought processes such as ordering, classification, seriation, and mathematics are possible, provided concrete objects are involved. The ability to think abstractly has not yet begun to appear.

Between eleven and fifteen years of age, the individual enters the stage of *formal operations*. In this stage students come to understand highly abstract concepts, such as justice, love, and prejudice. Their thoughts are no longer tied to actual objects and experience; they can think about ideas and use logic. Until the child fully develops stage-four thought processes, therefore, he or she is incapable of certain intellectual activities that require abstract reasoning.

Whether or not one accepts Piaget's theory of cognitive development, it is crucially important to know where students are in terms of their intellectual growth and development. Students who may have the same potential for high achievement may be approaching it at different rates, or may differ in their past opportunities to learn. A suburban child, for example, may not know as much about animals and nature as a child who has grown up on a farm. An inner-city child may know little about raking leaves or fishing. A rural child may never have flown in an airplane or visited a large city. Although these children's horizons may be broadened through vicarious experiences on television, much remains to be learned about the impact of that medium on their cognitive development.

When teachers ask students to perform tasks they are not ready for—due to slower rates of maturation or absence of necessary experiences—they may create the conditions of failure and make it less likely that the individual's intelligence will be developed to its fullest potential. The challenge is to ask students to perform mental tasks that match their intellectual development. If we aim too high we can trigger feelings of frustration, self-doubt, and failure. If we aim too low the student may become frustrated, bored, and alienated.

Levels of Achievement and Aptitudes

Achievement level is defined as the knowledge a student has previously acquired that relates to what is being taught. Although this knowledge could include learning skills such as critical thinking and decision making, the emphasis here is on content, which consists of the concepts and generalizations within the subject matter.

What students already know about what we plan to teach is of obvious importance to their success in the classroom. Do they have the basic knowledge—the building blocks—needed to understand new material? Can they read musical notes? Can they comprehend the textbook? Have they mastered their multiplication facts? Do they already know most of what we plan to teach this year? Perhaps a student is obsessed with reading about space or dinosaurs, has had years of experience helping in a parent's store, is already an expert mechanic, is an authority on Beethoven, or has a hobby collecting fossils. Perhaps a student has grown up in a world of crime and injustice, or has developed more insight into the problems of alcohol and drug abuse than could be provided in any college text.

Aptitudes refer to special abilities, talents, or natural tendencies that enable one to learn or understand quickly. When students show a special aptitude for what is being taught, they will probably learn at a rapid rate. Students who show little aptitude for a subject will require more time to learn it. Teachers must be careful not to assume, however, that a slow rate of learning necessarily means low aptitude. It may be that other explanations are possible. The student may lack more basic knowledge; one cannot learn division, for example, until the multiplication facts are mastered. The learner may not be ready to handle abstractions or may lack self-confidence. Students may be reflective rather than impulsive learners, or may experience transitional trauma due to cultural conflict between home and school.

Teachers must recognize that students' learning rates may differ. If we assume that a slow rate of learning indicates low aptitude, however, we are lowering our expectations and probably the student's self-expectations for success. The challenge is knowing when it is necessary and fair to expect more, and when it is not.

Current research on gifted and talented children and youth can make teachers more alert to the special talents and aptitudes that many students possess. Current research indicates that gifted students are evenly distributed across all racial groups and socioeconomic levels.[2] The traditional conception that gifted students are those who score very high on intelligence tests has given way to a much broader view. Today, many kinds of giftedness are recognized: intellectual, academic (one or more specific subjects), creative thinking, leadership, visual and performing arts, athletic, and mechanical. Students in all these categories would score above average on an intelligence test, but not necessarily in the highest ranges. For example, a highly creative student with excellent critical thinking skills could score 115 on an IQ test (generally believed to be the lowest level possible for the gifted). Traditional intelligence tests "do not measure other critical characteristics such as artistic excellence, superior moral attitudes and behaviors, creative or divergent production behaviors, superior psychomotor abilities, or superior leadership abilities."[3]

When considering the levels of achievement and aptitudes of students whose cultural background differs from what predominates in school (the Anglo-European macroculture), it is important to remember the following factors.

- The past experiences and opportunities of ethnically different students are often not the ones teachers recognize and value.
- Measures of achievement and aptitude have traditionally been most appropriate for White middle-income groups.
- Instructional content and strategies have also been developed primarily for White middle-income students.
- Teachers often lack understanding of cultural difference and have lower expectations for student success.
- The student may not be fluent in standard English or may speak a dialect the teacher regards as slang.
- The student may have a learning style preference that is not accommodated by the teacher.
- The student may not be accepted by a majority of classmates, a factor that has been found to lower achievement levels among minority children.

Motivation

Motivation refers to the inner drive, the feeling of intent or desire, that causes the student to learn. There exists within students a natural reservoir of motivation.[4] Provided that children feel respected and cared for by their teachers, there are no racial or cultural differences in their basic love of learning in the early grades. Natural excitement, the love of learning, and the desire to know are seen most clearly among children in kindergarten and the primary grades. As students move through school, however, the excitement often dims and teachers typically have to do something to motivate students to learn.

In our efforts to motivate students, we find there are differences in what works. Some students respond to competition, for example; turn any learning activity into a competitive game and they thrive. For competition types, the boredom of a history review or spelling list disappears when the class plays "Double Jeopardy" or baseball; the chance to play Quiz Bowl can make the weekly reading of *Time* part of their routine. Other students, however, dislike competition and feel anxious and less able to learn or perform in a competitive situation. Even high-achieving students, who theoretically could survive the competition, would do better in a cooperative setting.

Peer approval is another prime motivator for some students. Whether or not a student achieves in a given class may depend on how a clique or peer reference group feels about the teacher and subject. It is common for high-ability students to suppress their school achievements in order to be accepted by their peers. Those students who are moved by adult or teacher approval may be easier to motivate, though in some cases pressure from parents can cause undue tension and anxiety.

Younger students may be motivated by consumable rewards such as candy or other treats. Older students can often be motivated by opportunities for making choices, experiencing greater independence, or assuming new responsibilities, particularly if the options have real meaning for them.

Many of these strategies may sound like manipulation, especially if we accept the view of Maslow and other humanists who believe that all humans by nature continually search for growth and self-expansion. The question for teachers is: How can we act to utilize the natural motivation that exists within the students we teach?

Maslow states that human needs are organized into a "hierarchy of relative prepotency: physical needs, safety needs, belongingness and love needs, esteem needs, and the need for self-actualization."[5] Ordinarily, the needs at one level must be partially satisfied before the individual seeks to satisfy needs at the next level. Once the basic "lower" needs are met (food and water, protection, love, and self-esteem), there exists within everyone the compelling desire to grow and expand to his or her fullest potential, to be what Maslow refers to as self-actualized. A self-actualized person is one who is self-directed and grows by using all of his or her natural abilities. Self-actualized persons search to fulfill their highest needs through aesthetic experiences and a concern for ethics.

This theory has important implications for teaching. Only when students' basic needs are met are they ready to learn at their fullest potential. Their needs for food, water, shelter, clothing, and protection from harm must be satisfied before they can be concerned about love and belonging. The sense of belonging is necessary for building the self-esteem that is, in turn, necessary for self-actualization. As the individual begins to become self-actualized, the desire for knowledge, understanding, and aesthetic experiences intensifies.

Teachers obviously cannot control the student's world outside the classroom. We cannot solve problems such as poverty and hunger, family conflicts, child abuse, or a child's inability to make friends. Neither a hungry child nor a rejected child is likely to place a high priority on learning. Teachers, nevertheless, are in a prime position for helping students meet needs at all levels. We must do what we can to work toward the goal of helping all students reach their fullest potential. Suggestions such as in Box 5.1 are some of the strategies known to maximize motivation, development, and achievement among students. These suggestions are arranged in four categories: instructional qualities, personal qualities, content, and classroom climate.

Self-Concept

The self-concept, or self-image, is a complex set of beliefs that an individual holds true about himself or herself. This set of beliefs may be

Box 5.1

Teaching
Strategies

INSTRUCTIONAL QUALITIES

- Provide each student with an opportunity to make an important contribution to class activities.
- Provide each student with an opportunity to experience success.
- Provide students with effective feedback or helpful information about their progress; be prompt; be clear about the criteria for success.
- Shift patterns of instruction; use a variety of strategies and sensory channels.
- Alter the physical learning environment when necessary to make it compatible with the purpose of the lesson. (For example, desks in a circle facilitate equal communication, rows may be more effective for a film, and opposing blocks of chairs can enhance a classroom debate).

SUGGESTIONS ABOUT CONTENT

- Begin with clear objectives that are challenging but attainable.
- Make clear why the objectives are important and worth attaining.
- Cultivate curiosity and creativity.
- Invite students to participate in planning and evaluating their curriculum.
- Build on students' existing interests while trying to create new ones.
- Organize at least part of the curriculum around real life problems.

SUGGESTIONS ABOUT PERSONAL QUALITIES

- Search for ways to express care for each student.
- Never belittle or ridicule a student.
- Project enthusiasm.
- Avoid distracting behaviors and overuse of terms such as "uh" and "you know."
- Use movement—don't stay behind the desk.
- Be genuine.

SUGGESTIONS ABOUT CLIMATE

- Get to know students. Learn their names right away.
- Find ways to help students know each other.
- Insist that students show respect for each other; create a classroom climate of trust and acceptance.

viewed globally or may be broken down into components. For example, we have beliefs about our achievement abilities, both overall and in specific areas. We have beliefs about our character, such as our integrity or compassion. We have beliefs about our physical attractiveness, strength, and coordination.

How we see ourselves develops out of our interactions with others, the way we feel others perceive us and treat us. This self-image influences our behaviors, which, in turn, affect the way others see us and treat us, and the cycle (be it benevolent or vicious) is complete.

It appears that a positive self-image is a necessary though not sufficient condition for school success. Students with a negative self-image seldom achieve at above-average levels. On the other hand, many students with positive self-concepts do not achieve at high or above-average levels, as we might expect. Feeling good about oneself does not guarantee being a top student, but feeling bad nearly guarantees doing poorly.

When a student with low self-esteem enters a classroom, self-concept becomes one of the most challenging individual differences in how he or she will learn. Because students with a negative self-image are not fully able to learn, school becomes an arena for failure that prevents them from achieving the success needed for high self-esteem. A vicious cycle develops whereby the school itself, by providing experiences of failure, helps keep the student's self-image deflated.

> Once a child is convinced he cannot learn in school, the task of educators becomes almost impossible. He may well make trouble for his classmates, his teachers, and himself. A negative self-concept is just as crippling and just as hard to overcome as any physical handicap. In fact, a negative self-image may be even more crippling, because it is often hidden from the view of the naive or untrained observer. Most children who hate themselves act out this self-hatred by kicking the world around them. They are abusive, aggressive, hard to control, and full of anger and hostility at a world which has told them that they are not valued, are not good, and are not going to be given a chance. Such attitudes often continue to cripple an adult life.[6]

Do the children and youth of ethnic-minority backgrounds tend to have less positive self-images than those of nonminorities? The answer to this question is debatable. Research findings to date are contradictory and inconclusive.[7] Some have assumed, for example, that Black self-concepts would be lower because of the history of slavery and oppression Blacks have experienced in this society.[8] Although some research tends to support this view, other researchers have discovered that Black students' self-concepts are as high or higher than their White counterparts.[9]

A number of researchers have studied the impact of school desegregation on the self-concepts of minority students. In his extensive review of recent research on minority student self-concepts, Meyer Weinberg concludes that evidence supports the proposition that attendance at an interracial school benefits Black students' self-conceptions.[10] However, Weinberg cautions against artificial self-esteem programs that do not offer minority students the opportunities to acquire the knowledge and skills needed for school and occupational successes.

Others assert that Black students benefit more from the historically Black schools, where Black teachers are more caring and supportive of Black students, have high academic expectations, and provide Black students with positive role models as well as a knowledge of Black history and achievements. Such schools are unavailable to the majority of Black students today, and Weinberg seems justified in his conclusions.

In his book *Inviting School Success: A Self-Concept Approach to Teaching*,[11] William Purkey develops the conception of teaching as inviting. Teachers have the capacity to invite or disinvite, to encourage or discourage, student development and achievement. Purkey explains that invitations are the verbal and nonverbal, formal and informal, messages that make students feel responsible, able, and valuable. (Conversely, a *disinvitation* is a message that makes students feel that they are irresponsible, incapable, and worthless.) Even a child with a very low sense of self-esteem can be invited to learn by a caring teacher. No matter how bad the overall school situation is, the teacher always has the power to invite and disinvite students.

The authors of *Perceiving, Behaving, and Becoming* agree that a positive self is teachable, and that self-knowledge and growth as education goals are as important as the acquisition of subject matter.[12] They call for classroom climates that are free from destructive competition, prejudice, bigotry, and vicious conflict between opposing interest groups; for teachers who behave as friendly representatives of society; and for social experiences that make students feel acceptable, liked, wanted, able, respected, worthy, and important.[13]

Special Interests

Students' special interests refer to the hobbies and recreational activities students enjoy most and pursue whenever they can. Interests may also refer to personal concerns and problems the student faces. Wise teachers attempt to discover their students' special interests because outside interests can become a catalyst for student learning in the classroom.

Experienced teachers can supply numerous examples of reaching the "unreachable" by relating course content and activities to the student's special interest. Fractions can be taught through musical rhythms, history through sports, science through the outdoors, reading through motorcycle manuals, personal accounting through part-time jobs such as paper routes or child care, and civics through community issues and problems.

A classic case of building on student interest is described by Daniel Fader and Elton McNeil in *Hooked on Books*.[14] By instituting an extensive reading program based on paperbacks, magazines, and newspapers that most teachers would frown upon but that are related to the students' lives, Fader and McNeil were able to motivate even the most bored and apathetic students.

Physical Characteristics

Physical characteristics (the body itself) are closely related to the other individual differences being considered. Physical health and maturation, for example, affect intellectual and emotional growth and development; attractiveness, health and vitality, size, age, strength, agility, coordination, and gender can all affect self-perception, peer acceptance, and readiness for learning. When the individual is perceived as being different from what is believed to be normal, physical differences must be considered.

During the years of emerging adolescence, typically between ages ten and fourteen, physical differences are especially important. Tremendous physical changes take place with the onset of puberty among males and females. Bones lengthen, muscles enlarge, the endocrine glands produce hormones, and the individual develops sexually. Thomas Curtis and Wilma Bidwell wrote:

> This interrelationship between the hormonal balance of the body and the nervous system of the brain has certain implications for the development of the educational system for emerging adolescents. The possibility of extreme changes in mood and volatility found in many emerging adolescents becomes much more easily explained when the possibility of temporary chemical imbalance due to temporarily uneven hormonal secretions is noted. The concerns of the emerging adolescent about his or her physical body may create psychosomatic problems which, while not noted by adult observers, may have great impact upon the emotions of the emerging adolescent. Last, since the emotions are affected to some extent by the hypothalamus, it is not unreasonable to expect that the emotions of the emerging adolescent might be less predictable than in childhood or in later adolescence when hormonal secretions become less of a factor in the physical development of the youngster.[15]

Physical differences are often associated with various ethnic groups. Research on prejudice shows that in United States society skin color is the most salient characteristic that influences peoples' perceptions and judgments of each other.[16] Historically, lighter-skinned individuals have been favored over those with dark skin, sometimes even among Black Americans and Hispanics. Even though the civil rights movement of the 1960s helped to expand social recognition that Black is beautiful, skin color often makes a difference in the classroom. Studies of classroom interaction show that many teachers have higher expectations for the achievement of their White or lighter-skinned students than for Black, Hispanic, or darker-skinned students, and they interact with White students in more positive ways.[17]

Although they may be unaware of their prejudices, these teachers have accepted the racist view that a student's physical traits associated with race determine that student's social behavior, character, and intellectual abilities. This view leads to actions that subordinate students of another race.

Peer Relations

The social structure of the classroom and the social status of the individual student with respect to classmates can have an impact on student learning. In the vignette of Max Britten in the opening section of Part II, rejection and scapegoating by his peers had a negative impact on his school achievement. His schoolwork improved during those periods when he was accepted by the neighborhood clique. A single student in Warren Benson's class who decided to get serious about learning might face the rejection of peers. Warren would have to find a way to motivate certain cliques and make class attendance and learning socially acceptable.

Some researchers have discovered a positive relationship between a student's popularity among classmates and social interactions; others have found that social acceptability is also related to achievement.[18] School desegregation research has shown that school and classroom climates of acceptance have a significant impact on the academic achievement of minority students.[19] Students who represent a numerical minority tend to achieve better in classroom climates of acceptance.

One recent study of classroom climate in over forty desegregated seventh- and eighth-grade classrooms in Indianapolis showed that in classroom climates of acceptance, both Black and White students selected many friends of their own and different races.[20] Students also frequently initiated conversations with students of both races. In the low-acceptance classrooms, both Black and White students tended to limit their conversations and friendship choices to their own race. This study did not analyze the relationship between student interracial popularity (that is, interracial friendship choices and conversations) and achievement, but teachers in the high-acceptance classrooms felt there were no important racial differences in student achievement or aptitude. Teachers in the low-acceptance classrooms reported that White students were higher achievers than Black students. The study suggests that teachers themselves have a lot to do with the type of climate that is established. When compared with their peers, teachers in high-acceptance classrooms tended to be strong and directing, fair, warm, spontaneous, and involved in the teaching profession.

How can teachers discover peer relationships and the social status of individual students in their classrooms? A variety of sociometric techniques are available to collect these data. Typically, each student is asked to select other students in class for a specific reason, such as the student(s) they would most like to work with or sit next to, or the student(s) they like best or would most prefer as a friend. Other measures ask the student to select the classmate who best fits a certain role or description, such as class president, beauty queen, best athlete, smartest, or most friendly. Sometimes students will be asked to identify their least preferred choice or select students for negative roles or qualities, such as troublemaker or least liked. Such negative approaches are questionable. Keep in mind that simply using a sociogram may affect the social network of the classroom and could have a negative impact on the overall climate as well as on individual students. Socially isolated individuals in particular could be vulnerable. A sensitive and caring teacher, however, can use sociometric data as a base line for establishing a more accepting environment. Chapter 8 will explain strategies designed to help accomplish this.

Family Conditions

Family conditions refer to the child's experiences at home and include a wide range of factors such as love and emotional support, sibling relationships, parents' occupations, special learning experiences, economic resources, ethnicity, and so on.

The family's influence on the child's sense of ethnicity is of special interest. Wilma Longstreet pointed out the strong relationships between family and ethnicity when she defined ethnicity as "that portion of cultural development that occurs before the individual is in complete command of his or her abstract intellectual powers and that is formed primarily through the individual's early contact with family, neighbors, friends, teachers, and others, as well as with his or her immediate environment of the home and neighborhood."[21] Until the time a child can think abstractly, he or she naturally develops certain food and clothing preferences, ways of talking, body language, and values. Later, these cultural ways could be changed if the individual would choose to do so.

But for most of the time a child attends school, ethnic origins have a strong influence. How similar these cultural ways are to the macroculture is a factor in school success.

Although teachers often have no idea about what their students' home conditions are like, they make assumptions. Marcia comes from a rich family and has all the advantages; the fact that she's not doing well in school must be due to poor aptitude. Rachael lives in the poor section, has not been exposed to good books or music, and does not value school; thus little can be expected from her. Max comes from a split home; therefore, he feels rejected and needs extra attention in school, but a teacher with thirty-three other students can't provide it.

Too often, we assume that children and youth from low-income backgrounds or single-parent homes receive insufficient love and support from their families. We tend to assume the opposite for the child from the typical all-American family in suburbia. While there is some truth to these stereotypes, parents and students are rightfully offended when schools assume that children from low-income backgrounds are deprived of love and emotional support. Divorced parents are also rightly offended at the single-parent stereotypes. Research on the long-term effects of divorce on children shows that divorce is indeed traumatic for children, particularly male children under age six.[22] During the immediate crisis, many children do not achieve in school. Typically, at least a year is needed to adjust even under the best of conditions. Research also shows that after a period of transition and under supportive conditions some children recover sufficiently to resume progress in school, and that children raised in single-parent homes often develop greater independence, responsibility, and initiative.[23]

It would be impossible to know and fully understand the family conditions of all students. Teachers can realize, however, that sometimes a student is unable to learn in school because of problems at home, or a conflict between home and school. Teachers can avoid diminished expectations based on erroneous assumptions that a student is simply slow or unmotivated. We can provide encouragement and support in school and better the chances that eventually the child will be resilient and catch up. We can avoid stereotypes and misconceptions by asking ourselves the following questions:

1. Does the family provide love and emotional support?
2. Does the family provide adequate food and shelter?
3. Does the student have unusual family responsibilities?
4. Are there mutual feelings of respect and ease between family members and school personnel?
5. Is there any cultural conflict between home and school expectations?

Beliefs, Attitudes, and Values

Beliefs, attitudes, and values are at the heart of what is meant by culture. They are also at the heart of concern about individual differences within cultural similarities. Beliefs, attitudes, and values have developed out of shared and unique past experiences, and they strongly influence (while being influenced by) behavior and perceptions of the world.

A person's beliefs, attitudes, and values may be viewed together as an integrated cognitive system; change in any one of the three parts of the system will affect other parts, and is likely to result in a change of behavior.[24] *A belief refers to an opinion, expectation, or judgment that a person accepts as true.* Not all beliefs are equally important to the individual; they vary along a central-peripheral dimension. Central beliefs are most resistant to change, and the more central the belief that is changed, the more widespread the repercussions in the rest of the belief system.[25]

An attitude may be defined as a relatively stable organization of interrelated beliefs that describe, evaluate, and advocate action with respect to a person, object, or situation.[26] This definition suggests that attitudes have three components: an idea or thought component; a feeling or emotional component; and a readiness to respond or predisposition to action.[27] An attitude is thus a package of beliefs about what is true or false, desirable and undesirable.

As stated in Chapter 1, *values are beliefs about how one ought or ought not to behave, or about some end state of existence worth or not worth attaining.* Values are abstract ideals, positive or negative, that represent a person's beliefs about ideal modes of conduct and ideal terminal goals.[28] *A value is a standard we use to influence the values, attitudes, and actions of others;* it is like a yardstick we use to guide the actions, attitudes, comparisons, evaluations, and justifications of ourselves and others.[29]

Consider some examples that illustrate the complex cognitive system of beliefs, attitudes, and values. The first situation involves drug usage; the second, racial discrimination in the collegiate Greek system; and the third, cultural conflict between a teacher and a student.

In the first situation, two young high school students attend an unsupervised party where everyone is smoking pot. Neither student has ever used drugs before and for various reasons feels hesitant about doing so. They are both encouraged to join in the activity, and it appears that they would be excluded from the group if the invitation were refused. What do they decide to do and how are they likely to feel after the decision? (See Box 5.2.)

Because each person's beliefs are highly consistent in this example, and no value conflicts were presented, it is easy to infer what each person will do. In reality, however, the relationship between attitudes and behavior is usually not so clear cut.

Box 5.2

Cognitive
Systems—
Drugs

STUDENT A	STUDENT B
BELIEFS	
• Pot is not harmful; it is neither physically nor psychologically addictive. • My parents will be angry if I smoke pot. • Almost everybody smokes pot. • The laws against marijuana are unfair, and they aren't strictly enforced in this town anyway. • I will be accepted by this group if I smoke pot. • Pot makes a person feel more relaxed and euphoric.	• Pot can become psychologically addicting. • Sometimes pot contains lethal additives. • People who use pot suffer from feelings of inadequacy or boredom with life. • Pot is illegal. • It is possible that this party could be busted by police. • I will be accepted by this group if I smoke pot.
ATTITUDES	
• The idea of smoking pot with these friends feels good and I want to stay and accept the invitation.	• The idea of smoking pot with these friends feels bad and I want to leave.
VALUES	
• Personal enjoyment and friendship are more important than obeying a foolish law.	• Health and self-respect are more important than social acceptance.

The next example in Box 5.3 takes place on a college campus during rush. The illustration could also apply to many noncollegiate situations such as housing developments, apartment complexes, fraternal organizations, and social clubs. The situation takes place in a college fraternity or sorority that has historically been for one ethnic group: all-Jewish, all-White, or all-Black, and so on. A student from a different ethnic background has made it to the final selection stage and may be invited to join the organization. The students described in Box 5.3 are in a unique position to influence others. How do you think each will act?

It seems clear that student D would take a stand in favor of inviting the person to join. But what about student A, B, or C? The value conflicts seems stronger with those students who believe in a person's right to associate with whomever they choose, but who do not wish to be seen as prejudiced by close associates. These students seem unaware

Box 5.3

Cognitive Systems— Racial Discrimination

STUDENT A

STUDENT B

BELIEFS

STUDENT A

- Blacks are immoral and sexually promiscuous.
- Blacks are dirty.
- Blacks are lazy and never on time.
- Blacks are loud and violent.
- Blacks are less intelligent.
- Blacks are poor.
- Blacks are not like me.
- I'm not prejudiced; I can't help the way other people are.
- If I express my honest beliefs, some people will like me; others will dislike me.

STUDENT B

- Whites are stupid about life.
- Whites are intellectually superior.
- Whites are prejudiced against Blacks.
- Whites are dirty, especially in preparation of foods.
- Whites are emotionally cold and colorless.
- Whites are not like me.
- I'm not prejudiced; I can't help the way other people are.
- If I express my honest beliefs, some people will like me; others will dislike me.

STUDENT C

STUDENT D

BELIEFS

STUDENT C

- Jews are bookworms.
- Jews are mercenary and out to get all they can for themselves.
- Jews are loud and obnoxious.
- Jews are aggressive.
- Jews can't be trusted.
- Jews like to stick together.
- Jews are not like me.
- I'm not prejudiced; I can't help the way other people are.
- If I express my honest beliefs, some people will like me and others will dislike me.

STUDENT D

- Humans are basically the same.
- Nonphysical differences among humans develop from different experiences.
- Cultural differences enrich the human experience.
- Cultural differences can lead to conflict and stereotypes if they are not understood.
- United States society has a history of white racism, which affects the way different ethnic groups see each other.
- Humans learn to be prejudiced and they can learn to be antiprejudiced.

STUDENTS A, B, C

STUDENT D

ATTITUDES

STUDENTS A, B, C

- I will feel terrible if this person is allowed to join my group.

STUDENT D

- I will feel good if this person is allowed to join my group.

Continued

Box 5.3

Continued

- I will feel embarrassed if my friends disagree with me.
- I don't want others to think I'm prejudiced.

- I will feel ashamed if I don't say what I really believe.
- I don't want to lose my friends.

VALUES

- I have the freedom and right to associate with whomever I choose, especially in the private domain of my life.
- I want to be liked, accepted, and respected by my friends and associates.
- My own self-respect is more important than the acceptance of those who won't stand up for the right of individual freedom and choice.

- I should always take a stand against human injustice wherever it occurs.
- My own self-respect is more important than the acceptance of those who don't take a stand for social justice.
- I want to be liked, accepted, and respected by my friends and associates.

that the beliefs that underlie their attitudes and possible behavior are based on stereotypes.

The third situation in Box 5.4 takes place in the classroom. Sherri, a third-generation Japanese American whose family has retained many Japanese traditions, attends a school where most of her classmates have grown up within the macroculture. Once again the teacher is conducting a lively discussion. The students are actively involved and frequently challenge each other's ideas as well as the teacher. Sherri views the situation differently from many of her classmates and the teacher.

The case of Sherri shows how different beliefs based on cultural differences can lead to conflict in the classroom. Had the teacher known something about Japanese culture she might have responded more effectively to Sherri. Of course, not all teachers in United States society stress student involvement to the degree that this teacher does, and not all third-generation Japanese Americans would be as reticent as Sherri about class participation. Much depends on the individual's sense of ethnic identity, or the degree to which a person retains his or her ethnic origins.

Sense of Ethnic Identity

Sense of ethnic identity refers to the degree to which a member of any particular ethnic group retains the original culture that was learned from family and closest childhood associates. Original culture may refer to national origins such as Polish or Italian macrocultures or to a culture created within the context of generations of segregation from the United

SHERRI	TEACHER
BELIEFS	
• Teachers possess great knowledge. • The teacher is an authority. • It would show disrespect to question a teacher. • Careful reflection is required before one speaks out publicly. • It is rude and disrespectful to interrupt others.	• I am not the "fountain of all knowledge." • Students learn best when they are actively involved. • By challenging an authority, students learn to think critically. • Students who don't participate are either shy, bored, or not prepared for class. • Students are truly motivated when they initiate comments and questions on their own, without teacher intervention.
ATTITUDES	
• I feel uncomfortable in this classroom because the students are rude and disrespectful. • I want to be a good student. • I feel frustrated because I never get an opportunity to express my ideas.	• I feel uncomfortable with Sherri's lack of participation. • I must work harder to get her to speak up, to express her views and support them.
VALUES	
• Being educated is one of life's highest virtues. • As educators, teachers deserve the highest respect.	• Being educated is one of life's highest virtues. • My most important role as a teacher is to encourage students to think critically.

Box 5.4

Cognitive Systems—Cultural Conflict

States macroculture, as with Afro-Americans. All people belong to an ethnic group, but we may differ from other members of our group in terms of how closely we follow the original verbal language, body language, social values, and traditions. These differences in ethnic identity lead to the great differences found within any one ethnic group.

Consider again the example of Sherri. Many Sansei, or third-generation Japanese Americans, may retain the cultural values of the traditional middle-class agricultural system of Japan. Such values include education, hard work, achievement, patience, and respect for elders. Educational authorities were to be honored, obeyed, and respected without question.[30] Sherri apparently had retained many traditional Japanese values and beliefs. Many other Sansei, however, could be expected to be comfortable with the teacher's expectations.

One of the most promising conceptualizations of ethnic identity is in terms of developmental stages. A number of different conceptions of ethnicity stages exist, but the six-stage typology developed by James A. Banks is particularly helpful because of its well-developed implications for the classroom. Banks's typology is based on "existing and emerging theory and research" and on his own "observations and study of ethnic behaviors."[31]

In stage one, *ethnic psychological captivity*, "the individual has internalized the negative ideologies and beliefs about his or her ethnic group that are institutionalized within the society."[32] The stage-one person feels ethnic self-rejection and low self-esteem, and is ashamed of his or her ethnic group identity. Typically, such a person tries to avoid situations that lead to contact with other ethnic groups or strives aggressively to become highly culturally assimilated. Examples would be the Black person who passes for White, the guilt-ridden White liberal who tries too hard to be accepted in the Black community, the Mexican American who is afraid to leave the barrio, or the Polish American who anglicizes his or her name out of embarrassment.

Stage two, *ethnic encapsulation*, is characterized by ethnic exclusiveness and separatism. "The individual participates primarily within his or her own ethnic community and believes that his or her ethnic group is superior to that of others. Many stage-two individuals, such as many Anglo-Saxon Protestants, have internalized the dominant societal myths about the superiority of their ethnic or racial group and the innate inferiority of other ethnic groups and races. Many individuals who are socialized within all-White suburban communities and who live highly ethnocentric and encapsulated lives may be described as stage-two individuals.[33] Members of the Ku Klux Klan are ethnically encapsulated, as were Black Muslim followers of Elijah Muhammad. Both groups appealed to stage-one individuals who feel the pain of low self-esteem and are thus susceptible to groups that preach the supremacy of their special group.

In stage three, *ethnic identity clarification*, the individual is able to clarify personal attitudes and develops a healthy sense of self and ethnic identity. Once the individual learns to accept self, it is possible to accept and respond more positively to outside ethnic groups. According to Maslow's theories of human development, until a person has met basic human needs and is becoming self-actualized, ethnic identity clarification is not likely. The individual feels ethnic pride, but at the same time feels respect for different ethnic groups.

Stage four is *biethnicity*. "Individuals within this stage have a healthy sense of ethnic identity and the psychological characteristics and skills needed to participate in their own ethnic culture, as well as in another ethnic culture. The individual also has a strong desire to function effectively in two ethnic cultures," and may thus be described as biethnic.[34] According to Banks, levels of biethnicity vary greatly. Many Afro-Americans, for example, "learn to function effectively in Anglo-American culture during the formal working day" in order to attain social and economic gains. In private, however, their lives "may be highly black and monocultural."[35] All ethnic minorities, White and non-White alike, who wish to make social and economic advances are forced to become biethnic to some degree. This is not the case for members of the macroculture who "can and often do live almost exclusive monocultural and highly ethnocentric lives."[36]

Stage five is *multiethnicity.*

> The individual at this stage is able to function, at least at minimal levels, within several ethnic sociocultural environments and to understand, appreciate, and share the values, symbols, and institutions of several ethnic cultures. Such multiethnic perspectives and feelings . . . help the individual to live a more enriched and fulfilling life and to formulate more creative and novel solutions to personal and public problems.[37]

Stage six is one of *globalism and global competency.*

> Individuals within stage six have clarified, reflective, and positive ethnic, national, and global identifications and the knowledge, skills, attitudes, and abilities needed to function in ethnic cultures within their own nation as well as in cultures within other nations. These individuals have the ideal delicate balance of ethnic, national, and global identifications, commitments, literacy, and behaviors. They have internalized the universalistic ethical values and principles of humankind and have the skills, competencies, and commitments needed to act on these values.[38]

Although Banks stresses the "tentative and hypothetical" nature of his typology, even in its rough form it helps illuminate important socio-psychological differences between individual members of an ethnic group. Inside any particular school, we may find the entire array of stages within each ethnic group on campus. An awareness of this ethnic group diversity helps destroy ethnic stereotypes. Individuals do not become open to different ethnic groups until and unless they develop a positive sense of self, including an awareness and acceptance of their own ethnic group. This is an extension of the basic psychological principle that self-acceptance is a necessary condition for accepting others. The typology should not be viewed as a hierarchy; people do not necessarily begin at stage one and progress to stage six. Individuals can move from one stage to another, and depending upon personal experiences could become less open-minded as they go through life. Stages five and six are ideals that help us describe and visualize the goals of multicultural education.

In 1979 Margaret Ford and H. Prentice Baptiste developed the Teacher Student Interaction (TSI) instrument, which was designed to measure teachers' stages of ethnicity according to the first five stages of Banks's model.[39] Continuing research with the TSI has led them to conclude that teachers who are at a level of multiethnicity, Banks's fifth stage, are more effective teachers with culturally diverse students than are students at any of the four lower stages. Although Banks suggests that biethnic persons may well grow into a level of multiethnicity, Ford warns that the biethnic people may favor their two preferred ethnic groups and be more "encapsulated" vis-à-vis other groups.

Other research has explored the idea of stages of ethnic identity using Banks's model. In a recent study of undergraduates at a predominantly White university, this author found that Black students in higher stages of ethnicity felt less trauma on campus, were more satisfied with their decision to come to the university, and were more certain they would graduate there than were Black students in the lower stages.[40] She also found that among all the groups studied (Asian American, Blacks, Latinos, and Whites) a history of positive interracial contact experiences before college was related to higher stages of ethnicity. Furthermore, Latino males and females were most open to human diversity (that is, higher stages of ethnicity) while White males were least open.

William Cross has developed a somewhat different conception of stages of ethnic identity.[41] Cross focuses on what he sees as the "Negro to Black conversion experience," which occurred as Afro-Americans lived through the civil rights movement of the 1960s. Although his typology focuses on the Black psyche, it is applicable to any group that has experienced oppression and is moving toward liberation, for example other ethnic minority groups and women.

Black persons who are in stage one, or *pre-encounter*, accept the Euro-American world view. They seek to be assimilated into the White macroculture and could be described as anti-Black and anti-African. The second stage is *encounter*. Stage two is triggered by a shattering experience that destroys the person's previous ethnic self-image and changes his or her interpretation of the conditions of Black people in America. For many Black Americans the murder of Martin Luther King, Jr., was such an experience. White violence and outrage over the busing of Black school children to historically White schools provides another example for many Black youth.

A person who enters stage three, *immersion–emersion*, desires to enter totally into the world of Blackness. The individual feels Black rage and Black pride and may engage in a "kill Whitey" fantasy. Cross describes the stage-three person as having a pseudo-Black identity because it is based on hatred and negation of Whites rather than on the affirmation of a pro-Black perspective. Stage-three Blacks often engage in "Blacker than thou" antics and view those Blacks who are accepting of Whites as Uncle Toms. Immersion–emersion is similar to Banks's stage two of ethnic encapsulation, in its orientations of separatism and superiority.

Stage four, *internalization*, resembles Banks's ethnic identity clarification. The individual in internalization achieves greater inner security and self-satisfaction and may be characterized as the nice Black person with an Afro hair style and an attachment to Black things. There is a nealthy sense of Black identity and pride, and less hostility toward Whites.

The individual who moves into stage five, *internalization-commitment*, differs from the one who remains in stage four by becoming actively involved in plans to bring about social changes. The uncontrolled rage toward Whites is transformed into a conscious anger toward oppressive and racist institutions, from symbolic rhetoric to quiet dedicated long-term commitment. Stage-five individuals feel compassion toward those who have not completed the process. They watch over new recruits, helping them conquer hatred of Whites and the "pitfalls of Black pride" without Black skills. The super-Black revolutionary of stage three gives way to the Black humanist in stage five.[42]

Conceptions of stages of ethnic identity, such as those just described, need further refinement and may not prove to be the most valid approach for understanding sense of ethnic identity. Enough is known, however, to realize that students differ in their psychological readiness for interacting with people from different ethnic groups. This is true whether this meeting occurs through actual experience, or through texts and media. Students and teachers who are ethnically encapsulated will hold more negative prejudices against different ethnic groups than will others. Individuals who are in psychological captivity may be embarrassed by discussions of their group's contributions and characteristics, and may reject or deny evidence of individual and institutional racism. Individuals in the highest stages may, if permitted to voice their views, serve as models for others. However, they could be totally rejected by individuals in stage one or two.

Teacher Perceptions of Individual Differences

Teachers tend to regard individual differences based on cultural differences as deficits or disadvantages. The fact that disproportionately large numbers of ethnic minorities are below the United States poverty level reinforces the idea that ethnic differences represent cultural disadvantages. Even though approximately half of the nation's poverty children are low-income Whites, non-Whites are vastly overrepresented. As shown in Table 5.1, for example, 29.9 percent of all Blacks lived below the poverty level, compared to 9.4 percent of all Whites, 27.5 percent of American Indians, 35.5 percent of Vietnamese, 23.3 percent of Mexican Americans, and 36.3 percent of Puerto Ricans.

An analysis of the origins and conditions of poverty is beyond the scope of this book. What is important is that approximately 27.4 million persons are living at or below the poverty level ($12,412 for a family of four), and that this figure represents over 20 percent of United States children, including 30 percent of the children who live in large urban areas.[43] What is important is that most of those who are failing in school are from poverty backgrounds. What is important is how the teacher perceives and receives the poverty child. Teachers must ask themselves the following question:

> Are we talking about groups of individuals whose backgrounds, attitudes, and general capabilities have failed to equip them adequately for a life of opportunities or are we talking about minority cultures of a country where the attitudes of the majority have inhibited the participation of the minorities in these opportunities?[44]

Do these children fail because their intellectual development is deficient from what is expected at school? Or do they fail because they can't fit in?

Failure, the Deficit Argument

The deficit position argues that the poverty child is failing in school because he or she is unready for school. The poverty home is viewed as an environment that retards children's overall development and leads to their disadvantage in school.

Much of the research and related literature published in the 1960s contains evidence that consistently points out developmental lags in the cognitive development of the poverty child. Quotes from some of these works will illustrate the philosophy.

> More than a million children starting to school each fall are disadvantaged, victims of too little too late. The impoverishment of their lives is so severe that failure is a natural consequence. For those caught up in this most vicious of cycles, compensatory education is desperately needed to preclude tragedy.[45]

> Perhaps the most serious deficiencies occur in the area of cognitive functioning: in the processes of thinking, in language skills and reading. . . . The consequences of cognitive deficiencies in culturally deprived children are complicated by their pattern of motivation

Table 5.1   *Poverty in the United States, by Ethnic Group*

ETHNIC GROUP	PERCENTAGE OF PERSONS BELOW OFFICIAL POVERTY LEVEL*
American Indian	27.5%
Eskimo	28.8
Aleut	19.5
Asian and Pacific Island	**13.1**
Japanese	6.5
Chinese	13.5
Filipino	7.1
Korean	11.1
Asian Indian	9.9
Vietnamese	35.5
Hawaiian	15.8
Guamanian	13.9
Samoan	29.5
Spanish Origin	**23.5**
Mexican	23.3
Puerto Rican	36.3
Cuban	13.2
Black	**29.9**
Central city	30.1
Urban fringe	20.2
Rural	36.4
White	**9.4**
Central city	11.1
Urban fringe	6.1
Rural	11.2
White ethnic groups (selected)	
English	11.3
German	8.1
French	10.7
Irish	9.6
Italian	7.3
Polish	7.0

Source: Based on the 1980 U.S. Census Summary Report of General Social and Economic Characteristics, Tables 129, 139, 149, 165, and 171.

*The official poverty level was defined, as of 1980, as $7,412 for a family of four.

and attitudes. . . . Such children have a feeling of alienation induced by family climate and experience combined with a debilitatingly low self-concept; they tend to question their own worth, to fear being challenged, and to exhibit a desire to cling to their families; they have many feelings of guilt and shame. . . . These children are wary and their trust in adults is limited; they are hyperactive . . . quick to vent their hostility, orally and physically. In other ways they are apathetic, unresponsive, and lack initiative. It is difficult for them to form meaningful relationships.[46]

These are socially disadvantaged children because they are denied the experiences of normal children. They lack toys and challenging objects to play with; they lack conversation models and, thus, develop a poor vocabulary.[47]

Negro scores averaging about fifteen points below the white average on I.Q. tests must be taken seriously as evidence of genetic differences between the two races in learning patterns. Research suggests that such a difference would tend to work against Negroes and against the "disadvantaged" generally when it comes to "cognitive" learning—abstract reasoning—which forms the basis for intelligence measurements and for the higher mental skills. Conversely, Negroes and other "disadvantaged" children tend to do well in tasks involving rote learning—memorizing mainly through repetition—and some other skills, and these aptitudes can be used to help raise their scholastic achievement and job potential.[48]

Failure, the Difference Argument

This position argues that the United States is a polycultural society with monocultural schools, and accuses the school, rather than the child of unreadiness. Its proponents claim that the deficit view is based on ethnocentric research; that is, research based on Anglo-middle-class norms and values. Furthermore, they claim that the deficit view damages the learner's self-esteem because school success requires a denial of family and community. They cite as evidence teachers who, operating out of the deficit position, often make statements like, "If only we didn't have to send the children home at night," or "What can we expect of kids with parents like that?" Given a choice of fitting in at home or school, most children choose the former; thus the conflict between home and school expectations must be lessened. Because the child is powerless to change the school, it is the teacher's responsibility to find out where the child is and build from there.

Frank Riessman typifies the difference position in his explanation of the hidden I.Q. and cultural positives of poverty children and youth.[49] According to Riessman, mainstream schools put a premium on speed and tend to equate slowness with dullness. He claims that the assumption that the slow pupil is not bright functions as a self-fulfilling prophecy; it is important to recognize that there are weaknesses in speed and strengths in slowness. Recognizing that many of these children have serious skill deficiencies and undesirable anti-intellectual attitudes, Riessman urges teachers to build upon the cultural positives that poverty children bring to school. He includes the following in his list of positives:

> Cooperativeness and mutual aid that mark the extended family; the avoidance of the strain accompanying competitiveness and individualism; the equalitarianism, informality, and humor; the freedom from self-blame and parental overprotection; the children's enjoyment of each other's company and lessened sibling rivalry; the security found in the extended family and traditional outlook; the enjoyment of music, games, sports, and cards; the ability to express anger; the freedom from being word-bound; an externally oriented rather than an introspective outlook; a spatial rather than temporal perspective; an expressive orientation in contrast to an instrumental one; content-centered not a form-centered mental style; a problem-centered rather than an abstract-centered approach; and finally, the use of physical and visual style in learning.[50]

Riessman argues that disadvantaged children often do poorly on tests because they lack meaningful, directed practice; they lack motivation, and they are typically fearful of the examiner. Reviewing a study by Ernest Haggard, he wrote:

> Haggard decided to control each of these factors [practice, motivation, rapport]. He gave both low-income and middle-class children three one-hour training periods in taking I.Q. tests. These periods included careful explanations of what was involved in each of the different types of problems found on the I.Q. tests. The examinations were given in words that were familiar to both groups. Haggard also offered special rewards for doing well, and he trained his examiners to be responsive to the inner-city children as well as to the middle-class youngsters, thus, greatly enhancing the rapport.
> Under these conditions the I.Q.'s of the inner-city children improved sharply. This occurred even on the old I.Q. tests with the middle-class biased items. Apparently more important than the content of the test items was the attitude of the children toward the test situation and the examiner. . . .
> It is noteworthy that the middle-class youngsters improved far less than the inner-city youngsters in the Haggard experiment. This is because they were already working nearer their capacity, and the new environmental input—that is, the equalization of the test environment did not [expand the gap] between the two groups; rather it led to a sharp reduction of the difference.[51]

Typically, proponents of the deficit view propose school reforms that focus on remediation. They suggest a cultural injection as an antidote for poverty—the earlier the better—and advocate compensatory education programs.

Typically, programs based on the deficit view of reform place the burden of change on the child. Preschool programs assume that poverty children lag behind their middle-class counterparts in preparation for school, and propose a preschool compensatory program designed to make them learn at an even greater rate because their problem is essentially one of catching up. Since language development is crucial for school success, some programs recommend preschools that concentrate directly on language (for example, drill and rote memorization activities in standard English) rather than the indirect learning readiness emphasis of Head Start (such as tasting and learning about new foods).[52]

Reforms proposed by the difference advocates, on the other hand, focus on changing the school rather than the child. To date, large-scale programs modeled on this approach are rare. But there are some. Bicultural schools exist in several states where learning a second or third language is expected of everyone. Reading programs designed for the linguistically different begin with primers in the vernacular, and then systematically work toward teaching contrasts between the dialect and standard English.

Who are the disadvantaged in the United States schools? Mario Fantini and Gerald Weinstein wrote that the disadvantaged are those for whom the curriculum is outdated, inadequate, or irrelevant. They also include anyone who is unable to attain the basic goals of physical comfort and survival; feelings of potency, self-worth, and connection with others; and concern for the common good of humanity.[53]

There is a tendency for many of us to be ethnocentric and see the disadvantaged as being primarily minorities and lower-income people. Anyone who has not had the "normal" advantages of a middle-income home life is a potential candidate for being labeled disadvantaged. This is not a helpful attitude because it focuses on where our students *aren't*, and this blinds us to where our students *are*.

A good example of this is a young elementary school teacher in Chicago who was appalled to learn that some of her inner-city children did not know that beds go in a bedroom. What she did not realize is that many of her children's homes had beds in the kitchen, as a matter of course, particularly in the cold of winter. Furthermore, she confused and degraded (however unintentionally) her children with such comments as "Johnny! We don't speak that way!" Johnny is speaking the way all the important people in his life speak.

This does not mean that we can ignore the fact that the achievement levels of students like Kevin and Rachael are deficient. This does not mean that expectations or standards of achievement should be lowered.

The question is: How can we reverse the existing patterns of failure in schools and equalize the chances of all students to achieve success?

The deficit position breeds insensitivity and blindness to students' strengths, but the difference position isn't free from problems either. The simple notion of differences implies the question, "Different from what?" The human tendency is to view whatever is different from *me* in less positive terms.

In the attempt to find out how students learn best, it seems more helpful to see them as representing alternatives rather than as beings that are deficient or different. Alternatives connote the coexistence of worthy options, and open us to the various ways our students have learned to perceive, evaluate, believe, and behave. As Mario Benitez has stated, "Teachers must be helped to understand that the poor and racial or ethnic minorities can and actually have been able to learn at the same level as others when the proper environmental support was provided."[54]

Conclusion

This and the preceding chapter examined some of the individual differences that exist within the broader pools of culture. These characteristics are common to the human condition. Each student has special interests and aptitudes, preferred ways of learning, levels of skills, personal values, various self-images, a family and peers, and the potential to become self-actualized.

Teachers cannot assume that because students are members of a certain ethnic group they will be a certain way. We cannot, for example, assume that Carmen Hernandez knows Spanish or that Isaac Washington, who lives near Sixty-third and Halstead in Chicago, is not an expert on Beethoven. On the other hand, we know that cultures provide the context within which our lives unfold. The more that is known about culture, therefore, the better we can interpret student differences that *are* linked to cultural ways that differ from what is expected in school.

1. Learning skills and learning styles
2. Concrete and formal operations
3. Achievements and aptitudes and learning skills
4. Self-concept and motivation
5. Attitudes and beliefs
6. Ethnic encapsulation and ethnic identity clarification
7. The cultural deficit and cultural difference explanations of school failure

**Compare
and
Contrast**

Activities and Questions

1. Consider the following guidelines for understanding individual and cultural differences in the classroom.

INDIVIDUAL DIFFERENCES THAT CAN MAKE A DIFFERENCE IN HOW STUDENTS LEARN

- Learning styles
- Need for structure
- Learning skills
- Achievements and aptitudes
- Self-concept
- Peer relationships
- Motivation
- Physical attributes
- Special interests
- Family backgrounds
- Beliefs, attitudes, and values
- Sense of ethnic identity

ASPECTS OF ETHNICITY THAT CAN LEAD TO CULTURAL CONFLICT OR "TRANSITIONAL TRAUMA" IN THE CLASSROOM

- Verbal communication
- Nonverbal communication
- Orientation modes (e.g., conception of time, room arrangement, relaxation position)
- Social values
- Intellectual modes

Reconsider the vignettes on pages 81 to 84 and answer the following questions, using the preceding guidelines. Share your ideas in small and large groups.

THE CASE OF KEVIN ARMSTRONG

a. Why did Mrs. Dixon perceive that Kevin was not ready for third grade? (List as many reasons as you can think of.)

b. Assume that, like Mrs. Dixon, you know Kevin only in the "school arena." To what extent do you agree with her decision? Explain.

c. From Kevin's point of view, what are some possible explanations for his behavior? (List as many as you can think of.)

d. What are some of the strengths or personal positives Kevin brought to the classroom that his teacher was unaware of?

e. How do you suppose Kevin's parents feel about the school's action concerning their son?

f. If you were Kevin's teacher, how would you handle the situation?

THE CASE OF WARREN BENSON'S CLASSROOM

a. What two or three student behaviors do you find most disturbing? Briefly, what are some probable reasons for these behaviors?

b. What evidence of possible cultural conflict do you find in this classroom? How have these students probably experienced cultural conflict in their previous schooling? List as many possible examples of intercultural conflict and/or misunderstandings as you can. Be specific.

c. To what degree is it possible for you to analyze Warren Benson's classroom without falling into ethnic stereotypes about the teacher and the students? Do the guidelines help?

2. Read the *Autobiography of Malcolm X* and analyze the extent to which Banks's typology of ethnicity stages accurately describes the life of Malcolm X. What stage or stages of ethnicity are reflected in his life experiences. Use specific examples from the autobiography to support your arguments. Note those experiences that you believe produced a change to a different stage of ethnicity (in either direction) for Malcolm X.

3. Apply Banks's typology to yourself. Choose the stage that best describes you at your present level of ethnicity. Describe those important life experiences and circumstances that help explain where you are in terms of your ethnicity. If you have experienced more than one stage, explain why.

4. Read *The Doll Maker*, a novel by Harriet Arnow, which portrays the life of an Appalachian family that migrates to Detroit after World War II. What does the book reveal about the cultures of many of the geographically isolated Appalachian families? Specifically, what did you learn about verbal and nonverbal communication, social values, and approaches to learning? What are some of the cultural strengths, which many teachers might overlook, that Gertie's children bring to the classroom? What are some possible sources of transitional trauma her children could face when they enter an urban school?

Notes

1. Jean Piaget, "The Genetic Approach to the Psychology of Thought," *Journal of Educational Psychology* 52 (December 1961):277; Piaget, *The Psychology of Intelligence* (Paterson, N.J.: Littlefield, Adams, 1963); and John H. Flavell, *The Developmental Psychology of Jean Piaget* (Princeton, N.J.: Van Nostrand Reinhold, 1973).

2. Gilbert Clark, "Examining Some Myths About Gifted and Talented Students" (faculty guest editorial, *The Herald Telephone*, Bloomington, Ind., Summer 1982).

3. Ibid.

4. Arthur W. Combs, Chairman, *Perceiving, Behaving, Becoming*, ASCD Yearbook, 1962 (Alexandria, Va.: Association for Supervision and Curriculum Development, 1962).

5. Abraham Maslow, *Motivation and Personality* (New York: Harper and Brothers, 1954), p. 83.

6. F. Patterson, "The Purpose and Trend of the Conference," *Negro Self-Concept: Implications for School and Citizenship,* ed. W. C. Kvaraceus et al. (New York: McGraw-Hill, 1965).

7. Meyer Weinberg, *Minority Students: A Research Appraisal* (Washington, D.C.: National Institute of Education, 1977).

8. Patterson, "Purpose and Trend of the Conference," pp. 4–5.

9. Morris Daniel Caplin, "The Relationship Between Self-Concept and Academic Achievement," *Journal of Experimental Education* 37 (Spring 1969):13–16; P. Zerkel and E. Moser, "Self Concept and Ethnic Group Membership Among Public School Students," *American Educational Research Journal* 8 (March 1971):253–65; A. Soares and L. Soares, "Self-perceptions of Culturally Disadvantaged Children," *American Educational Research Journal* 6, no. 1 (1969):31–45.

10. Weinberg, *Minority Students.*

11. William Purkey, *Inviting School Success: A Self-Concept Approach to Teaching* (Belmont, Calif.: Wadsworth, 1978).

12. *Perceiving, Behaving, Becoming.*

13. Ibid.

14. Daniel N. Fader and Elton B. McNeil, *Hooked on Books: Program and Proof* (New York: Berkley Medallion Edition, 1968).

15. Thomas E. Curtis and Wilma W. Bidwell, *Curriculum and Instruction for Emerging Adolescents* (Reading, Mass.: Addison-Wesley, 1977).

16. H. J. Ehrlich, *The Social Psychology of Prejudice* (New York: John Wiley and Sons, 1973).

17. Christine Bennett and J. John Harris III, "Suspensions and Expulsions of Male and Black Students: A Study of the Causes of Disproportionality," *Urban Education* 16, no. 4 (January 1982):399–423; Geneva Gay, "Differential Dyadic Interactions of Black and White Teachers with Black and White Pupils in Recently Desegregated Social Studies Classrooms: A Function of Teacher and Pupil Ethnicity," OE Project no. 2F113 (January 1974); U.S. Civil Rights Commission, *Teachers and Students. Report V: Mexican-American Education Study. Differences in Teacher Interaction with Mexican-American and Anglo Students* (Washington, D.C.: Government Printing Office, March 1973); and Ray Rist, "Student Social Class and Teacher Expectations: The Self-fulfilling Prophecy in Ghetto Education," *Harvard Education Review* 40 (August 1970):411–51.

18. Walter R. Borg and Meredith Damien Gall, *Educational Research: An Introduction,* 3d ed. (New York: Longman, 1979).

19. Nancy St. John, "School Integration, Classroom Climate, and Achievement," ERIC ED 052 269, (January 1971); and idem., *School Desegregation: Outcomes for Children* (New York: John Wiley and Sons, 1975).

20. Christine Bennett, "A Study of Classroom Climate in Desegregated Schools," *Urban Review* 13 (Winter 1981); and idem, "Student Initiated Interaction as an Indicator of Interracial Acceptance," *Journal of Classroom Interaction* 15 (Summer 1980).

21. Wilma Longstreet, *Aspects of Ethnicity: Understanding Differences in Pluralistic Classrooms* (New York: Teachers College Press, 1978).

22. J. S. Wallerstein, "Children of Divorce: The Psychological Tasks of the Child," *American Journal of Orthopsychiatry* 53 (April 1983):230–43; and Mavis Hetherington and Ron Parke, *Child Psychology: A Contemporary Viewpoint* (New York: McGraw-Hill, 1979), pp. 431–64.

23. Wallerstein, "Children of Divorce."

24. Milton Rokeach, *Beliefs, Attitudes and Values* (San Francisco: Jossey-Bass, 1969).

25. Ibid., p. 3.

26. Ibid., p. 132.

27. Harry C. Triandis, *Attitude and Attitude Change* (New York: John Wiley and Sons, 1971), p. 8.

28. Rokeach, *Beliefs, Attitudes, and Values*, p. 124.

29. Ibid., p. 160.

30. George T. Endo and Connie Kubo Della-Piana, "Japanese Americans, Pluralism, and the Model Minority Myth," *Theory into Practice* 20 (Winter 1981):45–51.

31. James A. Banks, *Teaching Strategies for Ethnic Studies*, 3d ed. (Boston: Allyn and Bacon, 1984). Synopsis and quotations from this work are used by permission of Allyn and Bacon, Inc., and James A. Banks. Copyright © 1984 by Allyn and Bacon, Inc.

32. Ibid., pp. 55–56.

33. Ibid., p. 56.

34. Ibid.

35. James A. Banks, *Multiethnic Education: Theory and Practice* (Boston: Allyn and Bacon, 1981), p. 132.

36. Ibid.

37. Banks, *Teaching Strategies*, p. 56.

38. Ibid.

39. Margaret L. Ford, "The Development of an Instrument for Assessing Levels of Ethnicity in Public School Teachers" (unpublished Ph.D. diss., University of Houston, 1979).

40. Christine Bennett and John Bean, "A Conceptual Model of Black Student Attrition in Predominantly White Institutions," *The Journal of Educational Equity and Leadership* 4 (Fall 1984).

41. William Cross, "The Negro-to-Black Conversion Experience: Toward a Psychology of Black Liberation," *Black World* 20 (July 1979). Synopsis used by permission of the author.

42. Ibid.

43. Frederick Williams, ed., *Language and Poverty* (Chicago: Markham, 1970), p. 2.

44. Ibid.

45. Joe L. Frost and Glenn R. Hawkes, *The Disadvantaged Child* (Boston: Houghton Mifflin, 1966), preface.

46. Hilda Taba and Deborah Elkins, *Teaching Strategies for the Culturally Disadvantaged* (Chicago: Rand McNally, 1966).

47. John M. Beck and Richard W. Saxe, *Teaching the Culturally Disadvantaged Pupil* (Springfield, Ill.: C. C. Thomas, 1969).

48. Arthur Jensen, quoted in *U.S. News and World Report* 66 (March 10, 1969):48–51.

49. Frank Riessman, "The Overlooked Positives of Disadvantaged Groups," *Journal of Negro Education* 33 (Summer 1964).

50. Ibid.

51. Frank Riessman, *The Inner-City Child* (New York: Harper and Row, 1976).

52. Carl Bereiter and Siegfried Engleman, *Teaching Disadvantaged Children in the Pre-School* (New York: Prentice-Hall, 1966).

53. Mario Fantini and Gerald Weinstein, *The Disadvantaged: Challenge to Education* (New York: Harper and Row, 1968).

54. Mario Benitez, "A Blueprint for the Education of the Mexican American," ERIC ED 076 294 (March 1973).

Part Three

Curriculum Reform

A multicultural curriculum is one that develops competencies in "multiple systems of standards for perceiving, evaluating, believing, and doing."* How can the traditional curriculum be revised to include this multicultural dimension without sacrificing other basic skills, concepts, and understandings? How can the traditional disciplines and subjects be revised to include multicultural subject matter? The purpose of Chapters 6 and 7 is to provide answers to these questions.

Chapter 6 begins with four major aspects of curriculum reform: racism, minority perspectives, ethnic diversity, and basic human similarities. These aspects of reform help develop a rationale and foundation for the multicultural curriculum goals and classroom strategies presented in Chapter 7.

*Margaret Gibson, "Approaches to Multicultural Education in the United States: Some Concepts and Assumptions," *Anthropology and Education Quarterly* 7, no. 4 (November 1976):15.

Chapter 6

Aspects of Reform: A Rationale for a Multicultural Curriculum

Most of us tend to be ahistorical when it comes to Third World nations and ethnic minorities within our own society. It is difficult to be otherwise, given the nature of the traditional curriculum, which emphasizes the political development of Euro-American civilization. This chapter, therefore, provides a historical context drawn from various ethnic group experiences related to each aspect of reform. It would be a mistake, however, to regard the inclusion of history as an indication that multicultural education belongs primarily to the social studies. This is an unfortunate misconception that many schools accept. Every discipline has a history; every discipline relates to contemporary society; and every discipline is touched by racism, minority perspectives, ethnic diversity, and human similarities. This will become clearer in the following two chapters; the main point here is that if we are to change the curriculum, we must know where we have been, how we got there, and why revision is necessary.

The major purpose of this chapter, therefore, is to expand consciousness of racism, minority perspectives, ethnic diversity, and basic human similarities and how each aspect interacts with the curriculum. This will lay a foundation for revision in all areas of the traditional curriculum, and open the way for ideas beyond what can be proposed in this text.

Racism

The traditional curriculum in most schools in the United States is a classic example of institutional and cultural racism. From elementary school, where uncounted numbers of children have been taught to sit like an Indian (and have accepted the racial stereotype), to colleges and universities, where thousands more have learned the misconception that IQ differences are caused by race, schools have fostered the belief in

White supremacy. The traditional monoethnic curriculum has presented one way of perceiving, behaving, and evaluating: the Anglo–Western European way of the macroculture. School texts and educational media have presented negative myths and stereotypes about most of our ethnic minorities, have overlooked important contributions, and have presented a distorted view of past and current history that reinforces the doctrine of White supremacy. The case of Africa and the cultural roots of Afro-Americans provides one example.

The Case of Africa

The truth about Africa has been so distorted among non-Africans that with the emergence of Africa on the world scene in 1960 (the year most contemporary African nations achieved independence and sent representatives to the United Nations) most Westerners were almost totally ignorant about the earth's second largest continent. For centuries perceptions of the "Dark Continent" had been clouded over with myths and stereotypes, and Africa was greeted then as now with all the myths and stereotypes intact. Some of the simplest myths are most common: lions in the jungles, the isolated Dark Continent, inferior savages, a race of Negroes—heathens developed only by the grace of God and the White man—and land of turmoil, incapable of self-government. Because these myths and stereotypes are alive today in the school's curriculum (however unintentional the distortions and omissions may be), in the hands of unaware and unskilled teachers the curriculum continues to feed the racist doctrines and practices of White supremacy.

Some Common Misconceptions

Raised on a diet of Westernized history, Tarzan books and films, and sensationalized news media, many in the United States believe Africa to be a primitive land of hot, steamy jungles inhabited by wild animals and savages. In truth, less than 10 percent of the African continent is jungle. (Of course, lions live in grasslands not jungles.) Nearly half of the African continent consists of grassy savannah, and approximately a third is searing desert.[1]

The idea that Africa has been isolated until recently is also false. Ancient Africans had contact with the Greeks, Romans, Chinese, and early Indonesians, and there is evidence that they may have entered the Western Hemisphere long before the Spaniards. Archaeological evidence reveals active trade with Arabs and Indians via the Indian Ocean and the Sahara, which was at one time a lush fertile nursery of African civilizations. For example, cave paintings and chariot tracks preserved in rock attest to a lively commerce that began before the Sahara dried up and became a desert. Europeans traded with the Moroccans, probably without knowing that many goods (primarily gold, salt, and ivory) originated south of the Sahara. Davidson describes the bustling Port of Kilwa from the twelfth to the fifteenth centuries as the chief trading center of East Africa and one of the liveliest in the entire world. "On any given day . . . workers could be seen loading their masters' dhows with African gold, iron, ivory and coconuts, and unloading textiles and jewelry from India and exquisite porcelain from China."[2]

Related to the misconception that Africa was an isolated Dark Continent prior to the arrival of the Europeans is the belief that Africans were uncivilized savages. Early writings of Muslim scholars who traveled throughout Africa in the tenth and eleventh centuries, however, provide evidence that African civilization was as advanced, or more so, than contemporary Europeans, even according to the material standards typically used by Westerners. The Arab geographer al-Bakri, for example, wrote in 1067 (one year after twenty thousand Normans conquered England) that "the king of Ghana . . . can raise 200,000 warriors, 40,000 of them being armed with bows and arrows."[3] Mali's king, Mansa Musa, made his pilgrimage to Mecca in 1324.

> [His] entourage was composed of 60,000 persons, a large portion of which constituted a military escort. No less than 12,000 were servants, 500 of whom marched ahead of their king, each bearing a staff of pure gold. Books, baggage men, and royal secretaries there were in abundance. To finance the pilgrimage, the king carried 80 camels to bear his more than 24,000 pounds of gold.[4]

Because King Musa spent so much money in the Middle East, the value of gold in the great commercial center of Cairo was depressed for at least twelve years.[5]

Yet few people have learned about the achievements of the early West African kingdoms of Ghana, Mali, and Songhai, the forest kingdom of Benin, or Kanem-Bornu in the interior. The prosperity and power of the great West African empires, which covered an area almost as large as the United States, arose from the agricultural base of the Niger River Valley; their control of the gold and salt trade between North African Arabs; the existence of the open savannah that foot and horse soldiers could quickly traverse; and their rulers' adoption of Islam, which brought them aid, allies, and smoother trade among Muslims of North Africa and the Middle East.[6]

Although ancient Egypt is a staple of world history and art history courses, and a source of fascination for young children and youth, the Black African origin of Egyptian civilization, and therefore Anglo-European civilization, has been hidden. Few people have heard about the ancient kingdom of Kush, which thrived during the Ptolemaic era, was a center of extensive iron smelting, and developed the Meroitic alphabet.

Africa's record of achievement is not limited to the large kingdoms, however. Elaborate social and political systems, complex religions (frequently dismissed as animism), effective health care practices (for example, the herbal-psychological services of the traditional doctor), and advanced expressions of music and art, all developed in African villages as well as in large empires. Some scholars assert that the greatest genius of the African peoples was their capacity for social organization, a talent that operated at the village level and in the complex kingdoms.[7] In community attitude that "joined man to man in a brotherhood of equals, in moral attitudes that guided social behavior, in beliefs that exalted the spiritual aspects of life above the material," many Africans achieved a kind of social harmony that could exist without the power of a centralized authority.[8] This is not to overlook the fact that prior to European invasions nearly all ethnic groups in Africa practiced some form of slavery. It is important to recognize, however, that although they suffered great liabilities, African slaves were guaranteed extensive rights, had a relatively stable family life, and often experienced a great deal of social mobility. In fact, ultimate freedom was often presumed.[9]

Ibn Battuta, a Berber scholar and theologian from Tangiers who crossed the Sahara in 1352 and spent a year in Mali, found some of his hosts' customs unpleasant, but he wrote about the high sense of justice among the people. "Of all peoples, the Negroes are those who most abhor injustice. The Sultan pardons no one who is guilty of it. There is complete and general safety throughout the land. The traveler here has no more reason than the man who stays at home to fear brigands, thieves or ravishers."[10] Furthermore, "the blacks do not confiscate the goods of any North Africans who may die in their country, not even when these consist of large treasures. On the contrary, they deposit these goods with a man of confidence . . . until those who have a right to the goods present themselves and take possession."[11]

In the late fifteenth century, Europeans did not need to rely on the travelogs of Muslim scholars and could see for themselves that Africa was not a primeval wilderness inhabited by savages. Instead, these visitors discovered "prosperous, self-contained cities linked to each other by a busy, carefully ordered trade. Their inhabitants—merchants, artisans, laborers, clerks—lived comfortable lives. Their pleasures were the familiar ones cherished by all people—feasting and family gatherings. Africa was in many ways no more savage than Europe—at the time just concluding the Hundred Years' War and only recently occupied with burning Joan of Arc."[12]

Nevertheless, myths about Africa continued to flourish in Europe and eventually were transported to the colonies in North America. These myths conjured visions of the great White hunter facing primitive tribes with their cannibalism, depraved customs, loincloths, and spears. Early slave-ship records promoted the view that it was only through the grace of God and the White man that these heathen savages would be Christianized and civilized. Sensationalized news stories and films have helped keep the Tarzan image alive, as well as images of the noble savage unspoiled by the evils of industrialized society.

How and why did these myths develop? First, competition among the emerging European nations and houses of commerce led to practices of secrecy lest rivals benefit from knowledge gained through the early explorations of lands unknown to Europe. Second was the blatant "dishonesty of literary hacks who concocted all sorts of nonsense for a gullible public."[13] Third was the need to justify slave trade in the minds of Christians and the enlightened. Assurances that slaves were heathen savages who would benefit by becoming Christianized and civilized became the basic rationalization. Related to this is the fact that Europeans launched into an era of imperialism and the quest for new lands and natural resources. To control new colonies, in this case the African colonies, traditional history, culture, and sources of group identity had to be suppressed and were replaced (at least temporarily) by the colonialists' culture, history, and doctrines of White supremacy.

Today, many textbooks contain outdated information about African nations. Rapidly changing events on that continent make maps and other content obsolete even in relatively new texts. Furthermore, news media and periodicals, which could be used to supplement outdated materials, are often inadequate sources for understanding current and past events in Africa.

> *The Washington Post*, probably the most important news source of American political decision makers, covers Africa's fifty-two nations and 350,000,000 people with one reporter, who, within a few days was ordered to cover the independence of Mozambique, the coup against the Emperor of Ethiopia, and the Ali-Foreman fight in Zaire. This is an impossible assignment! (As one Madison, Wisconsin newspaper editor noted, there is more and better reporting on Africa in one weekly airmail issue edition of the British *Manchester Guardian* than in all the American national press combined.) Those who know Africa and read the U.S. Press' political reporting frequently find that the stories are shallow, and stereotypical, overemphasizing the importance of ethnicity and tribe, fixated on the bizarre and exotic, primarily dependent on white expatriates for information and sometimes covertly allied with white racialist interests.[14]

In addition to outdated content, most current textbooks that attempt to present Africans to elementary and secondary school students are subject to emphasis on exotic and irrelevant information about race, and overemphasis on small groups of people such as the Mbuti, San, and Khoi peoples, commonly referred to as Pygmies, Bushmen, and

Hottentots. The combined population of these three groups is estimated to be between 25,000 and 250,000, or approximately .007 to .7 percent of the total population of Africa (over 350 million).[15]

> The names chosen to describe these people—"Bushmen," "Pygmies" and "Hottentots"—are not names which are used by the people themselves; rather, they are deprecating and unflattering terms given to them by Europeans who . . . did not learn or use the appropriate names. Pygmy comes from a Greek word meaning short or dwarf. The name Bushman was given to the San people by South African whites who exterminated many of them and drove others from their fertile lands into the desert bush areas. . . . Many young Americans come to believe that many or most African people live like these exotic, small atypical groups because so much of the curriculum is devoted to their study.[16]

Given the vast reservoir of African history and cultures available and yet unknown by most people in the United States, the textbook emphasis on "Pygmies" and "Bushmen" is telling. While these peoples exemplify survival in an inhospitable environment and may be more spiritually developed than many humans who live in higher technological societies, the texts neither point this out nor establish the array of humanity found on the African continent. Thus the unsophisticated non-African reader who comes across illustrations and texts that only show Africans in the bush perceives emotionally and physically uncomfortable conditions and "improper behavior" (scanty clothes, scarification, dipping food from a common bowl) and evaluates the people as inferior. American children and youth need to understand the basic human characteristics they share with the various peoples of Africa. This is not achieved by emphasizing exoticism and cultural differences associated with "primitive" humanity.

Some Effects of Misconceptions About Africa

One result of this deformed view of past and present Africa is that it promotes ignorance and disdain of Africans. These are dangerous outcomes in a world whose peoples are growing closer and more interdependent. Another obvious result of ignorance about Africa is that it feeds the doctrine of White supremacy and the belief that Afro-Americans as a group are inferior because they are genetically related to Africans. Myths and theories from the past that were used to justify slavery continued to serve as a rationalization for inferior schools, substandard homes, low-paying jobs, and segregated restaurants, rest rooms, and transportation.

> To justify the treatment of the African slave, and later of the Afro-American citizen, white society encouraged an army of propagan-

dists to "scientifically" prove the inferiority of Black people. While this ideology of racism was applied to all people of color with whom Euro-American society came into contact, its severest application was against Afro-Americans. Because they were the most physically different from whites, because their numbers were the second largest to whites, and because of their geographical and social proximity to whites, Black people have been perceived as the greatest threat.

White supremacist ideology has infected every level of national life. Government officials, social scientists, ministers, teachers, journalists and doctors have all played a part, as new and more sophisticated revisions of the myths and rationalizations of white supremacy keep reappearing. Whether it is religious leaders in colonial days pointing to Biblical passages damning Ham; biologists of a hundred years ago "studying" cranial structures; Social Darwinists utilizing theories of evolution and survival of the fittest; geneticists of the 1920's "proving" inborn moral inferiority; Moynihan-like theories of Black "pathology"; recent genetic pronouncements of Shockley and Jensen about Black IQ—all serve as pseudo-scientific apologies for the ongoing oppression directed against Black people.[17]

Another effect of these deformed images of Africa is the misconceptions about Black Africans that crop up in textbooks and other educational materials. These misconceptions about Black African peoples are then transferred to Afro-Americans. According to Beryle Banfield, president of the Council on Interracial Books for Children, "Racism in textbooks is usually most evident in five important areas: the historical perspective from which the material is presented; the characterization of Third World peoples; the manner in which their customs and traditions are depicted; the terminology used to describe the peoples and their culture and the type of language ascribed to them; and the nature of the illustrations."[18]

In an excellent essay on racism in the English language, Robert B. Moore uses "A Short Play on Black and White Words" to illustrate some examples of racist terminology in the English language (see Box 6.1). When we consider that language is more than a vehicle for communication, that it actually shapes our ways of thinking and feeling, we realize that many texts and written materials help keep racism alive. Racism in the English language can to some degree be attributed to early misconceptions about Africa.

Facing Facts: The Impact of White Racism on Oppressors and Oppressed

A necessary first step in creating a revised curriculum is to face the facts of a racist past and present. It is essential to recognize the impact of racism on the oppressor as well as on the oppressed.

Box 6.1

A Short Play
on Black and
White
Words

Some may blackly (angrily) accuse him of trying to blacken (defame) the English language, to give it a black eye (a mark of shame) by writing such black words (hostile). They may denigrate (to cast aspersions; to darken) him by accusing him of being blackhearted (malevolent), of having a black outlook (pessimistic, dismal) on life, of being a blackguard (scoundrel)—which would certainly be a black mark (detrimental fact) against him. Some may blackbrow (scowl at) him and hope that a black cat crosses in front of him because of this black deed. He may become a black sheep (one who causes shame or embarrassment because of deviation from the accepted standards), who will be blackballed (ostracized) by being placed on a blacklist (list of undesirables) in an attempt to blackmail (to force or coerce into a particular action) him to retract his words. But attempts to blackjack (to compel by threat) him will have a Chinaman's chance of success, for he is not a yellow-bellied Indian-giver of words, who will whitewash (cover up or gloss over vices or crimes) a black lie (harmful, inexcusable). He challenges the purity and innocence (white) of the English language. He doesn't see things in black and white (entirely bad or entirely good) terms, for he is a white man (marked by upright firmness) if there ever was one. However, it would be a black day when he would not "call a spade a spade," even though some will suggest a white man calling the English language racist is like the pot calling the kettle black. While many may be niggardly (grudging, scanty) in their support, others will be honest and decent—and to them he says, that's very white of you (honest, decent).

Source: Robert B. Moore, "Racism in the English Language," pamphlet published by The Council on Interracial Books for Children, 1841 Broadway, New York, NY 10023. The Council offers a free catalog of its print and audiovisual materials on racism, sexism, and other forms of bias.

Most race relations experts have studied racism in terms of the costs of racism to the victims, especially the denial of equal access to educational, economic, and political power. Other deleterious effects include loss of role models and knowledge of the past, physical and mental suffering, and even loss of life. Scholars have begun to recognize that racism victimizes Whites as well. Jack Forbes, for example, in his studies of Indian and Chicano peoples, wrote that "Anglo American young people grow up in a never-never land of mythology as regards nonwhites and it is crucial for our society's future that damaging myths be exposed and eliminated."[19]

In a discussion of the effects of racism on White children, Rutledge Dennis stresses ignorance of other people, development of a double social psychological consciousness, group conformity, and moral confusion and social ambivalence.[20] A dual consciousness develops within

White children who are taught to hate and fear others and to conform to racial etiquette on the one hand, while being taught Christian love on the other. Because racism deprives Whites of getting to know Blacks, it fosters "their ignorance of the many-sidedness of the Black population" and thus reinforces stereotypes.[21] Given the interdependency of the human race and the great variety of cultures on earth, this ignorance is not only senseless but also dangerous.

Among adults, Dennis sees three effects of racism on the White population: irrationality, inhibition of intellectual growth, and negation of democracy. He refers to J. W. Silver's assertion that White supremacy contributes to "the basic immaturity of the White population and the inability of Whites 'to grow up, to accept the judgements of civilization.' "[22] He has put forth the words Booker T. Washington spoke in 1911: "It is a grave mistake for the vast majority of Whites to assume that they can remain free and enjoy democracy while they are denying it to Blacks. The antidemocrat not only wants to ensure that Blacks do not enjoy certain rights, he also wants to ensure that no White is free to question or challenge this denial."[23]

It is essential to recognize, however, that even individuals who are psychologically free of racial prejudices today are still victims of racist practices that are engrained within many social institutions. Everyone shares in a history of institutionalized racism. The United States Constitution defined a slave as three-fifths of a man and denied Black men the right to vote until 1865. (Black women gained the right to vote along with all female citizens in 1922.) In 1896 the Supreme Court ruled against Homer Plessy and declared that separate-but-equal facilities for Blacks and Whites were constitutional. Segregation remained legal in public facilities until 1954, when the decision was reversed in Brown v. the Board of Education of Topeka, which ruled that separate facilities were inherently unequal.

The doctrine of White racism was also institutionalized in national legislation concerning immigration. In 1793 George Washington proclaimed that the "bosom of America is open to receive not only the Opulent and respectable Stranger, but the oppressed and persecuted of all Nations and Religions whom we shall wellcome to a participation of all our rights and privileges."[24] Obviously, slaves and free people of color were not to be included in this policy, nor were the Indians or Mexicans of the Southwest. In 1882 Chinese people were excluded, and in 1908 the exclusion was extended to Japanese immigrants. The National Origins acts passed in 1924 and 1929 restricted the number of immigrants to 150,000 annually and set up quotas that favored people from Northern and Western Europe. About 70 percent of those allowed to enter were from Britain, Ireland, Scandinavia, and Germany. The remaining 30 percent came from Southern and Eastern Europe. The Walter-McCarran Act, passed in 1952, did little to change these discriminatory quotas. In 1965 the quota system was abolished. Each year,

170,000 immigrants can now enter the United States from Africa, Asia, Australia, and Europe, and another 120,000 can enter from North and South America.

Referring to the immigration law of 1965, President Lyndon Johnson announced: "It does repair a very deep and painful flaw in the fabric of American Justice. It corrects a cruel and enduring wrong in the conduct of the American nation. The days of unlimited immigration are past, but those who come will come because of what they are and not because of the land from which they sprung."

After the Civil War and up until World War II, lynching became a major means of keeping Blacks "in their place." Between 1892 and 1921, nearly 2,400 Black Americans were lynched, and it is estimated that at least a third of the victims were falsely accused. Most of the vigilantes were never punished for their actions; in some cases local police officers were involved in these crimes.[25] (Of course, many Whites, particularly Jews and Italians, were also lynched, but the disproportionality is greatest among Black Americans.) Mexican American citizens have been the victims of racism as well, for example in the outrageous Sleepy Lagoon incident and the zootsuit riots in Los Angeles during World War II. Today, disproportionately higher numbers of Black and Latino soldiers are given the most dangerous combat duties, as in Vietnam, are overrepresented in prisons and on death row, and are overrepresented among students who are suspended, expelled, or placed in classes for the retarded. The fact that upper- and middle-income Whites could often secure draft deferments and skilled lawyers, while low-income Whites and non-Whites could not, exemplifies institutionalized bias.

As painful as it may be, children and young adults must face facts about the racist past. Under the guidance of knowledgeable and caring teachers, minorities and nonminorities can gain insight into a social context that helps explain current patterns of poverty, protest, and apathy as well as interracial isolation, stereotypes, misconceptions, and conflict. These insights can help convert anger, rage, denial, guilt, and paternalism into the commitment and knowledge needed to combat racism and social injustice wherever it occurs.

Conclusions

The illustrations used in this discussion of racism have emphasized Africa and Afro-Americans. We must be careful, however, not to regard racism strictly as a Black-White issue. There are parallels to the case of Africa all over the world. The results of ignorance and misunderstanding have been seen in Southeast Asia during the Vietnamese War and its aftermath—and again in Central America, an area many perceive simplistically as the region of the banana republics.

Likewise, all non-White ethnic groups in United States society are affected by racism; many White immigrants, such as the Irish, Italians, Jews from Eastern Europe, and Croatians, also have experienced cruel discrimination. Today, for example, immigration officials in California sometimes violate the civil rights of Latinos who are assumed to be illegal aliens. Immigrants from Asia—the Vietnamese and Chinese—now face resentment and racial prejudices in many aspects of their lives.

Because space does not permit all-inclusive illustrations, the focus on Africa and Afro-Americans is appropriate. In terms of numbers, Afro-Americans represent the largest ethnic minority. More important, however, is the fact that no other group entered this society primarily as slaves. The experience of slavery and its justification firmly entrenched the doctrine of White supremacy in the predominant minds and institutions that shaped United States history and led to the overall suppression of dark-skinned citizens.

Obviously, schools do not exist in a vacuum. They are only one aspect of a broader social context that, despite many changes that help guarantee social justice for everyone, is still racist in many ways because it supports White supremacy. How do we proceed in the face of this? First of all, we must accept that schools can and should make a difference. Those who would equate a stand against racism with preaching values can be told that it is un-American and antihuman to be racist. We can then proceed as follows:

- Recognize racist history and its impact on oppressors and victims.
- Examine our own attitudes, experiences, and behaviors concerning racism.
- Understand the origins of racism and why people hold racial prejudices and stereotypes.
- Understand the differences among individual, institutional, and cultural racism.
- Be able to identify racist images in the language and illustration of books, films, television, news media, and advertising.
- Be able to identify current examples of racism in our immediate community and society as a whole.
- Identify specific ways of combatting racism.
- Become antiracist in our own behavior.

Minority Perspectives

Efforts to correct the Anglo–Western European bias that pervades the traditional curriculum requires careful planning. If textbook distortion, stereotypes, and serious omissions surrounding non–Anglo-European minorities are to be corrected, revisions must be guided by an understanding of ethnic minority perspectives as well as the traditional majority perspective.

Consider a few examples of events that have traditionally been examined only from the Anglo-European viewpoint. The Texas revolt and its aftermath is a classic example.

Rebellion in Texas

The Texas revolt has been rationalized in persisting myths about heroic Texans.* The famous legend of the Alamo portrays 187 principled native Texans courageously fighting 5,000 Mexican troops. But the reality was somewhat different. Most men at the Alamo mission, in what is now San Antonio, were not native Texans, but newcomers. As the conflict developed, adventurers and fortune seekers poured into Texas. Many of the men in the Alamo were not men of principle defending their homes but adventurers or brawlers such as James Bowie, William Travis, and Davy Crockett. In addition, the mythmakers do not mention that the Alamo was one of the best-fortified sites in the West; indeed, the defenders had twice as many cannon, much better rifles, and much better training in riflery than the poorly equipped and poorly fed Mexican recruits. Another part of the myth suggests that all the defenders died fighting heroically. In fact, seven defenders surrendered, including Crockett. After a series of further skirmishes General Sam Houston managed a surprise attack which wiped out much of the Mexican army in the north; the captured General Santa Anna was forced to sign over what was now the Republic of Texas to the insurgents.[26]

The United States government's annexation of Texas in 1845, which triggered war with Mexico and resulted in the United States takeover of nearly half of Mexico's territory, is traditionally viewed from the framework of expansionism or manifest destiny. This part of history is a classic example of where dual or multiple perspectives are required. Certainly the Mexican American or Chicano perspective of events following the war would differ from what appears in textbooks. Although the Treaty of Guadalupe Hidalgo guaranteed Mexican residents who chose to remain in the United States full rights of citizenship and protection of property, most Mexican landowners lost their lands to Anglo-European Americans. The methods of takeover ranged from "lynching, to armed theft, to quasi-legal and legal means such as forcing expensive litigation in American courts to prove land titles."[27]

Many of the villagers neglected to bring their papers into court and often had lost evidences of title. Most of them lacked funds to defend titles; or, if they retained an Anglo-American lawyer, a large part of the land went in payment of court costs and fees. . . .

*This extract from Joe R. Feagin, *Racial and Ethnic Relations*, © 1978, is reprinted by permission of Prentice-Hall, Inc., Englewood Cliffs, N.J.

Litigation over land titles was highly technical and involved; cases dragged on in the courts for years; and . . . control of resources shifted to the Anglo-Americans.[28]

One of the more popular techniques for expropriating land was taxation. "American politicians would levy property tax rates at levels that only the largest of Spanish landholders could afford, thereby forcing small Hispanic entrepreneurs off their land and into wage labor."[29] Without knowledge of this aspect of history, one cannot possibly understand the border phenomenon of Mexico and contemporary society in the Southwest.

The Relocation of Japanese Americans

On February 19, 1942, President Roosevelt signed Executive Order 9066, which mandated the relocation of Japanese people living on the West Coast. More than 110,000 of the 126,000 Japanese in the United States were affected, two-thirds of whom were native-born U.S. citizens.[30] Initially, the evacuees were housed in temporary centers that had been hurriedly converted from fairgrounds, racetracks, and livestock exposition halls. The conditions were described by Mine Okubo:

> The guide left us at the door of Stall 50. We walked in and dropped our things inside the entrance. The place was in semidarkness; light barely came through the dirty window on either side of the entrance. A swinging half-door divided the 20 by 9 foot stall into two rooms. . . . The rear room had housed the horse and the front room the fodder. Both rooms showed signs of a hurried whitewashing. Spider webs, horse hair, and hay had been whitewashed with the walls. A two-inch layer of dust covered the floor, but on removing it we discovered that linoleum . . . had been placed over the rough manure-covered boards. We opened the folded cots lying on the floor of the rear room and sat on them in the semidarkness. We heard someone crying in the next stall.[31]

Later, the Japanese Americans were shifted to one of ten permanent camps that sometimes housed as many as 20,000 people. Germans, Italians, and Japanese in Hawaii were also threatened, but none were actually relocated into the concentration camps. The camps were bordered with barbed wire, guarded by the military, and offered little privacy. Some object to the label *concentration camp* because it associates the Japanese American relocation experiences with the Holocaust in Germany, which exterminated six million Jews. There are, of course, significant differences in the two experiences: The Japanese were not exterminated, and many who could prove their loyalty were released to fight in the war, participate in work-release programs, or move east.

Nevertheless, the experience represents a massive civil rights violation of over 100,000 people and brought injustifiable personal tragedy and financial ruin to many of them. Even though the War Relocation Authority (WRA) was established to supervise the evacuations and the Federal Reserve Bank was ordered to protect their property, most evacuated Japanese Americans suffered great financial losses, which mounted to over $400 million and have never been fully repaid.

Why did it happen? The forced imprisonment of Japanese Americans has traditionally been explained from a military viewpoint. Japan had attacked the United States and the West Coast was particularly vulnerable to sabotage because of the military facilities concentrated along the coastline. It was feared that the Japanese (as well as Germans and Italians) were engaged in spy activities. Others have emphasized strong racist anti-Japanese prejudice that had long infected California as well as the federal government. (See anti-Japanese legislation at both the federal and state levels.)[32] Still others emphasize the role of farm and business elites eager to eliminate Japanese competition. Little understood by non-Japanese Americans is the impact of the relocation experience on the Japanese American community, for example the loosening of family ties between Issei and Nisei. Also little known is the fact that Japanese Americans did protest and resist their imprisonment, that many Japanese soldiers fought with great valor during the war, and that returning home after 1945, many Japanese Americans could not regain their farms and businesses and faced violence and discrimination in their communities. These considerations help make up the Japanese perspective that must be heard, to deneutralize past atrocities and to prevent their recurrence.

In "Teaching the Asian-American Experience," Lowell Chun-Hoon wrote:

> The greatest danger to an open society is an education that homogenizes its people into limited and fixed conformity; the greatest danger to a small minority like Asian-Americans is that they will be imprisoned in the images created for them by mass society and that their own personal reality will not be able to transcend the imposed psychological colonization of society-as-a-whole.[33]

Chun-Hoon asserts that schools bear a large responsibility for ensuring that minorities are accurately represented, and this can happen only when "the experience of minority groups in the United States is taught from both a majority and minority perspective."[34]

> Unless, for example, we can understand the relocation of Japanese-Americans during World War II, both from the perspective of those who were interned as well as from the perspective of those who interned them, we achieve only a partial understanding of the event

itself. For in this instance, the fullness of the historical event is not measured by the inconsequential effects experienced by the over-whelming American majority, but the extreme effects experienced by the Japanese minority. History is not made or experienced impartially, and attempts to report it or teach it neutrally all too often merely neutralize the real significance of events themselves. Accordingly, *the major imperative of teaching the Asian-American experience, or any minority's history, is the ability to represent these dual perspectives fairly and completely* [italics added].[35]

Slavery

Slavery and emancipation are classic examples of how textbooks have excluded the Black point of view. Slavery is often introduced as an economic necessity. Later slavery is treated as a problem for Whites.

The Black perspective on slavery would include African cultural origins and histories of the array of African civilizations (just as England and Europe are discussed prior to colonization among Whites). It would also include evidence of Black people's strength under conditions of extreme oppression (in many cases the strongest and most intelligent Africans were sold into slavery and survived the middle passage), and of the expressions of Black culture that emerged in United States society.

A vivid example of how intelligence can be dulled by limited frames of reference is the erroneous assumption often made concerning the social status structure among American slaves: House slaves, drivers, artisans, and mulattoes are accorded higher status than field slaves. According to Berry and Blassingame, however, the social structure from the slaves' viewpoint was far more complex.

> Occupations translated into high social standing only if they combined two of the following features: mobility (frequently allowing the slave to leave the plantation); freedom from constant supervision by whites; opportunity to earn money; and provision of service to other blacks. . . . At the bottom of the ladder were those slaves who had the most personal contact or identified most closely with masters (house servants, concubines, drivers, mulattoes). Since conjurors and physicians helped to maintain the slave's mental and physical health, they received more deference than any other black.[36]

Native-born Africans were revered as links to the ancestral home, as were educators.

> Old men and women with great stores of riddles, proverbs, and folktales (creators and preservers of culture) played a crucial role in teaching morality and training youths to solve problems and to

develop their memories. Literate slaves had even more status than the sources of racial lore because they could read the Bible, tell the bondsmen what was transpiring in the newspapers, and write letters and passes.[37]

Rebel slaves who resisted floggings, violated racial taboos, or escaped from their masters were held in the highest esteem by the slaves, and were preserved as heroes in slave folktales and songs. "Physical strength, skill in outwitting whites, possession of attractive clothes, and ability to read signs and interpret dreams also contributed to a slave's social standing."[38]

Charles Hamilton has described the lack of Black perspectives in the curriculum as part of the reason many Black parents give up on traditional desegregated schools and prefer Black community control of schools serving Black children and youth (see Box 6.2).

The Case of American Indians

One of the most blatant examples of Anglo-European bias in the curriculum is the fact that United States history is traditionally taught as an east-to-west phenomenon. The northward flow of peoples and cultures from central Mexico is largely overlooked. Our legacy from the Spanish colonizers who imposed Catholicism, the Spanish language, an economic system of mining and agriculture on the Indian populations, and who helped create Mestizo and Creole populations is largely ignored. If, on the other hand, history were taught according to a greater-America frame of reference, alternative perspectives to "manifest destiny" could be presented, particularly Chicano and Native American perspectives. Our legacy from the Indians, which is just being discovered, would be recognized. People would realize that Native American contributions penetrate all aspects of society, including our form of government, a federation copied after the Iroquois League.[39]

Estimates of the Native American population size at the time of the European invasion of North America vary greatly. Early analysts have estimated the indigenous population of North America at between 500,000 and 1,150,000, but more recently the figure has been estimated at nearly 10 million.[40] Current scholars believe that the early estimates did not consider factors such as European diseases, especially smallpox, measles, and syphilis, which wiped out large portions of the Native American population during early years of contact. Furthermore, lower estimates had helped legitimize European takeover of unsettled territories.

At the time of the European invasion there were hundreds of different Native American societies. Over 200 different languages were spoken, and political, social, and economic systems differed dramatically. Despite this great cultural diversity, however, a unifying world view,

Box 6.2

Race and
Education: A
Search for
Legitimacy

The schools serve as a major instrument to transmit such a common homogeneous culture. And yet, we are beginning to see black Americans call for the recognition of other heroes: Frederick Douglass, Martin Luther King, Jr., Malcolm X, and so forth. Students are demanding that the traditional Awards Day programs at their schools include such awards as a Malcolm X Manliness Award, a Marcus Garvey Citizenship Award, and Frederick Douglass and Martin Luther King, Jr. Human Rights Awards. We see black writers challenging the idea of a common secular political culture. John Oliver Killens and Lerone Bennett, Jr., are two prominent examples. Killens captured the mood when he wrote:

> We [black Americans] even have a different historical perspective. Most white Americans, even today, look upon the Reconstruction period as a horrible time of "carpetbagging," and "black politicians," and "black corruption," the absolutely lowest ebb in the Great American Story. . . .
>
> We black folk, however, look upon Reconstruction as the most democratic period in the history of this nation; a time when the dream the founders dreamed was almost within reach and right there for the taking; a time of democratic fervor the like of which was never seen before and never since. . . .
>
> For us, Reconstruction was the time when two black men were Senators in the Congress of the United States from the State of Mississippi; when black men served in the legislatures of all the states in Dixie; and when those "corrupt" legislatures gave to the South its first public-school education. . . .*
>
> Even our white hero symbols are different from yours. You give us moody Abe Lincoln, but many of us prefer John Brown, whom most of you hold in contempt as a fanatic; meaning of course, that the firm dedication of any white man to the freedom of the black man is *prima-facie* evidence of perversion or insanity.†

And Lerone Bennett, Jr. challenged much of American historical scholarship when he challenged the role and image of Abraham Lincoln:

> Abraham Lincoln was *not* the Great Emancipator. As we shall see, there is abundant evidence to indicate that the Emancipation Proclamation was not what people think it is and that Lincoln issued it with extreme misgivings and reservations.‡

*John Oliver Killens, *Black Man's Burden* (New York: Trident Press, 1965), pp. 14–15.
†Ibid., p. 17.
‡Lerone Bennett, Jr., "Was Abe Lincoln a White Supremacist?" *Ebony*, 23, no. 4 (February 1968):35.

Continued

Box 6.2

Continued

A growing number of black Americans are insisting that the schools begin to reflect this new concern, this new tension. We simply cannot assume a common secular political culture. If we continue to operate on such false assumptions, we will continue to misunderstand the very deep feeling of alienation in the black community. And misunderstanding cannot be a viable basis for enlightened public policy. Likewise, it is not only important that Afro-American history be taught in the black schools, but that it also be incorporated into the curriculum of white schools throughout this country. It is not sufficient that only black children be given an accurate historical picture of the race; all Americans must have this exposure—in the inner city, the suburbs, the rural schools.

Source: Charles V. Hamilton, "Race and Education: A Search for Legitimacy," in *Issues in Race and Ethnic Relations*, ed. Jack Rothman (Itasca, Ill.: F. E. Peacock, 1977), pp. 101–15. Originally published in *Harvard Educational Review* 38, no. 4, pp. 669, 684. Copyright © by President and Fellows of Harvard College. Reprinted by permission.

which had grown out of Indian values, allowed them to live in relative harmony with each other and with the earth.

They had what the world has lost. They have it now. What the world has lost, the world must have again lest it die. Not many years are left to have or have not, to recapture the lost ingredient. . . . What, in our human world, is this power to live? It is the ancient, lost reverence and passion for human personality, joined with the ancient, lost reverence and passion for the earth and its web of life.

This indivisible reverence and passion is what the American Indian almost universally had; and representative groups of them have it still.

If our modern world should be able to recapture this power, the earth's natural resources and web of life would not be irrevocably wasted within the twentieth century, which is the prospect now.

True democracy, founded in the neighborhoods and reaching over the world, would become the realized heaven on earth. And living peace—not just an interlude between wars–would be born and would last through ages.[41]

Today, many Indian leaders openly criticize the Anglo-European core culture and its religion. Christianity is sometimes criticized "as a crude religion stressing blood, crucifixion, and bureaucratized charity rather than practicing sharing and compassion for people."[42] Other criticisms of White Europeans are that they are newcomers to the continent, they sharply accelerated war on the continent, killed off many animal species, betrayed the Native Americans who had aided them in establishing a place on the continent, destroyed the ecosystem, polluted the environment, and became slaves to technology.[43]

The first 250 years of European contacts with Native Americans included accommodation as well as conflict. In the eastern portions of the continent, American, British, Dutch, French, and Spanish powers fought each other and Native Americans for control of the land. As long as the Indians controlled the balance of power in North America, the European and American governments recognized them (at least on paper) as the "rightful owners of land in the Americas. Land was not to be taken from Indians except in fair exchange. Indians were needed not only as military allies, but also as producers and suppliers."[44] This philosophy was reflected in words from the Northwest Ordinance.

> Article III . . . The utmost good faith shall always be observed towards the Indians; their land property shall never be taken from them without their consent; and in their property, rights, and liberty, they never shall be invaded or disturbed, unless in just and lawful wars authorized by Congress; but laws founded in justice and humanity shall from time to time be made, for preventing wrongs being done to them and for preserving peace and friendship with them.[45]

With the era of westward expansion came the image of the Indians as a savage race attacking helpless settlers as they resisted the pressures of farmers and missionaries on the frontiers. Although the Indian Removal Act passed in 1830 stipulated that Indians could be relocated only on condition of their consent, the end result was that the federal government forcibly removed those Indians living east of the Mississippi to reservations in the West. In the "trail of tears," for example, 4,000 Cherokees died during the forced march out of the South to Indian territory in present-day Oklahoma. "Oklahoma, already the home of the Five Civilized Tribes of the Southwest, was soon to become a vast concentration camp into which Indians from tribes as far apart as the New York Seneca and the West Coast Modace were to be squeezed."[46]

According to Hraba, ethnocentrism and cultural conflict played a large role in the bitter land conflict between the Euro-American and the Native American.

> It was the permanent settler who transplanted the European market economy and brought the legacy of private property. Sizable investments of labor and capital were made by settlers, for land had to be cleared, homes and whole towns built, and a system of transportation constructed on the frontier. . . . [It is] estimated that each homestead site required an initial investment of $1,000 to bring it into production. Private ownership of the land gave a settler some

sense of security that he would realize a return on his investments, for he had legal title to the land, and the land and the improvements he made on it could not be capriciously taken from him.[47]

Many European settlers had experienced the oppression of serfdom and found security in the ownership of private property.

The Anglo-European world view concerning land, private property, and exclusive ownership was incompatible with the Indian world view, which stressed egalitarianism, nonmaterialism, and opposition to the unnecessary alteration of nature or destruction of any part of the earth. Given these divergent perspectives, the era of treaties would seem to have been doomed by misunderstanding if not deceit. The impact of the Dawes Act passed by Congress in 1887 further illustrates these conflicting world views. The act provided each Indian family 160 acres of reservation land, with the titles held in trust by the federal government for 25 years. Furthermore, every attempt was made to suppress Indian traditions, especially native religions and education. The Indian boarding schools that were established required elementary school-age children to leave their families for the academic year. "Reservation Indians were expected to emulate white settlers . . . by becoming farmers and tilling allotments of privately owned land . . . [and] would eventually assimilate into American society."[48] Those expectations clearly violated Indian cultural values, and the results were disastrous for the Indians whose numbers shrank drastically and who lost over 90 million acres of land to the Whites.

Indians were declared citizens of the United States in 1924, and since the 1930s Indian nations have been recognized as legally autonomous self-governing territories, separate from any state. The Indian Reorganization Act of 1934, which established current policies, can be viewed from several angles. In one sense, the act indicates a return to the early principle that Indians have a right to self-determination: Reservation lands have been returned to tribal management, community day schools have replaced distant boarding schools, and traditional cultures, including the Indian religions, are encouraged.

On the other hand, the illegally seized lands have not been restored, many treaty agreements are still ignored, and the reservations are in a sense colonies subjected to the political and economic policies of a foreign ruler in Washington, D.C. Most reservations are located on barren land; compared to all other ethnic groups in the United States, the Indian population suffers the poorest health, the shortest life span, and the greatest economic impoverishment.

It must be openly acknowledged that Indians are poor because white people are rich, that the land, timber and minerals which white people use to produce their wealth were virtually all taken by force or deception. It must be recognized that Indian reservations usually exist in marginal land, not originally of value from the perspective of white economic development.[49]

What is the Indian perspective that should become part of the revised curriculum? Jack Forbes provides excellent guidance in his illustrations of what teachers must do to teach the history of Indian people from the Indian viewpoint (see Box 6.3).

Establishing Multiple Perspectives: The Challenge

An accurate representation of minority perspectives is not always possible. Even when one wants a full, unbiased depiction of minority viewpoints and experiences, lack of available knowledge is a major problem. Recorded history has emphasized White males in power positions, and past omissions and inaccuracies make it difficult to establish the experiences and contributions of all groups. Racist and sexist practices of the past make rediscovery of history difficult. Because copyrights and patents were not available to women and non-Whites until relatively recently, many early contributions remain unrecognized. The type of literature published, the forms of art created, even the nature of historic monuments, are all tainted with bias. One example is Black soldiers in World War I. Of the 200,000 Afro-Americans sent to France, nearly 30,000 fought in the front lines and received high accolades from the French. Yet no Black American soldiers were permitted to march in the glorious victory parade up the Champs Élysées. "The ultimate injustice was the War Department's insistence that Afro-American soldiers not be depicted in the heroic frieze displayed in France's Pantheon de la Guerre."[50]

Chinese Americans experienced a similar fate after contributing most of the labor needed to complete the western portion of the transcontinental railroad. Nearly 10,000 Chinese workers had been involved, and much of their labor was high risk using explosives and working at dangerous heights. Yet not a single Chinese face appears in a famous photograph that captured the first meeting of locomotives from east and west.[51]

Although oral history and folklore are not free of distortions and are often inaccessible to outsiders, oral literature and oral history along with music and the visual arts remain some of the best means of discovering minority perspectives. The fact that most slaves were barred from learning to read or write and that many immigrant groups such as the Chinese, Japanese, Mexicans, and Eastern European Jews entered initially as illiterate laborers means that few pieces of literature or documents written by these people for themselves are available. Oral history, including songs, folk tales, jokes, proverbs, aphorisms, verbal games, and

Box 6.3

Teaching
Native
American
Values and
Cultures

1. The unsubstantiated theories of white anthropologists need to be treated as such. For example, Native Americans are not "mongoloid" because, first, there is no such thing as a "mongoloid" and, second, because there is not a shred of evidence linking Indians exclusively with any single "race."

2. The "Bering Straits" migration theory needs to be treated with great skepticism, since there is absolutely no evidence (except logic) to support it. Indian people generally believe that they evolved or were created in the Americas. This viewpoint should be respected although it is acceptable to discuss the possibility of migration as an alternative explanation. The point is that there is no empirical evidence to support any particular migration theory.

3. Indians should be treated as the original Americans and the first 20,000 years of American history need to be discussed *prior* to any discussion of European, African, or Asian migrations to the Americas. Likewise, in the discussion of the pre-European period, data derived from archaeology should be supplemented by Indian traditional literature (as found in *The Book of the Hopi, The Sacred Pipe, The Constitution of the Six Nations*, and other available paperback books).

4. The on-going evolution of Indian groups needs to be dealt with, from 1492 to the present. That is, one needs to deal with the *internal* history of Native tribes and not merely with European relations. For example, the development of the Iroquois confederation, the Cherokee Constitution of 1824, the Handsome Lake religion, the Comanche-Kiowa-Kiowa Apache-Cheyenne-Arapaho alliance system, the westward movements of the Otchipwe, Cree, Dakotas and others, the teachings of the Shawnee Prophet, the Kickapoo Prophet, and so on, need to be discussed as significant developments in the *heartland* of America at a time when Europeans are only marginal (i.e., along the Atlantic Coast).

5. The teacher needs to deal truthfully with European expansion. Native wars of liberation and independence need to be dealt with as such and not as acts of aggression carried out against "peaceful" (but invading) whites.

6. The teacher will want to try to use accurate names for the Indian groups in his or her region (such as Otchipwe in place of Chippewa). The correct names can usually be found in Hodge's *Handbook of Indians North of Mexico.*

7. Native heroes and resistance leaders of the post-1890 period (such as Carlos Montezuma and Yukioma) need to be dealt with—Indian resistance *did not* cease with the "last Indian war."

8. American history, from the Native perspective, is not merely a material "success story" (bigger and bigger, more and more,

better and better), nor does it consist solely in the reverse (that whites have actually brought about the near-destruction of this land). History is not progressive, but cyclical. That is, the evils of the white man and some Indians and others is a repetition of previous eras wherein other people went astray and contributed to the destruction of a cycle. We are now in the fourth or fifth world from the Native perspective.

This world may be self-destroyed because of man's evil. More and more inventions, etc., may not lead to any great "utopia" in the future, but simply to the end of this epoch. Furthermore, what really matters is the spiritual struggle of all creatures, the struggle for perfect "character development," not a great invention.

White people, for example, may exalt over the development of a new type of rocket ship and regard a flight to the moon as an event worth recording in a history book. But from a wholly different perspective the decision of an "ordinary" man to give up a needed job whose demands run counter to his ethics is more significant because it is a "spiritual" act directly relevant to man's highest level of aspiration. From the traditional Indian perspective, at least, the history of America should focus on man's spiritual development and not on his material "progress."

Source: Jack D. Forbes, "Teaching Native American Values and Cultures," in *Teaching Ethnic Studies: Concepts and Strategies,* ed. James A. Banks (Washington, D.C.: National Council for the Social Studies, 1973), pp. 218–19. Reprinted by permission.

(among Afro-Americans) toasts offer the richest sources for understanding their ethnic perspectives. Lawrence Levine's exceptionally rich study of Black folklore, for example, has led him to paint a picture of slavery that differs dramatically from the view traditionally accepted by popular culture as well as by many scholars.

I have only begun to touch upon the reservoir of tales and reminiscences which stress slave courage, self-respect, sacrifice, and boldness. The accuracy of this picture is less important for our purposes than its existence. These stories were told and accepted as true—a fact of crucial importance for any understanding of post-slavery Afro-American consciousness. Once again a vibrant and central body of black thought has been ignored while learned discussions of the lack of positive reference group figures among Negroes, the absence of any pride in the Afro-American past, the complete ignorance Negroes have concerning their own history, have gone on and on. The concept of Negro history was not invented by modern educators. Black men and women dwelt upon their past and filled their lore with stories of slaves who, regardless of their condition, retained a sense of dignity and group pride. Family legends of slave ancestors were cherished and handed down from generation to generation. Postbellum Negroes told each other of fathers and mothers, relatives and friends who committed sacrifices worth remembering, who performed deeds worth celebrating, and who endured hardships that have not been forgotten.[52]

It should be clear that minority perspectives are not built only from heroes and success stories, or from an emphasis on foods, fads, and festivals. Carlos Cortez cautions against this in "Teaching the Chicano Experience" with words that can be applied to every ethnic group.

> Certainly heroes and success stories comprise *part* of the Chicano experience. Chicanos can develop greater pride and non-Chicanos can develop greater respect by learning of Chicano lawyers, doctors, educators, athletes, musicians, artists, writers, businessmen, etc., as well as Mexican and Chicano heroes (heroes either to their own culture or to the nation at large). However, the teaching of the Chicano experience often becomes little more than the display of Emiliano Zapata, Pancho Villa, Benito Juarez, and Miguel Hidalgo posters or an extended exercise in "me too-ism"—the list of Mexican Americans who have "made it" according to Anglo standards.
>   In falling into these educational cliches, the very essence of the Chicano experience is overlooked. For this essence is neither heroes nor "me too" success stories, but rather the masses of Mexican-American people. The . . . teacher should focus on these Chicanos, their way of life, their activities, their culture, their joys and sufferings, their conflicts, and their adaptation to an often hostile societal environment. Such an examination of the lives of Mexican Americans—not Chicano heroes or "successes"—can provide new dimensions for the understanding of and sensitivity to this important part of our nation's heritage.[53]

Obviously, people disagree about present awareness of alternative ethnic perspectives. Most of us are more aware of some minority perspectives than others, particularly if we have lived a minority experience. Each of us, however, needs to become more informed about ethnic perspectives beyond our own—especially when we have grown up in a racist society, with an incomplete, biased curriculum.

The challenge to become knowledgeable about new ethnic perspectives may seem overwhelming at first. It is a challenge that teachers are obliged to meet. The following suggestions are offered as possible ways of proceeding; with effective guidance, students can participate in all of these steps.

- Start small. Begin by selecting one or two ethnic groups, preferably those that hold special meaning for your students, community, and yourself.

- Become informed about this group's perspectives regarding current events and the subject areas you teach. Consult ethnic primary source materials, such as literature, films, art, news media, and music. A list of key questions can help guide the research or you may prefer to avoid preconceptions and let the issues emerge.
- Become acquainted with community resources (both people and organizations) in your area that can provide knowledge about this ethnic group. Complete a list of local residents who would be willing to visit your school or be interviewed by students.
- Examine your texts and supplementary materials for bias.
- Develop a resource file of primary source materials and teaching strategies that will help you present the group's perspectives to your students. Everything from news articles containing statistics that can be converted into math problems, to songs, speeches, and cartoons can be collected.
- Select one or more areas of your course in which the group's contributions and viewpoints have been overlooked. Create and teach a lesson that provides more accurate knowledge by including the group's perspectives.

Ethnic Diversity

We run the risk of stereotyping when we seek the perspective of a particular ethnic group. People within every ethnic group differ from each other in important ways. Not all White Anglo-Saxon Protestants are racially prejudiced. Not all Mexican Americans identify with their Indian heritage. Not all Black Americans are knowledgeable about life in the Black ghetto or can speak for the Black community on race relations issues. Not everyone who speaks Spanish is from Mexico.

Within any one ethnic group, social conflicts and different viewpoints emerge due to factors such as geographic origins, social class, and gender. Personal qualities such as aptitude, personality, and appearance also make a difference. All these factors interact with the individual's sense of ethnic identity; some individuals tend to be assimilated into the macroculture, others are more ethnically encapsulated, and still others are bicultural or even global in perspective.

Geographic origins, social class, and sense of ethnic identity are especially helpful in explaining ethnic diversity. Consider the cases of Jewish Americans and Black Americans.

Jewish American Origins

The origins of Jewish Americans are unique among American immigrants in that their sense of peoplehood was not linked to a nationality. The Jews are unified by religion and tradition rather than by national origins.

Jews are descendants of the Hebrews, a people who in ancient times lived in what is now Israel and its immediate neighbors. After the Roman Empire conquered their homeland in 70 A.D., Jews were eventually scattered all over the world (although mainly across Europe and the Mediterranean), where they remained a minority wherever they lived.

Despite long centuries of political fragmentation and persecution, Jews have kept alive their religion and cultural traditions. Judaism is one of the world's oldest religions and was the first to teach the existence of one God, giving birth to both Christianity and Islam. Jews were persecuted along with the early Christians prior to the Christianization of the Roman Empire. During the Middle Ages, Renaissance, and Enlightenment, they were attacked as heretics by Christians and have been the victims of scapegoating and discrimination up to the present. Of the estimated fourteen to twenty million people killed by the Nazis in World War II concentration camps, at least six million were Jews. The Holocaust exterminated three-fifths of the Jewish population in Europe; approximately one and a half million of the victims were Jewish children. Because Jews maintained their own religion, language, and traditions and lived in segregated communities or ghettos, they became "a marked people—natural targets for whatever passions or fears might sweep over an ignorant and superstitious population."[54] Furthermore, because Jews were typically barred from owning land, they often worked as middlemen, particularly money lenders, tax collectors, and small businessmen, performing the economic functions that "are almost universally unpopular around the world," as seen in the case of the Chinese in Southeast Asia, the East Indians in Uganda, and the Ibos in Nigeria.[55]

Restrictions on Jews were most relaxed in Western Europe, and many Jews began to assimilate to some degree into their host society. In Western Europe Jews could retain the Jewish religion and still be perceived as French, German, or English. Germany was one of the most liberal countries toward Jews, and it was there in the early 1800s that Reform Judaism originated. National policies toward Jews were more restrictive in Russia and Eastern Europe, and most Jews there remained Orthodox.

The Jewish people are divided into two broad groups, the Ashkenazic and Sephardic. Sephardic Jews had settled in the Mediterranean countries and are distinguished from the Ashkenazic Jews of Central and Eastern Europe in terms of language, food, dress, and art. Most Jewish Americans are Ashkenazic and originally spoke Yiddish, while many Sephardic Jews spoke Ladino. Each group also had its own pronunciation of the Hebrew language.

The first group of Jewish immigrants who came to America were Sephardic, coming primarily from Spain and Portugal. Prior to the Spanish Inquisition, Sephardic Jews in Spain enjoyed more freedom and attained greater positions of wealth and power than Jews anywhere else in Europe. Many owned large landed estates and were important political figures, bankers, and industrialists. Jewish wealth, in fact, was used to help finance the explorations of Columbus. Conditions changed suddenly in 1492 when Ferdinand and Isabella decreed that Jews convert to Christianity or be expelled. Some Jews pretended to convert, remained in Spain, and practiced their faith in secret. Others fled to the eastern Mediterranean, and still others came to the American colonies, which were known for greater religious freedom.

The stream of German Jews began soon after the arrival of Sephardic Jews. Quickly the German Jews came to predominate within the Jewish American population, which grew from approximately three thousand at the time of the Revolution to over a half million by 1880.[56] Differences existed between Sephardic and German Jews, and those differences are still evident today. According to Thomas Sowell, Sephardic Jews tended to emphasize business over scholarship. Drawing upon their expertise developed in Spain, most recovered from their earlier financial losses and were economically prosperous by the time of the American Revolution. Furthermore, they tended to look down on other Jews who were not of Sephardic origins, particularly the German Jewish immigrants.[57]

German Jews differed from later Jewish immigrants in that they did not settle in concentrated Jewish communities. Instead they spread out across the nation, working as "small tradesmen and professionals scattered among their non-Jewish clientele."[58] By the time the third wave of Jewish immigrants began in the 1880s (escapees from persecution in Russia), German Jews had become well established. "The German Jews were active, not only in their own communities but also in American society at large as businessmen and bankers. . . . Many Jews were destined to play important roles in developing such major American institutions as Macy's Department Store chain, Sears Roebuck, and the *New York Times*. As of 1880, 40 percent of all German-Jewish families had at least one servant. Only 1 percent of the heads of Jewish families were still peddlers, and fewer than 1 percent worked as laborers or domestic servants."[59]

The third (and largest) group of Jewish immigrants came from Eastern Europe, particularly from Russia where Jews were the victims of Russification and of peasant massacres called *pogroms*. Between 1880 and World War I, approximately two million Jews fled to the United States. Sowell writes that their arrival was an acute embarrassment to the German Jews in America.

The size of the eastern European Jewish immigration swamped the existing American Jewish community of largely German origin. The eastern European Jews were also heavily concentrated in New York City and, in fact, were even more localized on the lower east side of Manhattan, which contained the largest number of Jews ever assembled in one place on earth in thousands of years. The German Jews already established in America were appalled not only by the numbers but also by the way of life of the eastern European Jews. The eastern Jews were not only poorer—most arrived destitute, with less money than any other immigrant group—but were also far less educated (a 50 percent illiteracy rate), and with rougher manners than the more sophisticated and Americanized German Jews. Eastern European Jews had lived a provincial life, outside the mainstream of the general European culture in which German Jews were immersed. Eastern Europeans even looked different— earlocks, skull caps, beards, old-fashioned Russian-style clothing, scarves about the women's heads, and a general demeanor reminiscent of a painful past that German Jews had long ago left behind. The Orthodox Jewish religious services were full of traditions and practices long abandoned by the modern Reform Judaism of Germans. The very language of the eastern European Jews—Yiddish— was a folk dialect disdained by more educated Jews, who used either the language of the country or classical Hebrew.[60]

At times the Jewish philanthropic tradition overcame these negative attitudes, however. "German Jewish organizations made strenuous efforts to aid, and especially to Americanize, the eastern Jewish immigrants. Schools, libraries, hospitals, and community centers were established to serve 'downtown' Jews, financed by 'uptown' Jews."[61] However, the lines of distinction between German Jews and Eastern European Jews remained visible.

Most of the Eastern Jewish immigrants worked in manual labor, particularly the garment industries, where they met the demands for cheap labor in the notorious sweatshops. These Jews lived in crowded filthy slums that averaged more than 700 people per acre and were infested with tuberculosis and other diseases. Because of their religious orthodoxy, Jews from Eastern Europe lived and worked in close proximity with other Jews to satisfy their need for kosher food, a synagogue, and recognition of the Sabbath (many non-Jewish businesses and factories operated on Saturdays). Thus there were large concentrations of Jews in New York, Chicago, and Philadelphia.

The Jewish American community today reflects both the unity and diversity of its origins in Europe and the Mediterranean. Contrary to popular myths and stereotypes of wealthy Jews in control of United States finance, business, and industry, the Jewish community contains sharp socioeconomic differences. It is true that as a group Jewish Americans show the highest family income index of any major ethnic group in this society.[62] However, it is also estimated that out of a population of six million, over half a million Jewish Americans are below the nation's poverty level. While the percentage of Jews on college and university faculties and in other professions is much higher than their 2.6 percent of the United States population, very few occupy top executive positions or positions of political power. The widely held belief that Jews control the nation's business, banking, and finance is a misconception. Most Jewish Americans fall into middle-income categories that include middle management jobs and small business.[63]

As a group Jewish Americans have a tradition of humanitarianism, commitment to civil rights issues for all peoples, and political support for most liberal candidates. In contrast to some other groups, Jewish Americans have not become more conservative as they move up the socioeconomic ladder. Many Jews were active in the civil rights movement of the 1960s and in protests against the Vietnamese war. Jews are noted for their support of the Anti-Defamation League and numerous other civil rights organizations. On the other hand, friction has developed between portions of the Jewish and Black communities over issues such as Israel and Zionism, inner-city reforms, and affirmative-action programs. Jews also differ among themselves on the issue of Zionism and Arab-Israeli relations.

The Jewish religion itself remains a major source of diversity among Jews. The major religious movements (Orthodox, Conservative, and Reform) differ sharply in their degree of adaptation to the non-Jewish macroculture, and there are secular Jews who maintain their Jewish identity even though they do not accept any form of Judaism. This becomes a complex issue because for many Jews Judaism is the essence of being Jewish.

Although differences exist within each response, retentions of the original Jewish faith and tradition are strongest among the Orthodox Jews and weakest among Reform Jews. Conservative Judaism developed in the nineteenth century as an attempt to balance the Reform movement, which many Jews felt had become too secular. The numerical strength of these different responses is difficult to establish, but it seems evident that Orthodox Judaism is declining in this society.

Among Orthodox Jews the Sabbath is kept from sundown on Friday until sundown on Saturday. Religious services are in Hebrew and daily prayers are said in the morning, late afternoon, and after sunset. Dietary rules are strictly observed; for example, neither pork nor shellfish are eaten, and milk and meat are not consumed at the same meal. Only kosher food, that prepared in accordance with Jewish law, may be eaten. For example, meat may be eaten only if it comes from a healthy animal that has been killed quickly and painlessly.

Religious services among Reform and Conservative Jews contain much more English than do traditional Orthodox services. Men and women worship together, and organ music may be part of the service. Conservative Jews generally observe Jewish dietary laws in all public functions of the synagogue, while they may or may not keep a kosher kitchen at home. Reform Jews are least likely to keep kosher, are more likely to attend a synagogue (which they call "temple") only on high holidays (Rosh Hashanah and Yom Kippur), and are more likely to marry non-Jews than are Orthodox or Conservative Jews.

The Jewish American perspective emerges out of this array of past experiences, beliefs, and opinions from a Jewish point of view. All Jewish Americans are influenced by the challenge of living within a macroculture that is predominantly Christian. As part of a worldwide Jewish community, Jewish Americans are influenced by a long history of discrimination, which was experienced most recently in the horror of the Holocaust. They are influenced by the existence of Jewish communities in the modern state of Israel and elsewhere, such as the Soviet Union. These influences help to unify Jewish Americans despite their individual and group differences.

Diversity Among Afro-Americans

Differences within the Afro-American population are also overlooked, especially if one is not Black or has not had close contact with a Black community. Images of slavery and its aftermath of oppression have created the perception of a monolithic Black experience of poverty, social problems, and despair.

The point was illustrated recently in a teacher preparation class at a midwestern university. A small group presentation on "Black American Experiences: Implications for Teaching and Learning," which was given by six White members of the class, painted a picture of poverty, broken homes, welfare, poor self-concepts, and school dropout. However well intentioned the presentation may have been, its paternalistic tone and negative image outraged certain members of the class (mainly Black students) and amazed others. It became a lesson in misconceptions and stereotypes so prevalent in traditional social science literature, a lesson in ethnic encapsulation (none of the six White student presenters had even talked with a Black person prior to the class), and a lesson in diversity within the Black population. Of the four Black students in that class, one had grown up in the Chicago projects and had never really seen a White person before coming to college. Another had attended an elite, predominantly White prep school where she had been president of her class. Still another, a brilliant student and gifted musician from Detroit, had grown up in a Black community that represented every conceivable occupation, level of income, and level of education; both of his parents were college professors. The fourth student had been raised by a very strict family in a Black ghetto neighborhood where the children were bussed to predominantly White schools. Both parents had worked long hours to provide for their four children, who ranged from very light pink skin to pecan tan.

Three Black Histories[64]

One way to understand some of the differences among Black Americans today is to examine different origins among "free persons of color," emancipated slaves and their descendants, and West Indian immigrants.[65] It is estimated that between 10 and 14 percent of the Black population was legally free prior to the Civil War. Their origins were varied.

The earliest Africans came as indentured servants and gained their freedom after a fixed number of years. Children of Black servants were automatically free from birth. In the late seventeenth century, when the concept of chattel slavery evolved, slaves became property in perpetuity. Freedom could be attained, however, through voluntary manumission by slave owners, escape, self-purchase, or purchase by already free relatives or philanthropic Whites, or through special legislation as a reward for unusual service to the community.[66] Mulatto children of White mothers were also automatically free from birth.

The status of free Negroes was precarious at best, particularly in the South. Free Blacks could be kidnapped and sold into slavery, especially after the Fugitive Slave Law was passed in 1850. Free people of color were denied voting rights, excluded from the militia and from carrying United States mail, and were permitted to bear arms only if they could obtain a permit. Free Blacks could, however, own real estate and some attained great wealth. A Black elite developed in the lower South, for example, where Afro-Americans (formerly subjects of France and Spain) had more legal and customary rights than elsewhere in the South. In the state of Louisiana, there developed a large group of prosperous free Negro planters as well as a highly educated free Negro elite.[67] Furthermore, in Louisiana free Negroes traveled freely and could testify in court.

"Unlike other societies in the New World, in the United States the social distinctions between blacks and mulattoes and between free Negroes and slaves were fluid. Mulattoes generally did not constitute a separate caste."[68] Free persons of color differed from the slave population in both racial mixture (37 percent of the free were mulattoes, compared to 8 percent of the slaves) and in geographic distribution.[69] The slave population was southern and largely rural, while the free Black population was relatively evenly split between North and South, and nearly half were urbanized.

Referring to the massive migration of southern Black people to northern cities in the twentieth century, Sowell points out that

> much of the later cultural contrast between the established Negro elite and underprepared black migrants to the cities had its origins in this difference between their respective ancestors. Many of the outstanding Negroes of the post–Civil War period and early twentieth century were descendants of the "free persons of color."

Whites who pointed to those individual successes and asked, "Why can't the *others* do it?" were usually unaware that the other blacks were at an entirely different point in their social evolution.[70]

Although only about 1 percent of the Afro-American population originated in the West Indies, West Indians have long been greatly overrepresented among prominent Afro-Americans. Furthermore, compared with the overall Afro-American population, West Indian Blacks tend to have higher incomes, greater education, higher occupational status, and are far more likely to own their own businesses. Even today West Indian Blacks tend to remain socially distinct from other Afro-Americans in their selection of friends or marriage partners.[71]

Afro-Americans whose origins include the West Indies are significant not only because of their prominent leadership role, but also because they help destroy the myth that the greater successes of mulattoes (compared with "purer" Black Africans) is explained by an infusion of "superior White Blood." West African Blacks have a higher proportion of Black African ancestry than do American Blacks; therefore, biological differences (White ancestry) cannot accurately explain the greater achievement of mulattoes in United States society. The explanation would seem to rest in the different socioeconomic conditions of West Indian slavery. Black people were the majority population in the West Indies and thus slave escapes and rebellions were both more frequent and more successful. Furthermore, Black West Indians were assigned individual family plots of land that provided food for the family and marketplace. Finally, once slavery was abolished Black West Indians had access to a wide range of occupations, though, as in the United States, top positions were reserved for Whites.[72]

Socioeconomic Differences

Social class distinctions, relating to the different origins of free people of color, emancipated slaves, and people from the West Indies, contribute to differences within the Afro-American population today. Thomas Sowell reports that prior to the Civil War approximately 10 percent of the Black population held 70 percent of Black wealth and that this pattern continues. Today Black wealth tends to be distributed slightly more unequally than White wealth, and there remains a highly affluent group of Afro-Americans. Other achievements also tend to be concentrated among a small group of Afro-Americans. For example, the alumni of 5.2 percent of the Black high schools received 20.8 percent of all doctoral degrees awarded to Afro-Americans between 1957 and 1962, and of the 4.3 million Afro-American families in 1966, only 5.2 *thousand* families produced *all* of the Black physicians, dentists, lawyers, and academic doctorates in the country.[73] In those cases where it has been possible to trace ancestry, the continued prominence of free people of color has been striking.[74]

It is important to recognize that from an Afro-American perspective, most Blacks have grown up in middle-class families. Material prosperity is not always a necessary condition for class.

> One measure of a male's status in the Black community historically was his ability to provide for his family, to educate his children, and to support his church. It mattered not, for example, that barbers, mailmen, carpenters or porters were considered "lower class" by Whites, they were ascribed "middle-class" status if they held steady jobs enabling them to provide for their families.[75]

Education has traditionally been an important source of status in the Black community; thus an educated female teacher or school principal could provide upper-middle-class status to a husband who might work as a porter or custodian.

The stereotypical Black lower-class matriarchal family also exists, but it does not represent the majority of Black families. The number of Black families headed by single females has been steadily increasing, and by the mid-1980s, when unemployment rates peaked among Afro-Americans, it was estimated to be over 40 percent, compared with 22.4 percent in 1960 and 33 percent in 1976.[76] Ironically, the nation's welfare system itself has contributed to the breakdown of low-income families because of regulations that prohibit payments to women and children if a husband is present. During times of unemployment, it was often true that the only way a man could feed his family was to desert them.[77]

Differences over Color

Skin color provides another source of diversity within the Afro-American population. It is safe to assume that most Black Americans believe that most White Americans are racially prejudiced against Blacks. Blacks, therefore, hold negative attitudes about White society in general. There are, however, sharp degrees of difference in Black attitudes toward White folk, ranging from genuine love and acceptance of some White persons by some Blacks to rabid hatred of all Whites by other Blacks.

In his powerful self-portrait of Black America, John Langston Gwaltney illustrates the range of attitudes among Blacks toward Whites.*

---

*The following quotations from *Drylongso: A Self-Portrait of Black America*, by John Langston Gwaltney, are reprinted by permission of Random House, Inc., and John Brockman Associates. Copyright © 1980 by John Langston Gwaltney.

Given the negative conditioning of the Afro-American historical experience, it is astounding that so many black people are prepared to deal with white people as individuals. "If you are wrong, you are not right, I don't care what color you are. Should I not speak to some white person who is polite to me just because some other person that looks like that was nasty to me? All kinds of people have tried to make a fool of me, so if I went by that I wouldn't speak to anybody. I know it's hard to do, but I guess you just have to take people as you find them" (Iris McCrae).[78]

On the other hand, Gwaltney also quotes Erica Allen:

My uncle is a preacher and he says that white people are born evil. He'll tell you in a minute that the Bible says that the wicked are estranged from the womb. Now, as far as he is concerned, when you say "the wicked," you have said "the white race." He cannot stand white people, and although he is a man with good common sense most of the time, you cannot make him see reason about this race thing. He looks as white as any white person, but you'd better not tell him that unless you are ready to go to war. He won't even call them men. He says, "The beni did this" or "The beni have said so-and-so."

His daughter married a white boy about five years ago. They have two nice kids and are getting along fine, but Uncle Josiah acts like they're dead. She was—I mean, she is—his only girl and they were very close, so it's hard for everybody. It's been about five years now and you could count the weeks on the fingers of your hand that Felicity has not come to see him. He just won't have anything to do with her. She said that she'd keep coming to see him, and I guess she will because she's just as stubborn as he is.[79]

Black America's focus on skin color is not only a matter of interracial relations with Whites. There are clear skin color preferences and prejudices among Blacks toward other Blacks as well. Those people who have grown up in isolation from a Black community are often shocked to learn that Black folks perceive many shades of Black and that skin tone differences are often a source of prejudice or envy.

Skin lightening creams and the conks for hair straightening are continually in and out of fashion. Historically, however, the lighter-skinned child was often favored, especially in upper-income families where skin shade was a factor to consider in selecting friends and a marriage partner. On the other hand, the "high yaller" individual who could pass for White has often faced rejection and ridicule from other Blacks, as is vividly portrayed in Rudolph Fisher's prize-winning short story "High Yaller."[80]

Cecelia Delaney shares some valuable insights about skin color in her narrative with Gwaltney.

> I distinguished between us and them. Most white people I know are darker than I am. Even when I was most firm in my allegiance to my better-class-of-colored-people values, there was still the black-versus-white thing. I was far from a black nationalist then. My aunts had taught me that the better-class-of-colored-people had a responsibility to lead the less fortunate of our race. They didn't only mean poor black people, but darker black people, who, despite their unfortunate dark-brownness, had many things going for them—they were honest, clean, resourceful and strong. Actually, we lived among people of all colors. We told each other jokes about white people and black people, but I can't remember any jokes about yellow people versus dark brown people. These crazy things I and my relatives thought about dark brown people then was a part of the whole thing.
>
> You know that dark brown people have their insanities also. Astrid Haley's dark brown father would resort to almost any stratagem to avoid eating any food in the house of the most proper members of the better-class-of-colored-people. He shared the prejudice which so many dark people have about paler black people—you know, "Yaller's so low-down," as they say in the street. Both Astrid and I were under strict orders not to play with certain black kids. This off-limits group were, of course, the people we were most interested in. This group consisted of all kinds of black people. Some of those who were out looked like Astrid and some like me.[81]

Even though she describes intragroup prejudices and conflicts, there is also evidence of a clear Black American perspective in these remarks by Cecelia Delaney. The Black perspective emerges out of a kaleidoscope of opinion from a Black point of view. Despite the individual and cultural differences, all Afro-Americans are influenced by a "double-consciousness," an expression first used by W.E.B. DuBois in *Souls of Black Folk* to describe the experience of being Black in a White society. Most Afro-Americans are influenced by a core Black culture that differs from Euro-American culture in terms of language, values, and "soul." Most Afro-Americans are influenced by feelings of Black solidarity born out of abhorrence of slavery and a hatred of subordination by White society that is passed from one generation to the next.

Conclusions

Awareness of ethnic diversity can be developed along with the understanding of a minority perspective. The following suggestions extend those provided on pages 182 and 183 and illustrate how minority perspectives and ethnic diversity can be considered simultaneously.

- Select an ethnic group and plan ways of portraying the diversity within it. Include male and female viewpoints; different generations and age groups; dissimilar occupations, geographical regions, socioeconomic backgrounds, neighborhoods, and intergroup experiences.
- When social issues are debated, or when students are asked to play roles, include a realistic mix of opinions that portray the different viewpoints within many ethnic groups.
- Help students identify diversity within their own ethnic group, including physical features associated with different races, attitudes, opinions, and socioeconomic factors.
- Provide a variety of role models from each ethnic group present in the school.
- When tracking of students and ability grouping is used, avoid ethnically identifiable groups.

Human Similarities and Empathy

Too often in our attempts to foster understanding of cultural diversity, we focus on group differences and overlook the basic similarities of being human. The concept of humanity and feelings of unity with other humans must become a central aspect of the curriculum.

An understanding of three aspects of curriculum revision—racism, majority perspectives, and ethnic diversity—aids awareness of human similarities. All humans hold stereotypes and tend to be ethnocentric. Racism harms and dehumanizes the oppressor as well as the oppressed. Everyone is a minority in some aspect of life and needs the skills and freedom for self-expression. There are aspects of being human that transcend all cultures and ethnic groups, such as the need for food, shelter, and love.

Teachers must ensure that students get this message. Past experience shows that the realization does not happen automatically. Consider *The Human Manifesto*, which is an eloquent statement of human values and common concerns regarding survival of the human race on earth (see Box 6.4). If students are to develop this kind of global perspective and allegiance to humanity, or even the ability to harmonize with different groups in their classrooms and community, we must be concerned with their ability to feel what other people feel, and to understand the viewpoints of others they may disagree with.

Informed Empathy

It is one thing to develop knowledge and awareness of human similarities and another to develop empathy. Knowledge is a necessary but insufficient ingredient. The goal is informed empathy, or "knowl-

Box 6.4

The Human
Manifesto

Human life on our planet is in jeopardy.

It is in jeopardy from war that could pulverize the human habitat. It is in jeopardy from preparations for war that destroy or diminish the prospects of decent existence.

It is in jeopardy because of the denial of human rights.

It is in jeopardy because the air is being fouled and the waters and soil are being poisoned.

If these dangers are to be removed and if human development is to be assured, we the peoples of this planet must accept obligations to each other and to the generations of human beings to come.

We have the obligation to free our world of war by creating an enduring basis for worldwide peace.

We have the obligation to safeguard the delicate balance of the natural environment and to develop the world's resources for the human good.

We have the obligation to place the human interest above the national interest, and human sovereignty above national sovereignty.

We have the obligation to make human rights the primary concern of society.

We have the obligation to create a world order in which man neither has to kill or be killed.

In order to carry out these obligations, we the people of this world assert our primary allegiance to each other in the family of man. We declare our individual citizenship in the world community and our support for a United Nations capable of governing our planet in the common human interest.

Life in the universe is unimaginably rare. It must be protected, respected, cherished.

We pledge our energies and resources of spirit to the preservation of the human habitat and to the infinite possibilities of human betterment in our time.

Source: Planetary Citizens Registry, P.O. Box 2722, San Anselmo, Calif. 94960, as quoted in David Dufty, Susan Sawkins, Neil Pickard, Jim Power, and Ann Bowe, *Seeing It Their Way: Ideas, Activities and Resources for Intercultural Studies* (London: Reed Education, 1976), p. 29. Reprinted by permission.

edge plus sensitivity in trying to imagine oneself in another's shoes or bare feet. Empathy varies from trying to understand how other people think and view the world to how other people emote, feel or sense."[82]

Consider the following three responses made by students as part of a test that asked them to imagine themselves as someone else.[83]

What Would You Call THIS?

RESPONSE A

The holy man came to ward off the spirits which were giving my daughter headaches.

RESPONSE B

When I die I hope my body will be cremated and my ashes thrown into the sacred Godavari River.

As Compared with THIS?

RESPONSE C

I live in a typical agricultural village in a crude mud hut. I am a New Guinea highlander. Our tribe's religion is animism. My diet is essentially vegetative. The natural vegetation is chopped away with primitive stone axes, the lower storey plants are burnt producing nutrient for the soil. After fifty years the ecology of my area returns to its original state.

Responses A and B exemplify *informed empathy* while response C seems totally lacking in empathy, however informed it may be. Negative empathy or nonempathy, as illustrated in response C, shows "a lack of skill in identifying with others, a lack of cultural imagination, or an inability to think in terms other than those of your own culture."[84]

Building Empathy Through Language and Literature

Language is one of the great barriers to cultural pluralism in United States society, and to empathy and respect among culturally different people. Standard English is the predominant language, particularly in our schools. Writing from a Chicano perspective, Feliciano Rivera has stated:

> Historically, state and local institutions have insisted that to become "good Americans" all minority and immigrant groups have to abandon their native languages and cultures, give up their group identity, and become absorbed as individuals into the dominant group. If any group has resisted . . . it has been regarded as uncivilized, un-American, and potentially subversive. Furthermore, it is difficult for many people to accept the idea that a native-born Mexican American who happens to speak Spanish and who retains many of the values of his native culture might well be a loyal American. As a result, social and educational institutions in the Southwest and California have directed their activities toward the elimination of both the Spanish language and Mexican culture.[85]

On the other hand, in a striking contradiction, millions of dollars are spent to encourage schoolchildren to learn a foreign language.

A multicultural curriculum offers guidelines for moving beyond these contradictions. When teachers accept the goal of developing competencies in multiple systems of standards for perceiving, evaluating, believing and doing, it becomes obvious that knowledge about multiple dialects and languages is part of becoming educated. A society and a world comprised of linguistically different peoples require the ability to interpret an array of verbal and nonverbal communication modes to at least minimal degrees, and accurate interpretation requires some degree of empathy. Of course, it is unrealistic to expect that most people could ever become proficient in more than a few languages. Most North Americans can thrive with only one language, provided that language is English, so there is often little motivation to become bilingual or multilingual. The opportunity exists, however. Consider Table 6.1, which gives some indication of the language diversity within the United States.

At the very least, it is possible and imperative that we become proficient with one or more of the most prevalent dialects or languages that co-exist with our native tongue, be it English, Spanish, Chinese, or Appalachian dialect. The process of adding even one new dialect or language to our repertoire strengthens awareness of cultural conflicts and misconceptions that emerge from verbal and nonverbal cues associated with different languages. It becomes easier to understand how others misperceive and are misperceived.

The important role of language instruction in developing intercultural competence is discussed in the next chapter, and Chapter 8 will develop the concept of bilingual education more fully.

Literature and the arts provide other rich sources for developing informed student empathy. Short stories, poems, song lyrics, drama, and pieces of visual art often hold messages about universal human experiences and emotions such as love, grief, anger, protest, and death. Testaments to the human spirit, which thrives under even the most oppressive conditions, are found in spirituals created by Black people during slavery in the American South and in poems and drawings created by young Japanese American children and Jewish children who were imprisoned in concentration camps during World War II. A story such as *Annie and the Old One* can help young non-Indian children relate to humans who live in a culture that differs from their own.[86] Annie is a young Navajo girl who tries to halt time to delay the death of her beloved grandmother, whose time to die is drawing near. Each night Annie unravels the rug her grandmother is weaving in order to delay her grandmother's death, which will come when the rug is completed. Although Annie is unable to prevent the inevitable, her grandmother teaches her how to face life and accept death. The experience or fear of losing a loved one is something with which most children can empathize.

Literature and artistic achievements by one's own people provide sources of identity and pride within the individual, and sources of respect from others. They can help expand students' readiness for em-

Table 6.1 *Language Diversity in the United States: Percentage of School-Age Population Speaking Language Other Than English at Home*

LOCATION	LANGUAGE
15% and Over	
California	German, Italian, Spanish, Polish, Yiddish, French, Russian, Hungarian, Swedish, Greek, Norwegian, Dutch, Japanese, Chinese, Serbo-Croatian, Portuguese, Danish, Arabic, Tagalog, Armenian, Turkish, Persian, Malay (Indonesian), Scandinavian, Basque, Mandarin, Gypsy (Romani)
Arizona	Spanish, Uto-Aztecan
New Mexico	Spanish
Texas	Spanish
Alaska	South Alaskan, Eskimo, North Mexico
Florida	Spanish
New York	German, Italian, Spanish, Polish, Yiddish, French, Russian, Hungarian, Swedish, Greek, Norwegian, Slovak, Dutch, Ukrainian, Lithuanian, Czech, Chinese, Portuguese, Danish, Finnish, Arabic, Rumanian, Balto-Slavic, Celtic, Hebrew, Armenian, Near Eastern Arabic dialects, Turkish, Uralic, Albanian, Persian, Scandinavian, Amerindian, Dalmatian, Breton, Mandarin, Egyptian, Georgian, Gypsy (Romani), Athabascan
Hawaii	Japanese, Tagalog, Polynesian
10.0–14.9%	
Nevada	Spanish
Colorado	Spanish
Illinois	German, Italian, Spanish, Polish, Yiddish, Russian, Swedish, Greek, Norwegian, Slovak, Dutch, Ukrainian, Lithuanian, Czech, Serbo-Croatian, Danish, Balto-Slavic
New Jersey	German, Italian, Polish, Yiddish, Russian. Hungarian, Slovak, Dutch, Ukrainian
Connecticut	Italian, Polish, French

Sources: Theodore Andersson and Mildred Boyer, *Bilingual Schooling in the United States* (Washington, D.C.: U.S. Office of Education, 1970), pp. 26–27; and U.S. Bureau of the Census, *General Social and Economic Characteristics* (Washington, D.C., 1980), Figure 7, p. 10g.

pathy. Self-knowledge, self-acceptance, and security are necessary before people can understand and accept others with whom they may disagree. Furthermore, literature and the arts provide numerous opportunities for asking students to imagine themselves as someone else. What is a certain character feeling? What is the artist or composer expressing?

The selection and interpretation of appropriate materials from literature can be problematic, however. In an excellent publication by the National Council of Teachers of English, *Black Literature for High School Students*, authors Barbara Dodds Stanford and Karima Amin state that most teachers agree that Black literature can help foster interracial understanding. However, teachers differ in their interpretations of literature and in their views about what literature is appropriate.

> Whites tend to react favorably to books in which white people behave generously and kindly, and often do not notice when behavior is somewhat patronizing and fails to bring about meaningful change for black people. *To Kill a Mockingbird . . .* is probably the best example of a book which many white teachers feel promotes positive interracial attitudes by showing Atticus' courage. Most black teachers, however, point out that Atticus, in fact, compromised and survived in a destructive social system, and that for the blacks in the novel, Atticus' "heroism" was a paternalistic insult. In a just system, Tom Robinson would never have needed defending—and Atticus would not have been a hero.[87]

These caveats are not limited to Black literature. They apply to all literature, where racist or sexist themes are evident.

On the other hand, in books that avoid White paternalism and provide the realities of barrio, reservation, or ghetto life—such as *The Autobiography of Malcolm X* and Dick Gregory's *Nigger*—four-letter words and dialect are often objected to. Some teachers, minority and nonminority alike, fear these works will reinforce negative stereotypes about the ethnic groups portrayed. They also find that White students are sometimes so disturbed by Black, Chicano, or American Indian hatred of Whites that they cannot get beyond feelings of anger, grief, or guilt. Such reactions are understandable and need to be expressed, provided the environment is caring and supportive. However, there is often a danger that students will remain in a state of either nonempathy or overempathizing.

These risks can be minimized with careful instruction. For example, among ethnically encapsulated students whose only contact with culturally different people has been through myths and cruel stereotypes, it may be helpful to begin with ethnically different people of similar backgrounds, values, and social class. Regional and class prejudices will then not have to be dealt with along with their ethnic bias.

> White middle-class students, even if they are from prejudiced backgrounds, should be able to empathize with the characters in *It's Good to Be Black, Mary McLeod Bethune,* and *My Life with Dr. Martin King, Jr.* Working-class, urban white students may find that they can identify with Althea Gibson, Connie Hawkins, or Gordon Parks.[88]

Conclusions

The concept of unity through human similarities is undoubtedly the most important aspect of curriculum reform. Awareness of the common features of human life and the ways humans are interconnected is vitally necessary to achieving intergroup cooperation and harmony. The possibilities of what might be achieved are vividly illustrated by Lee Anderson's "World-Centered Schools" in *Schooling and Citizenship in a Global Age: An Exploration of the Meaning and Significance of Global Education.*[89] The philosophy behind his world-centered schools generated five overarching purposes:

- To develop students' understanding of themselves as individuals.
- To develop students' understanding of themselves as members of the human species.
- To develop students' understanding of themselves as inhabitants and dependents of planet Earth.
- To develop students' understanding of themselves as participants in global society.
- To develop within students the competencies requisite to living intelligently and responsibly as individuals, human beings, earthlings, and members of global society.[90]

How these purposes came to life in elementary schools is captured by the following chart, which was dramatically displayed in one of the classrooms.

What Do You Know About Being Human?

1. How are human beings like all other living things?
2. How are human beings more like some living things than others?

   Are you more like animals than plants? How?
   Are you more like a jelly fish or a bird? How?
   Are you more like a bear or a lizard? How?
   Are you more like a monkey or a cow? How?

3. How are human beings unlike all other living things?[91]

At World Middle School, the emphasis was understanding human culture, a program called "The Human Way of Living." The high school's curriculum was organized around five major programs.

- Studies of individual development and behavior
- Studies of the human species
- Studies of humankind's planetary and cosmic environments
- Development of human competencies
- Social service, political action, and work-study[92]

How can we develop this perspective in the absence of adequate resources and curriculum materials? Considerations such as the following can become instructional tools when used as evaluative criteria with even the weakest materials.

1. Look for evidence of ethnocentrism, the view that one's culture is the standard by which other cultures should be judged.
2. Look for evidence that foreign countries are seen too simplistically, with no discussion of the various microcultures within each society. Make the same evaluation with respect to ethnic groups: Are all members of a particular group assumed to share similar ideas, habits, and values, or is the diversity within each group recognized?
3. Consider whether the text presents conflicts between groups, nations, or cultures in an overly simple manner: White settlers versus Indians, the North versus the South during the American Civil War, labor versus management, the Communists versus the "Free World."
4. Watch for subtle suggestions that the so-called advanced civilizations are superior to, or must offer guidance to, less modern societies.
5. Look for evidence of confusion arising from ignorance of specific cultures: for example, traditional Chinese women pictured in the dress of traditional Japanese women.
6. Look for the erroneous use of Western assumptions to evaluate non-Western settings. For example, if an author states that "Many Islamic males are non-monogamous," does the word "non-monogamous" itself carry overtones that may mislead the reader?
7. Consider whether the learner is encouraged to imagine the world as others might see it, to understand the perceptions and interpretations of other cultures.
8. Look for a recognition that, despite cultural differences, people in all societies share the basic similarities of being human.[93]

---

1. Minority perspective and ethnic diversity
2. Ethnic diversity and stereotype
3. Jewish American origins and African American origins
4. Orthodox, Conservative, and Reform Jews
5. Black American perspectives and American Indian perspectives
6. Mexican American and Japanese American perspectives
7. Impact of racism on Whites and on non-Whites in the United States

Compare and Contrast

Activities and Questions

1. How have distortions of African history contributed to racism? Which came first, racism or distortion? Explain.

2. Read *Black Elk Speaks* by John G. Neihardt. How would you describe the great Sioux leaders? How did they become powerful? In your opinion, how did the sacred hoop become broken? Could it ever be restored?

3. Read *Further Reflections on Ethnicity*, a collection of essays by Michael Novak, author of *Rise of the Unmeltable Ethnics*. Describe the White ethnic perspective. To what degree is this perspective compatible with non-White ethnic perspectives in this society?

4. What are some ways courses outside the humanities and social sciences (particularly physical sciences, mathematics, and physical education) can help develop informed empathy? Brainstorm in small groups to generate lists of ideas and share the results with the other participants in your class or workshop.

5. A common misconception is that pride in one's own culture and ethnic group breeds intolerance and ethnocentrism toward other cultures and ethnic groups. How would you clear up this misinterpretation about interethnic relations?

6. How do you respond to Jack Forbes's statement on the usurpation of Indian lands and resources? As quoted earlier, Forbes wrote: "It must be openly acknowledged that Indians are poor because white people are rich, that the land, timber and minerals which white people use to produce their wealth were virtually all taken by force or deception. It must be recognized that Indian reservations usually exist in marginal land, not originally of value from the perspective of white economic development."[94] Is there any way of resolving this conflict? Explain.

7. Freedom of thought and expression sometimes conflicts with school censorship policies as well as the desire to eliminate racism from the curriculum. Questions such as the following need to be addressed. Explain your answers.

   a. Should racist books be eliminated from schools, including the library shelves?
   b. Can books that contain profanity and ethnic dialects be used without reinforcing negative stereotypes? Should they be used?

8. Given the fact that approximately 90 percent of our genetic makeup is identical to that of other humans, and less than 3 percent determines biological characteristics associated with race, why is race so important in our society today?

Notes

1. Basil Davidson, *African Kingdoms* (New York: Time-Life Books, 1966).
2. Ibid., p. 29.

3. Edgar A. Toppin, "The Forgotten People," *Christian Science Monitor*, March 6, 1969.

4. John Hope Franklin, *From Slavery to Freedom* (New York: Alfred A. Knopf, 1967), p. 15.

5. Davidson, *African Kingdoms*, pp. 83–84.

6. Toppin, "Forgotten People."

7. Davidson, *African Kingdoms*, p. 22.

8. Ibid.

9. Mary Frances Berry and John W. Blassingame, *Long Memory: The Black Experience in America* (New York: Oxford University Press, 1982), pp. 1–6.

10. Davidson, *African Kingdoms*, p. 82.

11. Ibid.

12. Ibid., p. 21.

13. Ibid.

14. David Wiley, "The African Connection," *Wisconsin Alumnus* 77, no. 2 (January 1976):7–11.

15. Astair Zikiros and Marylee Wiley, *Africa in Social Studies Textbooks* (East Lansing: African Studies Center, Michigan State University, 1978), p. 15.

16. Ibid.

17. *Stereotypes, Distortions and Omissions in U.S. History Textbooks* (New York: Council on Interracial Books for Children, 1977), p. 16.

18. Beryle Banfield, "How Racism Takes Root," *The UNESCO Courier*, March 1979, p. 31.

19. Jack Forbes, *Education of the Culturally Different: A Multi-Cultural Approach* (San Francisco: Far West Laboratory for Educational Research and Development, 1969), p. 50.

20. Rutledge M. Dennis, "Socialization and Racism: The White Experience," in *Impacts of Racism on White Americans*, ed. Benjamin P. Bowser and Raymond G. Hunt (Beverly Hills, Calif.: Sage Publications, 1981), pp. 71–85.

21. Ibid.

22. Ibid., p. 82.

23. Ibid.

24. Maldwyn Allen Jones, *American Immigration* (Chicago: University of Chicago Press, 1960), p. 79.

25. Joe R. Feagin, *Racial and Ethnic Relations* (Englewood Cliffs, N.J.: Prentice-Hall, 1978), p. 247.

26. Ibid., pp. 287–88.

27. Ibid., pp. 288–89.

28. Carey McWilliams, *North from Mexico: The Spanish-Speaking People of the United States* (New York: Greenwood Press, 1968), p. 77.

29. Joseph Hraba, *American Ethnicity* (Itasca, Ill.: F. E. Peacock, 1979), p. 241.

30. Feagin, *Racial and Ethnic Relations*, p. 338.

31. Bill Hosokawa, *NISEI: The Quiet Americans* (New York: William Morrow, 1969), pp. 329–30.

32. M. Browning Carrott, "Prejudice Goes to Court. The Japanese and the Supreme Court of the 1920s," *California History* (Summer 1983):122–39.

33. Lowell K. Y. Chun-Hoon, "Teaching the Asian-American Experience," in *Teaching Ethnic Studies: Concepts and Strategies*, ed. James A. Banks (Washington, D.C.: National Council for the Social Studies, 1973), p. 139. Quotations from this source, the NCSS 43rd Yearbook, are reprinted by permission of the publisher.

34. Ibid., p. 122.

35. Ibid.

36. Berry and Blassingame, *Long Memory*, p. 30. Quotations from this source are reprinted by permission.

37. Ibid., p. 31.

38. Ibid.

39. *More Than Bows and Arrows*, Cinema Associates, Seattle, Wash., 1978.

40. Hraba, *American Ethnicity*, p. 212; and Feagin, *Racial and Ethnic Relations*, p. 120.

41. John Collier, *Indians of the Americas* (New York: New American Library, 1947), p. 4.

42. Feagin, *Racial and Ethnic Relations*, p. 219.

43. Ibid.

44. Hraba, *American Ethnicity*, pp. 212–13.

45. D'Arcy McNickle, "Indian and European: Indian-White Relations from Discovery to 1887," in *The Emergent Native Americans*, ed. Deward E. Walker, Jr. (Boston: Little, Brown, 1972), pp. 75–86.

46. Virgil J. Vogel, *This Country Was Ours* (New York: Harper and Row, 1972), p. 70.

47. Hraba, *American Ethnicity*, p. 214.

48. Ibid., p. 225.

49. Jack D. Forbes, "Teaching Native American Values and Cultures," in *Teaching Ethnic Studies: Concepts and Strategies*, ed. James A. Banks (Washington, D.C.: National Council for the Social Studies, 1973), p. 217.

50. David Levering Lewis, *When Harlem Was in Vogue* (New York: Alfred A. Knopf, 1981), p. 15.

51. *Chinese Americans, Realities and Myths*, multimedia kit, The Association of Chinese Teachers (TACT) Curriculum Materials, 74-6A Ninth Avenue, San Francisco, Calif. 94118; Stan Steiner, *Fusang: The Chinese Who Built America* (New York: Harper and Row, 1979).

52. Lawrence W. Levine, *Black Culture and Black Consciousness* (Oxford, Eng.: Oxford University Press, 1977), p. 397.

53. Carlos E. Cortez, "Teaching the Chicano Experience," in *Teaching Ethnic Studies: Concepts and Strategies*, ed. James A. Banks (Washington, D.C.: National Council for the Social Studies, 1973), p. 191.

54. Thomas Sowell, *Ethnic America: A History* (New York: Basic Books, 1981), pp. 71–72. Quotations from this source are reprinted by permission of the publisher. Copyright © 1981 by Basic Books, Inc.

55. Ibid., p. 72.

56. Ibid., p. 77.

57. Ibid., p. 76.

58. Ibid., p. 77.

59. Ibid., p. 78.

60. Ibid., p. 80.

61. Ibid., p. 81.

62. Ibid., index.

63. Feagin, *Racial and Ethnic Relations*, p. 170.

64. See Thomas Sowell, ed., *Essays and Data on American Ethnic Groups* (Washington, D.C.: The Urban Institute, 1978), pp. 7–64.

65. Ibid., p. 7.

66. Ibid., p. 9.

67. Berry and Blassingame, *Long Memory*, p. 37.

68. Ibid., p. 36.

69. Sowell, *Ethnic America*, p. 10.

70. Ibid., p. 11.

71. Ibid., p. 41.

72. Ibid., p. 46.

73. Ibid., p. 22.

74. Ibid., p. 23.

75. Berry and Blassingame, *Long Memory*, pp. 80–81.

76. Ibid., p. 80.

77. Ibid., p. 84.

78. John Langston Gwaltney, *Drylongso: A Self-Portrait of Black America* (New York: Vintage Books, 1980), p. xxviii.

79. Ibid., pp. 73–74.

80. Rudolph Fisher, "High Yaller," *The Crisis* (NAACP), 1925.

81. Gwaltney, *Drylongso*, pp. 85–86.

82. David Dufty, Susan Sawkins, Neil Pickard, Jim Power, and Ann Bowe, *Seeing It Their Way: Ideas, Activities and Resources for Intercultural Studies* (London: Reed Education, 1976), p. 42.

83. Ibid.

84. Ibid.

85. Feliciano Rivera, "The Teaching of Chicano History," in *The Chicanos: Mexican American Voices*, ed. Edward W. Ludwig and James Santibañez (New York: Penguin, 1971), p. 200.

86. Miska Miles, *Annie and the Old One*, ill. Peter Parnall (Boston: Little, Brown, 1971).

87. Barbara Dodds Stanford and Karima Amin, *Black Literature for High School Students* (Urbana, Ill.: National Council of Teachers of English, 1978), p. 10.

88. Ibid., pp. 11–12.

89. Lee Anderson, *Schooling and Citizenship in a Global Age: An Exploration of the Meaning and Significance of Global Education* (Bloomington: Social Studies Development Center, Indiana University, 1979).

90. Ibid., pp. 438–39.

91. Ibid., p. 447.

92. Ibid., p. 464.

93. This list is based in part on Dufty et al., *Seeing It Their Way*, p. 149.

94. Forbes, "Teaching Native American Values and Cultures," p. 217.

Chapter 7

A Multicultural Curriculum: Goals, Assumptions, and Strategies

What does it mean to teach from a multicultural perspective? What are the goals, the intended outcomes? What crucial assumptions are made when these goals are accepted? What evidence, if any, indicates that these goals are attainable? The purpose of this chapter is to provide answers to these questions.

Goals and Assumptions[1]

Curriculum can be viewed as all the experiences, both planned and unplanned, that learners have under the auspices of the school. Following this definition, a pluralistic curriculum is one that must attend to the operations of the school's hidden curriculum—for example, teacher's values and expectations, student cliques and peer groupings, and school regulations. It must also attend to the values, learning styles, knowledge, and perceptions that all students bring to the school. A pluralistic curriculum, in its broadest sense, influences the total school environment.

Here, however, the focus will be limited to those planned experiences in school that are intended to develop student understandings, values, attitudes, and behaviors related to four interrelated goals of multicultural education: (1) the development of historical perspectives and cultural consciousness, (2) the development of intercultural competence, (3) the reduction of racism and ethnic prejudice and discrimination, and (4) the development of social action skills (see Figure 7.1). In combination these goals provide guidelines for helping students expand their capacity to perceive, evaluate, and comprehend different beliefs and behaviors.

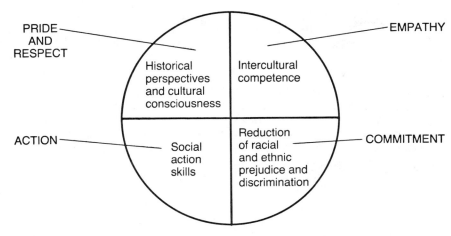

Figure 7.1   *Goals of a Multicultural Approach to Teaching*

Goal One:
The Development of Historical Perspectives and Cultural Consciousness

Historical and anthropological perspectives involve knowledge of the world views, heritage, and contributions of diverse cultures, including consciousness of one's own culture. Subject matter from the fields of history, literature, and the arts can be used to provide understanding about an ethnic group's contemporary culture, world view, and differing interpretations of human events. This knowledge builds an awareness of historical and contemporary developments among the nation's diverse ethnic groups, awareness of traditional and contemporary attitudes held by the members of the macroculture with respect to these groups, and knowledge about minority perspectives.

Content that builds within each student a sense of pride and ethnic identity is central, as is content about the achievements of other cultures. Therefore, teachers could use subject matter that has traditionally been confined to ethnic studies courses such as Black history, Mexican American literature, Native American cultures, and White ethnics, as well as world culture courses. Teachers would use this content in ways that would encourage students to get at the underlying values and patterns of socialization of a particular culture rather than focusing only on the more superficial cultural trappings (such as foods and holidays), heroes, and historical events.

Every classroom offers opportunities for developing historical perspectives and cultural consciousness. Students can interview family members about their own ethnic roots and experiences. Bulletin boards can display people of the week or points of view on a variety of topics, or who's who in math, music, science, and so on. A multicultural calendar provides an excellent way to introduce students to people from many ethnic groups.

> Celebrating the birthdays of specific men and women can bring these people to life as students learn about their contributions. Focusing on events significant in the history of various ethnic groups in the United States is an effective way of informing all students about this country's multiethnic heritage. Information about these groups will provide the minority group student special opportunities to identify with his or her history.[2]

The multicultural calendar is a useful teaching aid that can be used for immediate reference and display. The calendar could be modified for junior and senior high school students to highlight people who have contributed to specific fields, such as sports and athletics, science and industry, mathematics, literature, politics, and the arts. Students can help create the calendar by doing research, planning the displays, and doing the art work.

Among the assumptions underlying this goal are the following:

1. People must possess a degree of self- and group esteem, as well as personal security, before they can be empathetic in their interrelations with others.
2. Awareness of the achievements of one's culture group will enhance one's self- and group esteem.
3. Knowledge that corrects misconceptions about certain people (that non-industrialized people, for example, are less civilized than industrialized people) helps destroy the myth of Euro-American superiority.
4. Persons can achieve a psychological balance between cultural pride and identity on the one hand and appreciation of cultures different from their own on the other. (For example, increased group pride does not preclude reduced ethnocentrism.)

Goal Two:
The Development of Intercultural Competence

Intercultural competence is the ability to interpret intentional communications (language, signs, gestures), some unconscious cues (such as body language), and customs in cultural styles different from one's own. The emphasis is on empathy and communication. This goal recognizes that communication among persons of different cultural backgrounds can be hindered by culturally conditioned assumptions made about each other's behavior and cognitions. It is also based on the fact that "the effects of cultural conditioning are sometimes so pervasive that people whose experience has been limited to the norms of their own culture simply cannot understand a communication based on a different set of norms . . . [and] cannot understand why a 'self-evident' communication from them cannot be comprehended by others."[3]

Although this goal clearly overlaps the goal of developing historical perspectives and cultural consciousness, to teach for intercultural competence means going beyond the study of world views, heritage, and contributions associated with a particular people. It means building an understanding of how one is shaped by the values, priorities, language, and norms of one's culture. This knowledge then can grow into the realization that every person's perception of reality is shaped by experience. Once people understand how their own language, experience, and current modes of cognition relate to their own culture, contrasts may be made with the cultural experience and modes of cognition of culturally different others.

The goal of intercultural competence is a major objective of curriculum writers connected with UNESCO's efforts toward international understanding through education.[4] Although these educators have limited the scope of intercultural competence to the international scene, many of the accompanying theories and practices are appropriate for education in a domestic multicultural society.

The work of Harry Triandis and his associates has led to a form of cross-cultural training called a "culture assimilator," a programmed learning approach designed to increase understanding between members of two cultures.

> As the reader of the assimilator goes through the items, he learns to what features in the episodes he should attend, and which aspects he should ignore (discrimination learning). The episodes are selected so that they expose the trainee to situations that emphasize the distinctive features of social situations which he must learn to discriminate. The items are also selected to give the trainee contrasting experiences with situations differing sharply on such features. The training, then, emphasizes the distinctive features of events which make the situation in the other culture most different from the situations that the trainee has already learned in his own culture. As he receives more and more training with related items, he can abstract features which such items have in common. We call such invariances "cultural principles." After the trainee goes through a half a dozen items featuring the same principle, he is presented with a summary sheet in which the principle is stated as a conclusion. Thus, if he has not abstracted the principle by that point, it is given to him.

As an example . . . consider some recent work on black/white subcultural differences. Black subjects have a tendency to assume that all white persons are prejudiced against blacks. This has major implications for social perception in interracial encounters. Almost any behavior of the white can be misinterpreted, if the context in which it is seen reflects prejudice.[5]

Culture assimilators have been developed for a number of nations (such as Israel and Iran) and for Black and White cultures within United States society. To date, these assimilators have been developed entirely for industrial work settings. Similar approaches to multicultural education, however, can be developed for school settings.

While the culture assimilator can alert teachers to potential sources of misunderstanding in verbal and nonverbal communication, it typically does not provide instruction in the host language or host dialect. Language, chorus, drama, and speech teachers have multiple opportunities for building intercultural competence by teaching accurate pronunciation, intonation, syntax, and word meanings associated with different languages and dialects. In classrooms where multiple dialects of English are spoken, for example, teachers can draw from each one to teach the parts of speech and rules of grammar. Similarly, they can build up student vocabulary and analytical thinking skills. Speech teachers can develop understandings of culturally different styles of posturing and other nonverbal cues. Business teachers could include instruction on culturally different expectations concerning punctuality, eye contact, and handshaking or bows during job interviews. Physical educators and directors of athletic events can alert students to culturally different rules, notions of fair play, and body moves associated with certain sports.

Some of the assumptions underlying this goal are as follows:

1. Language is at the heart of culture and cognition.
2. People's effectiveness in multicultural communication can be improved by developing their cultural self-awareness (their abilities to recognize cultural differences in their own cognitions).
3. There are modes of human communication that can transcend cultural barriers.
4. Certain dimensions of the different cultures in our society, such as the Black experience, are static enough to be identified, defined, and taught.
5. Persons can achieve a psychological balance between cultural pride and identity on the one hand, and appreciation of cultures very different from their own on the other (that is, increased intercultural contact will not necessarily lead to cultural assimilation).

Goal Three:
The Reduction of Racism and Ethnic Prejudices and Discrimination

This goal is directed at developing greater awareness of the existence and impact of racism and ethnic prejudice and discrimination in American society as well as within other nations. Distinctions between individual and institutional racism are important. Prejudice and discrimination are studied within the contexts of American and world history, science, literature, and the arts. Teaching efforts aimed at the reduction of racial and cultural prejudice and discrimination are directed at clarifying students' values and at building moral reasoning skills intended to develop understandings, attitudes, and behaviors that are consistent with society's basic ideals, such as liberty, justice, and equal opportunity.

Science and health teachers can teach facts and myths surrounding the concept of race, as well as the biological attributes shared by all humans. Scientists estimate that 90 percent of one's genetic makeup is shared with all members of the human species, leaving only 6 to 7 percent related to gender and racial attributes and the remainder to individual variance. Misconceptions about the origins of the races and erroneous beliefs about the superiority of some races must be cleared up.

Teachers in all content areas can help students develop skills in detecting bias in texts and media. Math and general business teachers can create lessons along the lines of "the loan shark" to teach how racist practices keep some people in a poverty trap, at the same time they teach skills in using percentages and understanding interest rates. Typing teachers can include news articles that discuss racism in their typing skill assignments. Teachers in the humanities can use selected pieces of literature, art, and music to discuss themes related to racism and prejudice.

Positive interracial attitudes can also be fostered without modifying the curriculum extensively if the school population is racially and culturally diverse. Wherever students have a chance to work together to achieve a common goal, chances are excellent for improving mutual respect and appreciation. Sports and team efforts of every kind, musical or dramatic performances, and cooperative class projects are examples of activities many teachers use to develop positive interracial contact experiences. (The necessary ingredients for positive contact will be provided in the next chapter.)

Several crucial assumptions that underlie this goal are:

1. It is worthwhile for educators to focus on the reduction of racial/ethnic prejudice and discrimination even though powerful sectors of the society and the world do not presently value this goal.

2. It is appropriate for schools to teach certain humanistic values, such as the negative effects of racial and ethnic prejudice and discrimination.
3. A reduction of racial/ethnic prejudice and discrimination is possible through appropriate educational experiences.

Goal Four:
Development of Social Action Skills

The goal of developing within all students the knowledge, attitudes, and skills needed to help bring about political, social, and economic changes should not be limited to multicultural education. To the extent that educators value a sense of personal and political efficacy and a participatory orientation among all members of a society, this goal should also be part of any citizenship education program (as should the preceding multicultural goals). However, in view of the fact that certain ethnic groups are unable to gain, maintain, and effectively use political power, to ignore this goal is to make a sham out of the three goals that remain in the cluster.

Although a number of educators have pointed out the necessity for schools to help youth become more effective agents of change, very few curricula have been developed toward this end. Political socialization research, however, offers numerous insights indicating the types of curricula that may be effective in giving youth the knowledge, skills, and attitudes necessary to achieve the role of change agents (active participators within and outside the classroom).[6] Bradbury Seasholes expressed the essence of this goal when he wrote:

> Perhaps the greatest contribution educators can make to school-age . . . [youth] who will be tomorrow's adult citizens is to reorient their thinking about the development and use of political strategy. This means spelling out with approval the various techniques of bargaining, forced demands, concession and occasional retreat that are used by politically successful subgroups in our society. It means being candid on two scores when dealing with heterogeneous groups of students in the classroom—candid about the probable maximum of political potential that a given subgroup could have (just how successful groups can expect to be, given their total resources of numbers, money, effort, education, and so forth) and candid about the kinds of political techniques that are in fact being used currently or may be used in the reasonably near future.
>
> Political activity in this day and age, after all, involves not only voting, contributing money, and writing letters to congressmen. It sometimes involves street demonstrations and civil disobedience. These need talking out in the classroom, too, not in normative terms but in terms of strategies which sometimes succeed or fail

because they tread so close to the border of normatively acceptable political behavior.[7]

In addition to these facts, students need opportunities to make choices and evaluate their decisions. They need to practice self-expression, decision-making skills, and problem resolution. This practice can begin in kindergarten with opportunities to make simple choices, express opinions, set goals, and discuss classroom rules.

Underlying this focus are the following assumptions:

1. The subjugation and unjust treatment of any cultural group dehumanizes everyone.
2. Most people will, at some time in their lives, find themselves in the position of being a political minority.
3. All groups in society should have equal opportunity to bring about social and political change.
4. We value political access and participation for all citizens.
5. The more learners can actively participate in decision-making activities and work on self-selected problems beyond the classroom, the more likely they are to increase their feelings of personal and political effectiveness.

These four goals are overlapping, and each one individually represents a necessary but insufficient focus for multicultural education. For example, to increase cultural consciousness without also developing the understanding, skills, and attitudes that cluster around intercultural competence might lead to greater ethnocentrism and polarization. It would be impossible to develop people's intercultural competence (such as empathy) without also developing their senses of personal identity and security, which come with cultural consciousness. Furthermore, both these goals should foster an appreciation of both human similarities and ethnic diversity and an awareness of how racism and certain prejudices originate and subjugate. The fourth goal, enabling people to become change agents, goes beyond study and discussion and deals with the skills and behaviors needed to eradicate discriminatory practices as well as to bring about other desired changes.

This conceptualization of multicultural education as a cluster of goals does not mean that in individual courses teachers must stress each goal equally. What it does mean is that these four goals must be woven into an overall curriculum design that allows separate subject areas and courses to emphasize those goals that are most effectively dealt with inside the subject matter boundaries and age groupings of a particular school system. In some school settings, for example, historical perspectives and cultural consciousness might be emphasized in literature and the arts; intercultural competence in language and communications; reduction of racial/ethnic prejudice and discrimination in biology and world and United States history; and social action skills in government, business, or economics.

As another example, a careful sequence of learning experiences designed to foster social action skills could begin in kindergarten with simple decision-making activities and culminate in the final year of high school with a community action project. Ideally, teams of teachers within a school, school system, college, or university would collaborate on the sequencing and articulation of the multicultural curriculum objectives, strategies, and materials.

Strategies for Implementing Multicultural Curriculum Goals: A Sample Decision-Making Guide

With clarification of multicultural education goals, it becomes possible to build them into the curriculum. The following curriculum decision-making worksheet has been used by numerous teachers (kindergarten to adult) as a guide for change. In some cases interdisciplinary teams have worked together to create plans for a single age group. In others, representatives from each grade level have worked together to develop a multicultural content sequence for one or more subject areas.

The decision-making activity is introduced with a brief explanation of the five goals. Initially, full definitions are not provided and participants are encouraged to modify and refine the goals as they wish. Note that the wording for the decision worksheet goals is not identical to the multicultural education goals. This difference is intended to lead to fuller clarification and consideration of wording that is troubling for some, for example, "acceptance and trust," "eradication," and "change agent."

Once the small groups have reached a consensus and have shared their decisions for step one, a fuller explanation of the goals as previously provided should be presented. Participants may then work alone or with others who teach similar content to complete steps two and three. A fourth step may be added to allow participants time to implement, evaluate, and revise their lessons. Problems and successes can be discussed in a group, and a resource booklet of lesson ideas can be printed and distributed.

Plans for Pluralizing the Curriculum: Decision-Making Worksheet

Step One:
Clarifying the Goals
of a Multicultural Curriculum

Listed below are five goal statements concerning some purposes of education necessary in a society comprised of diverse racial and cultural groups. Rank these from one to five, with the first indicating the goal you value most and the fifth, the goal you value least.

Work alone first, then try to reach a consensus with other members of your group. You will have about thirty minutes to complete step one. Choose one member of your group to share your decisions with the large group.

_____ 1. To preserve ethnic heritage, promote ethnic identification, and raise ethnic consciousness.

_____ 2. To increase intercultural competence, including empathy, acceptance, and trust of those from other culture groups, and the ability to interpret customs and nonverbal behavior in differing cultural styles.

_____ 3. To build the skills, knowledge, and values that predominate in the mainstream culture.

_____ 4. To eradicate ethnic and racial prejudice.

_____ 5. To strengthen the social action skills that will enable students to become effective change agents.

The statement we believe identifies the most important goal of a

multicultural curriculum is: _____

_____

Our reasons are the following:

1. _____

2. _____

3. _____

The goal we value least is: _____

_____

Our reasons are the following:

1. _____

2. _____

3. _____

Step Two:
Identifying Objectives for Student Learning

My teaching area is _____. I can pluralize the curriculum in this area by using objectives for student learning such as the following ones.

OBJECTIVE	STUDENT ACTIVITY	EVALUATION
(What I hope will happen to students as a result of the lesson.) Skill, attitude, and/or knowledge based.	(What students will be doing to accomplish my objective.)	(How I will know students have accomplished my objective.)
1. _____	1. _____	1. _____
2. _____	2. _____	2. _____
3. _____	3. _____	3. _____

Step Three:
Writing the Lesson Plan

By yourself or in a small group, write a lesson plan that will help you begin to realize your objectives.

How can these goals be transformed into classroom strategies? This is up to the teacher who is most in tune with the special needs of a particular classroom. The following lesson illustrations are examples that can be modified as needed for any classroom. A number of the lessons have been developed by practicing or preservice teachers who used the multicultural education decision-making worksheet as a guide. The individuals named in the following passages have graciously consented to share their ideas. The lessons, largely unedited, are included here to help illustrate a variety of teacher perspectives.

Historical Perspectives and Cultural Consciousness

Illustration One

What Happens When Different Cultures Meet?

This lesson was developed for high school students. If simplified by the teacher, the overall concepts could be developed among much younger children. The lesson could be incorporated into many disciplines as a guide for understanding the absence or presence of contributions and achievements of various ethnic groups in, for example, the arts, sports, literature, science, or politics.

INSTRUCTIONS

The continuum shown in the following Decision Sheet diagrams what happens in a society where there is one predominant macroculture and any number of microcultures. Point A, cultural assimilation, represents an extreme where the predominant culture (sometimes called the host society) completely absorbs the microculture(s). Point C, suppression, represents the other extreme where the predominant culture keeps the microculture(s) totally separate and suppressed. Point B, cultural pluralism, represents a compromise. Everyone is governed according to laws established by the macroculture, and everyone must follow certain customs as is necessary for harmonious living in one society. At the same time, members of the various ethnic groups or microcultures are encouraged to retain their traditions (such as language, religion, and artistic expressions) if they wish to do so.

Also listed in the Decision Sheet are some of the important ethnic groups that help make up our society. Working together with other members of your group, try to agree on which point on the continuum is the *best* indicator of each group's experience. (We know that most groups have experienced all three, but try to select the most typical experience.) Write the name of the ethnic group on the line above the continuum at the appropriate point. If anyone in your group identifies with one or more of these ethnic groups, mark it with an asterisk (*). Choose one member of your group to share your decisions with the rest of us.

Decision Sheet

Place each of the following groups on the most accurate point on the continuum. Consult the Definition Guide on the next page for the meanings of cultural assimilation, cultural pluralism, and cultural suppression.

SOME IMPORTANT ETHNIC GROUPS IN OUR SOCIETY
LISTED BY NATIONAL ORIGIN OR RELIGION

Irish	Norwegian	Chinese	Amish
Afro-American[a]	Danish	English	Spanish
Jewish	Czechoslovakian	Puerto Rican	Greek
Japanese	Polish	German	Cuban
Italian	Navajo	Sioux	Vietnamese
Mexican			

A   B   C

←————————————————————————————→

Assimilation   Pluralism   Suppression

[a]Refers to people who trace their heritage to a number of different sub-Saharan nations.

Definition Guide

ASSIMILATION	PLURALISM	SUPPRESSION
The ethnic minority group:	*The ethnic minority group:*	*The ethnic minority group:*
• Gives up its original culture • Identifies with and is absorbed into the predominant Anglo–Western European culture • Is no longer identifiable as distinct from the predominant Anglo–Western European culture	• Retains many of its traditions, such as language, religion, artistic expression, and social customs • Adopts many aspects of the predominant Anglo–Western European culture such as language; monogamy; military service; local, state, and federal laws; and full civil rights of citizenship • Develops an ethnic perspective and also identifies with the nation as a whole • Respects and appreciates different ethnic traditions that they may or may not choose to experience	• Is segregated from the rest of society, including schools, churches, jobs, housing, restaurants, etc. • Develops a unique culture, or retains its original culture, or a combination of both • May develop a "dual consciousness" in order to survive
The macroculture:	*The macroculture:*	*The macroculture:*
• Accepts members of other ethnic groups once they give up their original ethnic identity • Views other cultures as unacceptable, inferior, or a threat to social harmony and national unity • Suppresses the culture and contributions of other groups	• Respects and appreciates ethnic diversity • Encourages ethnic minorities to keep many of their traditions alive • May or may not adopt some of society's different ethnic traditions and current way of life	• Regards the ethnic minority as inferior beings • Controls society's economy, government, schools, churches, news and other media • Accepts the doctrine of White supremacy and sets up policies to preserve it • Suppresses the culture and contributions of other groups

The following lesson, by Gayle Reiten, is intended for high school classes in American history, anthropology, literature, or art.

OBJECTIVES
1. Students will develop some familiarity with the traditional cultural values of the northern Great Plains Sioux that still govern and influence their society today.
2. Students will understand how these values shape the world view of the Sioux and influence their response, both individually and as a group, to the macroculture in the United States.

INTRODUCTION

The primary cultural symbol among the Sioux is the circle. It represents Wakan Tanka, the Great Spirit, and is found everywhere within the Lakota world view. The horizon and the four directions form a circle. The traditional dwelling house, the tipi, is a circle. All nature is circular. This circularity means that the Lakota view the world as a whole, not in parts and pieces to be separately analyzed. In this lesson plan the Siouan values will be examined separately, but it is important to remind the class of their interrelatedness.

THE FIRST GREAT VALUE: GENEROSITY AND SHARING

Among the Sioux people the idea of the value of generosity and sharing is very strong. This idea springs from their belief that the earth was the mother from whom they all came. Therefore the land and the food to be found upon it belonged to all; the food that resulted from the hunt or from gathering was shared with all others in the band who needed it.

Generosity and sharing as an ideal led to the custom of the Give-Away, in which any or all of one's possessions are given away in a ceremony to honor someone. The honoree could be a recent college graduate, a young man home from the army, or a dead relative. In this process one honors the Great Spirit, the person to whom one gives, and lastly oneself. However, paradoxical as this may seem, if one gives or shares with the idea of getting honor in return, one destroys the essence of sharing.

For this reason, when someone does something for you unasked, out of kindness, it is very rude to thank the person, for it is as if you were paying for the generosity, a terrible insult among the Sioux. However, if you ask someone to do something for you and the person complies, a thank-you is acceptable.

Another aspect of sharing is that doing and giving of oneself for the benefit of the group is a requirement in Siouan culture. If one has a talent or talents and denies these to one's people, it is wrong. As a result, the Sioux share both praise and shame. For instance, they share in pride for Ben Reifel, one-time congressman from South Dakota, and they share the shame of Siouan drunks lying in the gutter.

Historically: Since the land belonged to all, the Sioux had no concept of property ownership, and often believed when they signed treaties that they were ceding use of the land rather than ownership.

Currently: When a Siouan family moves to an urban area from the reservation in order to better their economic well-being, they often "fail" by non-Indian standards. Many family and friends will come to visit, spend time, create an extended family. However, this may lead to crowded housing conditions and financial strain as all are given enough money to function within the urban environment.

Questions: For the Lakota, what are the strengths connected with holding the value of generosity and sharing in the modern world? What are the weaknesses?

Activity: Some members of the class might wish to research the lives of famous Sioux such as Crazy Horse, Red Cloud, Sitting Bull, Spotted Tail, Billy Mills, Ben Reifel, Ella Deloria, and Vine Deloria (both senior and junior).

THE SECOND GREAT VALUE: RESPECT FOR OLD ONES

The Lakota Sioux have always had great respect for their old ones. The Lakota believed one could not speak from ignorance, and wisdom came only with age. One would be considered a young man or woman until the age of 45 or 50; then perhaps one might be considered a "wicasa"—a man—and to become "really a man" one needed to be more than 60.

This respect for the old ones has led to respect for anyone in authority—a priest, a teacher, a policeman, a judge. One way respect is shown is through aversion of the eyes. Another consequence of respect for elders is the custom whereby children of hospitalized parents spend much of their time, if not all their time, in the hospital with their parents. This is a matter both of respect and of generosity and sharing—the Lakota seldom leave a sick member of the family alone.

Historically: Early missionaries and teachers were confused by the Sioux. "They seem so shifty and dishonest!" "William Noheart never looks me in the eye." These comments reflected non-Indians' lack of understanding of behavior meant to reflect respect. It is still a problem.

Currently: A few years ago, the federal government gave the tribal government of the Standing Rock Sioux money to build a nursing home for the elderly on the reservation. But the home stood empty for years and was finally converted to government offices.

Questions: Why did the Standing Rock Sioux not make use of the government-built nursing home? In what ways does our macroculture treat older ones with respect? In what ways does it not? Do others of us have the same respect for the elderly as do the Sioux? Do we express it differently? In what ways do we show respect to authority, and what kinds of body language do we use?

Activity: Demonstrate the difference between a non-Indian greeting a stranger and the way a Sioux would greet a stranger.

THE THIRD GREAT VALUE: GETTING ALONG WITH NATURE

For the Sioux, getting along with nature meant more than not misusing the natural world. The Lakota people traditionally believed that Wakan Tanka, the Great Spirit, was in all things, in a rock or tree as much as in a person. And this being, this existence of the Great Spirit within each thing, was called that entity's "Innermost"—a concept that might be compared to the non-Indian idea of a soul or spirit. Furthermore, the Sioux saw the earth, through the Great Spirit's power, as mother to all—and all therefore are related to each other.

This leads to the Siouan ideas about respect for the Innermost. Since everyone's Innermost should be respected, out of politeness the Sioux will tell others what they want to hear, and never with the feeling that this is untruthful. They will also avoid telling someone what that person doesn't want to hear. The Sioux believe that when the Innermost is not respected, hurt is always the result. From this develops their great desire to get along with one another and to respect each person's Innermost.

Historically: The buffalo was the heart of the Siouan culture in the eighteenth and nineteenth centuries. Every part of the buffalo was used in some way. Nonetheless, because the Sioux people believed they were related to the buffalo, it could not be wantonly slaughtered. The Sioux would pray for understanding and forgiveness on the part of the buffalo before they began the hunt, and the entire process had a sense of sacred ritual about it.

Currently: Because of the belief among the Sioux that they must "get along together," one will often observe group togetherness, especially among children. But the group togetherness ideal, while a strength, can also be a weakness. For example, there is strong peer pressure among the reservation Sioux not to appear "better" or "different." And the ideal is often shattered by problems with drug and alcohol abuse, the biggest Native American health problem.

Questions: Can you think of some other ways the value of getting along with nature is a strength? A weakness? How does the non-Indian react to these ideas?

Activities: Research the buffalo's history and find out why these animals are now so few in number. Art classes might want to research paintings that portray the Sioux and the buffalo.

On the subject of current Sioux life, learn more about Native American problems with substance abuse, or about the adjustments that urban Indians must make in cities such as Minneapolis, Oakland, Boston, Chicago, and Cleveland.

THE FOURTH GREAT VALUE: INDIVIDUAL FREEDOM

Individual freedom is strongly related to all the other values, for it involves the essence of choice. No one can ever force anyone else's decision. But this is not freedom to run amok. Individual freedom for the Sioux meant freedom to choose to do the right thing. And the most important thing, the most right thing, was whatever would enable survival of the group. The value of sharing was also involved in choosing to help one's relatives and friends.

Since no Sioux had any right to impose his or her will upon another, the Lakota form of government was the most basic of democracies, with all the men and older women meeting together and making decisions. If any of those within the group did not agree with the decisions made, they were free to go. Many times this is exactly what happened, and new bands of the Sioux were created out of disagreement over some fundamental decision.

The respect for individual rights and abilities also led to the Siouan style of leadership. The idea of a "chief," one overall leader, really came from the non-Indian. Leadership depended upon the situation. One man might be best at leading raids on other tribes for horses. Another might be called upon to lead and organize the buffalo hunt. The style of making war was also not forced. If a man wanted to get up a raiding party, only those who chose to go went with him.

There were never any jails among the Sioux. They had two primary methods of social control: ridicule and banishment. Ridicule could run the gamut from gentle teasing of an adolescent who had behaved in a socially unacceptable manner to intense ridicule for an adult who had committed a more serious offense. Stealing among the Sioux was practically unknown, and still is to this day, because of the great respect for the individual. Serious crimes, such as murder, were punished by banishment. Survival on the northern Great Plains without the group was difficult at best—therefore banishment could be equivalent to a death sentence.

Historically: Sitting Bull is among the most famous of Sioux leaders, but few non-Indians know that he was not a great warrior leader. Rather, Sitting Bull was a "wicasa wakan," a holy man. Others were the military leaders during the Battle of the Little Big Horn.

Currently: The style of government on Sioux Indian reservations today often leads to a virulent form of reservation politics. Tribal government has democratic forms based on the past; and because of the strong belief in individual freedom, political disagreements can be strong.

However, groups who disagree with one another are no longer free to move.

Questions: In what ways are macroculture beliefs about individual rights the same as the beliefs the Sioux held? In what ways are they different? Does the macroculture value social freedom more than individual freedom, or vice versa? Give examples.

Activity: Read Mari Sandoz's novel *Crazy Horse* and try to determine how Lakota values functioned in making Crazy Horse one of the greatest Sioux leaders.

THE FIFTH GREAT VALUE: BRAVERY

For the Sioux, eagle feathers were the mark of bravery, and they had to be earned. Bravery was a matter of individual freedom; one had to choose to do the right thing. One could never boast about one's own exploits in battle; one allowed someone else, a friend or relative, to do so. Training for bravery began young. Little babies were not allowed to cry, for their cry could give away the location of the people in a tight situation.

A famous war cry the Sioux gave at the Battle of the Little Big Horn was: "Today is a good day to die!" This can only be understood within the context of the Lakota value of bravery. The Sioux believed that if the worst thing one had to fear was death—and if death itself was not really something to be afraid of—then if one died in the process of protecting one's family and people, today was indeed a good day to die. But the Sioux were not fanatic about death, as in some other cultures, and were as afraid of battle as any humans might be. Life itself was the most precious thing the old-time Sioux had, and to give it was the greatest sharing a Sioux warrior could offer.

Historically: The image of the war bonnet with many eagle feathers sweeping down to the ground is basically incorrect. Seldom did any warrior earn enough eagle feathers to create such a bonnet, though headdresses with a number of eagle feathers were possible. Young women could also earn eagle feathers, or wear them by inheritance.

Currently: The Sioux people are intensely patriotic, and in the twentieth century have contributed soldiers for American wars out of all proportion to their population. To fight in the American armed forces for them is still the way to protect the people.

Questions: Is our definition of bravery in the macroculture the same as or different from that of the Sioux? Are some or all of the Siouan values found within the American macroculture? To what degree are these values visible within the macroculture's literary and film images of the Indians?

Activity: Obtain Arthur Kopit's play *Indians* and have the class read, discuss, and/or present it using Sioux values as a basis for the discussion.

ADDITIONAL RESOURCES

Brown, Dee. *Bury My Heart at Wounded Knee.* New York: Holt, Rinehart and Winston, 1970.

Bryde, John F. *Modern Indian Psychology.* Vermillion: University of South Dakota Press, 1971.

Malan, Vernon D., and Jesser, Clinton J. *The Dakota Indian Religion.* Bulletin 473. Brookings: South Dakota State College, 1959.

Illustration Three

Three Views of History

This lesson was developed by David Page for use in a high school journalism or social studies class. The lesson could also fit under the goal of reducing racism, but is included here to exemplify how different ethnic perspectives can be brought to bear on many historic events. Furthermore, racist values are an integral part of United States history and culture.

On December 7, 1941, Japanese armed forces attacked Pearl Harbor. That night 600 Japanese immigrants were picked up by the FBI and held in detention centers. Two months later President Roosevelt signed Executive Order 9066 authorizing exclusion of all people with Japanese ancestry from the West Coast, and their relocation into internment camps. One hundred twenty thousand people were forced from home and put into these camps. Sixty percent of these people were American citizens. Personal possessions of those evacuated were either confiscated by the government, or sold at a fraction of their real worth. Over 30,000 Japanese and Japanese American families were forced to live in these camps from 1942 until 1945. The ostensible reason for their imprisonment was national security. A closer look reveals that many other forces were at work.

OBJECTIVES

1. Students should be able to understand some of the many factors that enable institutionalized racism to exist.
2. Students should be able to identify with victims of racism as fellow human beings.
3. Students should be able to see that not all laws are necessarily just, and that in some cases we must work to change laws for the better.

MATERIALS NEEDED

1. Copies of Executive Order 9066, which gives the U.S. Military the right to exclude any person from any area during wartime.
2. Video recording: *The Politics of War: Japanese Americans 1941–1945,* Chelsea House Educational Communications, 1970, ten minutes. Nonethnic narrator portrays situation of native Ameri-

cans of Japanese ancestry in the wake of Pearl Harbor, explaining war relocation and authority activities, such as Nisei detention camps, property losses, and abridgement of civil rights.

3. Sound recording: *They Chose America: Conversations with Japanese Immigrants*, Princeton, N.J.: Visual Education 5302-05-p 1975 (twenty-nine minutes, use side one only). A Japanese American talks about his experiences in America, before, during and after the war.

The three items listed above give three very different views of the same event. All are true, but all are incomplete when viewed alone.

Executive Order 9066 gives the official view for the internment. It bases its reason for enactment on national security and the right of the federal government to enact such a law during wartime.

The video recording details the events that preceded the enactment of Order 9066; it starts with a description of the social and political position of Japanese and Japanese Americans living on the West Coast before and during the war. This video recording provides an impersonal view of the Japanese internment. It speaks of the Japanese only as a group, not as individual people. The only people who speak are Caucasian historians and a narrator.

The sound recording features an older Japanese American man who was sent to an internment camp as a young adult during the war. He gives his view of what it was like to lose one's home and possessions, and the uncertainty he felt about his future.

Each of the three materials will be presented to the student separately, after which the student will be asked to rate seven statements about the internment of Japanese aliens and Japanese Americans. The statements are as follows:

Strongly agree   1   2   3   4   5   Strongly disagree

1. Japanese and Japanese Americans were interned mainly for national security.
2. Japanese and Japanese Americans were interned mainly for their own safety because Caucasians might think they were the enemy.
3. Japanese and Japanese Americans were interned because of racism.
4. Japanese and Japanese Americans were interned because of scapegoating.
5. Japanese and Japanese Americans were interned because of the economic competition experienced with Caucasians.
6. Americans of Japanese descent were more dangerous than citizens of Italian or German descent.
7. The internment of Japanese Americans during World War II was justified.

EVALUATION

After all questions have been answered, students should compare the three ratings to each other. In most cases students will have changed answers for at least a couple of the questions. Ask the students to write a short paper that details how and why their answers changed.

Illustration Four

Modeling Toward Understanding

This lesson was developed by Elizabeth Ellis for freshmen or sophomores in general ability groups. Prior to this lesson students ask parents and grandparents about the countries of their ancestry. Through this vehicle, with library research if necessary as a supplement, students are to bring to class at least eight facts about one country of their ancestors. Six of these facts should pertain to the physical characteristics of the country and two should be emotional, feelings these families carry about those roots. This plan is designed to develop culture consciousness.

OBJECTIVES

The twofold goal is to let students begin to look into their own cultural backgrounds and to take the first step of writing poetry through imitation. On a larger scale, they will become aware of their classmates' cultural backgrounds.

STRATEGY

Using the following outline, students will plug in the information indicated to complete the poem. Their role will be to assume the guise of someone who really knows and loves the country in question. Sentences do not have to be complete, and traditional grammar concerns fall secondary to creativity. They will be given a copy of my attempt as a guide to show the task does not need to be difficult, and to provide motivation through that reassurance. At the end, copies of Hughes's poem will be distributed for comparison and discussion. Also, each student will later receive copies of the entire class collection of poems.

OUTLINE

I've known _____(place)_____ .
I've known ___(physical fact)___ and ___(physical fact)___ .
_____(emotion—translate feelings about place)_____ .
I ___(verb)___ in ___(physical fact)___ when
_____(time)_____ .
I ___(verb)___ and ___(verb)___ .
I looked ___(physical fact)___ and _____(verb)_____ .
I heard ___(physical fact)___ when _____ .

I've known _____ (place) _____ .

_____ (physical fact) _____ .

____ (emotion—summarize feelings about place) ____ .

MATERIALS
Copies of outline and of teacher's trial run
Copies of Langston Hughes's "The Negro Speaks of Rivers"

Teacher's Try

I've known Ireland.
I've known the interminable staunch greenness and the endless
    drifting rain.
The pall of its rain echoes the cloud of upheaval lying over it.
I cry in Ireland when the bombs rip through.
I learned of the desperation and how it destroys the proud history.
I looked at Dublin and saw a girl sobbing as she walked by the
    Liffey.
I heard the anger and boredom of its young when all seems fruitless
    and false.
I've known Ireland.
Poor, sad, endlessly proud in its ballys and knocks.
Does the horror ever end?

*The Negro Speaks of Rivers**
LANGSTON HUGHES

I've known rivers.
I've known rivers ancient as the world and older than the flow
    of human blood in human veins.

My soul has grown deep like the rivers.

I bathed in the Euphrates when dawns were young.
I built my hut near the Congo and it lulled me to sleep.
I looked upon the Nile and raised the pyramids.
I heard the singing of the Mississippi when
    Abe Lincoln went down to New Orleans,
    and I've seen its muddy bosom turn
    all golden in the sunset.

I've known rivers:
Ancient, dusky rivers.

My soul has grown deep like the rivers.

Evaluation

Students will be asked in a writing assignment for their journals or a similar nongraded (nonthreatening) situation to point out any new facts that they learned about themselves through this assignment and what they learned about their classmates. This would tell me if the poem was worth writing.

Illustration Five

Introduction to the Blues

The purpose of this lesson plan for a music listening class is to expand the student's understanding and enjoyment of the art of music through the development of perceptive listening abilities. This course, developed by Allison Hoadley, is designed for high school juniors and seniors. There is a fairly even distribution of Blacks and Whites, males and females.

Multicultural Goals
- To develop Black and White culture consciousness through the study of a form of music originated by Afro-Americans as an expression of their own emotions and experiences, and through investigating the influence of this musical form on the music of both White and Black Americans.
- To increase intercultural competence through understanding how Blacks and Whites use music as a form of communication to express their attitudes and beliefs.
- To help eradicate racial prejudice through:
  learning a little of the history of Black people in America;
  recognizing the widespread influence of a Black style of music;
  working with students of another race to achieve a common goal.

Behavioral Objectives
1. The student will demonstrate his or her knowledge of how the blues style originated in America by getting at least 75 percent of the answers correct on a short quiz to be given the following class period.
2. The student will be able to accurately describe the general harmonic structure of a standard twelve-bar blues progression on the above quiz.
3. The student will be able to correctly harmonically analyze a twelve-bar progression in a blues song through listening.
4. The student will be able to describe the characteristics of a blues melody and explain how these characteristics affect the moods of the style.
5. Students will create, with the help of a few fellow students, their own blues with original words and melody, to be performed the next class period.

MOTIVATION
A recording of Black blues music—"That's All Right" (Louis Myers)

ACTIVITIES
1. Introduce students to the blues and rouse their interest in the topic by playing a recording of Louis Myers singing "That's All Right." Discuss with them in general terms the type of music they just heard, and briefly define the blues as a form of Afro-American folk music that later gave birth to jazz.
2. Play the recording again; instruct the class to listen for a pattern in the harmony. Once they can perceive the repeating harmonic pattern, play part of the recording once more and tell students to listen for the number of measures of the harmonic pattern. Introduce the term "twelve-bar blues."
3. Play the chord progression slowly on the piano. Students will listen and write out the chords being played in each bar:

1	2	3	4	5	6	7	8	9	10	11	12
I^7	I^7	I^7	I^7	IV^7	IV^7	I^7	I^7	V^7	IV^7	I^7	V^7

Discuss the chord progression in a standard twelve-bar blues.
4. Play a recording of "Graveyard Dream Blues" (Bessie Smith). Instruct the students to hold up one, four, or five fingers according to the I, IV, and V chords they hear. Play part of the recording again; instruct students to listen to the melody and determine what mood they think is being conveyed, and how the melody contributes to that mood. Discuss briefly melodic differences between this song and the second movement of Haydn's Symphony no. 94 (*Surprise*). Show them the first few bars of the blues melody written out on a blackboard; have students give the pitch inventory. Show and explain the blues scale (with flatted third and seventh); explain how the use of blues notes contributes to the overall mood.
5. Explain the historical development of the blues, importance of emotion in presentation, development of performance practices.
6. Expose the class to additional recordings:
   "Billie's Blues"—Billie Holiday
   "It Ain't Necessarily So"—*Porgy and Bess*, George Gershwin
   "The South's Gonna Do It Again"—Charlie Daniels Band
   Discuss similarities and differences between these and previous examples.
7. Have students team up with one or two other students to create their own blues on a standard progression with words that reflect their own personal feelings and experiences. This will be performed later in the week.

MATERIALS

Recordings:

"That's All Right," Louis Myers, from *Sweet Home Chicago*

"Graveyard Dream Blues," Bessie Smith, from *Any Woman's Blues*

"Billie's Blues," Billie Holiday, from *Billie Holiday's Greatest Hits*

"It Ain't Necessarily So," George Gershwin, *Porgy and Bess* (Odyssey Records)

"The South's Gonna Do It Again," Charlie Daniels Band, from *Fire on the Mountain* (Epic Records)

A piano

Melodies and notation written on blackboard

EVALUATION

1. Students' knowledge concerning the origin, historic developments, and structure of the blues will be assessed through a short quiz to be given the next class period.

2. Students' understanding of the terms and concepts presented will be evaluated through their participation or lack of participation in the discussion.

3. Students' harmonic listening ability may be perceived through checking their written analysis of the chords of a blues progression played on the piano and through watching them raise the correct number of fingers when listening to a recording.

4. Students' ultimate understanding of the nature of blues can be observed through experiencing their own original performance in this style.

Illustration Six

Folk Dancing

This lesson was developed by Rhea Townley for use in physical education programs.

MULTIETHNIC GOALS

1. Develop cultural consciousness for both German culture and Israeli culture.

2. Build social action skills by pairing students of different races, sexes, and ethnic groups for dancing and by the whole group working together in a circle dance.

3. Build acceptance interpretation of nonverbal behavior of these cultures.

OBJECTIVES

1. Student will be able to perform the German dance Ländler and the Israeli dance Cherkessia.

2. Student will be able to understand the movements in the dance as it is understood by these two different cultures.

LESSON OPENER

Discuss square dancing and tell students that American square dancing is composed of international dances. The Americans changed them to fit their personality and characteristics.

Much personality and character is seen in dances. While we learn the two following dances, let's see what we can learn about these people and their cultures.

ACTIVITY

1. Teach the Ländler.
2. Divide the class in small groups and discuss what this dance can tell them about the German people. Have the students make a list.
3. Teach the Cherkessia.
4. Divide into small groups, as previously done, and discuss the meaning of this dance. Have students make another list as before.
5. Now, have class members discuss their feelings on both dances. Emphasize that the Ländler shows us the Germans are happy, hardy, fun-loving people who love to stomp out a good tune. The Cherkessia shows the joy and sadness of the tragic Jewish past.

MATERIALS

1. *Teaching Physical Education in Elementary Schools* by Vannier and Gallahue is a useful book for the teacher.
2. Records:
   Sonart Folk Dance Album M8
   Victor 20448

EVALUATION

1. Have students perform both dances in small groups.
2. Have students choose one dance and write a one-page paper about what the dance tells them about that specific culture.

This lesson plan was written by Brad Purlee.

Illustration Seven

Heart Attack!

OBJECTIVES

1. The student should be able to describe what happens to the body during a heart attack. Minimum acceptable performance would include the description of at least three of the items discussed in class.
2. The student should be able to describe the emergency treatment and medical care for victims of a heart attack. Minimum accept-

able performance would include the description of at least three of the treatments discussed in class.

3. Given a model of the heart, the student should be able to identify the atria, ventricles, and valves and describe their functions. Minimum acceptable performance would include correctly identifying and describing the function of four of the six components of the heart.

4. The student should be able to describe Dr. Daniel Hale Williams's contribution to heart surgery, to the schooling of Black women wishing to become nurses, and the effects of these contributions on the medical profession. Minimum acceptable performance would include a brief report discussing each item.

STRATEGY

1. What causes heart attacks?
   a. Discussion of the importance of oxygen to cells and how the oxygen gets to the individual cells.
   b. Have members of the class take their pulse rate and compare their results to that of the average healthy person.
   c. Describe what happens to the cells around a blood vessel when it becomes blocked.
   d. Explain some of the causes of blockage.
2. Heart Attack—Care and Treatment
   a. Emphasize the importance of immediate medical attention.
   b. Types of medical personnel qualified to give treatment:
      i. ambulance team
      ii. hospital technicians
      iii. nurses
      iv. doctors
   c. Types of medical treatment:
      i. monitor heartbeat
      ii. give intravenous medication
      iii. administer oxygen
      iv. administer counter shock
      v. open-heart surgery
   d. Guest speaker—local doctor who can explain about open-heart surgery, the recovery process, and give suggestions for good health for people who are recovering from a heart attack.
3. The Heart—its components
   a. Film—*The Heart—An Inside Story.*
   b. The four chambers of the heart—see model of the heart.
      i. location
      ii. function
   c. The two valves of the heart—see model of the heart.
      i. location
      ii. function

     d. The vessels leading to and from the heart—see model of the
        heart.
        i. location
        ii. function
  4. Dr. Daniel Hale Williams—first surgeon to perform open-heart
    surgery.
     a. Born January 18, 1858, in Hollidaysburg, Pennsylvania.
     b. Began his study of medicine in 1878.
     c. In 1883 graduated from Chicago Medical College (now North-
       western University) and opened a practice on the south side
       of Chicago.
     d. Founded Provident Hospital in 1891—included in its organi-
       zation was the first nurse's training school for Black women
       in the United States.
     e. In 1893, performed the first open-heart surgery—saving the
       patient's life.
     f. Later worked to further the cause of civil rights.
     g. Only Black charter member of American College of Surgeons.
     h. Died August 4, 1931.

MATERIALS
Stopwatches
Guest speaker
Film—*The Heart—An Inside Story* (available from the Southern In-
    diana Education Film Center)
Film projector and screen
Model of the heart

EVALUATION STRATEGY
    A short multiple-choice test will be given to test the student's
achievement on each of the four segments in the strategy section. In
addition, a brief report on the contributions of Dr. Daniel Hale Williams
will be required.

Intercultural Competence

These lessons were developed by Pamela L. and Iris M. Tiedt in their
handbook of activities for multicultural teaching. In the following passage, the Tiedts focus on Spanish and suggest activities that could be
adapted to any language.*

**Illustration
Eight**

Focusing on
Language

*Excerpt from Pamela L. Tiedt and Iris M. Tiedt, *Multicultural Teaching: A
Handbook of Activities, Information, and Resources* (Boston: Allyn and Bacon, 1979),
pp. 80–84. Reprinted by permission.

NOBODY SPEAKS MY LANGUAGE

Give students a taste of what foreigners experience by setting up the classroom as a foreign country. For a brief period, everyone (including the teacher) will pretend that they cannot understand what anyone else says (or writes). Hide all written material so that students will not see anything in a familiar language. Students will have to communicate by pointing, gesturing, and acting out.

At the end of the specified time, discuss how everyone felt. How would this experience be similar to or different from that of a foreigner coming to this country for the first time? Was there anything they wanted to communicate but could not? How could they help someone in a similar situation?

A LOCAL LANGUAGE SURVEY

Do students know what languages are spoken in their area? Begin with the local place names. What languages have influenced local names? Ask families. What languages are spoken in the students' families? Do students know people who speak different languages?

Make a map or chart of the area on which to record the information students find. Have them research local history to see what the earliest languages were. Were there any native American groups living nearby? What language did they speak and what happened to them? Ask who the first settlers were and what languages they brought with them. Trace the language history down to the present time. Students should be able to discover what the major local language groups are and how long their speakers have been in the area.

Once the major languages are identified, this can become an important resource for further study. Plan lessons around examples from these languages. Bring people in who speak various languages so that students can hear what the languages sound like.

FOCUSING ON SPANISH

Spanish is the most commonly spoken language in the United States other than English. Spanish-speaking Americans have their roots in Mexico, Spain, Puerto Rico, Cuba, and other countries. Most Spanish speakers are spread throughout California and the Southwest. However, students may be surprised to learn that there are large groups of Spanish speakers in Colorado, Massachusetts, and Florida, for example. In addition, almost all major cities such as Chicago and New York have large Spanish-speaking communities. All children should be aware of the Spanish language and the variety of Spanish-speaking cultures represented in the United States.

The following activities are designed to acquaint all students with the Spanish language. They can be used with bilingual programs or classrooms in which only English is spoken. You can use these activities easily whether or not you know Spanish. Encourage Spanish-speaking students to contribute vocabulary and pronunciation information and reward them for their knowledge. If you have no Spanish-speaking students, bring in Spanish language teaching tapes or records for the class to become accustomed to Spanish sounds. The activities given here are not intended to teach students Spanish. They are useful to make non-Spanish speakers aware of Spanish as an interesting and important language and to assure Spanish-speaking students that their ability to speak two languages is valued. Although the activities refer specifically to Spanish, they can be adapted for use with any language. . . .

COMPARING ALPHABETS

Show students how the Spanish alphabet is similar to the English alphabet. Show them how it differs. Write or print the letters on the board, circling the letters that are added, thus:

a	b	c	(ch)	d	e	f
g	h	i	j	k	l	(ll)
m	n	(ñ)	o	p	q	r
(rr)	s	t	u	v	w	x
y	z					

Explain that the letters k and w are used in the Spanish language only when words have been borrowed from other languages (kilómetro and Washington).

LETTER NAMES

What are the names of the letters of the alphabet? English-speaking children will be interested in learning how Spanish-speaking children say the alphabet. Have a child who speaks Spanish say these letters slowly for the group. This is more effective than reading or saying them yourself, for it makes the student aware that knowledge of Spanish can be important in school.

Spanish Letter Names

a	ä	g	hā
b	bā	h	ächā
c	sā	i	ē
ch	chā	j	hōtä
d	dā	k	kä
e	ā	l	ālā
f	äffä	ll	āyā

m	āmā	s	āsā
n	ānā	t	tā
ñ	ānyā	u	ü
o	ō	v	bā
p	pā	w	düblä bā
q	kü	x	ākēs
r	ārā	y	ē grē · āgä (Greek i)
rr	ārrā	z	sätä

COMPARING PHONEMES AND GRAPHEMES

After examining the alphabet letters that are used in writing Spanish, show students the phonemes used in speaking Spanish, some of which are similar to English but none of which are exactly the same. Also show them corresponding graphemes for these phonemes. Here they will notice many differences between Spanish and English, as shown in Box 7.1.

SPANISH PRONUNCIATION

Whether or not you have ever studied Spanish, it is important to be able to pronounce the Spanish that you introduce in your classroom as easily as possible. Use the chart of Spanish phonemes to become familiar with Spanish sounds. Ask Spanish-speaking students to share their knowledge of Spanish and contribute words or demonstrate pronunciations. There is no reason for you as the teacher to be afraid of making mistakes. You can help by making an effort to try Spanish words without having to speak Spanish fluently. Taking at least an introductory Spanish class is, of course, recommended for any teacher's professional development.

VARIETIES OF SPANISH

The information on Spanish presented in this book is very general. There are many varieties of Spanish spoken in the United States, depending on where the speakers live, how long they have lived in this country, and where they came from originally. Spanish in the Southwest is different from Spanish in the Midwest (Chicago), the Northeast, and Florida. Even in New York City, there are important cultural and linguistic differences between persons from Puerto Rico, Cuba, Dominican Republic, Colombia, Ecuador, Peru, Mexico, Venezuela, Bolivia, and other South American communities.

The differences in the Spanish of Latin America are primarily vocabulary and pronunciation. Some vocabulary differences are due to influence from local Indian languages, others to independent development of Spanish.

Box 7.1

Spanish-
English
Phonemes

CONSONANTS	SPANISH	ENGLISH
b	también	rib
	abrir	like v, but with lips almost touching
c	casa	case (before a, o, u)
	nación	cent (before e, i)
ch	chico	church
d	donde	down
	madre	the
f	familia	family
g	gente	like exaggerated h (before e, i)
	gordo	game
h	hacer	silent
j	jugar	like exaggerated h
k	kilómetro	kitchen
l	lástima	little
ll	llena	yellow ⎫ (regional variation)
		million ⎭
m	mañana	morning
n	nada	nothing
ñ	niño	canyon
p	piña	supper
q	queso	key
r	pero	rich
	rico	trilled r
rr	perro	trilled r
s	sala	sad
t	trabajar	time
v	enviar	like b in también
	la vaca	like b in abrir
w	Wáshington	wash
x	examen	exam
	extranjero	sound
	México	hit
y	yo	yes
z	zapato	save

VOWELS		
a	padre	father
e	es	they
i	nida	police
o	poco	poem
u	luna	spoon
	querer	silent after q
ai, ay	traiga	nice

Continued

Box 7.1

Continued

au	auto	m<u>ou</u>se
ei, ey	aceituna	tr<u>ay</u>
eu	deuda	<u>ay</u> plus <u>oo</u>
ia, ya	hacia	<u>y</u>onder
ie, ye	nieve	<u>y</u>es
io, yo	dios	<u>y</u>olk
iu	ciudad	<u>y</u>ule
oi, oy	soy	b<u>oy</u>
ua	guante	<u>w</u>ander
ue	vuelve	<u>w</u>eight
y	y	<u>e</u>ven
ui, uy	muy	<u>we</u>
uo	cuota	<u>woe</u>

The following are examples of different words used in Latin America for *boy*.

Mexico	chamaco	Panama	chico
Cuba	chico	Colombia	pelado
Guatemala	patojo	Argentina	pibe
El Salvador	cipote	Chile	cabro

Pronunciation also varies regionally. The following are some of the differences found.

syllable final *s* becomes *h* or disappears—*estos* is [éhtoh] or [éto]
ll becomes same as *y*—*valla* and *vaya* are alike
syllable final *r* sounds like *l*—*puerta* is [pwelta], *comer* is [komel]

Introduce vocabulary specific to local Spanish-speaking groups by having a variety of children's books available. Many books, written about members of particular groups, take pride in presenting common Spanish words that are special to that group.

Illustration Nine

Negro Spirituals for the School Choir

This multicultural lesson for the high school choir, developed by Arlessa Barnes, is primarily an introduction to the teaching of one or two Negro Spiritual selections to add to the choral repertoire. The plan, of course, would extend beyond one lesson.

MULTICULTURAL GOAL
Developing culture consciousness and intercultural competence.

OBJECTIVE

To understand and become aware of the unique characteristics evident in Negro Spirituals and to become aware of the contributions made to the Spiritual movement by several Black composers and artists. To develop skill in correct pronunciation of Black dialect used in the Spirituals.

PROCEDURE

1. Listen to and discuss the characteristics of one or two Negro Spirituals that have been passed down from the African tradition.

   Suggested listening: any of the below or selected from the Materials (discography).

   Note to teacher: Spirituals have certain distinctive features, syncopated rhythms, call and response technique (or leader and chorus), rich harmonies, etc. Spirituals are emotional expressions of Negro individuals about their particular experiences (an example of an emotional Spiritual is "Sometimes I Feel Like a Motherless Child"). Spirituals also tell of biblical incidents, for example "Joshua Fought the Battle of Jericho." The call and response song form, which is directly of African origin, is present throughout the Afro-American repertoire. A song that employs the leader and chorus arrangement is "Swing Low, Sweet Chariot." Some of the Spirituals undoubtedly had hidden or double meanings and served as signals for escape purposes. "Steal Away to Jesus" is a classic example.

2. Select one or two Negro Spirituals to teach to your choir. Stress the importance that the Spiritual is a part of our American heritage.

   Suggested songs: see Materials (song collections)

   Note to teacher: Stress that your singers use proper Negro dialect when singing Spirituals. Negro dialect may present some difficulties to White people who have never lived in the South, but most of the Spirituals lose charm when they are sung in straight English. Examples:

(dialect)	"I ain't gonna study war no mo"
(English)	"I am not going to study war anymore"
(dialect)	"Gaud's go'nuh trouble duh watah"
(English)	"God's going to trouble the water"

3. Discuss the Fisk Jubilee Singers, who acquainted the masses with Spirituals during their American and European tours from 1871 to 1878.

4. Discuss Marion Anderson, who perfected these songs with her skilled technique and culture.

5. Discuss J. Rosamond Johnson and Harry T. Burleigh (Spiritual composers).

Suggested Motivating Activities

1. Visit a Black church choir rehearsal or service. For those students who are unfamiliar with Black Gospel music, observing the emotional energy will help them relate to the Black aesthetic.
2. Attend a Black religious choral concert if one is scheduled nearby.
3. Have students attempt to harmonize by ear.
4. Allow students to move. Movement, such as foot tapping, swaying, facial expressions, and clapping, is an important part of the Afro-American music culture and shows a true Black aesthetic.

Materials

1. Discography:
   Fisk Jubilee Singers (Folkways FA 2372) and (Word Records W 4007 LP)
   Tuskegee Institute Choir (Westminster 9633)
   He's Got the World, Marion Anderson (Victor LSC 2592)
2. Song Collections:
   Chambers, H. A., ed. *The Treasury of Negro Spirituals*. New York: Emerson Books, 1963. The book is divided in two sections: "Traditional Spirituals" and "Modern Compositions." The Spirituals are tastefully arranged.
   Johnson, James Weldon, and J. Rosamond Johnson. *The Book of American Negro Spirituals*. New York: Viking Press, 1954. Very useful and most recommended.
   Landecks, Beatrice. *Echoes of Africa in Folk Songs of the Americas*. 2d rev. ed. New York: David McKay, 1969. Part Four, titled "Songs Roots of Jazz in the U.S.," has street cries, Spirituals, and shouts, work and minstrel songs, and blues. Good selections, with notes and suggestions for performance.
   Lloyd, Ruth Norma, comp. and arr. *The American Heritage Songbook*. New York: American Heritage, 1969. Part Seven of this book, "Songs of the American Negro," contains thirteen Spirituals and folk songs with information about each one.
3. Suggested reading (for the teacher who may not be familiar with Afro-American music):
   Heilbut, Tony. *The Gospel Sound*. New York: Simon and Schuster, 1971. A solid contribution to the literature, good discography.
   Marsh, J.B.T. *The Story of the Jubilee Singers: With Their Songs*. New York: Negro University Press, 1969.
   Reeder, Barbara. "Getting Involved in Shaping the Sounds of Black Music." *Music Educators Journal* 59 (October 1972):80. This article delineates pertinent rhythmic aspects in Black music with activities to help students feel and respond.
   Work, John Wesley. *American Negro Songs and Spirituals*. New York: Bonanza, 1940.

EVALUATION
1. Listening exam(s): Test can be matching, multiple choice, and/or short essay. Construct tests whereby students would be required to pinpoint and describe various characteristics of the Negro Spiritual.
2. Ask students to prepare reports on one of the artists/composers studied.
3. If you have an opportunity to observe a live performance of a Black religious choir, instruct students to do a report, critiquing the performance and discussing various characteristics.

The following lesson on slang and how it affects communication was prepared by Lori Bauer. It is designed for a unit on interpersonal relationships in ninth-grade home economics classes.

Illustration Ten

A Matter of Semantics

OBJECTIVES
1. Students will know that environment and one's experiences can influence one's reception or understanding of verbal messages.
2. Students will understand that communication affects interaction with others.
3. Students will become aware that communication with others can be affected by their self-perception and their perception of others.
4. Through group activities, students will understand how awareness and perception affect the receiving of a message.

ACTIVITIES

Lesson opener: Teacher walks in class and says "Hey man, gotta really heavy dude for you cats today. Dig it?" (Hopeful response would be they'd ask what are you talking about.) Teacher responds that he or she is talking about slang, words that all of us use but may not be aware of their effect on others. Many misunderstandings occur due to use of words that don't mean the same thing to all people. To illustrate this, students will be given a slang handout. Given the following list of words and phrases, students will individually define at least eighteen of the twenty-six. The list contains: ace, but, cop out, dig it, excel, far out, give me five, hangout, in, joint, knocked out, lay off, machine, neat, on the side, pop, quack, rags, skins, track, uppers, vibes, wind up, X, yellow, Zzzzzzz! Their responses will be discussed; then they should take this list and ask a parent, grandparent, or someone in a different age group how he or she would define the terms. A discussion the following day comparing different responses will take place. The purpose of this exercise is to demonstrate how messages could be miscommunicated between people of similar backgrounds but of different ages.

Next, students will receive the handout "Just What Do They Mean?" Individually, they should try to define as many of these terms as possible: talis, WASP, te amo, Cajun, rabbi, chalice, honky, eight-cow wife, monogamy, polygamy, cop a nod, lame, rat now, Abraham. Since these terms are comon to various groups of people around the world, it is expected that students will not be able to define many of them. Students then form groups of four and explain why they can't define some terms and how those words could frustrate persons from different cultures. They should also explain how they would feel if someone used these words around them often and they didn't understand. How would it affect their self-perception and perception of others?

At the end of the lesson, the teacher will write the objectives on the board, and students will copy them. Then the class will review each and how it applies to their own experience.

EVALUATION TECHNIQUE: SHORT ANSWER
1. Define in your own words what is meant by slang. Give two examples of slang and how it could cause a message to be miscommunicated.
2. List two words you commonly use that would be unfamiliar or cause bad feelings if used with someone from a different background.
3. How have the exercises in class made you more aware of the words you use and how these words can affect others who may be unfamiliar with them?

These types of questions work well, because they are easy to relate with class exercises. Achievement is usually high.

Illustration Eleven

For the Good of the People

This lesson plan for sixth-grade social studies was written by Susan Goodman.

OBJECTIVE
Students will gain an understanding of Indians' feelings about having to leave their land. Students will write a short paper comparing Indians' feelings about the loss of their land to the simulation of the student's own loss of land.

LESSON OPENER
Today we are going to use our time machine. First, we will visit the time period of the late 1700s to early 1800s. You will become a Cherokee Indian. Next, we will use the time machine to move into the future and you will become a small farmer in Switz City.

ACTIVITY

Read the following and discuss in small groups.

Part 1: You are an Indian named White Horse. You and your ancestors have lived in this section of land for many years. It has supported your every need for food, shelter, clothing. You respect and love the land. But now the white settlers are moving onto your land. They have built fences where you once freely traveled. They are killing the game— cutting the forests. The white men even complain of *your* existence there. Finally, a treaty has been signed, and you are told you must move "for the good of your people." How do you feel?

Now reenter the time machine for your trip to the future:

Part 2: For several years your family has owned a small farm in Switz City. It has been passed from generation to generation. You have a deep feeling of home and security here. You have made an acceptable living for your family on this farm. Now the Department of Natural Resources is planning to construct a huge reservoir. Your property will fall in about the middle of the lake. Your first angry inquiries are met by these facts:

Many of your neighbors are in the same position.

The state will pay you a fair price for your land. (The price actually turns out to be much less than a real estate agent said you could get.)

Your land has already been officially condemned.

Construction will begin in three months.

You have no appeal.

The state representative says he can do nothing to halt progress in the state.

The reservoir will "benefit all citizens of the state," says the governor in his form letter answering your angry telegram.

How do you feel? After fifteen to twenty minutes (or more) of discussion, write your paper, comparing your feelings as a farmer to those of the Indians. Point out any similarities and differences that you discover.

EVALUATION

Observation of group work and the written papers of the students.

MATERIALS

Handouts with parts 1 and 2 typed separately to hand out to different groups.

ENRICHMENT

Have groups of the sixth graders do skits showing these two scenes to younger students in the early elementary school grades. The performers should do research and try to dress in authentic clothing. Then, another class member can lead the younger students in a discussion of feelings.

Reducing Ethnic Prejudice and Discrimination

Illustration Twelve

Can You Recognize Racism?

This lesson has been used effectively with high school students, grades 9 to 12. The check-list section has also been used with advanced elementary school children. The lesson can be adapted to any subject area by modifying the content of the check-list quotations and descriptive statements. The check list could, for example, pertain only to sports and athletics, or the fields of business, science, or the performing arts.

INSTRUCTIONS

First work alone. Put a check before each statement you think is an example of racism. Then work with your small group and try to agree on the examples of racism. (Your group will receive a packet of statement cards to make the task easier.) Choose one member of your group to share your decisions with everyone.

1. Which of the following quotations or descriptive statements are examples of racism? Indicate these with a check (✔).

_____ "A Black family moved into our neighborhood this week."
_____ The principal interviewed two equally outstanding candidates, one Black and the other Latino. She selected the Black teacher because her school had several Latino teachers but no Black teachers.
_____ In 1882 immigration laws excluded the Chinese, and the Japanese were excluded in 1908.
_____ During the 1960s civil rights movement, Mrs. Viola Liuzzo, a White civil rights worker from Michigan, was shot by White southern segregationists.
_____ Between 1892 and 1921 nearly 2,400 Black Americans were lynched by vigilante mobs who were never brought to justice.
_____ "The best basketball players on our team this year are Black."
_____ The band director discouraged Black students from playing the flute or piccolo because he believed it was too difficult for them to excel on these instruments.
_____ When Mrs. Wallace, a Black woman from Detroit, visited a predominantly White university in northern Michigan to see her son play basketball, she was seriously injured in a

car accident. She refused a blood transfusion because she was afraid of being contaminated by White blood.

———— When Stacey Russell, a Black undergraduate, went through rush, the girls of an all-White sorority decided not to pledge her because several members threatened to move out if they did.

———— The geography textbook described the peoples of Nigeria as primitive and underdeveloped.

———— The children who attended an elementary school in southwest Texas spoke only Spanish at home. When they came to school all the books and intelligence tests were in English. Nearly all of the children were placed in remedial classes or in classes for the mentally retarded.

———— Mr. Jones said, "It is true that Indians who still live on reservations live in extreme poverty. But this is because they refuse to give up their traditions and a culture which is obsolete in the modern world."

———— The U.S. Constitution defined slaves as three-fifths of a man.

———— The reporter wrote that "Toni Morrison is a brilliant writer who accurately portrays much of the Black experience in America."

———— When John brought home a new friend, his father was shocked and angry. Peter, the new friend, was of Japanese origin and John's father had been seriously wounded by the Japanese in World War II. John's father refused to allow Peter to visit again.

———— In 1896 the Supreme Court ruled that separate facilities for the races were legal as long as they were *equal.* This resulted in separate schools, churches, restaurants, restrooms, swimming pools, theaters, doctors' offices, neighborhoods, Bibles used in court, etc.

———— When Mary Adams wanted to find a place in the school cafeteria the only vacant chair was at a table seating five Black girls. Mary, who is White, was afraid to join them.

———— In California today, approximately 10 percent of the population is Black, while 41 percent of those in prison are Black. Blacks generally have more financial difficulty than Whites in hiring a lawyer and plea bargaining.

2. *Small Group Decision Sheet*

Select one member of your group to write your group's decisions below and another person to share the results with the rest of us. Be prepared to explain your reasons if necessary.

a. The following statements are examples of either individual or institutional racism: (Write numbers and a word or two for description, and arrange them according to those that refer to racist individuals, and to racist policies and institutions.)

INDIVIDUAL RACISM	INSTITUTIONAL RACISM

b. Our group's definition of racism is:

_____

c. The main difference between individual and institutional racism is:

_____

d. Examples of individual and institutional racism that we know about in our community are:
Individual racism:

_____

_____

_____

Institutional racism:

_____

_____

_____

This lesson can be used at any grade level; the written decision-making sheet can be omitted for young children, and the wording made more appropriate for advanced high school youth. Eventually, the lesson could lead to an examination of ethnic bias in literature. Experience has shown that it is often most effective to begin with sex bias since everyone can identify with being either male or female. The lesson could fit into a variety of subjects. Possible units of study include images in literature or advertising, family relationships and sex role expectations, Title Nine and athletics, careers, and political behavior.

Illustration Thirteen

Hidden Messages in Children's Literature

GOALS
1. Students will analyze how children's literature and other socialization agents work to shape the attitudes and behaviors of male and female children.
2. Students will begin to develop strategies for detecting biased images in media.

STUDENT ACTIVITY
Each class member is given one or more children's stories.

FOR SEXISM	FOR RACISM
"Hansel and Gretel"	*Mary Poppins*
"Snow White"	*Robinson Crusoe*
"Little Red Riding Hood"	"The Ugly Duckling"
Policeman Small	*The Slave Dancer*
"Cinderella"	*Pippi Longstocking*
"Rumpelstiltskin"	*The Five Chinese Brothers*
"Sleeping Beauty"	*Charlie and the Chocolate Factory*
"The Three Little Pigs"	*Doctor Dolittle*
The Giving Tree	*Sounder*
I'm Glad I'm a Boy	*Magdalena*
I'm Glad I'm a Girl	
Pippi Longstocking	
Tamás Takes Charge	

1. I have examined the following books:

   _____

   _____

   I would like to include these other books I can remember:

   _____

   _____

2. Females tend to be described in these ways:

_____

Males tend to be described in these ways:

_____

3. One or more of these books try to make children think and behave in these ways: (list as many examples as possible)

_____

_____

_____

4. The five most common characteristics associated with women and girls are:

_____

_____

_____

_____

_____

In what ways does our society support these images of females?

_____

_____

_____

In what ways does our society reject these images of females?

_____

_____

_____

5. The five most common characteristics associated with men and boys are:

_____

_____

_____

_____

_____

In what ways does our society support these images of males?

_____

_____

_____

In what ways does our society reject these images of males?

_____

_____

_____

6. Based on this evidence, what differences do you predict between the behavior of males and females in our society?

These lessons, prepared by Jean Seger,* are designed to be taught to high school students. The time for teaching the lessons is approximately two periods. It is expected that the students will have had preliminary instruction on percents, elementary statistics, and the construction of bar, line, and circle graphs. The lessons are designed to instruct the student on constructing, reading, and interpreting graphs and tables while having the student formulate ideas on discrimination based on racial prejudices.

Illustration Fourteen

Reading, Constructing, and Interpreting Graphs

PERFORMANCE OBJECTIVES

1. The student will be able to correctly read Tables 7.1, 7.2, and 7.3. Upon looking at the tables the student will be able to answer orally or in writing questions concerning the information in the tables.
2. Given access to Table 7.1, the student will be able to construct a line graph comparing the income of Blacks to the total population with years of education completed.
3. Given access to Tables 7.2 and 7.3, the student will be able to choose three of six professions and the corresponding data and construct circle graphs for each one.
4. The student will be able to express his or her opinion either orally or in writing on the benefits that minority individuals receive by attending higher education institutions.
5. The student will be able to express his or her opinion either orally or in writing on the economic, social, and psychological ramifications for minority groups who are not adequately represented in higher education or the work force.

*Tables expanded and updated by C. Bennett.

Table 7.1   *Estimated Income of Regularly Employed Persons over 18, by Race, Sex and Schooling, 1980 (mean annual income in U.S. dollars)*

	WHITE FEMALE	WHITE MALE	BLACK FEMALE	BLACK MALE
Elementary School				
0–8 years	8,353	14,142	7,757	11,574
High School				
1–3 years	9,208	15,845	8,678	12,360
4 years	10,374	17,648	9,916	13,726
College				
1–3 years	11,688	19,849	11,317	15,541
4 years	13,833	25,943	13,550	18,223
5 or more years	16,958	31,092	16,872	23,400

Source: Adapted from U.S. Bureau of the Census, *Statistical Abstracts of the United States, 1985,* 105th edition (Washington, D.C., 1984).

Table 7.2   *Occupation of Employed Persons 16 Years Old and Over, by Race and Sex, 1983 (percentage of total)*

OCCUPATION	FEMALES	BLACKS	HISPANIC AMERICANS
Managerial and professional	40.9	5.6	2.6
Technical, sales, and administrative support	64.6	7.6	4.3
Service	60.1	16.6	6.8
Farming, forestry, and fishing occupations	16.0	7.5	8.2
Precision, production craft, and repair	8.1	6.8	6.2
Operators, fabrication, and laborers	26.6	14.0	8.3
All occupations combined	43.7	9.3	5.3

Source: Adapted from U.S. Bureau of Labor Statistics, *Employment and Earnings* (Washington, D.C., January 1984).

Table 7.3 *Profession of Employed Persons by Race and Sex, 1983, 50 States and District of Columbia (percentage of total)*

PROFESSION	FEMALES	BLACKS	HISPANIC AMERICANS
Dentists	6.7	2.4	1.0
Engineers	5.8	2.7	2.2
Lawyers and judges	15.8	2.7	1.0
Financial executives	38.6	3.5	3.1
Physicians	15.8	3.2	4.5
Teachers, college and university	36.3	4.4	1.8
Teachers, except college and university	70.9	9.1	2.7
All professions combined	40.9	9.3	5.3

Source: Adapted from U.S. Bureau of the Census, *Statistical Abstracts of the United States, 1985,* 105th edition (Washington, D.C., 1984), pp. 402–403.

STRATEGY
In all lessons students will work in groups of two.

DAY 1

MATERIALS

1. Poster displaying the information in Table 7.1
2. Individual copies of the table
3. Rulers

ACTIVITIES

1. Each group will receive a copy of Table 7.1 and a larger model of the table will appear on the front blackboard.
2. The teacher will direct students in the method for reading the chart to find the median income of individuals based on education completed.
3. The teacher will ask students to orally (a) state the median income earned by individual; (b) compare the incomes of Blacks and Whites with same educational experience, and repeat for males and females; and (c) compapre the incomes of Blacks and Whites with different educational experience.
4. Working in pairs, each group will construct a line graph based on the table.
5. Using the line graphs that students have constructed, the teacher will ask students to state their views on: (a) Is there a correlation between education completed and median income earned? (b) Is the discrimination in salaries between the total population and

the Black population with equal educational experience fair? (c) What about the income differences between males and females?

Day 2

MATERIALS

1. Poster displaying the information in Tables 7.2 and 7.3
2. Individual copies of the table
3. Rulers, protractors, and compasses

ACTIVITIES

1. Each group will receive a copy of Tables 7.2 and 7.3, and a larger model of these tables will appear on the front blackboard.
2. The teacher will direct students in the method of reading the chart to find the number and percent of population each racial group comprises in a profession.
3. The teacher will ask students to orally (a) state the percent of females, Whites, Blacks, and Hispanic Americans in each of the professions listed; (b) compare the percents between racial and gender groups; and (c) compare the percent of a race in each profession to the percent that race comprises of the U.S. population; repeat the comparison for gender.
4. Working in pairs, each group will construct circle graphs for three of the professions listed.
5. Using the circle graphs that groups have constructed, ask students to orally state their views on: (a) Are Blacks and Hispanic Americans adequately represented in professions based on their population in the United States? Are females? (b) What are the negative ramifications for groups who are not adequately represented in professions? Students should consider economic, social, and psychological ramifications. (c) Will the percent of women and minority races in professions increase or decrease in the future?

Illustration Fifteen

The Uniqueness of You

The goal of this lesson, as its author, Sally Goss, explained, is for the learner to be able to identify the unique and distinctive characteristics that make all individuals special. The activities should help to eradicate ethnic and racial prejudice by showing how we are all unique but similar at the same time.

MATERIALS
Baby pictures supplied by students
DNA structure kits

LEARNING ACTIVITY 1

Ask each student to bring in a baby picture and a recent photo. Arrange these randomly on the bulletin board. Have students match each baby picture with the correct recent photo. After giving the correct answers, discuss the following questions:

How much similarity is there among the baby pictures? Why?
How much similarity is there among the recent photos? Why?
Why are the baby pictures more similar than the recent photos?
How is the uniqueness of each individual demonstrated by the recent photos?

LEARNING ACTIVITY 2

After the teacher presents a lecture on the components of DNA, its functions, and the processes of its replication, students will construct their own DNA helixes and view first-hand how amines form unique DNA sequences.

OBJECTIVES

1. Student will master the following skills: (a) dribbling with right hand, (b) dribbling with left hand, (c) right-hand lay-ups, (d) left-hand lay-ups, (e) free-throw shots, (f) jump shots.
2. Students will practice cooperative team learning. (See Chapter 8.)
3. Students will develop more positive racial attitudes.

Illustration Sixteen

Basketball Skills

STRATEGIES

1. Students will be grouped into heterogeneous teams, comparable in terms of skill (as pretested), sex, ethnic group, and racial/ethnic attitude (as pretested).
2. Teams will rotate to the different skill stations set up in the gymnasium and practice the skills together as a team (approximately two weeks).
3. The team whose members show the greatest gains on the post-test wins.

MATERIALS

1. *Student Team Learning: An Overview and Practical Guide* by Robert E. Slavin (Washington, D.C.: National Education Association, 1983).
2. Basketball for each team.
3. Sociometric test or Borgardus Social Distance Scale.

EVALUATION
1. Scores on skill-based posttest.
2. Scores on attitudinal posttest.
3. Observation of intergroup cooperation.

Social Action Skills

Illustration Seventeen

The Cycle of Personal Alienation

Socialization can be defined as a sociopsychological process, whereby the personality is created under the influence of the educational institutions (and agents). Activities that help students understand this process should encourage students to use introspection to discover their own patterns of perception and work toward helping them become more empathetic. Thus the student begins within and moves outward. The examination of socialization processes, such as how persons become who they are and learn to perceive and behave as they do, appears to be a valuable means of helping to break down perceptual and communication barriers between different culture groups. The possibilities for using this strategy in working toward the goals of cultural consciousness, intercultural competency, and eradication of ethnic and racial prejudice and discrimination are obvious.

However, because of the impact of past behavior and experience on attitudes (including self-image) and future behavior, understanding of the socialization process is a crucial thread that ties the goal of social action skills to our conceptualization of multicultural education. If people are to become agents of change, they must understand the cycle of alienation (see Figure 7.2), how they might be socialized into this cycle, how it might operate in their own lives, and how it might be broken.

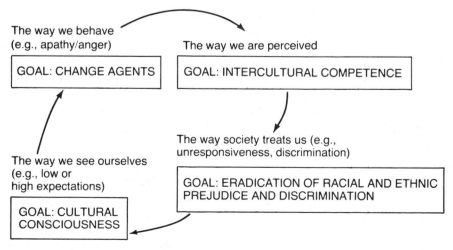

Figure 7.2   *The Cycle of Personal Alienation*

The activity that follows was designed specifically to develop students' understanding of this cycle. Although it focuses on attitudes about social or political issues, any feeling or belief can be substituted (for example, preferences in fashion, music, or food; concept of beauty; religion; attitudes toward different culture groups). When implemented among racially and culturally diverse students, the exercise proved to be a powerful means of enabling individuals to understand how they had been socialized politically, and the differences that exist in the political socialization of males, females, and different culture groups.

Students begin by examining their own values and attitudes, move on to analysis of how these attitudes and values developed (the socialization process), and are then asked to identify implications for their own lives. Once students have completed their individual reactions and recorded them on paper or tape, comparisons can be made across the lines of sex, race, and ethnicity.

SELF-ANALYSIS: HOW DID YOUR ATTITUDES DEVELOP?

The topic of the next few activities is you. You will be exploring your own political feelings and beliefs, and attempting to discover how you developed them. The questions will help you begin. Answer them in a way that is meaningful to you; be as brief or as lengthy as you wish.

1. Describe your feelings and beliefs about the following (these may be modified according to student interest and knowledge background).
   a. School desegregation
   b. Capital punishment
   c. Voting in presidential elections
   d. Government welfare for unemployed mothers with dependent children
   e. Participation in military service during time of war
   f. Your city's police force
   g. School prayer
   h. Bilingual education in public schools
2. How important have each of the following been in influencing the feelings and beliefs you expressed above? (Just comment on the important ones and include specific examples.)
   a. Your family (father, mother, other relatives)
   b. Teachers
   c. Friends
   d. Church
   e. Media (movies, TV, songs, books, newspapers)
   f. Events and/or experiences
   g. Other?
3. Considering the feelings and beliefs you have described, where would you place yourself on the following scales?

	STRONGLY AGREE	AGREE	UNSURE	DISAGREE	STRONGLY DISAGREE
I am completely satisfied with how our society works.					
I feel that I can make a significant difference in how our society works if I want to change things.					
I believe most government officials and politicians can be trusted to do what's best.					

4. How will these attitudes affect your life?

Illustration Eighteen

A Promise to Myself

Students of all ages can be asked to write a letter to themselves about an action they can take to help achieve a goal they have selected. (Nonwriters can dictate it to a classmate or adult.) The goal could pertain to self-growth or to a needed change in the classroom, school, or community. Letters are sealed and mailed or returned to the student after the specified amount of time has passed. This activity could, for example, be a follow-up to the small group activity on identifying racism on pages 244–246.

Illustration Nineteen

To Take a Stand or Not

Students can develop decision-making skills if they are given an opportunity to act out a problematic situation in role play before they actually encounter it. Young children can use dolls, puppets, or masks made of decorated paper plates during the role play. Older students can be given role cards that define their new personality or they can be asked to empathize with a person in an open-ended situation. Examples of role playing that help build decision-making skills related to multicultural education goals are listed below. Students can be asked whether they would take a stand or not, depending on who they are (themselves, another actual person, or a contrived character). Wording would be modified according to students' grade level.

• Your best friend uses a racial slur to insult a classmate.
• You feel that your teacher is racist because Black/White/Latino

students get away with murder in the classroom and you get punished for much less.

- Your parent tells a cruel ethnic joke that cuts down _____ at a family gathering.
- You find out that the sorority/fraternity you want to join will not pledge anyone from a different race. You are/are not a member of the same race.
- You are White and have a new job in a sporting-goods store. Your boss asks you to make a note of any Black person who cashes a check in the store.
- One of your best friends in school is Black/Latino/White. You want to invite this friend to your birthday party but your parent(s) says no.
- You catch a classmate cheating on an exam. The cheater is of a different race from you and you are afraid of being called prejudiced. Yet you know the cheater shared the exam with a small group of close friends, which raised the class curve causing you and others to do poorly.
- A teacher's purse was stolen by a tall Black person wearing an Afro. You are innocent, but because you fit the description you are called in for questioning and accused of the crime.
- You have just learned that you will be transported by bus to a new school next year in a distant part of town. You hear that the parents in that neighborhood are angry and upset that you and classmates from your neighborhood are being brought in.
- Before you came to the United States you loved school and were a good student. Now you understand little of what the teacher and classmates say, and you have been placed in a classroom for the mentally retarded.

Compare and Contrast

1. The ethnic studies approach and the multicultural approach
2. Informed empathy and intercultural consciousness
3. Historical perspectives and cultural consciousness
4. The curriculum goals of multicultural education and the underlying assumptions

---

Activities and Questions

1. Work alone or with other members of your class or workshop to complete the curriculum decision-making sheet on pages 214–216. Small groups could be based on similar teaching disciplines or on interdisciplinary teams from the same school or district.

2. Develop a multicultural calendar with other members of your class or workshop, or let your students help you. Individuals or small groups could focus on a different ethnic group and research people and events to be included in the calendar. At least one entry per month per

ethnic group could be the initial goal, with the number expanding as the data bank increases over the years. Both minority perspectives and ethnic diversity should be reflected in the calendar as it emerges. The calendar's people and events could be related to a specific subject (sports and athletics, music, literature, government, and so on).

3. Why does Black History Month sometimes trigger resentment among non-Black students? How might the goals and philosophy behind Black History Month be best achieved?

4. What are the arguments in favor of and against school programs that include Christian beliefs, music, and traditions, as, for example, at Christmas or Easter? How should schools handle the controversy?

5. It is sometimes argued that multicultural education belongs mainly, if not entirely, in the social sciences, literature, and the arts. Do you agree or disagree? Explain.

Notes

1. This section is adapted from a paper originally written by the author for presentation at a curriculum institute sponsored by the Association for Supervision and Curriculum Development, Boston, October 17–18, 1975. A later version was included in *Multi-Cultural Education*, comp. and ed. Margaret Cyrus Mills (Charleston: West Virginia Department of Education, 1976).

2. Pamela L. Tiedt and Iris M. Tiedt, *Multicultural Teaching: A Handbook of Activities, Information, and Resources* (Boston: Allyn and Bacon, 1979), p. 174.

3. Alfred J. Kraemer, "A Cultural Self-Awareness Approach to Improving Intercultural Communication Skills," ERIC ED 079 213 (April 1973), p. 2.

4. David Wolsk, "An Experience Centered Curriculum: Exercises in Personal and Social Reality," United Nations Education, Scientific and Cultural Organization, Paris, 1974, ERIC ED 099 269; and Doyle Castell, *Cross-Cultural Models of Teaching: Latin American Example* (Gainesville: University of Florida Press, 1976).

5. Harry C. Triandis, "Culture Training, Cognitive Complexity and Interpersonal Attitudes," in *Cross-Cultural Perspectives on Learning*, ed. Richard W. Brislin, Stephen Bochner, and Walter J. Lonner (New York: John Wiley and Sons, 1975), pp. 70–71.

6. See, for example, Robert D. Hess and Fred M. Newman, "Political Socialization in the Schools," *Harvard Education Review* 38 (Summer 1968):528–45; Bradbury Seasholes, "Political Socialization of Blacks: Implications for Self and Society," in *Black Self-Concept*, ed. James A. Banks and Jean D. Grambs (New York: McGraw-Hill, 1972); Lee H. Elman, "Political Socialization and the High School Social Studies Curriculum," unpublished Ph.D. diss., University of Michigan, 1970; and Christine Bennett Button, "Political Education and Minority Youth" in *New Views of Children and Politics*, ed. Richard G. Niemi (San Francisco: Jossey-Bass, 1974).

7. Seasholes, "Political Socialization of Blacks."

Part Four

Teaching Concepts and Strategies

What are some of the teaching concepts and strategies known to be effective in working with the cultural and individual differences students bring to the classroom? Is it possible to create a flexible learning environment without classroom chaos? Is it possible to allow students to learn in different ways and still maintain high standards of achievement? If so, is it possible to accomplish this without becoming exhausted over excess lesson planning and record keeping? The purpose of this chapter is to provide some affirmative answers to these questions.

Consider the example of a teacher whose classroom illustrates the possibilities. How Eric Jones, a Los Angeles high school teacher, implements individualization and establishes a pluralistic learning environment is illustrated in the following classroom description. His key concepts and strategies will then be analyzed, and their implementation in other classroom settings will be proposed.

Most teachers are in favor of individualizing instruction, even though many feel it is possible only with small numbers of students. Part of the problem is misunderstanding about what the concept means. "During the 1960s, individualized instruction was associated with teaching machines and programmed texts, and conjured up images of a single learner alone in timeless space, facing a panel board with several control knobs, and responding to lists of stimuli that had been previously tested and sequenced in a manner that ensured successful learning."[1] Most recently, individualized instruction may be defined as "any steps taken in planning and conducting programs of studies and lessons that suit them to the individual student's learning needs, learning readiness, and learner characteristics or 'learning style.' "[2]

A key to this teacher's success is the flexible learning environment that allows for individualized instruction. The concepts of mastery learning, experiential learning, and bilingual education are combined to provide the basic framework for individualized instruction in his classroom. These three concepts are implemented through a variety of teaching strategies including peer and cross-age tutoring, independent study,

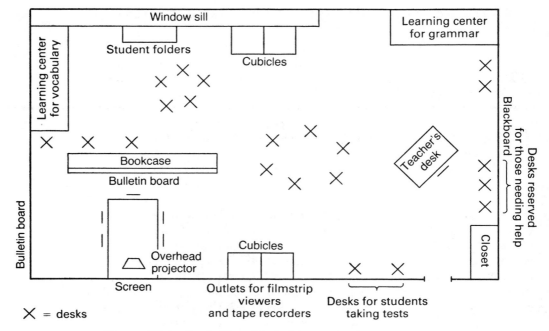

Figure IV.1   *Basic Floor Plan of Tenth-Grade English Classroom Arrangement. Adapted from Christine Bennett, "Individualized Instruction in the Secondary Schools," Viewpoints in Teaching and Learning 55, no. 2 (Spring 1979):77.*

learning centers, and learning activity packets. Other strategies not in evidence today include student team learning, lecture, and small-group discussion.

It is Thursday morning in November. Eric Jones, a tenth-grade English teacher in Los Angeles, arrives early to set up his classroom before the arrival of his first-period students.

Today, Eric is following up Monday and Tuesday's large-group activity, Bafá Bafá, a cross-cultural simulation.[3] Eric's classroom arrangement (Figure IV.1) differs sharply from most of the others in Green Grove High.

Eric's plan includes areas for quiet study. Cubicles are set up with large painted cardboard boxes lined with styrofoam egg cartons to absorb sound. These are placed on individual small tables, or several together on a long one. Eric creates other areas conducive to group work by arranging circles of desks or tables and chairs. His equipment is accessible and the students know how to operate it themselves. He stores student folders and answer keys for his self-directed learning centers in labeled boxes covered with brightly colored contact paper. These files are conveniently located since the students refer to them often.

Eric uses few partitions. He prefers to keep the classroom open so that he can keep an eye on what is going on and be available to help when students raise their hands or become frustrated with malfunctioning equipment. He uses movable bookcases set on wheels for placement of alternative textbooks and a good-sized paperback library. The bookcase can be swung around to quickly create more private areas for tutoring or small-group discussion.

Eric's students are a heterogeneous group in terms of ethnicity, family income level, values, interests, learning-style preferences, and achievement. He prefers this. Experience has taught him that human diversity in the classroom can be in itself motivating for students and can assist the teacher in reaching students who might otherwise be unteachable.

Take Tony Castillo and Tomás Cortez as examples. Neither speaks more than a few words of English. Although Eric has had two years of college Spanish at UCLA, he lacks the necessary fluency in oral Spanish to fully assist Tony and Tomás. The school does have a bilingual education program, but it is already overcrowded and understaffed. Neither Tomás nor Tony has been able to get into the program. Fortunately, Eric was able to schedule a bilingual student, Ricardo Juarez, into this class. In addition to benefiting Tony and Tomás, Ricardo's overall school achievement and attitude have improved markedly since he assumed the role of peer instructor.

The simulation Eric used on Monday was designed to enable his students to feel what it's like to visit another culture. The students were physically separated into two different cultures, the Alphas and Betas, and then were given approximately twenty minutes to learn and practice their new culture. Each culture had its own unique traditions, customs, language, and assumptions. Observers and visitors moved back and forth between the two cultures until everyone had an opportunity to visit the other culture.

Eric then allowed the class time to discuss what happened. Students were amazed to discover that a mere twenty minutes in their new culture had helped shape their perceptions and assumptions, and had made them rather ethnocentric. Alphas and Betas both felt strange, uncomfortable, unwelcome, confused, and even afraid when they visited each other. Each perceived the other as rude, stupid, and either greedy or nosy. Each made incorrect assumptions about the other, and the reporters made many errors in their interpretations of what they saw.

In the follow-up discussion on Tuesday, the class eagerly discussed what it felt like to visit another culture, to be misperceived by others, and to discover their own misperceptions and erroneous assumptions. They analyzed causes of the misperceptions and cultural conflicts that occurred. Implications for American society were analyzed, particularly those associated with ethnicity in Los Angeles, their school, and in their own classroom. Media coverage of two historic incidents in Los Angeles, the zootsuit riots during World War II and the shooting of Rubin Salazar, were described, analyzed, and discussed. Both incidents involved conflict between the Anglo and Chicano communities.

Several days after the introductory simulation, Eric's students are involved in small-group and independent learning activities that have grown out of Monday's experience (Figure IV.2). These activities have been carefully selected for each student on the basis of the student's mastery level of common core learnings (or mastery level of a student's self-selected learning) and the student's preferred style of learning.

Eric labels common core learnings those skills and understandings that everyone is expected to master. Examples of common core learnings for his course as a whole are basic vocabulary and acquisition of key concepts, plus interpersonal communication, decision-making, and thinking skills. Examples of common core learnings for the unit on "The News Media: Believe It or Not?" are the ability to distinguish facts from opinion in selected samples of printed, visual, and aural news media. Students who have achieved mastery of the unit's common core learning objectives are free to work toward mastery of self-selected learnings. Today, Stuart, Martha, Pat, Tom, Terri, and Diane are working in self-selected areas according to a contract set up with Eric. Ricardo has developed an original activity for Tomás and Tony to supplement Eric's vocabulary learning center. Everyone else is working toward common core mastery learning, although the methods and/or materials vary.

Eric has gathered diagnostic information on most of his students (approximately 140 in his 5 classes) during the past few months. He maintains a file for each student. These files contain information on the student's reading level, cognitive style (abstract or concrete), preferred mode of learning (visual, auditory, kinesthetic, mixed), need for structure, preferred mode of instruction (independent, one to one, small group, large group), and interests.

At first Eric found the gathering and storing of student information overwhelming, and he nearly gave up. Although the first month of each year is still demanding, he has worked out an efficient and effective system of record keeping that runs

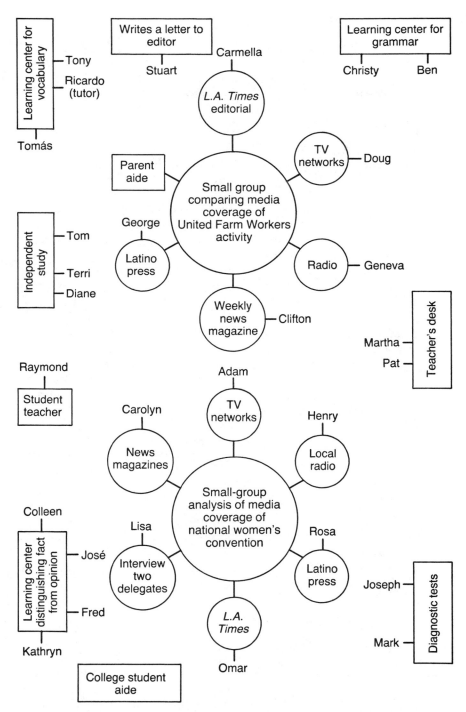

Figure IV.2 *Classroom Floor Plan in Use by Students. Adapted from Christine Bennett, "Individualized Instruction in the Secondary Schools,"* Viewpoints in Teaching and Learning *55, no. 2 (Spring 1979):80.*

smoothly and assists each student in understanding his or her progress.

Eric makes excellent use of aides from the community and participants from local schools. He finds that most of these people can come only one day a week for approximately three hours, and some valuable community resource people are free only one hour a week or less. To avoid confusion and the possible distraction of new people moving in and out of the room, he has developed a master schedule illustrating who comes when and for what purpose. He insists that his regular participants and volunteers be reliable and punctual, and participate in at least one class at the same time each week for one school semester. He categorizes his aides according to their areas of skill and interest and develops tasks accordingly. Every aide has a specific job to do whenever she or he is present in the classroom. Some of the tasks many aides, especially senior citizens, can do include typing or writing as the pupil dictates an original story, vocabulary card games, scrabble, conversing in Spanish and standard English, grading and recording tests, and discussing literature. Those participants who serve as tutors go through a twelve-hour training program that is coordinated by another teacher at school.

Occasionally, he sets up pot-luck or brown-bag lunches to allow his students to meet and talk with busy resource people from the community. This semester each of his five classes has a minimum of one aide for two days every week; some classes have an aide every day. Eric uses a grandmother, a former fifth-grade teacher, to help organize and coordinate the activities of all the other aides.

Involvement of outside persons might be more than many teachers can take, at least all at once. Eric has developed his organization and network of people over several years so that community people from the neighborhoods of all his students are an integral part of his classroom environment. And it isn't a one-way street. Many of his students voluntarily reciprocate with neighborhood clean-up, gardening projects, grocery shopping, and yard care.

This classroom exemplifies the use of a cluster of basic strategies for individualized instruction. First, in the simulation activity the teacher uses experiential learning in the large group to motivate students and introduce a new unit or topic. Teachers who use the experiential or do-look-learn approach select an experience situation as a springboard to discussion, analysis, and follow-up activities, which lead into the ongoing curriculum. Typical experience situations are simulations, role playing, or contrived activities that involve every student.

Second, the teacher's program includes mastery learning. Mastery learning is based on the premise that all but a few students are capable of learning the basic concepts and skills of a subject if they are given appropriate instruction. In this classroom, a common core of learning objectives is identified for each unit. With a few exceptions, no student moves on to a new unit until mastery (usually 85 percent correct on unit test) has been achieved. Rapid learners may spend most of their time working on self-selected objectives that allow them to pursue special interests related to the topic. Learners who are slow to master the first few units often begin to speed up as they experience learning success, many for the first time.

Third, the teacher has set up an extensive tutoring program that involves peers and community aides. Tutoring, especially cross-age tutoring, appears to be an effective strategy for raising student achievement levels. Research on the impact of tutoring programs indicates:

1. Training is necessary. Tutors must receive training in basic human relations and techniques appropriate for the content to be taught.
2. Tutors generally benefit more than tutees; however, tutees also benefit in terms of achievement gains.
3. Students who are failing in their own classwork can be helped to instruct younger learners in their regular schoolwork.

Finally, the teacher is also making effective use of the learning activity package (LAP), learning centers or stations, and independent study. These strategies are basic ways of building a more flexible learning environment.

Consider the description and analysis of each of these concepts and strategies in Chapter 8, which also presents student team learning, a strategy not evident in Eric's classroom. Sample lessons created by practicing teachers are also included to illustrate how a variety of teachers have moved to create more flexible learning environments.

Notes

1. Harriet Talmage, ed., *Systems of Individualized Education* (Berkeley: McCutchan, 1975), p. 36.

2. Glen Heathers, "A Working Definition of Individualized Instruction," *Educational Leadership* 34, no. 5 (February 1977):342.

3. R. Garry Shirts, *Bafá Bafá: A Cross Culture Simulation*, 1977, published by Simile 11, 218 Twelfth Street, P.O. Box 910, Del Mar, Calif. 92014.

Chapter 8

Educational Concepts and Teaching Strategies for Pluralistic Classrooms

Mastery Learning

Mastery learning refers to a teaching concept that breaks subject matter down into a series of units to be learned sequentially. The learner must achieve a high level of competency in one unit before moving on to the next unit in the sequence.

Proponents of mastery learning contend that the vast majority of students (90 to 95 percent) are capable of mastering most learning tasks in the school's basic curriculum if given sufficient time and appropriate instruction.[1] They believe that high standards (at least as high as the traditional grade levels) can be expected and achieved if the quality of instruction is adequate. Quality of instruction depends on factors such as the clarity of the learning task, appropriate sequencing of instructional materials, and effective use of tests to provide corrective feedback and motivational support. How quickly a student will learn new tasks depends on prior learning, aptitude, the task's complexity, perseverance, and the learner's ability to understand instructions, as well as the quality of teaching. The major point is, however, that nearly all students can eventually learn if they have good instructors.

Patricia Cross, a scholar who has focused on nontraditional students (those beyond the White middle class), believes that mastery learning is the missing link needed to foster academic success among those who have been overrepresented among the students who fail in school or drop out.[2] For one thing, mastery learning assumes that virtually all students can learn. For another, it helps school failures—those who have not mastered basic essentials—catch up.

For a variety of reasons many students are not ready to learn certain concepts or skills when they are introduced, or they are unable to master them as taught by a particular teacher. Yet these students are rushed through the curriculum, and the gap between school achievers and nonachievers widens every year. Proponents of mastery learning argue that the concept provides a solution to these problems because it lays the foundation for future learning by insisting that one unit must be mastered before the learner tackles the next. Furthermore, poor students discover that they are, in fact, capable of doing good work.

Some critics of the mastery learning approach fear that the overall levels of student achievement will decline because teachers will put most of their efforts into getting everyone up to a minimum standard. Other critics argue that it places too much burden on teachers by blaming them for student failures. Proponents, on the other hand, argue that the schools often do contribute to failure. In his introduction to *Schools Without Failure*, for example, William Glasser wrote:

> Much has been written on the difficulties of improving education in the central city. From personal experience, I believe that most people who write about these schools have not raised the critical issue. They have been so obsessed with the social, environmental and cultural factors affecting students that they have not looked deeply enough into *the role education itself has played in causing students to fail, not only in the central city but in all schools. . . .* Very few children come to school failures, none come labeled failures; *it is school and school alone which pins the label of failure on children.*[3]

Mastery learning's proponents believe they can provide at least a partial antidote to school failure. Benjamin Bloom claims, for example, that with appropriate instruction 95 percent of students can attain mastery and a grade of A. For Bloom, the notion of grading by the bell-shaped normal curve makes no sense in the classroom because it is a statistical tool designed to reflect random processes. To the degree that the teacher has purposeful impact on learners, the grading curve should depart from a chance distribution; thus Bloom asserts that the closer student achievement follows a normal distribution, the more unsuccessful are the teacher's efforts.[4]

The mastery learning literature has grown dramatically since the seminal works of John Carroll in 1963 and Bloom in 1968.[5] James Block has probably done more than anyone to date in helping educators transfer the theories of mastery learning into practice.[6] Typically, a course based on Bloom's mastery learning is developed according to the following steps:*

1. The course or subject is broken down into a series of learning units covering one or two weeks of instruction.
2. The instructional objectives, representing a wide range of learning outcomes (e.g., knowledge, comprehension, and application), are clearly specified for each unit.

---

*The list of steps is reprinted with permission of Macmillan Publishing Company from *Individualizing Classroom Instruction* by Norman E. Gronlund. Copyright © 1974 by Norman E. Gronlund.

3. The learning tasks within each unit are taught using regular group-based instruction.
4. Diagnostic-progress tests (formative tests) are administered at the end of each learning unit.
5. The results of the end-of-unit tests are used to reinforce the learning of students who have mastered the unit and to diagnose the learning errors of those who fail to demonstrate mastery.
6. Specific procedures for correcting learning deficiencies (e.g., re-reading particular pages, using programmed materials, and using audiovisual aids) and additional learning time are prescribed for those who do not achieve unit mastery. Retesting may be done after the corrective study. (See Table 8.1 on page 272 for types of correctives.)
7. Upon completion of all the units, an end-of-course (summary) test is administered to determine students' course grades. All students who perform at or above the predetermined mastery level (set at course's outset) receive a grade of A in the course. Lower grades are also assigned on the basis of absolute standards that have been set for the course.
8. The results of the unit tests (formative tests) and the final examination (summary tests) are used as a basis for improving the methods, materials, and sequencing of instruction.[7]

Eric is using a modified version of Bloom's mastery learning (see Figures 8.1 and 8.2). He identifies the learning goals and objectives in the common-core area, and divides his course into a sequence of cumulative units (Figure 8.1) designed to help students master the overarch-

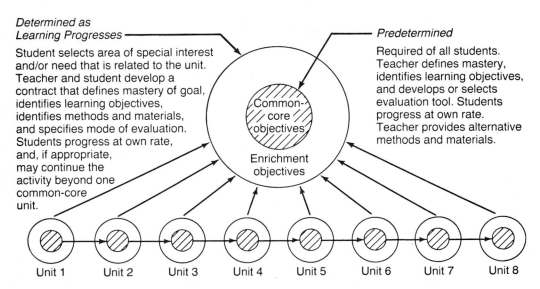

Determined as Learning Progresses

Student selects area of special interest and/or need that is related to the unit. Teacher and student develop a contract that defines mastery of goal, identifies learning objectives, identifies methods and materials, and specifies mode of evaluation. Students progress at own rate, and, if appropriate, may continue the activity beyond one common-core unit.

Common-core objectives

Enrichment objectives

Predetermined

Required of all students. Teacher defines mastery, identifies learning objectives, and develops or selects evaluation tool. Students progress at own rate. Teacher provides alternative methods and materials.

Unit 1   Unit 2   Unit 3   Unit 4   Unit 5   Unit 6   Unit 7   Unit 8

Figure 8.1 *Overview of Learning Objectives for Entire Course*

ing objects for the course. With a few exceptions, no student moves on to a new unit until mastery has been achieved. However, enrichment learning objectives also become a systematic part of his planning. These are developed, or emerge, in each unit for students who have already mastered the core material or who will learn it very quickly. In contrast to the core learning objectives, which are spelled out in advance, the enrichment learning objectives need not follow a cumulative sequence from unit to unit and are relatively open-ended to encourage student creativity and divergent thinking. In the case of short-term enrichment objectives, contracts are used, and they match the student's need for structure as well as the amount of time likely to be available before the entire class moves on to the next unit. It is possible, however, for some students to pursue enrichment learning objectives that span two or more common-core learning units.

Rapid learners may spend most of their time working on enrichment objectives. Students like Tony and Tomás, however, will also have some opportunity to work on student-selected enrichment objectives. A key to the success of Eric's program is the fact that the enrichment objectives are, in fact, enriching. Students do not regard them as extra or busy work.

In addition to including the student-selected enrichment objectives, Eric has modified Bloom's mastery learning in a second important way. Rather than using correctives to reteach students who do not achieve mastery on the unit test, he *continually* builds the correctives into his learning program. He uses group-based instruction largely for motivation, basic instructions, and occasional lectures. He feels this greater flexibility is necessary because of the strong cultural diversity and numerous individual differences among his students. Because he knows the students cannot all master the objectives in the same way with ease, he does not wait until a unit test has identified students who needed different strategies (see Figure 8.2).

Eric's floor plan illustrates how he organizes his classroom so that many of these correctives can be used throughout the unit as part of his original instructional plan.

One of the most important advantages of mastery learning is that it provides learners with a feeling of success and accomplishment. Furthermore, the feeling is based on actual achievement and new competence. These achievements generate feelings of confidence that are necessary for school success; because students are actually mastering the expected learning objectives, problems of social promotion are minimized or eliminated. It is no longer acceptable to cover material and move on if students have not learned.

As conceptualized by Bloom and Block, mastery learning is well suited for the constraints most teachers face—for example, large groups, required textbooks, grade-level groupings, and strict time schedules.[8]

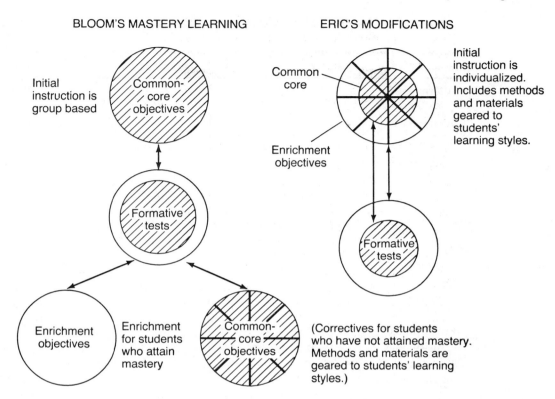

Figure 8.2   *Mastery Learning Modified*

Mastery learning allows us to teach a group of students in whatever way we wish. We are required to modify the large group plan by using one or more correctives (see Table 8.1) only for those students who did not learn during the initial group-based instruction. Furthermore, mastery learning is not all that new. Many textbooks and supplementary materials in all areas of the curriculum are already based on the mastery learning concept. Teachers just have not been expecting mastery on the part of most students.

The approach is not without problems, however. Teachers worry that too much time will be spent waiting for slower learners to catch up. (Experience shows, however, that once the fundamentals are learned in early units, high levels of mastery are achieved more quickly in subsequent units.) Parents and high-achieving students under the traditional approach often resent the lack of recognition and the fact that everyone can get A's. If mastery learning is to be successful, a careful orientation is necessary for students, parents, and teachers. Competition for grades must be replaced by shared responsibility for achievement and the recognition that everyone benefits when the overall level of learning is

Table 8.1 *A Summary of General Types of Correctives,*
by Block and Anderson

CORRECTIVE	INDIVIDUAL	GROUP	PRESENTATION	INVOLVEMENT
Alternative textbooks	✔		✔	
Workbooks	✔		✔	
Flashcards	✔		✔	
Reteaching		✔	✔	
Audio-visual materials*		✔	✔	
Token economies	✔			✔
Academic games		✔		✔
Group affective exercises*		✔		✔
Programmed instruction	✔		✔	✔
Tutoring	✔		✔	✔
Small group study sessions		✔	✔	✔

Source: Reprinted with permission of Macmillan Publishing Company from *Mastery Learning in Classroom Instruction* by James H. Block and Lorin W. Anderson. Copyright © 1975 Macmillan Publishing Company.

*These correctives might also be used on an individual basis in some situations.

significantly improved. There is still room for the development of individual talents and gifts, however, and this must be part of the plan.

Students who are accustomed to failure must be given encouragement, support, and the experience of success. Students who are accustomed to school success must continue to experience it. When genuine enrichment opportunities are available, learning expands and students need not suffer through redundant material. Report cards can be modified to record students' special achievements beyond the basic course requirements.

Teachers will need to rely on their common sense as they implement the concept of mastery learning in their own classrooms. Eric, for example, believes that mastery learning works best for those portions of the course in which concepts and skills are typically learned sequentially, complex behaviors depend on the previous learning of less complex behaviors, and students use convergent thinking (recall) rather than divergent thinking (synthesis). This is a clue that students who tend to be highly intuitive, approach learning holistically, or prefer inductive learning might become frustrated or uncomfortable with a total program comprised of performance-based sequential and convergent learning tasks. Higher-order thinking skills—including application, analysis, synthesis, and evaluation—can, however, be taught through the mastery learning approach.

Furthermore, there are important areas in Eric's course where predetermination of objectives and methods of evaluation associated with mastery learning are inappropriate because they cannot be specified prior to knowing the students personally; areas related to personal creativity and expression, special knowledge interests, and attitudes and behavior such as cooperation, empathy, and respect. Finally, some students with high aptitudes may lack requisite entry-level knowledge skills such as (for this classroom) standard English.

Experiential Learning

Experiential learning uses personal experience to engage the learner totally (physically, emotionally, and intellectually) in the discovery of new knowledge. Experiential learning is a teaching concept that is different from mastery learning. The two approaches to teaching can be compatible, as is the case in Eric's classroom.

Some make a distinction between the two concepts on the basis of the humanist-behaviorist controversy. To the degree that mastery learning is based on behavioral objectives and behavior modification, it falls into the psychological school of behaviorism. Experiential learning, on the other hand, falls into the school of humanism.

With mastery learning the knowledge goals and learning objectives are centered in the subject matter. With experiential learning, knowledge is centered in the pupil's behavior and personal and social reality. Knowledge is valued most when it is personally discovered, analyzed, and assimilated. The teacher acts as a fellow investigator rather than as an expert, but encourages students to observe and analyze their experiences.

Eric uses experiential learning to introduce traditional subject matter. His students are engaged in a variety of learning activities that have grown out of the simulation Bafá Bafá.[9]

An outstanding resource on the experience-centered curriculum has been developed by an international group of teachers from eight different countries who have worked with David Wolsk as part of a UNESCO-sponsored project for developing international understanding. These teachers have developed a total of fifty-eight units intended mainly for students between the ages of eleven and eighteen. They have also devel-

Box 8.1

Components
of Experien-
tial Learning

Step One: The experience situation

Step Two: Development of observation and description skills

Step Three: Development of analysis and decision-making skills

Step Four: Follow-up activities that link the experience situation and discussion with the ongoing curriculum

oped guidelines for applying the units to specific subject areas, including biology; mathematics; literature, writing, and language; social studies; physical sciences; physical education; and the arts.[10] Four required components are illustrated in Box 8.1. Typically, the teacher creates or selects an experience situation to introduce a new concept or unit. These experiences are designed to involve and stimulate students physically, emotionally, and intellectually, for example a simulation or contrived incident. A carefully developed discussion and appropriate follow-up activities are necessary bridges to the common-core learning objectives of the course; otherwise, the experience situation can degenerate into fun-and-games.

For example, the UNESCO project developed one simple exercise to illustrate the process of stereotyping. Students were asked to discuss their own answers to the question, "What is a (Dane)?"

> One Danish class recorded their discussion of "What is a Dane?" and exchanged it with a Hungarian class that had written their answers to "What is a Hungarian?" as well as their ideas about Danes. In the follow-up to the exchange, both classes were able to see how they look to others, how they tend to stereotype themselves, how misinformed were their expectations of national differences, and how it feels to be "judged" by others. This judging is what caused their biggest reaction.[11]

Another unit, Blind Trust, is based on a trust walk. Half the students are blindfolded and then led throughout the school and/or outdoors on a ten-minute walk by an unknown partner. Talking is not permitted. Later, the students exchange roles so that each experiences leadership and dependency. A third unit, Four Hands on the Clay, illustrates some of the practices involved in cooperative decision making. Students work in pairs on a large block of clay, with their eyes closed. After the students have removed watches and jewelry and have rolled up their sleeves, they are lined up along the walls; then they are instructed to close their eyes and keep them closed throughout the exercise. The students are instructed not to talk or laugh or make any noise that would allow others to identify them. Partners are then led one by one over to chairs next to large blocks of clay that have been distributed around the desks or tables so that partners can sit opposite each other with the clay between them. The partners are instructed to create something out of the clay, working and communicating only with their hands.[12]

Even if experience situations such as these do not turn out as the teacher expected, the activity cannot fail. Whatever happens should become the basis of the follow-up discussion in step two. Once class members have discussed their observations of what happened, they should move to a discussion of their feelings and analyses.

After a trust walk, students might be asked what influenced them to trust or not trust the other person. What cues from the other person did they tune into? How did the other person feel? Would it have helped to know who their partner was, or not? During the exercise Four Hands on the Clay, students could explain how they decided what would be created. Without the use of eyes and ears, how did communication take place? What was your partner feeling?

In the fourth stage, follow-up activities are needed to link the experience situation and discussions with important course objectives. Students should not regard these activities as just fun and frills. Independent study or small group projects are possible follow-ups, as well as large group instruction and lectures. Four Hands on the Clay, for example, could introduce students to a study of the nervous system. What was going on in the brain during their activity? All students experienced a visual image as they worked. How can this occur? Four Hands on the Clay could also motivate students to explore nonverbal communication, to develop their own creative expressions, or to increase their decision-making skill. (How did the partners communicate? Or did they? Could they cooperate?) Students might build upon their experiences in the trust walk to examine the role of trust in cross-cultural communication, international agreements, and the role of spotters in physical education classes

The curriculum developed by Wolsk and his team has been found to significantly increase pupils' readiness to associate with students and families of different nationalities. Positive impact has also been noted on students' feelings of acceptance by the teacher and other pupils, attitudes toward school learning, decreased levels of school and general anxiety, and increased social sensitivity through greater empathy, acceptance, respect, and genuineness. Thus, the approach clearly has implications for any teacher who wishes to decrease interpersonal and group barriers based on ethnic differences, and to increase empathy.

Wolsk's curriculum has also been found to enhance student achievement. The experiences of one eighth and ninth grade English teacher in the rural Midwest is typical of teachers everywhere who decide to implement experiential learners. In this teacher's classes, the students' writing skills improved dramatically during the program, particularly when compared with the skills of classmates who did not have an opportunity to discuss and write about experience situations. The teacher happened to be very creative in developing ingenious experience situations. However, other teachers in his school tended to be suspicious and even ridiculing of his approach until the student achievement results became obvious by the end of the year.

An experiential approach is especially effective with culturally diverse groups of students because (with the important exception of language) there are no specific knowledge, attitude, or skill prerequisites for the initial involvement. Students can participate in the introductory activity regardless of their achievement levels or cultural orientation. In fact, the greater the diversity of experiences among the students who participate, the richer the follow-up discussion and activities will be for all the students. As happened in Eric's second-period class, cultural patterns often emerge spontaneously and can be examined with less risk of stereotyping because these patterns coexist with individual variability.

The experience-centered curriculum is an approach to individualized instruction that works well in conjunction with mastery learning because it injects the motivation that is often necessary to move learners on to mastery.

> A class learning from a textbook and the teacher's lessons uses much of their time and energy in adjusting the structures of their own information processing systems, their individual classification structures, to the teacher's and textbook's classifications. Alternatively, when an experience situation is used as a starting point, and an open-ended discussion follows, the pupils are, in a sense, *being left alone to learn in their own style.* They individually put in and take out of the situation what they are ready for. When they follow this up with textbooks and teachers' lessons, it is with a series of questions stated in their own terms and linked to their own reactions to the experience situation and to their individual views of their own past, present and future lives.[13]

Bilingual Education[14]

Bilingual education is usually defined as the use of two languages as mediums of instruction. In this society, one of the two languages must be English and the student's home language becomes the second language of instruction. Bilingual education's major goals are (1) to help students identify their ethnicity, (2) to foster acculturation in the host culture and gain proficiency in the target language, and (3) to help students build on diversity and integrate their home culture and language with their new ones.

The concept of bilingual education rests upon two very basic and seemingly obvious assumptions:

1. People are more likely to learn anything, including English, if they understand what they are being taught.
2. Students with limited English ability will not fall behind their English-speaking peers if they can keep up with subject matter content through their native language while they are mastering English.[15]

Over a billion people worldwide speak a language other than English. Just within United States society, according to the 1980 census, 11 percent of Americans are from non-English-speaking homes. Further, Nancy Conklin and Margaret Lourie provide statistics that indicate that Limited English Proficient (LEP) or non-English-speaking populations are found in virtually every state (see Figure 8.3). As Brisk has suggested, "The history of American education is marked by attempts to grapple with our 'polyglot heritage.' "[16]

The United States is not the first country to formulate policy for a polyglot or multilingual society. Global strategies for language policy tend to fall into three categories: (1) emphasis on a national language at the expense of indigenous languages, (2) elevation of a local language (vernacular) that symbolizes sociocultural, religious, or political unity to the status of national language, or (3) retention of the language of a previously occupying nation, or colonial languages, as the official language when there are numerous traditional language groups competing for power. The history of language policy in the United States is best described by the first global strategy, emphasis on a national language at the expense of indigenous languages.

The nineteenth- and early twentieth-century waves of immigration from Europe, China, and Japan prior to World War I led initially to the establishment of private and public schools that used native languages as the primary mediums of instruction.[17] These multilingual education programs and a national tolerance for cultural diversity were soon submerged by Americanization programs in the schools. By 1923 thirty-two states had adopted English-only instruction for the schools. Some school systems attempted to prohibit any kind of foreign language instruction. This step, however, was ruled unconstitutional by the Supreme Court (Meyer v. Nebraska) in 1923. In part, a reaction to World War I, these English-only laws still exist in a few states today. Assessing their intent, Arnold Leibowitz states that they were designed "to limit access to economic and political life."[18] Although educational trends have moved away from the banning of foreign language instruction, an effort is being made to politically establish English as the official language of the United States. Though this type of bill has failed in Congress on numerous occasions, individual states have begun to investigate such legisla-

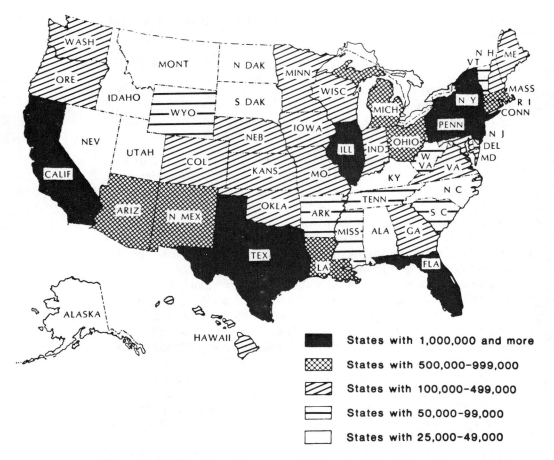

Figure 8.3 *Number of Persons with Non-English Mother Tongues, by State. Reprinted with permission of The Free Press, a Division of Macmillan, Inc., from* A Host of Tongues *by Nancy Faires Conklin and Margaret A. Lourie. Copyright © 1983 The Free Press.*

tion. In 1984 the state Senate passed a bill that established English as the official language of Indiana.

World War II led to the realization that the trend toward educational monolingualism had left the United States at a global disadvantage. It was not until 1958, however, after the Russians launched Sputnik, that the United States realized the disadvantage of a policy of linguistic isolation. The National Defense Education Act, passed that year, had as its primary goal the facilitation of foreign language instruction in the United States. One ramification of this act came in the form of assertive efforts on behalf of linguistic minorities during the 1960s.

The concept of bilingual education has steadily gained momentum in this society since the foundation of Miami's Coral Way School in 1963.

Established by the wave of Cuban immigrants who entered Florida in the early 1960s—most of whom were highly educated, skilled professionals who held social and educational values compatible with Miami's mainstream—the school provided Spanish-language-dominant and English-language-dominant children proficiency in two languages and an appreciation of knowledge of two cultures. The success of this Dade County, Florida, school greatly influenced language education policy over the next twenty years. A chronology follows:

1963   Dade County, Florida, initiated a bilingual program for Spanish-speaking Cuban children and English-dominant children who want to become bilingual.

1965   The Elementary and Secondary Education Act (ESEA) granted funds to schools to upgrade education, including the areas of languages and linguistics.

1966   The first Navajo/English school was created in Rough Rock, Arizona.

1968   The Bilingual Education Act was passed by Congress. Title VII of ESEA was created to promote bilingual schools. Seventy-two bilingual programs started in 1969.

1971   Massachusetts became the first state to pass a law mandating bilingual education for limited-English-proficient students.

1973   The Bilingual Education Reform Act updated the 1968 law and mandated the study of history and culture in bilingual programs.

1974   The United States Supreme Court Decision, Lau v. Nichols, decreed that limited-English-proficient students have a legal right to bilingual instruction as part of equal educational opportunity.

1974   The National Council of Teachers of English (NCTE) affirmed the right of a student to use his or her own language.

1979   Ann Arbor, Michigan, court decision on dialects stated that use of black English vernacular is not an indication of intellectual inferiority or learning disability.

1979   The President's Commission on Foreign Language and International Studies reported: "The inability of most Americans to speak or understand any language except English and to comprehend other cultures handicaps the U.S. seriously in the international arena."

1983   The National Commission on Excellence in Education called for renewed efforts in teaching foreign languages.

Although our national language policy has recently focused on the desirability of linguistic diversity, the concept of bilingual education is controversial. Unfortunately, the controversies associated with bilingual education are often rooted in a distinction between transitional and maintenance programs. Transitional programs focus on the transfer of native language competency skills to assist the learning of English, with the goal of the student functioning in an English-only classroom. Maintenance programs, however, are designed to help children develop cognitive skills in both their native language and in English. Often overlooked is the fact that maintenance of the native language actually supports and facilitates transition into English.[19] Finally, there are English as a Second Language (ESL) programs, which use only English as a medium of instruction. The ESL programs may be found as a language arts component of a bilingual education program or used alone to simultaneously teach English to students of different native language backgrounds.

Before examining the different philosophies and strategies associated with these competing approaches, consider an example of the LEP student who is usually the focus of the controversy.

> Josué sits silently in the back of the classroom. His book is closed; he stares at his new fifth grade surroundings. He has mastered the nuances of English. He nods his head appropriately when spoken to in a pleasant tone—looks downcast when an English voice is angry. He displays all the proper nonverbal cues in his new American school. He misses Puerto Rico and the familiar sound of Spanish in the classroom. The teacher likes Josué; thinks he is a good boy, but slow. Without assistance, Josué will become part of a forgotten minority—the Hispanic gifted.

By the age of three, a child has begun to master the phonological, semantic, and syntactic components that all languages must have. These sound, meaning, and grammar systems develop in generative stages referred to as holophrastic (one-word utterances), telegraphic ("me go home"), and pivot-open grammar ("allgone egg"). The vocabulary, intonation patterns, and nonverbal gestures that accompany language production are learned from models (parents, siblings, neighbors) and are culture bound. World view, perception, and intuition are reflected in the language-learning process. Josué's world view is being newly tested. His assumptions of nonverbal or socially directed verbal exchanges seem satisfactory. His intuition has told him that, but his rewards are strong. Sitting quietly in the back of the room does not get him the attention he needs, but he does get approving smiles. He has been taught to be polite and respectful and because of his intellectual gifts, he will one day catch on—perhaps in four months—perhaps next year; for now, he waits.

LEP students are often caught up in conflicts between personal language needs—for example, the need to consolidate cognitive skills in the native language—and a sociopolitical climate that views standard English as most desirable and prestigious. The ideal bilingual education program uses an eclectic tactic that approaches language learning holistically and incorporates first and second language learning pedagogy.[20] Bilingual education best serves the LEP student when only two language groups are involved: the home language and English. An ideal bilingual program would not isolate the LEP student, but would have a group of English-dominant students who want to become proficient in a second language.[21]

A maintenance program provides dual language instruction for students from kindergarten through twelfth grade. The student develops cognitively in both languages and is instructed in the history and culture of his or her ethnic group as well as that of the macroculture. The learner may therefore retain and expand the home language while also mastering standard English. A transitional program, on the other hand, focuses on the goal of mainstreaming LEP students into English-only classes as soon as they have the English proficiency to succeed, and cultural assimilation is often stressed. In transitional programs, dual language instruction may be instituted in grades kindergarten to four, and initially students are taught in their home language and the language of the host country or the target language. The child's cognitive skills, however, are eventually transferred from the home language to standard English. Unfortunately, this transference is expected prior to the consolidation of language skills in the native language, which typically occurs around the age of ten or eleven. This premature transference may harm the child's cognitive development by disallowing use of the home language as a cognitive tool.

English as a Second Language (ESL) is a method of teaching English based on theoretical principles of language acquisition. The goal is to assimilate learners into the English language as quickly as possible. ESL programs seem most effective when more than one home language is represented in a classroom. They provide English-only instruction but may include a multicultural emphasis. Troike cites research indicating that an English-only classroom is not as cognitively effective as a sound bilingual program.[22] ESL programs, however, can be highly effective and appropriate for students who are motivated to learn the new language in a mainstream English-only classroom. Whatever approach is used, motivation is the key to successful language learning. Richard Gardner and Wallace Lambert described integrative and instrumental motivation as being the determining factors in language learning.[23] Integrative motivation usually represents the learner's desire to incorporate both the target language and selected cultural aspects into his or her lifestyle. Instrumental motivation, however, is more single-goal oriented—learning the language to enhance career goals or academic success, for example.

A variety of factors affect the motivation of LEP students' desire to learn the English language as well as their motivation to retain their original language. Table 8.2 summarizes some of the major factors that

Table 8.2 *Factors Encouraging Language Retention and Loss*

Language Retention	Language Loss
Political, Social, and Demographic Factors	
Large number of speakers living in concentration (ghettos, reservations, ethnic neighborhoods, rural speech islands)	Small number of speakers, dispersed among speakers of other languages
Recent arrival and/or continuing immigration	Long, stable residence in the United States
Geographical proximity to the homeland; ease of travel to the homeland	Homeland remote and inaccessible
High rate of return to the homeland; intention to return to the homeland; homeland language community still intact	Low rate or impossibility of return to homeland (refugees, Indians displaced from their tribal territories)
Occupational continuity	Occupational shift, especially from rural to urban
Vocational concentration, i.e., employment where co-workers share language background; employment within the language community (stores serving the community, traditional crafts, homemaking, etc.)	Vocations in which some interaction with English or other languages is required; speakers dispersed by employers (e.g., African slaves)
Low social and economic mobility in mainstream occupations	High social and economic mobility in mainstream occupations
Low level of education, leading to low social and economic mobility; *but* educated and articulate community leaders, familiar with the English-speaking society and loyal to their own language community	Advanced level of education, leading to socioeconomic mobility; education that alienates potential community leaders
Nativism, racism, and ethnic discrimination as they serve to isolate a community and encourage identity only with the ethnic group rather than the nation at large	Nativism, racism, and ethnic discrimination, as they force individuals to deny their ethnic identity in order to make their way in society
Cultural Factors	
Mother-tongue institutions, including schools, churches, clubs, theaters, presses, broadcasts	Lack of mother-tongue institutions, from lack of interest or lack of resources
Religious and/or cultural ceremonies requiring command of the mother tongue	Ceremonial life institutionalized in another tongue or not requiring active use of mother tongue
Ethnic identity strongly tied to language; nationalistic aspirations as a language group; mother tongue, the homeland national language	Ethnic identity defined by factors other than language, as for those from multilingual countries or language groups spanning several nations; low level of nationalism
Emotional attachment to mother tongue as a defining characteristic of ethnicity, of self	Ethnic identity, sense of self derived from factors such as religion, custom, race rather than shared speech
Emphasis on family ties and position in kinship or community network	Low emphasis on family or community ties, high emphasis on individual achievement

Table 8.2   (Continued)

LANGUAGE RETENTION	LANGUAGE LOSS
Emphasis on education, if in mother-tongue or community-controlled schools, or used to enhance awareness of ethnic heritage; low emphasis on education otherwise	Emphasis on education and acceptance of public education in English
Culture unlike Anglo society	Culture and religion congruent with Anglo society

Linguistic Factors

Standard, written variety is mother tongue	Minor, nonstandard, and/or unwritten variety as mother tongue
Use of Latin alphabet in mother tongue, making reproduction inexpensive and second-language literacy relatively easy	Use of non-Latin writing system in mother tongue, especially if it is unusual, expensive to reproduce, or difficult for bilinguals to learn
Mother tongue with international status	Mother tongue of little international importance
Literacy in mother tongue, used for exchange within the community and with homeland	No literacy in mother tongue; illiteracy
Some tolerance for loan words, if they lead to flexibility of the language in its new setting	No tolerance for loan words, if no alternate ways of capturing new experience evolve; too much tolerance of loans, leading to mixing and eventual language loss

Source: Reprinted with permission of The Free Press, a Division of Macmillan, Inc., from *A Host of Tongues* by Nancy Faires Conklin and Margaret A. Lourie. Copyright © 1983 The Free Press.

encourage language retention and language loss. It is essential for teachers to recognize that some ethnic groups tend to be more motivated than others to learn standard English. The Spanish-speaking communities of the southwest, for example, were guaranteed the right to retain the Spanish language under the conditions of the Treaty of Guadalupe Hidalgo, and fluency in the Spanish language is essential to maintaining family and community bonds on both sides of the border. Newly arrived Vietnamese, on the other hand, who are eager to build a new life in the United States may also be eager to master English. When family members encourage the acquisition of English, or are themselves bilingual, the child's acquisition of the new language is enhanced. The mastery of standard English need not result in the loss of the home language. The knowledge of two or more languages or the ability to code switch from one variety of English grammar, pronunciation, and usage to another (bidialectalism) is very desirable in a pluralistic society.

Obviously, the best teachers for LEP students are bilingual teachers who can use the home language as well as English. Yet bilingual teachers for some languages are difficult to find. Therefore, more monolingual teachers will at some time have LEP students in their classroom. What can these teachers do? The full answer is beyond the scope of this book and may be pursued in the sources listed in the notes at the end of this chapter. Karen Webb's strategies for improving reading skills among dialect-dominant students, which follow, illustrate how bilingual education strategies have emerged out of foreign language pedagogy. Her guidelines also provide a sample of what is available. These teaching strategies may be modified to reach LEP students, whether or not the teacher is bilingual.

Strategies for Improving Reading Skills

GUIDELINES FOR TEACHERS WITH DIALECT-DOMINANT STUDENTS

1. Become familiar with features of the students' dialect. This will allow the teacher to better understand students and to recognize a reading miscue (a noncomprehension feature) from a comprehension error. Students should not be interrupted during the oral reading process. Correction of comprehension features are best done after the reading segment.
2. Allow students to listen to a passage or story first. This can be done in two ways: (1) finish the story and then ask comprehension questions or (2) interrupt the story at key comprehension segments and ask students to predict the outcome.
3. Use predictable stories, which can be familiar episodes in literature, music, or history. They can be original works or experiential readers.
4. Use visual aids to enhance comprehension. Visual images, whether pictures or words, will aid word recognition and comprehension.
5. Use cloze procedure deletions to focus on vocabulary and meaning. Cloze procedures are simply selected deletions of words from a passage in order to focus on a specific text feature.
   EXAMPLE: The little red hen found an ear of corn. The little red _____ said, "Who will dry the ear of _____ ?" (vocabulary focus)
   Today I feel like a (noun). (grammar focus)
   There was a (pain) in the pit of his stomach. (semantic focus)
6. Allow students to retell the story or passage in various speech styles. Have students select different people to whom they would like to retell the story (family member, principal, friend) and assist them in selecting synonyms most appropriate to each audience. This allows both teacher and student to become language authorities.
7. Integrate reading, speaking, and writing skills whenever possible.
8. Use the microcomputer (if available) as a time-on-task exercise.

The microcomputer can effectively assist in teaching the reading techniques of skimming (general idea), scanning (focused reference), reading for comprehension (master total message), and critical reading (inference and evaluation). Time on task is extremely important to skills development.

Learning Activity Packets and Learning Centers

Learning activity packets (LAPs) and learning centers are useful strategies for providing help to supplement large-group instruction. Both strategies are self-contained learning units for one or a small group of students, which require a minimum of teacher guidance if designed and implemented properly. Both can be designed as a single lesson or a series of lessons, or they may be integrated into an entire instructional program as part of the overall classroom organization plan. Learners are usually permitted to progress at their own rate.

The main difference between the two strategies is format. LAPs are typically designed for a single student and are usually packaged in a folder, envelope, or booklet. Centers, on the other hand, involve the creative use of some designated space to develop one or more stations that can be used by one student or a small group of students. For some it "may be a designated area of a room; on a wall, on a shelf, hanging from the ceiling, free standing in the room, or in folders in a box for portability. For others it may engulf the entire physical confines of an area allowing complete freedom of movement and encouraging all manner of learning modes."[24]

A second difference is that LAPs, sometimes referred to as modules or unipacs, represent mastery learning in microcosm, especially if they are performance based. The rationale underlying mastery learning and performance-based packets is identical: Simple concepts must be learned as a foundation for future complex learning, and most students are capable of high achievement although the rate of learning and approach may be different. LAPs are a useful tool for providing instructional alternatives because teachers can create or select LAPs to match the learning needs of an individual or a small group of students. Theoretically, it is possible to imagine thirty students in a self-contained classroom working independently in thirty different LAPs. One of the dangers of LAPs is an underemphasis on affective objectives, since the necessary measurement techniques are less readily available.

LAPs are used at all age levels (kindergarten to adult) and can be implemented in any subject area. Some are based primarily on the written word; others take the form of skill centers (such as physical education) or may even be extended into learning centers that include a variety of pictures and instructional media. Whatever the format, these learning units should contain the following components.

1. *Title.* This should arouse student interest.

2. *Motivating Rationale.* Often this is a very brief statement of purpose that tells why the unit is worth studying. Many teachers include some kind of motivational set or attention grabber.

3. *One or More Learning Objectives.* These objectives tell the learner what she or he must do in order to master the unit. Objectives should focus on the thinking, feeling, and acting dimensions of the learner. Too often, LAPs contain objectives aimed solely at knowledge recall.

4. *Pretest.* This activity enables the teacher to determine the learner's readiness for the unit. It also allows learners to see where they stand in relation to what they are expected to master. The pretest helps avoid redundancy for students who have already mastered the unit or portions of it. It also helps avoid a mismatch for students who lack prerequisite background of skill and information.

5. *Learning Activities.* Experiences and materials are selected or developed to assist the learner in achieving the unit objective(s). In some units students are expected to complete the same assignments in the same way, and the learning activities section might be relatively brief. Usually, it is desirable to provide alternative materials and activities to allow for differences in learning style and language. Gronlund suggests that the following list of activities be considered in planning assignments.*

> Read books
> Read magazine articles
> Read newspaper articles
> Use programmed materials
> View film or filmstrips
> Listen to tapes
> Conduct experiments
> Do projects
> Play games
> Take field trips
> Practice communication skills
> Practice physical skills
> Discuss questions with teacher or peers
> Take self-test on unit activities[25]

Special attention must be given to the level of the reading material. It may be necessary to write special instructional materials that can be read by everyone, including learners whose first language is not standard English.

*The list is reprinted with permission of Macmillan Publishing Company from *Individualizing Classroom Instruction* by Norman E. Gronlund. Copyright © 1974 by Norman E. Gronlund.

6. *Posttest.* The posttest measures learner attainment of the unit objective(s) and is usually an alternate form of the pretest. Unless it is used as a self-test, the posttest is not included in the packet itself and may be obtained from the teacher when the learner feels ready. Except for certain attitudinal and valuing measures, the posttest is typically criterion referenced (that is, absolute standards of mastery are established, usually 85 percent correct).

Learning centers may be modeled after mastery learning, depending on the purpose of the center, but typically they are not. Each station usually contains all the components needed in a LAP: title, rationale, learning objectives, pretest, learning activities (methods and materials), and means for determining student achievement. Rather than receiving a printed package from the instructor, as with the LAP, the student moves to a center and can receive audio or pictorial instructions and a variety of learning materials and activities. The amount of written explanation can vary from none to extensive. Up to six different learning centers might exist simultaneously in a self-contained classroom, and students might be required to complete any number of them.

> Centers can be *developmental,* presenting new understandings and skills; *functional,* providing opportunities to use newly acquired skills and understandings; and/or *recreational,* providing opportunities to engage in activities for the sake of creativity and pleasure. They should allow for exploration through open-endedness and afford opportunities to pursue the solution to problems in the learner's own way and should provide the child with the option of manipulating ideas and materials and sharing reactions of such manipulations with their peers and teachers.[26]

Whatever the purpose, successful centers contain three components. The first, clear directions, must tell the student where to place completed work and should guide self-evaluation and assessment. They may be written, flow charted, tape recorded, or given by the teacher or another student. The second component is alternative activities for learning, with emphasis on different learning styles. The third is a method of assessing and recording the learner's involvement in the center.

Both LAPs and learning centers are available commercially, although many teachers prefer to create their own materials. Two samples of teacher-created materials follow. The first is an excerpt from a LAP created by Teresa Hogue, a high school literature teacher. The second, by Janice Bristow, describes an eighth-grade foreign language teacher's experiences with learning centers. Following these examples, this section concludes with a listing of major advantages and disadvantages associated with LAPs and centers.

SHORT STORY PACKET II

SNEAKING A PEEK
at
★ *Setting* ★
by Teresa Hogue

I.   INTRODUCTION

Congratulations!! You are about to embark upon another
thrill-packed adventure into the realm of "literature."
(Now don't get too excited. . . .) By now you are a veteran
user of LAPs because you have survived the activities outlined for you in Short Story Packet I: The Plot Sickens.
Remember that in Packet II the learning activities branch out.
Our discussion will go beyond a simple definition of *SETTING*
and how it aids in understanding the short story. We will
examine a broader definition of *SETTING* and think about
how an individual's surroundings or environment can shape
the person he becomes.

Let's review the rules for using LAPs. Using the tape
is optional. If it helps you with your reading, continue to
listen to the tape as you read. If it bothers you, don't
use it. Different people learn in different ways, so choose
the way that you learn best.
        If you run across a word that you do not know
the meaning of--STOP--grab a copy of Brother Webster and look it up!
        If you don't understand an activity in the LAP--
STOP--get your hand in the air and I will come running.
Together we will clear up your problem.
        If you can think of an alternate activity that would
be more meaningful for you to do--STOP--get your hand in the
air and we will talk about it.
        When you are through working with this packet, return it
to the shelves INTACT--that means complete, the way you got
it, and with no pieces missing!! Failure to comply will
result in death by slow torture. . . . NEED
                                        I SAY
                                        MORE?

II.   INSTRUCTIONS

Short Story Packet II: Sneaking a Peek at *SETTING* contains
two major objectives. For each objective there are a variety
of learning activities designed to help you achieve that
objective. In this packet, you will be required to complete
all activities unless you are told otherwise.
        In addition to this packet, you will need your Self Journal,
probably another notebook, and writing implements. Unless a

formal writing assignment is indicated, you may use any color of pen you like. (Am I nice, or what?) Creativity in the completion of LAP activities will be rewarded with higher grades.

After you have completed all the activities in Packet II, it will be time for a conference with Ol' Lady Hogue. At that time we will evaluate your work and discuss moving on to the next packet.

All writing assignments, unless [Cat got your Pen?] appears next to the activity, may be taped on cassette. Remember that an outline of your work must accompany the tape!

III. OBJECTIVES

1. You will review the definition of *SETTING* and understand why it is an important element in the study of the short story. The following activities will help you achieve this objective:

    (a) Organizing a chapter in your Self Journal entitled *SETTING*; this will serve as the "vehicle" we'll use to present your work from Packet II.
    (b) Demonstrating your understanding of *SETTING* by reading two stories and analyzing their settings, and by making up your own settings from pictures that suggest a story.
    (c) Reading a third story and deciding why *SETTING* is crucial to that story and how the story would be different if either element of setting were changed.

2. You will broaden your definition of *SETTING* and think about how surroundings and environment affect people. These activities will help you achieve this objective:

    (a) Brainstorming as many broad definitions of *SETTING* as you can with your friends. This will be the springboard we'll use to understand ourselves in relation to our surroundings.
    (b) Researching (in the library!!) the life of a person whom you admire and deciding how environment shaped his or her achievements.
    (c) Outlining an assignment to demonstrate how your environment both stops you from doing some things and offers a wide variety of things you can do.
    (d) Writing (oh, boy!) a formal composition that discusses how your environment has affected you in the past and how it affects you at the present, and what your goals are for the future.

Don't Panic! Turn the Page!

IV. ACTIVITIES -- 1

A. In your journal, begin a chapter on *SETTING*. This chapter will include a title page, a definitions page, several activities pages.

SHOW TIME

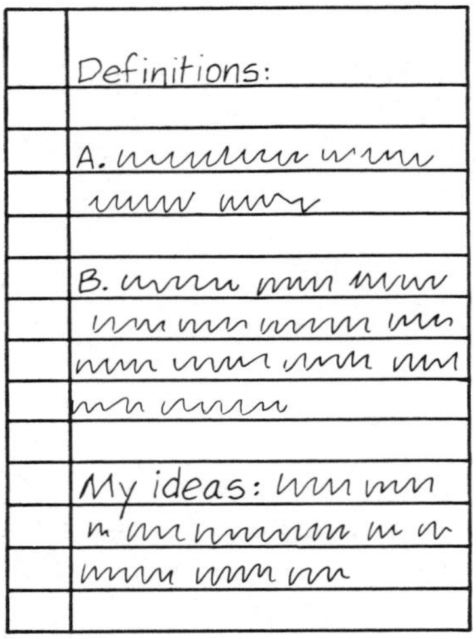
Definitions:
A.
B.
My ideas:

(1) Title Page. The word *SETTING* should be displayed in bold letters somewhere on the page. (Doesn't freedom make you feel giddy?) Persons in search of brownie points will want to tastefully illustrate the page.

(2) Definitions Page. In the glossary of your lit book, look up the definition of *SETTING*. Copy it into your journal. This will be definition "A."

Walk, don't run, to the bookshelves and latch onto a copy of Brother Webster. You'll find five definitions. Which one applies most closely to the study of literature? Copy it into your journal. This will be definition "B."

(3) Congratulations. You have just completed Activity A.

B. Firming It Up: Are you ready to continue? Of course you are! In your literature text, your assignment is to read "The Day We Flew the Kites" on p. 103 and "The Hunchback Madonna" on p. 156. Stop and Execute.

READ
AT YOUR
OWN
RISK

Welcome back. I'd suggest doing this activity on a piece of scrap paper and then copying the finished product into your journal. Listen up. . . . First, I want you to decide what the setting is for each story. If you need help ask for it now! Okay. Then tell me in which story you think setting is most important. Explain why setting is not as important or vital in the other story. Stop and Execute.

REMEMBER: SETTINGS CAN CHANGE WITHIN A STORY!!!!

C. Story Starters: In pocket 1 of the LAP folder, you will find three pictures.

→→ If these pictures were short story illustrations, what do you think the setting of each story might be?

Choose one of the pictures. Write the opening paragraphs of a short story suggested by the picture. You should

establish or explain the setting of the story in those
two paragraphs. This assignment should be about 200
words long.
--OR--
You may find your own picture and do the same assignment.
--OR--
You may draw or illustrate your own picture.
--OR--
You may creatively illustrate the setting of your story
starter by sculpting a statue.
--OR--
You may illustrate your started story with a ten-
frame storyboard. ★ Stop and Execute. 〜 〜〜

D. The Wizard of Frank

(1) In your literature text, turn to p. 308 and read
"The Diary of Anne Frank."

"Diary" is NOT a short story because it is non-fiction.

If it will help or entertain you, I have taped the
story on cassette 6 under Autobiography.

(2) What is the setting of this story?

(3) You may want to scribble the rest of this assignment on scrap paper and then recopy it into your
journal, because it is a formal writing assignment.
I want you to tell me about how time and place--or
Anne's environment--affected her life. What political events were going on around Anne as she wrote
in her diary? How did these events affect Anne and
her family? Why were they especially vulnerable
to the situation in Europe? In spite of the turmoil of Anne's surroundings, what were her major
concerns? Are they like or unlike the things that
are important to you?

(4) You will relish this exercise because it means you
get out of class to go to the library!! Listen
carefully to the assignment and take any notes you
may need. Remember that LAPs stay in the room.
    Imagine that you are a wizard. You have the
power to change time and place. See options for
completing this activity below:

(a) Change Place: You magically place Anne Frank
    in another city during World War II. Use at
    least two sources for a 300-word written report
    on what life would be like for a young person
    in that city. For example, you could describe
    Anne's life if she lived in London during the
    Blitz.

(b) Change Time: This one is a little more difficult but can be fun--especially if you are a
history buff. You will magically place Anne
in Amsterdam during another period in history.
For example, you could describe what life was
like for a young Jewish girl in Amsterdam
during World War I or during the Napoleonic
Wars.
The librarian is expecting you and can help you
with questions you might have on research. You
will be allowed one class period in the library to
research this assignment.

V.   ACTIVITIES -- 2

A.   Brainstorming: With your friends, your relatives, and
any stranger you meet on the street who is as excited
about broad definitions of *SETTING* as you are, brainstorm as many definitions of *SETTING* as you can.
Dedicate a page in your journal to the fruits of your
labors.

B.   Mirror, Mirror: In pocket 1, you will discover a mirror. . . . After you have admired yourself, take a
serious look at the person staring back at you.
     Consider the limits your environment places on what
you can do. Think also about the opportunities your
environment offers you.
     There are limits to what we can do because of when
and where we live, but there are also endless possibilities. In Central Indiana it is not possible to pile
in the car after school and go to the ocean or the
mountains. Nor can we visit with King Henry VIII or
vacation on Mars. But there are many opportunities
available to us in our place and time. Ten years ago,
you could not enroll in computer class. Fifty years
ago, you would not be listening to this tape.
     In your journal, introduce yourself and describe
your environment. You may be very specific or very
general. On the back of the page, make three columns.
In column I, list five things you can't do because your
environment doesn't offer them. Then list five things
you can do. In the third column, list four goals or
things that you would like to do sometime during your
lifetime.

	Mirror, Mirror		
	My name is Guy Smiley. I		
	live on the planet Earth in		
	the twentieth century.		
	CAN'T	CAN	WILL
	¹*Have lunch*	¹*Work on*	¹*Make*
	with Hitler	*my go-cart*	*$1,000,000*
	²*go surfing*	²*program*	²*Be a father*
		my Apple II	³*Found my*
			own racing
			team

CAUTION: POOR HANDWRITING

C. <u>Hero at Large</u>: In a magazine, find a picture of your favorite sports hero, rock star, actor, etc. Read about that person's life in newspapers and magazines, or call for an interview if you can arrange it. (You may have a study hall pass, if you need one.)

What happened early in life that led this person to success in his or her field? Did the environment offer special opportunities or obstacles that had to be overcome? After researching this person's life, do you admire him or her more, or are you disappointed? Record your ideas and reactions in a 200-word journal entry.

D. In a formal composition, discuss the environment you are growing up in. Talk about its effect on your past and your present. What are your goals for the future and how do your surroundings affect those goals?

NOW IT'S YOUR TURN TO WRITE!

<u>Further Instructions</u>: After you have finished all of the activities in this packet, prepare to turn in your journal. Make an appointment with your teacher for evaluation.

<u>Speaking of Evaluation</u>: Your grade will be based on how neatly, creatively, and completely you have completed the packet activities. Each LAP will count as a test grade.

PATIENTLY AWAITING YOUR LAP!

Learning Centers in a Foreign Language Classroom

Janice K. Bristow

I have always pictured learning centers as places to go when finished with work, a place for extra information and enjoyment. Naturally, I decided to create a learning center for recreation and enrichment. I never have enough time to present the cultural information I should, so I decided the emphasis of my center would be daily life in Germany. I planned the center to be used specifically with my German 8B class, which is the class for all eighth graders who did not make it into the two-year language program.

There were many problems. Even with the center stuck in a corner, there was always too much noise and confusion. Many students would want to use the center at the same time, and only students who finish work quickly could get a chance. There were no evaluations, as the material was intended for enjoyment, so students did not take the center seriously. Generally, the center became a place for conversation and discipline problems.

My solution was drastic. I threw out the center and started over. I felt I needed a clear plan with clear objectives. I decided upon a learning center to be used for reinforcement of skills taught through lecture and through the text. All students would use the center; in fact, it would become part of the regular class work. Students would be evaluated by the quizzes and tests I normally give after lecture and text exercises.

There were again many problems. Since I share a room with another teacher, and since I teach four different classes, the center for German 8B had to be portable—easily assembled and taken apart, as well as easily stored. (See Figure 8.4 for room plans for the arrangements

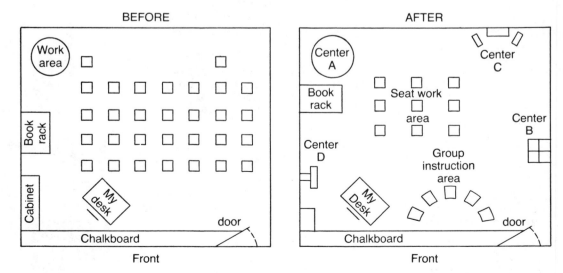

Figure 8.4   *Room Plans*

made.) Since I wanted to use the center with each chapter of the book, the materials had to be simple and easily changed. (See Table 8.3 on the next page for examples of materials.) The next problem was dealing with twenty-one students using the center. To solve this, I first divided the class into three ability groups. Then, I divided class time into three sections. Then, instead of one center, I created four centers. Each center deals with a component of the text chapter—for instance, grammar, vocabulary, culture, and oral comprehension. I made a rotation chart (see Figure 8.5), so that during a class period each group would work with the centers, work on assignments at their seats, and work with me on reinforcement of class lecture. Working with seven students at a time, I felt I could better meet their needs. This way, with four centers, there would only be two students per center per time unit. In one day each student only gets to one center, so I have included a rotation of centers to my chart. We spend three weeks on each unit. During those three weeks, we spend four days on this new schedule so that everyone gets to all centers and gets four days of small-group work with me.

There are still a few details to be worked on, but so far the plan is

DAY →		1	2	3	4
Eva Jeff C Elaine Kim Brian E→ Stephen		A	B	C	D
Steve Jim R. N Mingo Chris S. Missy T Ernest		B	C	D	A
Jenny Jill E William Mark Kerry R Chris B.		C	D	A	B
Ihab Jim D. S John		D	A	B	C

	group	seatwork	LC's
	purple	red	orange
	red	orange	purple
	orange	purple	red

Today's order
of instruction

Purple: Eva, Steve, Jenny, Ihab,
          Jeff, Jim R., Jill
Red: Elaine, Mingo, William,
          Jim D., Brian, Ernest, Kerry
Orange: Kim, Missy, Mark, John,
          Stephen, Chris S., Chris B.
(Names are color coded on chart.)

Figure 8.5   *Rotation Chart and Ability Groups*

Table 8.3 *Example Activities for Learning Centers, Chapter 3*

STATION A: CLASSROOM VOCABULARY

Materials:
Flashcards with a picture, the English and German words
Blank cards, markers, tape
White 9 × 12″ paper, crayons
Textbooks
Cassette player with tape of vocabulary
Large sign with instructions

Students are instructed to choose between:
Memorizing vocabulary with cards
Making labels and placing them around the room on classroom objects
Drawing and labeling vocabulary
Listening and repeating tape presentation of vocabulary

STATION B: VERB CONJUGATION

Materials:
Chalkboard
Colored chalk, eraser
Answer key
Large sign with instructions

Students are instructed to:
Follow step-by-step instructions to write the different parts of several verbs in different colored chalk. They then check their work with the answer key.

STATION C: GERMAN SCHOOLS

Materials:
A description of German schools written on tagboard with pictures and photographs
Notebook paper and pencils
Large sign with instructions

Students are instructed to:
Read the description
Pretend they are a German student and write a brief report or skit about their typical day at school. These may be read or performed if the student desires

STATION D: LISTENING, COMPREHENSION, PRONUNCIATION

Materials:
Reel-to-reel tape player
Tape of dialogue with native German speakers
Textbook
Dittoes for dictation exercises
Large sign with instructions

Students are instructed to:
Follow the tape presentation with their text, repeating in the appropriate places. Then they are to close their books and write what is spoken on their dittoes. They then open the book and check their work.

working well. I get a chance to work with seven students instead of twenty-one, and each student gets a chance to become more responsible for his or her own learning at my four centers. The centers are simple enough to be set up before class, and simple enough to adapt for each chapter. I am also getting students involved with the setting up of the centers, which adds to their sense of responsibility and helps them understand that they are their centers, not the teacher's centers.

Both LAPs and learning centers offer advantages such as these:

- They allow students to work in their own learning styles and at their own levels of ability in achieving an objective.
- They enable students to work at their own rates.
- They permit self-pacing and self-evaluation without comparison with others.
- They encourage teachers to assess the interests, needs, and abilities of students before and during the learning activity.
- They help remove the fear of failure from the learning environment. Students can continue working until the desired competency has been reached.
- They encourage the student to take responsibility for learning and yet provide specific feedback and guidance through self-checking activities.
- They help teachers monitor student learning as it progresses, allowing modifications of instruction when required.
- They encourage teacher and student creativity in developing new centers and LAPs and in making existing ones more effective. Teachers can collaborate in creating and sharing new LAPs and centers.

These strategies are not free from problems, however:

- LAPs are sometimes viewed by students, colleagues, parents— and even teachers—as a factory-line approach to instruction that is inconsistent with the traditional role of the teacher as the sole distributor of knowledge. Centers are sometimes perceived to foster student socializing at the expense of learning.
- Students who are not accustomed to self-paced instruction and self-evaluation may feel uncomfortable or be unaccepting.
- Both strategies require a considerable amount of development and preparation time from teachers. Additional teacher time is also spent in supervising and orienting students, particularly during the introduction of the strategy.
  Because of time constraints teachers might be discouraged from doing the revision necessary to meet the changing needs and interests of new students.

Independent Study

Independent study means much more than simply allowing students to work alone on assignments. In its truest sense, independent study refers to that portion of the teacher's instructional program that permits students to choose their own learning objectives, as well as methods and materials of study. It is the strategy for individualized instruction that best satisfies a student's own interests, learning style, and learning rate.

Independent study is a necessary component of Eric Jones's instructional plans. It encourages students to pursue enrichment learning activities and provides the teacher with guidelines for classroom management through the use of contracts.

Independent study allows advanced students to explore a topic as deeply as they wish, and to be as creative as possible. Students are enabled to develop knowledge and skills that go far beyond what is possible in the large-group instructional setting. Their learning and experiences should be shared with other members of the class, during the study and after its completion.

Typically, independent study has been used only with students believed to be the most able; where accelerated courses are not available, independent study is essential. Even though students differ in their readiness to study and investigate on their own, every student can and should be encouraged to pursue independent study to some degree.

The rationale underlying independent study is the assumption that if students can learn how to learn in school, they will become life-long learners as adults. Independent study develops the sense of responsibility, direction, and self-motivation requisite to life-long learning. It also helps develop the requisite skills of inquiry.

It has been shown that independent study can be plugged into the ongoing curriculum as an outgrowth of experience situations. Furthermore, independent study projects can enhance students' motivation by allowing them to delve more deeply into topics that hold their interest. One of the advantages of independent study is that it can be extended beyond the classroom into the community itself. The approach can be used in any school, in any community, and in any subject area.

Independent study is most effective when teachers include the following activities:

- Identify individual students' interests and abilities through interviews, inventories, and tests.
- Make available materials and experiences that correspond to students' interests and abilities.
- Know the amount of structure each student needs. (David Hunt's description of students who require high, moderate, or low degrees of structure offers helpful guidelines; see pages 105–108.)
- Develop contracts and use progress reports that match the learner's need for structure and strengthen self-evaluation skills.

- Realize that some students do not understand contracts and the notion that they are responsible for meeting their commitment. Start small with these students.
- Do not expect the same type of contract to work with all students. It may take several years of trial and error to develop a repertoire of contracts that satisfy teacher and students.
- Do not use independent study as the only strategy for any student. All students need social interaction, especially recluses and shrinking violets who are most apt to enjoy independent work.

Sample Contracts and Progress Reports

The following example was developed by an algebra teacher and includes two contracts providing different degrees of structure.

Independent Study

Debra York-Heck

Because I was planning a unit on graphs/graphing in my algebra classes, I planned the following independent study project: Each student was supposed to select a topic of interest and study the relationship between a constant and some related variable. Then they were instructed to illustrate their results on a graph of their choice and supply a typed explanation of their procedures. This was the basis of evaluation. As an example, one student chose to determine what school fund raiser earned the most money. To illustrate the results, she constructed a broken line graph and attached to it a description of her procedures. The purpose of these projects was to strengthen the students' abilities in drawing information from graphs. By creating their own, I believed it would enable them to decipher information from graphs more easily. Once I decided on this project, I thought a contract between each student and myself would be of great convenience (see Tables 8.4 and 8.5 on pages 300–301.) Because each student's project would be different, I felt this would be the most practical method of recording their learning agreements, which we had discussed. I was right.

This project began October 25 and was not due until November 22. The results throughout were terrific. First of all, they loved the idea of having a contract. I thought it might make them uneasy since the use of one was foreign to them, but it didn't. It made them feel more responsible (and none of their friends ever used a contract before so they "had one on them"). By conferencing with each student at least once a week, I was able to determine their progress. I did not have to push any of them to begin, and they always had new results to report to me. They conducted their studies, the results of which were to be put into the required evaluative format. It was a new and welcome experience to see them so involved.

Table 8.4 *Algebra II—Contract 1 (Highly Structured)*

Name _____

Project beginning October 24, 1983, and ending November 21, 1983.

Purpose
To further the student's understanding of graph representations.

Criterion Performance
Create a graph illustrating the correlation between any constant and one or more variables. There must be a typed explanation of your procedures and the results illustrated on a poster unless negotiated otherwise.

Method
You may work alone or with a partner. Topics are optional. The following are only suggestions: mileage of various cars, number of various sandwiches sold at fast-food chains, food prices at different stores, clothing sales, basketball scores, couples vs. single guests at a bar, number of people attending movies on various nights and/or afternoons, annual snow/rainfall, average temperatures for various months, number of songs played in an hour on different radio stations, number of drunk-driving arrests since new law.

Resources
There will be three other sources available at the Resource Service Desk if you choose to utilize them.
1. *Career Mathematics: Industry and the Trades*
   Lying, Merwin J., Meconi, L. J., Zurck, Earl J.
2. *Essentials of Basic Mathematics*, 3d ed.
   Edmond, Carolyn E., Plotkin, Samuel H., Washington, Allyn J.
3. *Math Squared*
   Stern, David.

Student's choice of topic, working situation, and evaluation

Signed _____
(student)

Signed _____
(teacher)

Table 8.5   *Algebra II—Contract 2 (Less Structured)*

Name _____

Project beginning October 24, 1983, and ending November 21, 1983.

Purpose
To further the student's understanding of graph representations.

Criterion Performance
Create a graph illustrating the correlation between any constant and one or
more variables. There must be a typed explanation of your procedures and
the results illustrated on a poster unless negotiated otherwise.

Method
You may work alone or with a partner. Topics are optional.

Resources
The use of other resources is optional.

Student's choice of topic, working situation, and evaluation

Signed _____
(student)

Signed _____
(teacher)

Contracts can also be used in the primary grades, as illustrated in
Table 8.6 on the next page.

Cooperative Learning: Student Team Learning

Student team learning has emerged recently as one of the most promising strategies for working with diverse groups of students. Developed
originally for racially desegregated schools, the approach has been extended to virtually all types of schools. Most recently, student team
learning techniques have been used to help integrate mainstreamed
learners into the "least restrictive environments" with "normal-
progress" classmates.[27]

Various learning techniques have been developed as alternatives to
the competitive incentive structure and individualistic task structure of
traditional classrooms. The success of the student team learning approach developed by Robert Slavin, David DeVries, and Keith Edwards
at Johns Hopkins University, however, has been most fully documented.[28]

Research results show that student team learning improves both

Table 8.6 *Sample Contract, Grades 2 to 4 (teacher can fill in if necessary)*

Topic chosen by student:
What If I Had Been Born Fifty Years Ago?

I want to find out what it was like to live fifty years ago. This week I will do one/two/three things (pupil circles one) to find some answers.

_____ 1. I will talk to these people:

_____

_____

_____

_____ 2. I will read this book:

_____

_____ 3. I will watch this television program:

_____

_____ 4. I will visit this place:

_____

_____ 5. I will write a letter to:

_____

I will ask this question:

_____

_____

On ___(day)___ I will share what I find out. I will (pupil checks one):

_____ Write a paragraph   _____ Draw a picture

_____ Speak on a tape   _____ Speak to the class

_____ Put on a skit with these friends:

_____

_____

Signed _____
                              (pupil)

_____
                              (teacher)

Date _____

academic achievement and students' interpersonal relationships. All students (including high, average, and low achievers) appear to benefit. One of the most consistent findings is that Black students, and possibly Chicanos, "gain outstandingly in cooperative learning."[29] Further research is needed before these race-X treatment interactions can be fully explained. There is some evidence to support the possibility that children raised in Black and Hispanic cultures tend to be more motivated by cooperation than competition, while the reverse is often true for those raised in the White middle-class milieu.[30] In contrast to the orientations of many Black and Hispanic students, the traditional classrooms in United States society stress competition and individual achievement. This emphasis can be stressful when students are faced with the situation of "attempting to excell academically and risk alienating their peers, or to do the minimum needed to get by."[31]

Given the fact that disproportionate numbers of Black and Chicano students are low achievers, Slavin suggests that student team learning may help close the school success gap between minority and nonminority students. This is not to imply that the needs of White students are overlooked in the process. Although the achievement gains among nonminority White students tend to be less dramatic, their school achievement is not hindered by cooperative learning, and they reap many benefits in intergroup relations.

> For improving race relations, our results have been phenomenal. In seven field studies in desegregated schools, most of them inner-city Baltimore junior high schools, we found that team learning classes had much better racial attitudes and behaviors than traditional classes. In many cases, when we asked students to name their friends, they named as many or almost as many friends of other races as they would have if race were not a criterion. This was quite different from our pretests in these classes and in our control classes; in fact, in most of our control classes there were fewer cross-racial friendships on the posttest than there were on the pretest.
>
> In addition to positive effects on race relations the team classes learned as much or more than the traditional classes. In five of the seven studies in desegregated schools, the team classes learned significantly more language arts and mathematics than did the traditionally taught students. In many of the studies, students in the team classes engaged in less off-task behavior than did control students. This indicates that team learning techniques may also improve discipline in desegregated schools. Team learning techniques don't have to cost anything, and they are easy to learn and use. Instead of the usual one-day workshop in which speakers try to reduce teachers' prejudice, we can spend the same time to teach teachers to use an instructional system that is far more likely to improve students' racial attitudes and behaviors as well as their achievement.[32]

The three student team learning methods used most widely are: Student Teams–Achievement Divisions (or STAD), Teams-Games-Tournaments (TGT), and Jigsaw II. The following descriptions are taken from the teacher's manual available from the Johns Hopkins Team Learning Project.

In the *Jigsaw*, students are assigned to six-member teams. Academic material is broken down into as many parts as there are students on each team. For example, a biography might be broken into early life, first accomplishments, major setbacks, and so on. Members of the different teams who have the same section form "experts groups" and study together. Each then returns to his or her team and teaches the section to the team. Often, the students take a quiz on the entire set of material. The only way students can do well on this quiz is to pay close attention to their teammates' sections, so students are motivated to support and show interest in each other's work.

Teams-Games-Tournaments. Teams-Games-Tournaments (TGT) is the best researched of the classroom techniques that use teams. In TGT, students are assigned to four- or five-member learning teams. Each week, the teacher introduces new material in a lecture or discussion. The teams then study worksheets on the material together, and at the end of the week, team members compete in "tournaments" with members of other teams to add points to their team scores. In the tournaments, students compete on skill-exercise games with others who are comparable in past academic performance. This equal competition makes it possible for every student to have a good chance of contributing a maximum number of points to his or her team. A weekly newsletter, prepared by the teacher, recognizes successful teams and students who have contributed outstandingly to their team scores. The excitement and motivation generated by TGT is enormous. Teachers using this method have reported that students who were never particularly interested in school were coming in after class to get materials to take home to study, asking for special help, and becoming active in class discussions. In one project in a Baltimore junior high school that contains a large number of students bused from the inner city, almost every student in two classes stayed after school (and missed their buses) to attend a tie-breaker playoff in the TGT tournament competition [see Figure 8.6].

Student Teams–Achievement Divisions. Student Teams–Achievement Divisions (STAD) is a simple team technique in which students work in four- or five-member teams, and then take individual quizzes to make points for their team. Each student's score is compared to that of other students of similar past performance, so that in STAD, as in TGT, students of all ability levels have a good chance of earning maximum points for their teams. Thus, STAD is like TGT, except that it substitutes individual quizzes for the TGT game tournament.[33]

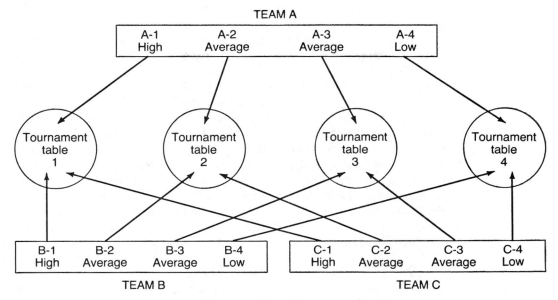

Figure 8.6 *Assignment to Tournament Tables. From Robert E. Slavin,* Teacher Manual for Student Team Learning *(Baltimore, Md.: Center for Social Organization of Schools, Johns Hopkins University, 1978), p. 10. Reprinted by permission of the author.*

A fourth technique, Team-Assisted Individualization (TAI), has been developed and evaluated more recently. Developed originally for math, TAI is a unique form of cooperative learning in that it uses individualized rather than class-paced instruction. TAI is designed especially for classrooms where students are too heterogeneous to progress at similar rates. In TAI, students are assigned to four- to five-member heterogeneous teams as in other forms of team learning. After diagnostic testing, each team member works through the appropriate set of programmed mathematic units at his or her own pace.[34]

Why is student team learning so successful? For one thing, the strategy avoids problems due to diffusion of responsibility often associated with small-group work. Many people have worked in groups where some individuals were rewarded even if they contributed little or nothing to the group and where those who contributed most, or who worked to their fullest potential, received no recognition. Team learning avoids these problems because *group rewards are based on each individual member's learning.* The strategy is structured so that "the achievement of all group members does in fact contribute to group success. . . . [Furthermore] the contributions of each group member can be easily seen, so that praise or blame among group members can be correctly applied."[35]

An important aspect of student team learning is equal-opportunity scoring. Team scores are derived from the improvement on test scores of individual members in STAD and Jigsaw II, and from game competition with equals in TGT. This enables all students, no matter what their entry-level skills, to contribute to the team if they do their best. This scoring system is believed to increase student achievement and is necessary for several reasons. First, it avoids the problem of low student motivation under traditional grading systems, in which some students are virtually guaranteed A's and B's while others do poorly no matter how hard they try. When grades correspond to ability rather than effort, high-ability students can often take things easy, while lower-ability students become discouraged over too-difficult tasks. When *improvement* is the criterion for success, both success and failure are within the reach of all students. This is believed to enhance motivation and personal responsibility.

A second advantage of equal-opportunity scoring is that it lessens the chances that the less able group members will be devalued by their group mates. A system that rewards performance increases makes every team member a potential contributor. Experience shows that more able team members often become motivated to tutor the less able students, who might otherwise be ignored or resented because they are perceived as a liability to the group.

Because equal-opportunity scoring is embedded in the student team learning strategies, its separate effect is difficult to determine. The results to date do suggest, however, that it may have a positive effect on student achievement.[36]

The effectiveness of task specialization, whereby each team member becomes an expert on one piece of the puzzle (i.e., Jigsaw) is not conclusive either. Positive results have been obtained in courses like social studies, science, and literature when content can be broken into subtopics. When the learning task requires mastery of a specific set of skills, concepts, or facts, as in a language, then group study (i.e., STAD and TGT) is more effective than task specialization.

Peer and Cross-Age Tutoring

Tutoring can be another effective strategy for providing individualized help to supplement large-group instruction. Peer tutoring involves students teaching students their same age, while cross-age tutoring involves older children teaching younger children. It is also conceivable for children to teach adults or older children when they have special skills or knowledge. Bilingual-bicultural individuals of any age, for example, can be invaluable in helping monolingual learners understand course content and make transitions between home environments and culturally different school environments.

Peer tutoring can be used at all levels above grades three or four in any subject area where one or more students are at a relatively advanced level of skill or understanding as compared with their classmates. Advanced students help instruct less advanced students. This is the simplest and most direct form of tutoring and can be monitored by one teacher. Typically, tutoring is one-on-one, but small groups are possible. Imagine a large class in tennis or gymnastics in which four or five highly skilled students are used to help instruct students grouped according to their skill level. Imagine a fifth-grade math class that has, instead of students in groups labeled high, average, or low, heterogeneous (mixed abilities) children grouped by modality strengths and working on fractions under the direction of a classmate who has mastered the concepts. Imagine a compulsory Spanish class in which native speakers of Spanish are helping small groups of non-Spanish-speaking classmates improve their conversational skill.

Although tutoring is conceived as a remedial measure designed to help low achievers, research shows that tutors are likely to improve their own learning and emotional development in the process. Being in the instructor role has obvious benefits that need not be limited to high achievers. Through cross-age tutoring, students who are failing in their own classwork can be helped to effectively instruct younger children in their schoolwork. The personal achievement gains of these tutors are sometimes dramatic.

Cross-age tutoring requires the cooperation of at least two teachers and therefore involves more complex management. One exemplary cross-age tutoring program has been developed by Peggy Lippitt and her associates at the University of Michigan, and it is available for dissemination.[37]

Effective tutoring programs do not happen automatically. They are effective only under proper conditions. First of all, teachers must accept the idea. Often it is difficult to give up the teacher role and admit that sometimes our students are better able to communicate a concept or an idea than we are. This is particularly true among peer-oriented learners. Second, the competitive structure of schools needs to be modified so that education can become what Jerome Bruner calls a "communal undertaking." Bruner proposes that teachers give students more responsibility for the education of their fellow students, especially younger students, as one means of controlling the psychological problems associated with prolonged adolescence.[38] Under the conditions of communal learning, advanced students do not resent sharing their expertise and parents do not feel their children are being exploited or held back.

Even when little can be done to change the school's competitive structure, the classroom environment can become relatively cooperative and accepting, and some degree of tutoring is possible.

In addition to these general theoretical considerations, there are the following specific conditions, which are discussed more fully in the excellent monograph *Peer and Cross-Age Tutoring in the Schools* by Sophie Bloom.

1. There is a structured situation in terms of a clearly specified task, time, material, and procedures.
2. There is a supportive teacher or supervisor—the tutor as well as the tutee needs sustained and continuous direction and encouragement.
3. The tutors and tutees support and reinforce each other.
4. While tutors do not need elaborate training, they do need clear directions and a model of appropriate behavior.
5. Both tutors and tutees need feedback and correction, and both need clearly perceived learning gains.[39]

Research into the effectiveness of tutoring programs in the schools underscores the importance of orientation and training of tutors. We cannot assume that untrained tutors, be they children or adults, will automatically use effective strategies; research and observation show the opposite.[40] On the other hand, research also shows that effective and manageable training programs have been developed and are available.[41] These programs have a dual focus. First, tutors need training in the content area they are teaching, and knowledge of the most effective techniques for the subject matter. Knowledge about the tutees' modality strengths may also prove helpful; for example, multiplication facts could be taught using flash cards, oral response, games, manipulatives, worksheets, or some combination of these. Second, tutors need to develop human relations skills to help them relate constructively with the learner. Tutors (including adults) may feel frustrated when learning progresses at a slow pace, and they need to avoid using ridicule or doing the work for the learner.

On the basis of his own research as well as that of others, Grant Von Harrison has asserted that "almost all upper-grade elementary children can be trained to use effective teaching skills when tutoring."[42] He found that the most effective procedure for training tutors consists of three steps: "First, the tutor reads instructions in simple expository text form concerning the task; second, the skills described by the written text are discussed and clarified; and, third, a role playing session follows with the trainer playing the part of the learner and tutors taking turns practicing the tutoring skills."[43]

In contrast to cooperative team learning, there is very little research to date on the effectiveness of peer tutoring in culturally pluralistic classrooms. It seems obvious, however, that an effective tutoring program must consider cultural differences based on language, nonverbal communication, social values, and learning styles. Where cultural traditions emphasize the authority of males or seniority, for example, female tutors for males or younger tutors are likely to be unacceptable.

Under the proper conditions, tutoring is an indispensable and effective resource for the teacher, tutor, and tutee; however, it is not without drawbacks. Perhaps the greatest of these are the burdens of training tutors and managing the program. Unless the school has a tutoring program managed by a supervisor available to all teachers, these burdens are likely to fall on the classroom teacher. In some cases, such as in the classroom of Eric Jones, it is possible to organize outside help. Sometimes only a few students in class require tutoring. Other times, particularly when students are tracked into low-achievement groups, an entire group of students would benefit. How one eighth-grade math teacher developed a tutoring program tailored to his particular situation is presented in the following illustration, which the teacher subtitled "A Sneaky Way to Identify and Train Peer Tutors for Interclass Tutoring."

Individualization Through Use of Partners

E. Van Campbell

Purpose: to use partners to develop tutor-tutee relationships in order to satisfy more of the individual needs of the students in attaining mastery of some basic math skills.

Rationale: Due to the shortcomings of group instruction in my classroom and the limits of my time and energy, some of my students need help that I alone cannot give them. I have found in the past that many students are willing to help their classmates learn a task. Research indicates that a tutor's knowledge alone does not yield positive effects. Successful tutors must have appropriate communication skills. Training has been effective in developing a positive tutor-tutee relationship. Intraclass peer tutoring fits my situation best, but I believe it would be counterproductive to formalize tutor-tutee roles. Training partners to use appropriate communication techniques should be good for both the tutor and tutee and enable each student to assume either role. Then, as my students naturally space themselves in the self-paced materials we use they will be more prepared to help their slower-paced classmates or work cooperatively with a partner.

Training of tutors: Ideally, the tutors learn as the trainer models the procedures. Each tutor is then given an opportunity to role play the procedure once, twice, or as many times as necessary. Tutors need to rehearse the specific material they will use in the tutoring session.

The minimum training would include the following subjects.

- How to begin the tutoring session and set a positive tone.
- A step-by-step procedure for the learning, practice, and application of a skill, using specific materials.
- What to do when the answer is right: Praise and reward.
- What to do when the answer is wrong: For incomplete answers, repeat the question in different words. For incorrect answers, model the correct answer by saying "my turn" and telling the answer; then say "your turn" and let the tutee repeat the correct answer. If the tutee almost knows the answer, contrast tutee's answer with the correct answer and let tutee discover the difference. Don't let tutee struggle too long to get the right answer. It wastes time and frustration sets in.
- What to do if the tutoring goes very badly: Ask the teacher or supervisor for suggestions.
- How to vary the tutoring session with suggestions for keeping high interest and good attention.
- How to end the session with a brief game, story, joke, riddle, or some other way of reducing the tension of intensive work.
- How to keep a simple checklist or other record form.[44]

SAMPLE TUTORING ACTIVITY:
AN INTRODUCTORY ACTIVITY TO NUMBER THEORY

Objective: to have all students master the following task. Mastery will be defined as 95 percent correct with a two-minute limit.

Task: to write the whole numbers one to sixty as the product of two whole numbers, using the number one only when necessary.

Required materials: pencil with eraser and then a worksheet (see Tables 8.7 and 8.8). Since this is a speed drill, notice all cumbersome symbols are already provided on the worksheet.

Suggested practice modes: using a designated partner
Oral-oral practice:

- Quizzer states number; quizzee responds with a product.
- Quizzer says "ok" after each correct response.
- Quizzer says "again" when an incorrect response is received.
- Quizzee should never guess; appropriate options are to say "help" or "skip" or be silent.
- Quizzer responds to "help" by repeating number, pausing, giving a correct response, and then repeating number for quizzee.
- Quizzer responds to "skip" by making a note and then repeating at end of the list.
- Quizzer also makes note of any number on which help was given.
- Quizzer reacts to a pause by saying "my turn," giving number, product, and repeating number to tutee.

Table 8.7   *Worksheet for Task in Number Theory*

Name _____   Date _____   Period _____

1 =	21 =	41 =
2 =	22 =	42 =
3 =	23 =	43 =
4 =	24 =	44 =
5 =	25 =	45 =
6 =	26 =	46 =
7 =	27 =	47 =
8 =	28 =	48 =
9 =	29 =	49 =
10 =	30 =	50 =
11 =	31 =	51 =
12 =	32 =	52 =
13 =	33 =	53 =
14 =	34 =	54 =
15 =	35 =	55 =
16 =	36 =	56 =
17 =	37 =	57 =
18 =	38 =	58 =
19 =	39 =	59 =
20 =	40 =	60 =

Oral–oral/written practice:

• Quizzer gives orally.
• Quizzee answers both orally and in writing.
• Only the expressed product is written.

Written practice:

• Quizzee to be provided with a worksheet-test.
• Quizzer watches as quizzee works on worksheet.
• Quizzer says correct answer when quizzee says "help."
• Quizzer, when seeing an incorrect response, says "my turn," erases incorrect response, and writes correct response.

Timed practice:

• Quizzer works as a timer.
• Quizzee skips any number that cannot be answered immediately.

Table 8.8 *Answers to Problems in Table 8.7*

Name _____   Date _____   Period _____

1 = 1 × 1	C21 = 3 × 7	P41 = 1 × 41
P2 = 1 × 2	C22 = 2 × 11	C42 = 2 × 21
P3 = 1 × 3	P23 = 1 × 23	P43 = 1 × 43
C4 = 2 × 2	C24 = 2 × 12, 3 × 8,	C44 = 2 × 22, 4 × 11
P5 = 1 × 5	4 × 6	C45 = 3 × 15, 5 × 9
C6 = 2 × 3	C25 = 5 × 5	C46 = 2 × 23
P7 = 1 × 7	C26 = 2 × 13	P47 = 1 × 47
C8 = 2 × 4	C27 = 3 × 9	C48 = 2 × 24, 3 × 16,
C9 = 3 × 3	C28 = 2 × 14, 4 × 7	4 × 12, 6 × 8
C10 = 2 × 5	P29 = 1 × 29	C49 = 7 × 7
P11 = 1 × 11	C30 = 2 × 15, 3 × 10,	C50 = 2 × 25, 5 × 10
C12 = 2 × 6, 3 × 4	5 × 6	C51 = 3 × 17
P13 = 1 × 13	P31 = 1 × 31	C52 = 2 × 26, 4 × 13
C14 = 2 × 7	C32 = 2 × 16, 4 × 8	P53 = 1 × 53
C15 = 3 × 5	C33 = 3 × 11	C54 = 2 × 27, 3 × 18,
C16 = 2 × 8, 4 × 4	C34 = 2 × 17	6 × 9
P17 = 1 × 17	C35 = 5 × 7	C55 = 5 × 11
C18 = 2 × 9, 3 × 6	C36 = 2 × 18, 3 × 12,	C56 = 2 × 28, 4 × 14,
P19 = 1 × 19	4 × 9, 6 × 6	7 × 8
C20 = 2 × 10, 4 × 5	P37 = 1 × 37	C57 = 3 × 19
	C38 = 2 × 19	C58 = 2 × 29
	C39 = 3 × 13	P59 = 1 × 59
	C40 = 2 × 20, 4 × 10,	C60 = 2 × 30, 3 × 20,
	5 × 8	4 × 15, 5 × 12,
		6 × 10

- Quizzee is allowed to go back at end.
- Quizzee says "stop" when finished.
- Quizzer responds with a positive statement, such as:
  "Your time really improved."
  "Wow, you really zipped through the first twenty."
  "Hey, you're almost there."
  "That'll be hard for me to beat."
- Quizzer and quizzee check work together.

Evaluation of task: Students will be given a timed test (same as worksheet) by the teacher in a group situation. Those who demonstrate mastery will be able to move into individually paced workbooks. Those who do not demonstrate mastery will consult with the teacher about a practice partner. The practice partner could be a student who has attained mastery. All students will be expected to demonstrate mastery on subsequent days before beginning workbooks.

Some suggested partner and helping techniques:

- Cross out the twenty most difficult—time yourself.
- Practice the twenty most difficult—time yourself.
- Practice the 30s only.
- Practice the rough spots.
- Tutor could write one factor as a hint.
- Tutee could practice the 2s, 3s, etc.
- Tutee could orally note the problem numbers before being timed.
- Don't race; speed up only when comfortable.

Summary and Conclusions

A small proportion of students can learn well no matter what teachers do. Most students, however, seem to require some form of individualized help beyond regular classroom instruction if they are to maximize their learning and development. The challenge to teachers of culturally diverse groups of students is tremendous, for added to the variety of individual differences always present is the factor of ethnicity.

This chapter has focused on teaching concepts and strategies that are known to be most effective with diverse groups of students. Certain concepts and strategies, namely experiential learning, bilingual education, and student team learning were developed especially to meet student needs based on cultural differences. Each of the five strategies presented offers a distinct way of supplementing large-group instruction in order to create greater flexibility in the learning environment. Some strategies will appeal to teachers and students more than others. None of the strategies represents a panacea; none would be effective and appropriate for all students all of the time. It is up to us as teachers to create our own clusters of strategies for a given group of students at a particular point in the curriculum.

Few of us would feel comfortable with the degree of flexibility evident in Eric Jones's classroom. The idea of managing, monitoring, and keeping records of students' learning can be overwhelming. The key is to start small. This chapter concludes with two approaches to getting started. Some teachers may prefer to begin with a small group of learners, those who are having the most difficulty or those who are far beyond their peers. Others may prefer to start with the total classroom environment. Still others may prefer some combination of the two.

Approach A: Focus on the Learner

1. Identify the students who are not achieving well under the present classroom conditions or who are exceptionally advanced.
2. Identify reasons for the students' difficulties. The list of twelve individual differences that affect student learning (pages 90–91), discussed in Chapters 4 and 5, can provide guidelines.
3. Identify the most essential learning goals and objectives for those students.
4. Select strategies to supplement large-group instruction, which are likely to meet students' learning needs.
5. Gather and assemble the needed materials and/or select necessary persons.
6. Plan the schedule, place, location of assembled materials, and record-keeping strategy.
7. Monitor students' progress and evaluate their success.
8. Revise the instructional plan as necessary.

Approach B: Focus on the Total Classroom Environment

1. Select one of the strategies presented in this chapter as a means of supplementing large-group instruction.
2. Based on the organization of the course, identify points at which to introduce the strategy.
3. Select one point and fully develop the strategy. Implement, evaluate, and revise your strategy as necessary.
4. Attempt to develop, implement, and revise one new version of the strategy each semester.
5. When possible, work with other teachers in the development, evaluation, and revising process. This can add depth to any one strategy, as, for example, when each teacher develops materials for a specific modality preference or for a different subtopic to be included in a LAP, learning center, or tutoring session. Interteacher cooperation can also expand the strategy repertoire of everyone in the group. Teachers can request that inservice days, or college course projects, be designed for this purpose.
6. Once the strategy is fully integrated into the instructional plan, select another strategy and repeat the process.

Compare and Contrast

1. Mastery learning and experiential learning
2. Peer tutoring and cooperative team learning
3. Independent study and individualized instruction
4. Bilingual education and multicultural education
5. Learning centers and learning activity packets

1. Consider the case of Eric Jones. What do you like and dislike about his classroom? In what ways is he responding to individual and/or cultural differences? To what degree, if any, would you be comfortable teaching in his classroom? What problems would you anticipate? How could you attempt to deal with them?

2. Compare and contrast the classrooms of Warren Benson and Eric Jones. What are the similarities? What are the differences?

3. Imagine that you are working with Warren Benson's students in your own area of specialization. Explain how you could structure the learning environment to individualize student learning to a greater degree. Be sensitive to the possibilities of both individual and cultural diversity. Would you reorganize your formal curriculum in any way? Explain. Would equal-opportunity scoring, as used in cooperative team learning, work in this classroom setting? Explain.

4. This book has taken the position that the teacher's major goal is to foster the intellectual, social, and personal development of students to their highest potential. Furthermore, this position is based on the assumption that virtually all students are capable of growth, development, and academic success. Would you qualify these assumptions in any way? Explain.

5. *Clarifying the sources of individualized instruction.* This year you have several students who are having great difficulty learning in your class. At least a few of them, you believe, are achieving far below their capabilities. You decide to restructure your learning environment to enable you to individualize instruction to a greater degree. Listed below are twelve sources that you could use as you develop plans for individualizing student learning. Work alone in part one and rank these from the information source you believe would be most helpful (1) to the source you believe would be least helpful (12). Complete part two with other members of your group. You may modify any of the source statements if necessary.

PART ONE

_____ 1. Measures that indicate each student's learning style.

_____ 2. Community goals and competency expectations for students.

_____ 3. Your own view of the needs of your students, which may be due in part to the views of previous teachers and cumulative records.

_____ 4. Inventories that measure students' personal values, goals, and attitudes.

_____ 5. Key concepts, generalizations, and skills that are germane to the subject area(s).

_____ 6. Knowledge about personal/family problems your students face.

_____ 7. Measures of student learning rate.

_____ 8. Pretests of student knowledge background.

_____ 9. Knowledge about the social climate (human dynamics) of your classroom and school.

_____ 10. The school district's curriculum guide, which lists knowledge and skills students are expected to attain.

_____ 11. Knowledge about students' ethnicity.

_____ 12. Other? Specify _____

PART TWO

1. The three information sources we believe would be helpful in planning for individualizing instruction are the following.

a. _____

b. _____

c. _____

Our reasons are: _____

_____

2. The three sources we believe would be least helpful are:

a. _____

b. _____

c. _____

Our reasons are: _____

_____

6. List five individual differences that you see as being important influences in how a student learns. Find out how you could diagnose or assess and respond to each one. Use specific examples in a content area of your choice.

7. Assume that you plan to include more individualized instruction in your classroom next year. What do you see as your major challenges? How could you meet them?

8. Given a situation where mastery learning is implemented in its classic form (that presented by Benjamin Bloom), which students are likely to benefit most—gifted, average, or low achievers? Would the result be different with the modified approach used by Eric Jones? Explain fully.

9. Read *Hunger of Memory* by Richard Rodriguez. In what ways did he experience transitional trauma between home and school, between the Mexican Catholic church and the Irish Catholic church, and within his family and neighborhood? What have been his deepest pains in growing up? His greatest joys? What does his life reveal about life in America? What are his views on bilingual education? Who finds his views controversial and why? How might he respond in the job interview outlined below?

10. Simulated job interview through role play and/or individual written response or small group discussion—setting and questions can be modified as desired.

Setting: You are a top candidate for an excellent teaching position in a large school corporation. As one of the three finalists, you have been asked to meet with the assistant superintendent in charge of curriculum and instruction. You have heard informally that you are the first choice of the principals who have already interviewed you and that whether or not you get the job depends on your interview with the assistant superintendent. You also know that to do well you must be able to think clearly and support your remarks with specifics, including noted authorities, wherever possible. You really want this job! How do you respond?

QUESTION: First of all, what have you learned about cross-cultural encounters that will help you in the classroom?

ANSWER: ?

QUESTION: In this district we need to do a better job of multicultural education. What expertise do *you* have in this area? How do you view multicultural education? What should our goals be?

ANSWER: ?

PROBE: What about schools where the student population is not diverse? Should we worry about multicultural education in an all-Black, all-White, or all-Hispanic school?

ANSWER: ?

PROBE: Let's get more specific. What are some important multicultural concepts that you could develop in your teaching area?

ANSWER: ?

PROBE: I like that. Now, what about strategies? What are some of the specific teaching strategies you would use in your classes? Remember, our students are very diverse.

ANSWER: ?

PROBE: What about the school or district as a whole? Give me some ideas about how we can avoid resegregation and move from desegregated to truly integrated learning environments. Give me some specific possibilities.

ANSWER: ?

QUESTION: Some of our parents and teachers are concerned about standards, particularly when it comes to bilingual education. What does the research say? Briefly, what is the issue concerning bilingual education, and where do you stand?

ANSWER: ?

QUESTION: Which ethnic groups in our society do you see as least assimilated?

ANSWER: ?

QUESTION: Don't you think it's about time they gave up their traditions and started to act like Americans?

ANSWER: ?

QUESTION: Explain.

ANSWER: ?

QUESTION: A lot of our students have misconceptions and stereotypes about each other and different peoples who make up society. Identify several stereotypes you see as being particularly troublesome, and tell me how you plan to deal with it in your classroom.

ANSWER: ?

QUESTION: One last question. You know that we are looking for someone who can meet the challenge of multicultural education in our schools. Why do you want the job?

ANSWER: ?

Notes

1. Benjamin S. Bloom, "Mastery Learning," In *Mastery Learning: Theory and Practice*, ed. J. H. Block (New York: Holt, Rinehart and Winston, 1971).

2. K. Patricia Cross, *Accent on Learning* (San Francisco: Jossey-Bass, 1976).

3. William Glasser, *Schools Without Failure* (New York: Harper and Row, 1969), p. 26.

4. Bloom, "Mastery Learning."

5. John B. Carroll, "A Model of School Learning," *Teachers College Record* 64 (May 1963):723–33; and Benjamin S. Bloom, "Learning for Mastery," *Evaluation Comment* 1, no. 2 (1968).

6. James H. Block, ed., *Mastery Learning: Theory and Practice* (New York: Holt, Rinehart and Winston, 1971).

7. Norman E. Gronlund, *Individualizing Classroom Instruction* (New York: Macmillan, 1974), p. 10.

8. See James H. Block and Lorin W. Anderson, *Mastery Learning in Classroom Instruction* (New York: Macmillan, 1975), p. 38.

9. R. Garry Shirts, *Bafá Bafá: A Cross Culture Simulation*, 1977, published by Simile 11, 218 Twelfth Street, P.O. Box 910, Del Mar, Calif. 92014.

10. David Wolsk, *An Experience Centered Curriculum: Exercises in Personal and Social Reality* (Paris: United Nations Educational, Scientific and Cultural Organization, 1974). ERIC ED 099 269.

11. Ibid., p. 2.

12. Ibid., p. 3.

13. Ibid., p. 8.

14. This section on bilingual education was contributed by Karen Schuster Webb, Assistant Professor in Language Education at Indiana University, Bloomington.

15. R. C. Troike, "Synthesis of Research on Bilingual Education," *Educational Leadership* 38 (March 1981):498–504.

16. M. Brisk, "Language Policies in American Education: A Historical Overview," in *Bilingual Education Teacher Handbook*, ed. Martha Montero (Cambridge, Mass.: Evaluation, Dissemination and Assessment Center for Bilingual Education, 1982).

17. R. Garcia, *Learning in Two Languages* (Bloomington, Ind.: Phi Delta Kappa Educational Foundation, 1976).

18. Arnold H. Leibowitz, "Language as a Means of Social Control: The United States Experience," unpublished manuscript, August 1974.

19. Troike, "Bilingual Education."

20. Roger W. Shuy, "A Holistic View of Language," *Research in the Teaching of English* 15, no. 2 (May 1981):101–11.

21. Troike, "Bilingual Education."

22. Ibid.

23. R. C. Gardner and W. E. Lambert, *Attitudes and Motivation in Second-Language Learning* (Rowley, Mass.: Newbury House, 1972).

24. Crystal Compton, "Learning Centers," Alachua County Public Schools, Gainesville, Fla., unpublished and undated reprint.

25. Gronlund, *Individualizing Classroom Instruction*, pp. 46–47.

26. Compton, "Learning Centers."

27. Robert Slavin, *Cooperative Learning* (New York: Longman, 1983).

28. Ibid.

29. Ibid., p. 61.

30. Ibid., p. 62.

31. Ibid.

32. Robert Slavin, *Using Student Team Learning*, rev. ed. (Baltimore: Center for Social Organization of Schools, Johns Hopkins University, 1980), pp. 2–3. Reprinted by permission of the author.

33. Robert Slavin, *Teacher Manual for Student Team Learning* (Baltimore: Center for Social Organization of Schools, Johns Hopkins University, 1978), pp. 6–7. Reprinted by permission of the author.

34. Slavin, *Cooperative Learning*, p. 27.

35. Ibid., pp. 32–33.

36. Ibid., pp. 52, 53.

37. Peggy Lippitt, Jeffrey Eiseman, and Donald Lippitt, *Cross-age Helping Program: Orientation, Training, and Related Materials* (Ann Arbor: University of Michigan, Center for Research on Utilization of Scientific Knowledge, Institute for Social Research, 1969). A cross-age helping package of dissemination materials is published by Xicom, RFD #1, Sterling Forest, Tuxedo, N.Y.

38. Jerome Bruner, "Immaturity—Its Uses, Nature and Management," *Times Educational Supplement* (London) October 27, 1972, pp. 62–63.

39. Sophie Bloom, *Peer and Cross-Age Tutoring in the Schools* (Washington, D.C.: National Institute of Education, December 1976).

40. Grant Von Harrison, "Structured Tutoring: Antidote for Low Achievement," in *Children as Teachers*, ed. Vernon L. Allen (New York: Academic Press, 1976), pp. 169–77.

41. Ibid.

42. Ibid., p. 171.

43. Ibid.

44. Bloom, *Peer and Cross-age Tutoring*, p. 30.

Bibliography

Abrahams, Roger D. "Cultural Conflict in the Classroom." Videotape from a symposium sponsored by the Alachna County Teacher Center, Gainesville, Fla., January 30, 1975.

Abrahams, Roger D., and Geneva Gay. "Talking Black in the Classroom." In *Language and Culture Diversity in American Education*, ed. Roger D. Abrahams and Rudolph C. Troike. Englewood Cliffs, N.J.: Prentice-Hall, 1976.

Allport, Gordon. *ABC's of Scapegoating*. New York: Anti-Defamation League of B'nai B'rith, 1979.

————. *The Nature of Prejudice*. Reading, Mass.: Addison-Wesley, 1979.

Anderson, Lee. *Schooling and Citizenship in a Global Age: An Exploration of the Meaning and Significance of Global Education*. Mid-America Program for Global Perspectives in Education. Bloomington: Social Studies Development Center at Indiana University, 1979.

Banfield, Beryle. "How Racism Takes Root." *The UNESCO Courier*, March 1979.

Banks, James A. *Multiethnic Education: Theory and Practice*. Boston: Allyn and Bacon, 1981.

————. *Teaching Strategies for Ethnic Studies*. 2d ed. Boston: Allyn and Bacon, 1979.

————. *Teaching Strategies for Ethnic Studies*. 3d ed. Boston: Allyn and Bacon, 1984.

Beck, John M., and Richard W. Saxe. *Teaching the Culturally Disadvantaged Pupil*. Springfield, Ill.: C. C. Thomas, 1969.

Benitez, Mario. "A Blueprint for the Education of the Mexican American." ERIC ED 076 294 (March 1973).

Bennett, Christine. "Student Initiated Interaction as an Indicator of Interracial Acceptance." *Journal of Classroom Interaction* 15 (Summer 1980).

————. "A Study of Classroom Climate in Desegregated Schools." *The Urban Review* 13, no. 3 (1981).

Bennett, Christine, and John Bean. "A Conceptual Model of Black Student Attrition in Predominantly White Institutions." *The Journal of Educational Equity and Leadership* 4 (Fall 1984).

Bennett, Christine, and J. John Harris III. "Suspensions and Expulsions of Male and Black Students: A Study of the Causes of Disproportionality." *Urban Education* 16, no. 4 (January 1982).

Bennett, Milton. "Culture and Changing Realities." Society of Intercultural Education Training and Research (SIETAR). Pre-Conference Workshop. Third Annual SIETAR Conference, Chicago, February 25, 1977.

Bereiter, Carl, and Siegfried Engleman. *Teaching Disadvantaged Children in the Pre-School*. New York: Prentice-Hall, 1966.

Berry, Mary Frances, and John W. Blassingame. *Long Memory: The Black Experience in America.* New York: Oxford University Press, 1982.

Block, James H., ed. *Mastery Learning: Theory and Practice.* New York: Holt, Rinehart and Winston, 1971.

Block, James H., and Lorin W. Anderson. *Mastery Learning in Classroom Instruction.* New York: Macmillan, 1975.

Bloom, Benjamin S. "Learning for Mastery." *Evaluation Comment* 1, no. 2 (1968).
———. "Mastery Learning." In *Mastery Learning: Theory and Practice,* ed. J. H. Block. New York: Holt, Rinehart and Winston, 1971.

Bloom, Sophie. *Peer and Cross-Age Tutoring in the Schools.* Washington, D.C.: National Institute of Education, December 1976.

Borg, Walter R., and Meredith Damien Gall. *Educational Research: An Introduction.* 3d ed. New York: Longman, 1979.

Brisk, M. "Language Policies in American Education: A Historical Overview." In *Bilingual Education Teacher Handbook,* ed. Martha Montero. Cambridge, Mass.: Evaluation, Dissemination and Assessment Center for Bilingual Education, 1982.

Bruner, Jerome. "Immaturity—Its Uses, Nature and Management." *Times Educational Supplement* (London). October 27, 1972.

Button, Christine Bennett. "Political Education and Minority Youth." In *New Views of Children and Politics,* ed. Richard G. Niemi. San Francisco: Jossey-Bass, 1974.

Caplin, Morris Daniel. "The Relationship Between Self-Concept and Academic Achievement." *Journal of Experimental Education* 37 (Spring 1969).

Carey, McWilliams. *North from Mexico.* New York: Greenwood Press, 1968.

Carroll, John B. "A Model of School Learning." *Teachers College Record* 64 (May 1963).

Carrott, M. Browning. "Prejudice Goes to Court: The Japanese and the Supreme Court of the 1920s." *California History* (Summer 1983).

Castañeda, Alfredo, and Tracy Gray. "Bicognitive Processes in Multicultural Education." *Educational Leadership* 32 (December 1974).

Castell, Doyle. *Cross-Cultural Models of Teaching: Latin American Example.* Gainesville: University of Florida Press, 1976.

Chinese Americans: Realities and Myths (multimedia kit). The Association of Chinese Teachers (TACT) Curriculum Materials 74-6A Ninth Avenue, San Francisco, Calif. 94118.

Chun-Hoon, Lowell K. Y. "Teaching the Asian-American Experience." In *Teaching Ethnic Studies: Concepts and Strategies,* ed. James A. Banks. 43d Yearbook. Washington, D.C.: National Council for the Social Studies, 1973.

Clark, Gilbert. "Examining Some Myths About Gifted and Talented Students." Faculty guest editorial, *The Herald Telephone,* Bloomington, Ind., Summer 1982.

Cohen, Elizabeth. "Status Equalization in the Desegregated School." Paper presented at the Annual Meeting of the American Educational Research Association, San Francisco, April 1979.

Cohen, M. W. "Student Influence in the Classroom." Paper presented at the Annual Meeting of the American Educational Research Association, Toronto, April 1978.

Collier, John. *Indians of the Americas.* New York: New American Library, 1947.

Combs, Arthur W., Chairman. *Perceiving, Behaving, Becoming.* ASCD Yearbook, 1962. Alexandria, Va.: Association for Supervision and Curriculum Development, 1962.

Compton, Crystal. "Learning Centers." Alachua County Public Schools, Gainesville, Fla. Unpublished and undated reprint.

Conklin, N., and M. Lourie. *A Host of Tongues.* New York: Free Press, 1983.

Cornbleth, C., O. L. Davis, Jr., and C. Bennett Button. "Expectations for Pupil Achievement and Teacher-Pupil Interaction." *Social Education* 38 (January 1974).

Cornett, Claudia E. *What You Should Know About Teaching and Learning Styles.* Fastback 191. Bloomington, Ind.: Phi Delta Kappa Educational Foundation, 1983.

Cortez, Carlos E. "Teaching the Chicano Experience." In *Teaching Ethnic Studies: Concepts and Strategies,* ed. James A. Banks. 43d Yearbook. Washington, D.C.: National Council for the Social Studies, 1973.

Cross, Patricia. *Accent on Learning.* San Francisco: Jossey-Bass, 1976.

Cross, William. "The Negro-to-Black Conversion Experience: Toward a Psychology of Black Liberation." *Black World* 20 (July 1979).

Cubberly, Ellwood P. *Changing Conceptions of Education.* Boston: Houghton Mifflin, 1909.

Curtis, Thomas E., and Wilma W. Bidwell. *Curriculum and Instruction for Emerging Adolescents.* Reading, Mass.: Addison-Wesley, 1977.

Daniels, Jack, et al. "Teaching Afro-American Communication." ERIC ED 082 247 (November 1972).

Davidson, Basil. *African Kingdoms.* New York: Time-Life Books, 1966.

Dennis, Rutledge M. "Socialization and Racism: The White Experience." In *Impacts of Racism on White Americans,* ed. Benjamin P. Bowser and Raymond G. Hunt. Beverly Hills, Calif.: Sage Publications, 1981.

Dufty, David, Susan Sawkins, Neil Pickard, Jim Power, and Ann Bowe. *Seeing It Their Way: Ideas, Activities and Resources for Intercultural Studies.* London: Reed Education, 1976.

Dunn, Rita, and Kenneth Dunn. "Learning Styles/Teaching Styles: Should They . . . Can They . . . Be Matched?" *Educational Leadership* 36 (1979).

Ehman, Lee H. "Political Socialization and the High School Social Studies Curriculum." Unpublished doctoral dissertation, University of Michigan, 1970.

Ehrlich, H. J. *The Social Psychology of Prejudice.* New York: John Wiley and Sons, 1973.

Elkins, Stanley. *Slavery: A Problem in American and Institutional Intellectual Life.* Chicago: University of Chicago Press, Universal Library ed., 1963.

Endo, George T., and Connie Kubo Della-Piana. "Japanese Americans, Pluralism, and the Model Minority Myth." *Theory into Practice* 20 (Winter 1981).

Fader, Daniel N., and Elton B. McNeil. *Hooked on Books: Program and Proof.* New York: Berkley Medallion Edition, 1968.

Fantini, Mario, and Gerald Weinstein. *The Disadvantaged: Challenge to Education.* New York: Harper and Row, 1968.

Feagin, Joe R. *Racial and Ethnic Relations.* Englewood Cliffs, N.J.: Prentice-Hall, 1978.

Fischer, Barbara Bree, and Louis Fischer. "Styles in Teaching and Learning." *Educational Leadership* 36 (January 1979).

Flavell, John H. *The Developmental Psychology of Jean Piaget.* Princeton, N.J.: Van Nostrand Reinhold, 1973.

Foner, Laura, and Eugene Genovese, eds. *Slavery in the New World.* Englewood Cliffs, N.J.: Prentice-Hall, 1969.

Forbes, Jack. *Education of the Culturally Different: A Multicultural Approach.* San Francisco: Far West Laboratory for Educational Research and Development, 1969.

———. "Teaching Native American Values and Cultures." In *Teaching Ethnic Studies: Concepts and Strategies,* ed. James A. Banks. 43d Yearbook. Washington, D.C.: National Council for the Social Studies, 1973.

Ford, Margaret L. "The Development of an Instrument for Assessing Levels of Ethnicity in Public School Teachers." Unpublished Ph.D. diss., University of Houston, 1979.

Forehand, G. A., and M. Ragosta. *A Handbook for Integrated Schooling.* Princeton, N.J.: Educational Testing Service, 1976.

Franklin, John Hope. *From Slavery to Freedom.* New York: Alfred A. Knopf, 1967.

Friedlander, Jonathan. *The Middle East: The Image and the Reality.* Los Angeles: University of California Press, 1980.

Frost, Joe L., and Glenn R. Hawkes. *The Disadvantaged Child.* Boston: Houghton Mifflin, 1966.

Garcia, R. *Learning in Two Languages.* Bloomington, Ind.: Phi Delta Kappa Educational Foundation, 1976.

Gardner, R. C., and W. E. Lambert. *Attitudes and Motivation in Second-Language Learning.* Rowley, Mass.: Newbury House, 1972.

Gay, Geneva. "Differential Dyadic Interactions of Black and White Teachers with Black and White Pupils in Recently Desegregated Social Studies Classrooms: A Function of Teacher and Pupil Ethnicity." OE Project no. 2F113, January 1974.

———. "Multiethnic Education; Historical Developments and Future Prospects." *Phi Delta Kappan* 64, no. 8 (April 1983).

Gay, Geneva, and Roger D. Abrahams. "Black Culture in the Classroom." In *Language and Cultural Diversity in American Education,* ed. Roger D. Abrahams and Rudolph C. Troike. Englewood Cliffs, N.J.: Prentice-Hall, 1976.

Gibson, Margaret. "Approaches to Multicultural Education in the United States: Some Concepts and Assumptions." *Anthropology and Education Quarterly* 7, no. 4 (November 1976). Reprinted in *Anthropology and Education Quarterly* 15, no. 1 (Spring 1984).

Glasser, William. *Schools Without Failure.* New York: Harper and Row, 1969.

Goodenough, Ward H. *Cultural Anthropology and Linguistics.* Georgetown University Monograph Series on Language and Linguistics, no. 9, 1957. Reprinted in *Language in Culture and Society: A Reader in Linguistics and Anthropology,* ed. Dell H. Hymes. New York: Harper and Row, 1964.

Gordon, Milton M. *Assimilation in American Life.* New York: Oxford University Press, 1966.

Gregorc, Anthony F. "Learning/Teaching Styles." In *Student Learning Styles: Diagnosing and Prescribing Programs.* Reston, Va.: National Association of Secondary School Principals, 1979.

Gronlund, Norman E. *Individualizing Classroom Instruction.* New York: Macmillan, 1974.

Gwaltney, John Langston. *Drylongso: A Self-Portrait of Black America.* New York: Vintage Books, 1980.

Hall, Susan J. *Africa in U.S. Schools, K–12: A Survey.* New York: The African Institute. 1978.

Hamilton, Charles V. "Race and Education: A Search for Legitimacy." In *Issues in Race and Ethnic Relations,* ed. Jack Rothman. Itasca, Ill.: F. E. Peacock, 1977.

Heathers, Glen. "A Working Definition of Individualized Instruction." *Educational Leadership* 34, no. 5 (February 1977).

Herskovitz, Melville I. *The Myth of the Negro Past.* Boston: Beacon Press, 1969.

Hess, Robert D., and Fred M. Newman. "Political Socialization in the Schools." *Harvard Education Review* 38 (Summer 1968).

Hetherington, Mavis, and Ron Parke. *Child Psychology: A Contemporary Viewpoint.* New York: McGraw-Hill, 1979.

Hidden Figures Test—Cf-1. *Kit of Factor Referenced Cognitive Tests.* Princeton, N.J.: Educational Testing Service, 1962.

Hilliard, Asa. "Alternatives to IQ Testing: An Approach to the Identification of Gifted Minority Children." Final report to the California State Department of Education, 1976.

Hosokawa, Bill. *NISEI: The Quiet Americans.* New York: William Morrow, 1969.

Hraba, Joseph. *American Ethnicity.* Itasca, Ill.: F. E. Peacock, 1979.

Hsu, Francis L. K. *The Study of Literate Civilizations.* New York: Holt, Rinehart and Winston, 1969.

Hunt, David E. "Learning Style and Student Needs: An Introduction to Conceptual Level." In *Student Learning Styles: Diagnosing and Prescribing Programs.* Reston, Va.: National Association of Secondary School Principals, 1979.

Hyman, Ronald, and Barbara Rosoff. "Matching Learning and Teaching Styles: The Jug and What's in It." *Theory into Practice* 23 (Winter 1984).

In Search of Mutual Understanding. Japan/United States Textbook Study Project, Joint Report. Washington, D.C.: National Council of the Social Studies, January 1981.

Jones, James M. "The Concept of Racism and Its Changing Reality." In *Impacts of Racism on White Americans,* ed. Benjamin D. Bowser and Raymond G. Hunt. Beverly Hills, Calif.: Sage, 1981.

Jones, Leroi. *Blues People: The Negro Experience in White America and the Music That Developed from It.* New York: William Morrow, 1963.

Jones, Maldwyn Allen. *American Immigration.* Chicago: University of Chicago Press, 1960.

Kallen, Horace M. *Culture and Democracy in the United States.* New York: Boni and Liveright, 1924.

Keefe, James. "Assessing Student Learning Styles: An Overview." In *Student Learning Styles and Brain Behavior.* Reston, Va.: National Association of Secondary School Principals, 1983.

Keefe, James W., and Marlin Languis. *Learning Stages Network Newsletter* (New York) 4, no. 2 (Summer 1983).

Kelso, Jack. "The Concept of Race." *Improving College and University Teaching* 15, no. 95 (Spring 1967).

Kluckholm, Clyde. *Mirror for Man.* Greenwich, Conn.: Fawcett, 1965.

Konvitz, Milton R. "Horace Meyer Kallen (1882–1974): Philosopher of the Hebraic American Idea." In *American Jewish Yearbook, 1974–1975*, ed. Morris Fine and Milton Himmelfarb. Philadelphia: Jewish Publication Society of America, 1974.

Kraemer, Alfred J. "A Cultural Self-Awareness Approach to Improving Intercultural Communication Skills." ERIC ED 079 213 (April 1973).

Kusler, Gerald E. "Getting to Know You." In *Student Learning Styles and Brain Behavior*. Reston, Va.: National Association of Secondary School Principals, 1983.

Leibowitz, Arnold H. "Language as a Means of Social Control: The United States Experience." Unpublished manuscript, August 1974.

Levine, Lawrence W. *Black Culture and Black Consciousness*. New York: Oxford University Press, 1977.

Levine, Robert A., and Donald Campbell. *Ethnocentrism: Theories of Conflict, Ethnic Attitudes and Group Behavior*. New York: John Wiley and Sons, 1942.

Lewis, David Levering. *When Harlem Was in Vogue*. New York: Alfred A. Knopf, 1981.

Lippitt, Peggy, Jeffrey Eiseman, and Ronald Lippitt. *Cross-age Helping Program: Orientation, Training, and Related Materials*. Ann Arbor: University of Michigan, Center for Research on Utilization of Scientific Knowledge, Institute for Social Research, 1969. A cross-age helping package of dissemination materials is published by Xicom, RFD #1, Sterling Forest, Tuxedo, N.Y.

Longstreet, Wilma. *Aspects of Ethnicity: Understanding Differences in Pluralistic Classrooms*. New York: Teachers College Press, 1978.

Lynd, Robert. *Knowledge for What? The Place of Social Science in American Culture*. Princeton, N.J.: Princeton University Press, 1939. Reprint. New York: Evergreen Black Cat edition. Grove Press, 1964.

Maslow, Abraham. *Motivation and Personality*. New York: Harper and Brothers, 1954.

McNickle, D'Arcy. "Indian and European: Indian-White Relations from Discovery to 1887." In *The Emergent Native Americans*, ed. Deward E. Walker, Jr. Boston: Little, Brown, 1972.

McWilliams, Carey. *North from Mexico: The Spanish-Speaking People of the United States*. New York: Greenwood Press, 1968.

Melendez, David, Donna Cole Melendez, and Angela Molina. "Pluralism and the Hispanic Student: Challenge to Educators." *Theory into Practice* 20, no. 1 (Winter 1981).

Messick, Samuel, ed. *Individuality in Learning*. San Francisco: Jossey-Bass, 1976.

Miles, Miska. *Annie and the Old One*. Ill. Peter Parnall. Boston: Little, Brown, 1971.

Mintz, Sidney W. "Creating Culture in the Americas." *Readings in Anthropology 75/76*. Guilford, Conn.: Dushkin, 1974.

Montagu, Ashley. *Man's Most Dangerous Myth: The Fallacy of Race*. 5th ed. New York: Oxford University Press, 1974.

———. "What Anthropology Is." *Instructor* 75 (November 1965).

Moore, Robert B. "Racism in the English Language." New York: Council on Interracial Books for Children, n.d.

More Than Bows and Arrows. Cinema Associates, Seattle, Wash., 1978.

Myers, Linda James. "The Nature of Pluralism and the African American Case." *Theory into Practice* 20 (Winter 1981).

Novak, Michael. *Further Reflections on Ethnicity.* Middletown, Pa.: EMPAC, Jednota Press, 1977.

Patterson, F. "The Purpose and Trend of the Conference." In *Negro Self-Concept: Implications for School and Citizenship,* ed. W. C. Kvaraceus et al. New York: McGraw-Hill, 1965.

Pettigrew, T. "The Case for the Racial Integration of the Schools." In *Report on the Future of School Desegregation in the United States,* ed. O. Duff. Pittsburgh: University of Pittsburgh, Consultative Resource Center on School Desegregation and Conflict, 1973.

Phillips, J. C. "College of, by and for Navajo Indians." *Chronicle of Higher Education* 15 (January 16, 1978).

Piaget, Jean. "The Genetic Approach to the Psychology of Thought." *Journal of Educational Psychology* 52 (December 1961).

———. *The Psychology of Intelligence.* Paterson, N.J.: Littlefield, Adams, 1963.

Purkey, William. *Inviting School Success: A Self-Concept Approach to Teaching.* Belmont, Calif.: Wadsworth, 1978.

Ramirez, Manuel, and Alfredo Castañeda. *Cultural Democracy, Bicognitive Development and Education.* New York: Academic Press, 1974.

Ramos, Reyes, and Martha Ramos. "The Mexican American: Am I Who They Say I Am?" In *Chicanos: As We See Ourselves,* ed. D. Trejo Arnulfo. Tucson: University of Arizona Press, 1979.

Reinert, Harry. "One Picture Is Worth a Thousand Words? Not Necessarily!" *The Modern Language Journal* 60 (April 1976).

Riessman, Frank. *The Inner-City Child.* New York: Harper and Row, 1976.

———. "The Overlooked Positives of Disadvantaged Groups." *Journal of Negro Education* 33 (Summer 1964).

Rist, Ray. "Student Social Class and Teacher Expectations: The Self-Fulfilling Prophecy in Ghetto Education." *Harvard Education Review* 40 (August 1970).

Roberts, Kenneth L. *Why Europe Leaves Home.* Reprinted in "Kenneth L. Roberts and the Threat of Mongrelization in America, 1922." In *In Their Place,* ed. Lewis H. Carlson and George A. Colburn. New York: John Wiley and Sons, 1972.

Rokeach, Milton. *Beliefs, Attitudes and Values.* San Francisco: Jossey-Bass, 1969.

Rose, Peter I. *The Study of Society: An Integrated Anthology.* New York: Random House, 1967.

Rosenthal, R., and L. Jacobson. *Pygmalion in the Classroom: Teacher Expectation and Pupils' Intellectual Development.* New York: Holt, Rinehart and Winston, 1968.

Sagar, H. A., and J. W. Schofield. "Integrating the Desegregated School: Problems and Possibilities." In *Advances in Motivation and Achievement: The Effects of School Desegregation on Motivation and Achievement,* ed. D. E. Bartz and M. L. Maehr. Greenwich, Conn.: JAI Press, 1984.

Saral, Tulsi B. "Consciousness Theory and Intercultural Communication." Paper presented at meeting of the International Communication Association, Portland, Oreg., April 14–17, 1976.

Seasholes, Bradbury. "Political Socialization of Blacks: Implications for Self and Society." In *Black Self Concept,* ed. James A. Banks and Jean D. Grambs. New York: McGraw-Hill, 1972.

Shade, Barbara J. "Afro-American Cognitive Style: A variable in School Success?" *Review of Educational Research* 52, no. 2 (Summer 1982).

Shirts, R. Garry. *Bafá Bafá: A Cross Culture Simulation*. 1977. Published by Simile 11, 218 Twelfth Street, P.O. Box 910, Del Mar, Calif. 92014.

Shuy, Roger W. "A Holistic View of Language." *Research in the Teaching of English* 15, no. 2 (May 1981).

Sills, David L., ed. "Assimilation." In *International Encyclopedia of the Social Sciences*. Vol. 1. New York: Macmillan/Free Press, 1968.

Slavin, Robert. *Cooperative Learning*. New York: Longman, 1983.

———. *Student Team Learning: An Overview and Practical Guide*. Washington, D.C.: National Education Association, 1983.

———. *Teacher Manual for Student Team Learning*. Baltimore: Center for Social Organization of Schools, Johns Hopkins University, 1978.

———. *Using Student Team Learning*. Rev. ed. Baltimore: Center for Social Organization of Schools, Johns Hopkins University, 1980.

Snow, R. "Unfinished Pygmalion." *Contemporary Psychology* 14 (April 1969).

Soares, A., and L. Soares. "Self-perceptions of Culturally Disadvantaged Children." *American Educational Research Journal* 6, no. 1 (1969).

Sowell, Thomas, ed. *Essays and Data on American Ethnic Groups*. Washington, D.C.: The Urban Institute, 1978.

———. *Ethnic America: A History*. New York: Basic Books, 1981.

Spradley, James P., and David W. McCurdy. *Anthropology: The Cultural Perspective*. New York: John Wiley and Sons, 1975.

Stanford, Barbara Dodds, and Karima Amin. *Black Literature for High School Students*. Urbana, Ill.: National Council of Teachers of English, 1978.

Steiner, Stan. *Fusang: The Chinese Who Built America*. New York: Harper and Row, 1979.

Stereotypes, Distortions and Omissions in U.S. History Textbooks. New York: Council on Interracial Books for Children, 1977.

St. John, Nancy. *School Desegregation: Outcomes for Children*. New York: John Wiley and Sons, 1975.

———. "School Integration, Classroom Climate, and Achievement," ERIC ED 052 269 (January 1971).

Taba, Hilda, and Deborah Elkins. *Teaching Strategies for the Culturally Disadvantaged*. Chicago: Rand McNally, 1966.

Talmage, Harriet, ed. *Systems of Individualized Education*. Berkeley, Calif.: McCutchan, 1975.

"Teacher-Aide Guide for Navajo Area," product of a conference at the DZILTH-NA-O-DITH-HLE Boarding School, Bloomfield, N.M., June 8–12, 1970.

Tiedt, Pamela L., and Iris M. Tiedt. *Multicultural Teaching: A Handbook of Activities, Information, and Resources*. Boston: Allyn and Bacon, 1979.

Toppin, Edgar A. "The Forgotten People." *Christian Science Monitor*, March 6, 1969.

Torrence, Paul. "Cultural Discontinuities and the Development of Originality of Thinking." *Exceptional Children* 29 (September 1962).

Triandis, Harry C. *Attitude and Attitude Change*. New York: John Wiley and Sons, 1971.

———. "Culture Training, Cognitive Complexity and Interpersonal Attitudes."

In *Cross-Cultural Perspectives on Learning,* ed. Richard W. Brislin, Stephen Bochner, and Walter J. Lonner. New York: John Wiley and Sons, 1975.

Troike, R. C. "Synthesis of Research on Bilingual Education." *Educational Leadership* 38 (March 1981).

Tylor, Sir Edward B. *Primitive Culture.* 2 vols. London: John Murray, 1871. Reprint, New York: Harper Torchbooks, 1958.

U.S. Civil Rights Commission. *Teachers and Students. Report V: Mexican-American Education Study. Differences in Teacher Interaction with Mexican-American and Anglo Students.* Washington, D.C.: Government Printing Office, March 1973.

Vogel, Virgil J. *This Country Was Ours.* New York: Harper and Row, 1972.

Von Harrison, Grant. "Structured Tutoring: Antidote for Low Achievement." In *Children as Teachers,* ed. Vernon L. Allen. New York: Academic Press, 1976.

Wallerstein, J. S. "Children of Divorce: The Psychological Tasks of the Child." *American Journal of Orthopsychiatry* 53 (April 1983).

Walzer, Michael, Edward T. Kantowicz, John Higham, and Mona Harrington. *The Politics of Ethnicity.* Cambridge, Mass.: Belknap Press of Harvard University Press, 1982.

Weinberg, Meyer. *Minority Students: A Research Appraisal.* Washington, D.C.: National Institute of Education, 1977.

Wiley, David. "The African Connection." *Wisconsin Alumnus* 77, no. 2 (January 1976).

Williams, Frederick, ed. *Language and Poverty.* Chicago: Markham, 1970.

Wirth, Louis. "The Problem of Minority Groups." In *The Science of Man in the World Crisis,* ed. Ralph Linton. New York: Columbia University Press, 1945.

Witkin, Herman A., Carol Ann Moore, and Frederick J. McDonald, "Cognitive Style and the Teaching/Learning Processes." American Educational Research Association. Cassette Series 3F, 1974.

Wojtan, Linda S. "The Immigrant Experience: A Polish-American Model." Funded by the Ethnic Heritage Studies Program Title IX, ESEA, 6008100438, Ethnic Heritage, October 1981–December 1982.

Wolsk, David. *An Experience Centered Curriculum: Exercises in Personal and Social Reality.* Paris: United Nations Educational Scientific and Cultural Organization, 1974. ERIC ED 099 269.

Zerkel, P., and E. Moser. "Self Concept and Ethnic Group Membership Among Public School Students." *American Educational Research Journal* 8 (March 1971).

Zikiros, Astair, and Marylee Wiley. *Africa in Social Studies Textbooks.* East Lansing: African Studies Center, Michigan State University, 1978.

Index